THE SHANNON NAVIGATION

IN MEMORIAM

Harry Rice and Vincent Delany

THE SHANNON NAVIGATION

RUTH DELANY

The Lilliput Press
in association with
Waterways Ireland

This publication has received support from
Waterways Ireland and from The Heritage Council
under the Publications Grants Scheme.

First published 2008 by
THE LILLIPUT PRESS LTD
62-63 Sitric Road, Arbour Hill, Dublin 7, Ireland.

A CIP record is available from the British Library.

1 3 5 7 9 10 8 6 4 2

ISBN 978 1 84351 132 8 (cased)
978 1 84351 128 1 (pbk)

Set in Riven. Design by Sharon O'Reilly at Neat Design.
Printed and bound by Estudios Gráficos Zure, Bizkaia, Spain.

CONTENTS

ACKNOWLEDGMENTS

I have been accumulating information for this book for many years and some of it has already been used in my earlier books. However, I am very conscious of the fact that there is still a great deal to be learnt about this great river navigation and I am hoping that this book will stimulate further research. I could not have achieved the publication I was striving for without the assistance of many people. My daughter, Hilary, and brother-in-law, Tom Kelly, patiently printed out and photocopied when I needed this assistance. Antony Farrell of The Lilliput Press has been a good friend over the years in helping me to publish my books on Ireland's inland waterways; these are of specialist interest with small print runs. I must also thank Delphine Lemoine and Siobán Devlin, The Lilliput Press for all their work in patiently inserting corrections. In particular I am most grateful to Waterways Ireland for agreeing to be associated with this publication that has enabled The Lilliput Press to publish it with many colour illustrations. The interest that Waterways Ireland has shown in this publication reflects the long association I have enjoyed with the several different bodies who have administered the Shannon over the years. I am also grateful to the Heritage Council for grant-aiding the publication through its publication grants scheme. I must thank Paul Kidney, Martin Critchley, Emma Jane Critchley and Eilis Vaughan of Era-Maptec. I have worked with Era-Maptec in the past in preparing Shannon guides and it was good to work with them again in the preparation of the illustrations, maps and origination of this publication. In particular I must thank Sharon O'Reilly who did the origination.

John Lewis agreed to read my first draft and not only made some very useful comments but gave me confidence to continue with the work. Brian D'Arcy and Ray Dunne, Waterways Ireland, also read the text. Brian D'Arcy made some very helpful suggestions, Ray Dunne showed a great interest in my efforts and was extremely helpful in providing information and illustrations and Eamon Horgan, Waterways Ireland, helped with photography. Paula Tracey and Liz Gabbett, Waterways Ireland, assisted me in looking through the archive in Enniskillen and arranged for copies to be made of some items, and Eanna Rowe was very helpful with the publication. As has always been the case in the past I have enjoyed great assistance from all the libraries: Trinity College, Dublin, the National Library of Ireland, the National Archives Ireland and Ken Bergin of the Special Collections, Glucksman Library, University College, Limerick. In the many years I have been travelling up and down the Shannon I have always received a warm welcome from the lock and bridge keepers. I would also particularly like to acknowledge Peter Quigley of Quigley's Marina and Paddy and Maria Gilboy of Tara Marina, Knockvicar, who always managed to find me a berth for *Harklow* and more recently *Arcady* when I needed one.

Over the years I have been collecting inland waterway illustrations, many of them my own photographs dating back to the 1950s but others from various sources. Many members of the IWAI have helped including Colin Becker, Brian Goggin and Niall Galway, who share my enthusiasm for waterway history and accompanied me on visits to waterway sites and helped with the photography. In particular I must thank Kevin Dwyer who allowed me to use some of the magnificent aerial photographs from his book on the Irish inland waterways *Ireland – the Inner Island*. I would like to thank all those who gave permission to use their photographs. I have tried to get in touch with as many people as possible to obtain permission to use the illustrations and if I have failed to acknowledge some of them or contact everyone I apologize; it has not been an easy task to identify where some of the illustrations I have collected came from. David Laing was most helpful in tracing the fine colour painting that I had hoped to use on the cover that was in the Victoria & Albert Museum in London. I was very fortunate to share many conversations about the early days of sailing on the Shannon with my brother-in-law, Alf Delany, who died recently, and he allowed me to borrow from his large collection of Shannon memorabilia to use as illustrations. I have also used a number from the late Walter Borner's extensive collection of Shannon photographs, which he had sent me over the years, and I know it would have given him much pleasure to know that they were being used; I have included them now in memory of Walter and Ruth. Peter Wilson helped with information about fishing on the river. I am also grateful to Sean Kierse, Killaloe, for his assistance in tracing illustrations, Mary Shackleton for allowing me to use some photographs from the Shackleton collection, Reggie and Michael Goodbody for access to the Goodbody Dromineer papers, Paul McMahon and Tony Roche for photographs from the Photographic Unit of the Department of the Environment, Heritage & Local Government, and Sean Fitzsimons, Athlone Branch, Inland Waterways Association of Ireland. I would also like to thank Brendan Delany, ESB, who arranged for Tony Fitzgibbon, Ardnacrusha civil engineer, to give me information about the hydro-electric works and who also arranged for Pat Yeates and Gerard Hampson to allow me access to the ESB archives. John Crowe, Shannnon Development, gave permission to use one of their photographs.

It should be noted that all money transactions in Ireland prior to January 1826 were made in Irish currency (£13 Irish equals £12 sterling). The use of statute miles or Irish miles (1 Irish mile equals 2240 yards [2048m]) was never very clearly defined with no official date of abandonment and unless otherwise indicated all measurements are imperial with approximate metric equivalent in brackets (1 foot equals 0.3048m).

FOREWORD

We in Waterways Ireland are delighted to welcome this important publication by Ruth Delany. It is the culmination of many years work and once again Ruth has woven together a wonderfully detailed history – this time a history of the mighty river Shannon. That history is expertly brought to the reader and is interwoven with stories, facts and lore. The understanding and the wealth of knowledge Ruth possesses comes leaping from every page. Her attention to detail, research expertise and scholarly ability are proof positive of her unwavering dedication to the inland waterways of Ireland.

As guardians of many of those inland waterways we in Waterways Ireland were delighted to collaborate and assist with this publication. It is an invaluable source of information, data and historical facts about Ireland's greatest river and will add to the knowledge and understanding of the waterway enthusiast as much as it will inform and educate the general reader.

Certainly the Shannon has made a significant contribution to the history and lives of many – from lore and folklore to prehistoric and historic, from commerce route and vital artery to leisure playground and cruising paradise.

Congratulations Ruth on this wonderful publication – your enthusiasm, drive and dedication leap forth from the pages.

Legend has it that the goddess Sionann devoured the salmon of wisdom and she in turn dissolved to become the greatest river in Ireland – the Shannon. Legend also has it that on hearing the news Sionann's father Lodán, desendant of Neachtain the Celtic God of Water, wept uncontrollably and from his tears formed the remaining rivers and lakes of the island of Ireland.

Sionann may have devoured the salmon of wisdom but Ruth must have encountered the salmon of knowledge.

John Martin
Chief Executive
Waterways Ireland

Brian D'Arcy
Director
Waterways Ireland

Martin Dennany
Director
Waterways Ireland

5th December 2007

THE SHANNON NAVIGATION

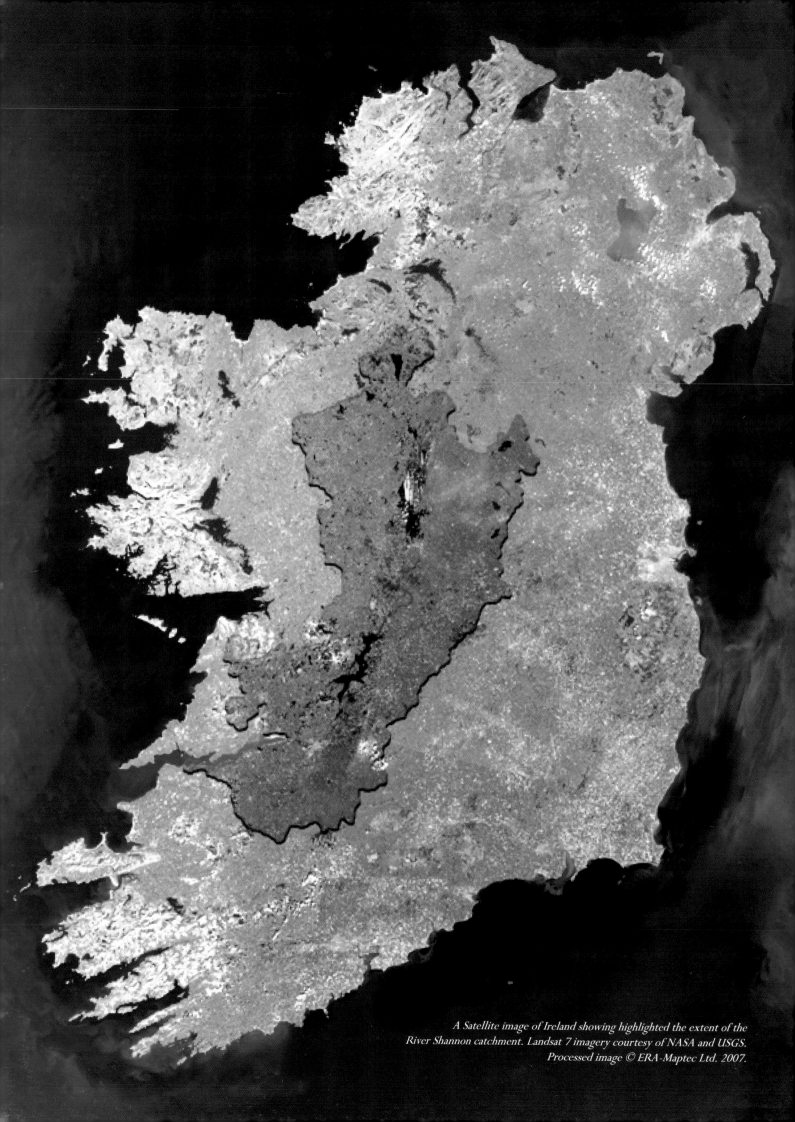

A Satellite image of Ireland showing highlighted the extent of the River Shannon catchment. Landsat 7 imagery courtesy of NASA and USGS. Processed image © ERA-Maptec Ltd. 2007.

INTRODUCTION

This book endeavours to tell the story of the Shannon Navigation from the mid-seventeenth century, when suggestions that something be done to make the River Shannon more navigable were made, up to the present day. The story of the development of the river as a navigation makes it possible to form a picture of what the river was like at any given time or place, and to some extent what sort of conditions people were living in. While the book covers some three hundred and seventy-five years in the history of the river, this represents a very small period in its overall existence.

Writing in the 1980s for the section on the landscape of the river for *The Shell Guide to the River Shannon*, the late John Weaving, the legendary figure who died in 1987 and who was 'at one' with the river and ever observant, described working on a new slipway near Drumsna on the north Shannon:

We dug down through 2m of blue clay, which contained neither sand, gravel nor stones. Underneath this there was 1m-depth of woodland peat containing sections of pine. This lay directly above the limestone bedrock. As the top peat was over 1m below the present summer water level, this would imply that, at some stage prior to the ice ages, the water level must have been considerably lower, or perhaps there might not have been a river in this area at all.

John also described evidence of a blockage left behind by glaciation at Rosebank, just downstream of Carrick-on-Shannon, with deep scouring below it that suggested to him that there was a waterfall formed here as the water, ponded back by the blockage and forming large lakes upstream, overflowed. These two examples show how modern development has helped to understand how the river evolved. Writers such as Frank Mitchell, who have traced the history of the Irish landscape, have put together the story of the river over the centuries.[1]

The central lowlands of Ireland were made up originally of carboniferous limestone and then, following periods of glaciation, with the ice ages waxing and waning, the ice ultimately receded about 10,000 years ago. It left behind a very different landscape, depositing glacial drift of one sort or another, and the Shannon as we know it today began to emerge. In the case of the upper Shannon, drumlins, small rounded hills of blue clay, sometimes caused temporary blockages to the run-off of water, which in turn ponded back into lakes, flooded out and deposited blue clay over wide areas. The lakes became shallower as the land dried out, reeds, sedges, rushes and willows grew and partly decayed, forming bogs that are still a feature in places along the river corridor today.

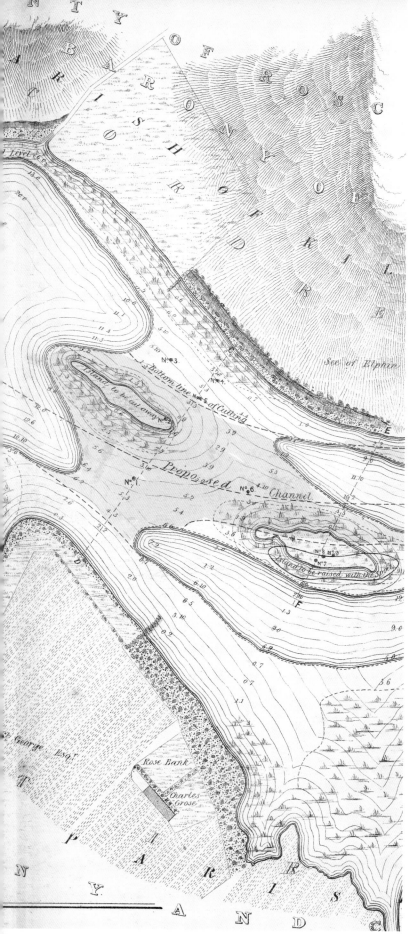

A drawing of Rosebank, downstream of Carrick-on-Shannon, prepared in the 1830s by Thomas Rhodes before the navigation channel was changed and deepened which illustrates John Weaving's interpretation of the geology.

Farther downstream, where the river meanders sluggishly, eskers were formed, crossing the river roughly in an east-west direction. As the ice melted, streams beneath the glaciers deposited sand, gravel and boulders filling the melt-water channels. The south Shannon posed some questions for the geologists as to why the river found its way to the sea through the hard sandstone and slate hills surrounding the southern end of Lough Derg instead of flowing westward into Galway Bay through Scarriff Bay. It is suggested that much earlier the central plain stood higher and the course through Killaloe offered the easiest access to the sea.[2] As the limestone plain was lowered by denudation, the river retained its course through the hills, even when sea levels rose with the melting of the ice. At Killaloe it plunged over a rock-sill, rather like a huge dam, before flowing rapidly out to sea at Limerick. This natural feature was removed in the 1920s and a new artificial dam erected farther downstream when the hydro-electric works were being carried out.

Today the source of the river is at the Shannon Pot on the slopes of the Cuilcagh Mountains 152m above sea level. The river falls 104m from here to Lough Allen and from Battlebridge, over the 185km of its course to Killaloe, it falls only 12m before dropping 30m in its final few kilometres to the sea. Thus the river as we know it today tells its own story of how it evolved. Emerging from the ice ages, slow flowing over much of its course, it broke down into a number of sections divided by stretches of impassable rapids, which in turn provided fording places, largely where the locks occur. Each of these sections were widely used as natural navigations from early times when movement around the country was very difficult, roads were few and inaccessible, and much of the land was covered with dense forests.

An interesting recent excavation arising out of the construction of a rising main at Hermitage, just downstream of Castleconnell, has demonstrated that the very earliest recorded inhabitants in the early Mesolithic Age settled here on the banks of the Shannon.[3] Cremation sites were found with flint points or microliths, which could have been used for fishing, and also stone axes of a much earlier date than previously found. It is suggested that this was a fording place and there are indications that it was a busy settlement for many centuries up to the Iron Age. Putting all the evidence together from geologists, annalists and historians over the years, a picture emerges of the importance of the river not only providing sites for monastic settlements and as a means of transport and commerce but also of its strategic importance in the continuing struggles for supremacy among the Irish chieftains, assisted from time to time by what the annalists referred to as 'the foreigners', a term used to describe the Vikings in the first instance and subsequently the Normans.[4]

The Shannon Pot, source of the Shannon, on the slopes of the Cuilceaghs.

Three of the most important monastic settlements in the country are to be found on Holy Island on Lough Derg, at Clonmacnois and on Inchcleraun on Lough Ree, with many other smaller sites including those on islands on Lough Key. Clonmacnois, founded in the sixth century at a point where the north-south route provided by the river met the east-west route along the esker ridges of the Eiscir Riada, is the site of an early bridge across the river. There is reference in the Annals of Clonmacnois in 1158 to a bridge here and research carried out in 1994-1995 by the Irish Underwater Archaeological Research Team revealed the piles of a bridge dating back to the eighth century, possibly one of a series of bridges.

The river also provided a natural frontier, and its fording places assumed great importance, none more so than Athlone with Lough Ree becoming the base of considerable fleets. The Danish invaders, driven from their own country by the centralizing policy of the kings of Norway, used estuaries and rivers to penetrate inland and on the Shannon overcame rapids by using rollers to work their boats upstream, enabling them to assemble fleets as far upstream as Lough Ree. The greatly feared Turgesius assembled a fleet on the lake in the mid-ninth century and held what was euphemistically called 'hostings' or military campaigns into Connacht and Meath, plundering the monastic settlements until his reign of terror came to an end when he was captured by Maelshechlainn II and drowned in Lough Ennel. There seems to have been little Viking presence for the next hundred years until it was recorded that the fleet of the Limerick-based invader, Olafr, on Lough Ree was attacked by the Dublin Vikings in 924. He warded them off successfully and held sway until 937, when he was finally defeated and carried off to Dublin.

Clonmacnois: the monastic settlement with the location of the remains of a bridge extending from near the castle, a short distance downstream of the moorings, to the Roscommon shore. (Dept. of the Environment, Heritage & Local Government)

Although this ended the Viking presence on Lough Ree, the struggle between the kings of Munster and Connaught continued with Irish chieftains competing for control of the river and continuing to plunder the monastic settlements. Brian Boru is reputed to have sailed up the river with a fleet of 300 boats to do battle with Maelshechlainn II until they agreed a truce at the mouth of the River Inny. Brian reneged but a new deal followed to fight the Vikings together, ending with Brian's death at the Battle of Clontarf in 1014. There are further accounts in the various Annals of fleets assembling, battles fought and storms resulting in shipwrecks and loss of life. Turlough O'Connor had a fleet on Lough Ree in 1137, there was a severe winter in 1156, storms in 1190 and, in 1201, Cathal Crobhderg and Norman 'foreigners' retreated eastward across the Shannon at Rindoon pursued by Cathal Carrach and his Connaught men, and many were drowned. Because of the strategic importance of Rindoon,

Clonmacnois: a model of the bridge was made based on underwater research carried out in 1994-1995. (Dept. of the Environment, Heritage & Local Government)

Lough Key: MacDermot's castle on an island known as 'The Rock' from Francis Grose Antiquities of Ireland 1792

the Normans erected a castle here in 1227, having built a bridge at Athlone in 1210 and a castle there to replace the earlier Irish stonghold of the O'Conchobairs. There were also battles fought on the upper Shannon and in 1235 the MacDermot stronghold, The Rock, on Lough Key on the Boyle Water, was attacked and burnt.[5] The Annals also record unusual weather conditions; in 1252 there was a great wind followed by a great heat and drought when people were said to have crossed the Shannon in places without wetting their feet and in 1586 there is a strange entry in the Annals that the river flowed upstream into Lough Ree from Athlone for a period.

Giraldus Cambrensis, who visited Ireland with Prince John in 1185, listed the principal rivers and described the Shannon: 'The Sinnenus [Shannon] deservedly claims first rank, both for its full and majestic stream, which flows through vast tracts of country and for the abundance of fish within its waters.'[6] Current excavations at Knockvicar on the Boyle River have revealed a mass grave of the early to mid-fourteenth century possibly linked to death arising out of the plague years of the Black Death.[7] The excavation is being carried out by a team from Sligo Institute of Technology at a site marked on old maps as 'Bishop's Seat'. It is thought that this might be the site of a bishop's palace dating back to the thirteenth century, which is mentioned in the Annals of Lough Key as being destroyed deliberately in 1259 to prevent it falling into the hands of the Anglo-Normans.

Lough Key: Castle Island as it is today.

Harman Murtagh in his *Athlone History and Settlement to 1800*[8] points out how in Elizabethan times the potential of the river had come to be recognized and in particular the importance of Athlone, where a stone bridge was erected in 1567. The military importance of the river was also being increasingly realized. The policy of having a water bailiff and a government galley on Lough Ree was revived in 1571 because of the great number of boats, some of which were being used to carry out robberies with groups of rebels occupying some of the islands. He was authorized to stamp the legally held boats and charge them a fee of 12 pence per quarter and confiscate the others. In 1580 Sir Edward Waterhouse, a secretary of state and a member of the Irish Privy Council, was appointed as water bailiff. He used Athlone as his base and a second galley was added. The vessels were used to transport men and supplies up and down the river. He was given wide powers to fine and punish offenders and to destroy those weirs that obstructed the navigation or affected fishing rights. He enjoyed fishing and fowling rights and also was overseer of swans, like his counterpart on the Thames. The government fleet was extended to four galleys and they continued to be used to control the river and convey supplies into the early 1600s.

It was also reported in 1580 to the English Privy Council that the surest way of sending letters from Munster was by water up the Shannon from Limerick to Athlone on 'the passenger boat and from there overland to Dublin'. In 1580 Sir William Pelham wrote to Sir Francis Walsingham, Queen Elizabeth's secretary of state, that if he 'did view the commodious havens and harbours, the beauty and commodity of this river Shannon, which I have seen from the head of it beyond Athlone to the ocean, you would say you have not in any region observed places of more pleasure or a river of more commodity', adding with feeling 'if the land were blessed with good people'.

Boats were variously described as 'boats, cotts, wherries and other vessels' and there is an interesting description of some of the different types of boats on Lough Ree written in 1682 by Nicholas Dowdall.[9] He described the river as:

... navigable for boats of about 10 or 20 tuns, but the vessels most made use of for fishing, portage of goods, etc., are made of one big tree like a trough, flatbottomed and some of them so large that they will carry 60 or 80 men and are called cotts. They usually carry horses and other cattle in them, besides they make use of them for carrying timber from the adjacent woods and by laying of long poles over across the said cotts and fastening great beams of timber across the said cotts they will carry 20 tun of timber or more.

Lough Key: Castle Island in the early 1900s with the nineteenth century folly built around the former castle in the 1820s. (Courtesy of the National Library of Ireland)

The strategic role of the Shannon in the Williamite struggles is well documented. After the battle of the Boyne in July 1690 the Jacobites fell back to west of the river and Sarsfield prevented the Williamite forces from crossing the river by fortifying the crossing places at Portumna, Meelick, Banagher, Shannonbridge, Athlone, Lanesborough and Jamestown.[10] Athlone was used as headquarters and the first siege of Athlone followed that summer with the second siege in June 1691 following a continuing winter campaign. During that winter an attack on Jamestown was repulsed as was an attack at Lanesborough, when part of the bridge was broken down but the Williamites failed to establish a bridgehead.

As the country became more stable there was an increase in trade and movement on the river. The islands on the lakes were no longer occupied by feudal lords and were settled by farmers and fishermen. Man's intervention on the river as a navigation so far had been limited to making weirs to create millraces and catch eels and other fish, upgrading natural shallows to create fords and the erection of many-arched stone bridges that impeded the flow. It is not surprising then, with political conditions in the country gradually improving in the seventeenth century and with examples of navigational improvements being tried in other countries, that linking up the navigable stretches of the Shannon began to exercise minds in Ireland.

Turf Boat.

An early turf boat.

It is beyond the scope of this book to include an account of the history of the Shannon Estuary or the port of Limerick except in so far as it affects inland navigation or comes within the remit of the Shannon Commissioners. The recent Discovery Programme intertidal archaeological survey of the Shannon Estuary, which it was considered opened up the need for further studies, shows how this coastal area evolved over the centuries from the earliest pre-historic Mesolithic period right through to medieval and post-medieval times.[11] The study demonstrates how the people, 'foragers, farmers and fishers', lived their lives in this estuary landscape over the years emerging into the conditions existing among the people the Shannon Commissioners were to find in the mid-eighteenth century.

Athlone: an early print showing the type of boats on the river in the 1850s.

CHAPTER ONE
THE EARLY WORKS TO 1800

EARLY NAVIGATION SCHEMES

Early estimates for making the Shannon navigable had tended to be rather far off the mark. In the seventeenth century the Lord Deputy Strafford proposed a scheme to link up the rivers Shannon, Brosna, Barrow and Boyne, a forerunner of the subsequent eighteenth-century inland waterway schemes, but no action was taken.[1] In a letter to the Earl of Thomond in 1683 he said: 'heere is one that offers to make the river Shannon navigable from Limericks to above the foord at Killalow, and he demands for his payment and charges therein £3,000'. In 1664 the Duke of Ormonde issued fourteen 'Instructions' for the Council of Trade, one of which stated: 'You are to consider by what ways and means commerce may be promoted, by the employment of some persons in the mending Highways and Bridges, and making Rivers navigable, and in draining bogs and loghs, and recovering land from the sea.'[2] Although meetings were held on a weekly basis for a number of years to discuss the implementation of the instructions, apart from producing reports for the Council no action followed.

A statement was made in 1697 in the Irish House of Commons that the development of inland navigation would be a means of achieving the general improvement of the country at large and on 9 September a petition was read from the Grand Jury of County Galway calling on the government to make the River Shannon navigable from Limerick to County Leitrim at an estimated cost of £14,000 (it must be remembered that all transactions carried out in Ireland until January 1826 were in Irish currency).[3] This was followed by the appointment of a committee by the Commons in 1697 to prepare a bill to improve the Shannon from Limerick to Jamestown. It did not make any parliamentary progress although a sum of £200 was allocated in 1705 for 'canal surveys' but no indication was given as to what these surveys were. It was not until 1709 that leave was given to Mortimer Heylen and Stephen Costilloe to bring in the heads of a bill. The committee recorded: 'That the petitioners have been at great Pains and charges for a Publick good to sound and fathom the River Shannon from the City of Limerick to the town of Carrick, in the County of Leitrim, and do find it practicable to make the said River navigable, and they considered that this could be achieved for 20-ton boats.[4] This might explain how the £200 allocated in 1705 had been expended. Six years later there was still no progress and George Frizell, Henry Croasdale and others undertook to parliament that they would make the Shannon navigable from Limerick to Carrick. This time an Act was passed that included general provisions for undertakings of this kind.[5]

A number of other navigation schemes had also been proposed and so the Act was wide ranging and was entitled: 'An Act to Encourage the Draining and Improving of the Bogs and Unprofitable Low Grounds, and for the Easing and Despatching the Inland Carriage and Conveyance of Goods from one part to another within this Kingdom'. The preamble recited:

Whereas the great tracts of bog and fenny waste grounds which encumber the midland parts of this Kingdom are not only useless to the owners, but an occasion of corrupt air and a retreat and harbour for malefactors, and whereas it has been ascertained that navigable and communicable passages for vessels of burthen to pass through might be made from and through the said midland counties into the principal rivers, and by the benefit of such master drains, the bogs and other lost grounds might be improved, and also a cheap and commodious communication betwixt His Majesty's subjects inhabiting the several parts of his said Kingdom might be opened.

In addition to the River Shannon from Limerick to Carrick, twenty other navigation schemes were listed with proposed links between some of them. For example work was authorized on a navigation from Castlerea to the River Shannon near Clonfert using the River Suck and also from Sligo to Carrick-on-Shannon via the Unshin, Lough Arrow and Boyle. Apart from some limited work at Adare on the River Maigue, which discharged into the Shannon Estuary, no further action was taken. Another Act was passed in 1721, 'continuing and amending several Acts near expiring', which made provision for the several undertakings by establishing separate bodies of undertakers for each of them.[6] These were made up of the local members of parliament and justices of the peace, who were invested with powers of settling issues with owners of land that might be required or of land affected if the works caused flooding. No commissioner was to act 'where he or they are any ways particularly interested or concerned'. It set out the tolls that could be charged on the completed navigations and it even stipulated that adjoining landowners would have the liberty to use pleasure boats without charge. However, the

ATHLONE.

Drawn by Samuel Lover, Esq., R.H.A.

Athlone: an early bridge with its three mills from a drawing by Samuel Lover.

Limerick: a Bartlett print of the old Baal's Bridge over the Abbey River which was replaced in the 1830s by a single arch bridge.

one thing it did not do was make public funding available for any of the works. Between 1721 and 1725 two further sums of £500 each were allocated for 'canal surveys', and a further Act in 1729 replaced the commissioners by four bodies, one for each of the provinces, and allowed them to raise money by what were called 'tillage duties' because it was considered that the drainage and improvement works were designed to encourage tillage.[7] These duties were to be levied on 'Coaches, Berlins, Chariots, Calashes, Chaises and Chairs, and upon Cards and Dice, and upon wrought and manufactured Gold and Silver Plate, imported into or made in Ireland for the Purposes therein mentioned'.

One ambitious scheme had been undertaken in the 1720s, when subscribers formed a company to make the River Liffey navigable, which ended in costly failure, and this acted as a severe deterrent to any further such private investment in waterways for some time. The tillage duties were expended to begin work on the Newry Canal and then on the Tyrone Navigation, in an attempt to provide access to the Tyrone coalfields, and subsequently for some works on the Boyne and on the Lagan. In 1751 the provincial commissioners were consolidated into one body, the

Corporation for the Promoting and Carrying on an Inland Navigation in Ireland (the Navigation Board), and the duties were extended for a further twenty-one years.[8] The Act gave them the authority to make over property to private undertakers together with grant aid not exceeding one sixth of sums expended by the undertakers on the works. The Shannon, which more than any other of the schemes would have met the criteria of relieving flooding and increasing land for tillage, had not received any funding from the money raised by the duties up to this time. However, it did continue to be the source of comment in pamphlets at the time although estimates for the work involved continued to greatly underestimate the costs, displaying a lack of understanding of what works were actually needed. A pamphlet in 1746, with reference to the difficulties for traffic interrupted in summer by rapids, stated that the 'curious and very learned Doctor Bolton, late Archbishop of Cashel, frequently declared that he would undertake to have all those difficulties removed, so that vessels of 30 tons might pass and re-pass easily at all times of the year, for the sum of £3,000', although a second edition of this pamphlet in 1755 omitted this boast.[9]

Limerick: the old Baal's Bridge at high water.

It was stated that a survey had been made of the river from Killaloe to Limerick with a plan and estimate of £11,488 and in 1742 'the ingenious Mr Gilbert', who together with Thomas Steers, a Liverpool engineer, was associated with the Newry Canal works, estimated that the scheme could be achieved for £20,359 15s 3d; the estimate was rising but still showed an ignorance of what was involved.

Between 1729 and 1755 the tillage duties had amounted to £88,893 which, together with £3,200 in grants, had been expended on navigation works but it is apparent that, with the small amount generated by the duties, inland navigation works in Ireland would have evolved at a very slow pace if it had not been for a sequence of events which arose in the Irish Parliament in the 1750s. Rather than surrender surplus funding to be administrated by the English Crown, a group of members in the Irish Parliament won sufficient support to allocate large amounts of funding to public works and for the encouragement of industry, thereby eliminating any surplus. Navigation works were an obvious choice with the legislation already existing and the Commissioners of Inland Navigation in a position to utilize the funding to add to the sums that continued to be raised by the tillage duties. It would appear that the commissioners had begun to do some survey work on the Shannon because in a pamphlet, written by Matthew Peters in 1755, he recounted that in the summer of 1753 he was ordered to leave his work on the Shannon 'being then employed by the Rt. Hon. the Navigation Board as Pay Clerk and Assistant to that Work, which was then under the direction of the late Mr Scanlan'. Now, finally, assured of funding, work to improve the navigation of the Shannon was about to begin in earnest.

The commissioners decided to undertake the Shannon works in two divisions. Thomas Omer, who they had appointed as their engineer in June 1754, was instructed to begin work on the Shannon to cover the river from Killaloe to Carrick and William Ockenden, another newly arrived engineer in Ireland, was put in charge of the Killaloe to Limerick stretch. Not much is known about these two engineers. A Thomas Omer had worked as a master carpenter on the Kennet Navigation in 1740 and there is a reference in the *Irish Commons Journal* to 'Thomas Omer, of Dutch descent', who had worked on the Newry Canal and the Newry Ship Canal in 1754. Ockenden had arrived in Ireland in the 1750s and remained until his death in 1761. The Commissioners of Inland Navigation employed them to supervise the new navigation works at this time and one writer, Henry Brooke, extolled their virtues in 1759:

Should these Men persevere, for a few years more, with the same Spirit and Success, they will be Instruments in the Hands of our Parliament and Commissioners for doing the greatest of Human works, that of making a great Little Nation, they will thereby entitle themselves to a National Acknowledgement, and the names of Omer and Ockenden will be honourable to our Posterity. [10]

In fact, much of their work was subsequently found to be suspect.

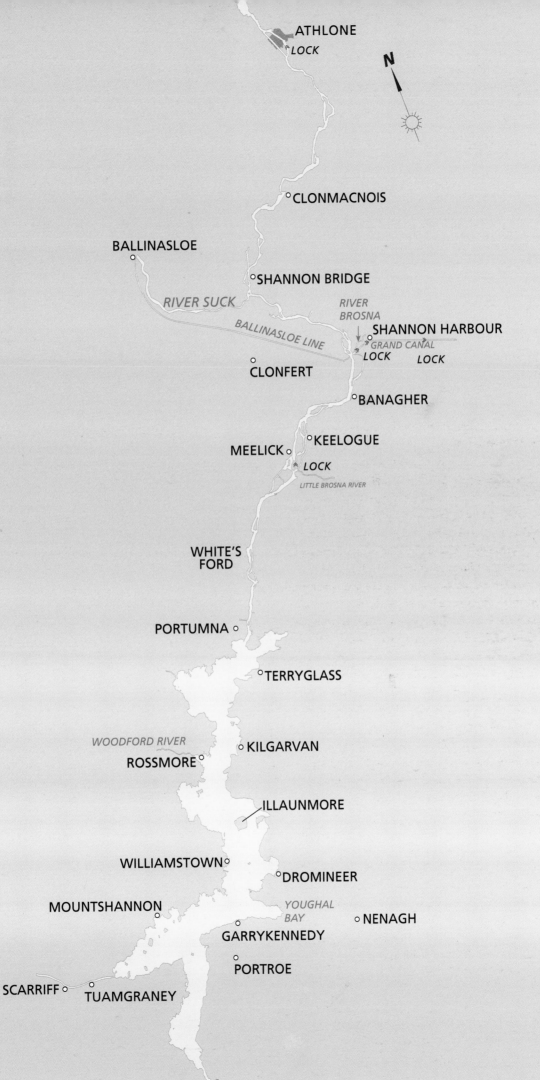

ATHLONE
LOCK

CLONMACNOIS

BALLINASLOE

SHANNON BRIDGE

RIVER SUCK

RIVER BROSNA

BALLINASLOE LINE

SHANNON HARBOUR

GRAND CANAL

LOCK   *LOCK*

CLONFERT

BANAGHER

KEELOGUE

MEELICK

LOCK

LITTLE BROSNA RIVER

WHITE'S FORD

PORTUMNA

TERRYGLASS

WOODFORD RIVER

KILGARVAN

ROSSMORE

ILLAUNMORE

WILLIAMSTOWN

DROMINEER

MOUNTSHANNON

YOUGHAL BAY

NENAGH

GARRYKENNEDY

PORTROE

SCARRIFF

TUAMGRANEY

KILLALOE

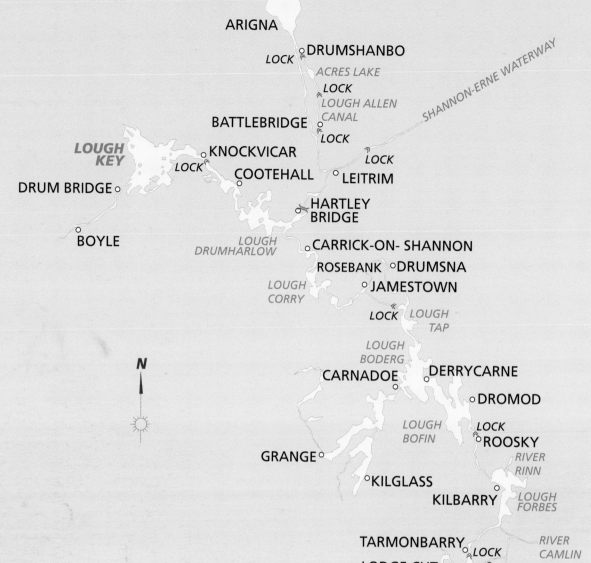

LOUGH ALLEN

ARIGNA

LOCK ○ DRUMSHANBO

ACRES LAKE

LOCK

LOUGH ALLEN CANAL

BATTLEBRIDGE

LOCK

SHANNON-ERNE WATERWAY

LOUGH KEY

KNOCKVICAR

LOCK

COOTEHALL ○ LEITRIM

LOCK

DRUM BRIDGE ○

HARTLEY BRIDGE

BOYLE ○

LOUGH DRUMHARLOW

CARRICK-ON- SHANNON

ROSEBANK ○ DRUMSNA

LOUGH CORRY

○ JAMESTOWN

LOCK *LOUGH TAP*

LOUGH BODERG

N

CARNADOE ○ DERRYCARNE

○ DROMOD

LOUGH BOFIN

LOCK

○ ROOSKY

RIVER RINN

GRANGE ○

○ KILGLASS

KILBARRY *LOUGH FORBES*

TARMONBARRY

LOCK *RIVER CAMLIN*

LODGE CUT

RICHMOND HARBOUR

STROKESTOWN ○

ROYAL CANAL

○ LANESBOROUGH

PORTRUNNY ○

GALEY BAY

BARLEY HARBOUR

RINDOON ○

R. INNY

LECARROW

DERRY BAY

LOUGH REE

INNER LAKES

HODSON BAY ○ ○ GLASSAN

○ BALLYGLASS

THE MIDDLE AND UPPER SHANNON
1755–1785

It is possible to build up some idea of how these works proceeded from the reports to parliament and also from subsequent surveys carried out in the years that followed. It seems to have been assumed that if the places where there were extensive shallows, which had divided the river up into separate navigable stretches in the past, were overcome by making lateral canals, the river could be made navigable throughout its length. No attempt was made to construct weirs to control the levels and the whole issue of drainage and the extensive flooding of the river basin did not appear to have been given any consideration. The many factors that were responsible for the flooding, such as the other stretches where there were less obvious shallows but where the channel was confined, the existence of extensive eel

weirs and the confining nature of the narrow arches of the bridges, were issues which were not to be addressed until the mid-1800s.

Omer began work in 1755 at Meelick where there were two areas of extensive shallows, Meelick and Keelogue, and he decided to construct a lateral canal to bypass these, which was to be some 2 miles (3.2km) long with a lock, 120ft (36.6m) long by 19ft (5.79m) wide which had a 7ft 3in (2.2m) fall, a single-storey lock house, three accommodation bridges and a guard lock at the upper end.[11] Omer was constructing the first locks on the Grand Canal at this time which were 137ft (41.7m) by 20ft (6.1m) to cater for boats carrying 170 tons. John Smeaton visited Meelick in 1773 and recorded: 'I saw a lock on the Shannon

Meelick: the lock house designed by Thomas Omer in 1755 with the date over the doorway inside the porch, which was added later.

about three miles and a half below Banagher, which has been in use eighteen years, it is built with the same kind of stones, hammer dressed, and has stood very well.'[12] It was reported to parliament that between 1757 and 1761 a total of £10,455 16s 6d had been expended by Thomas Mahon, Mr Clements and Mr Omer and that works were also being carried out on the whole river.[13] This would suggest that once work was underway at Meelick, Omer worked up river beginning works at Banagher, Shannonbridge and Athlone.

At Banagher a much shorter canal was needed to bypass the bridge and shallows but, although there was about a 3ft (0.9m) fall, he constructed the lock with just a single set of gates and made a harbour area in the canal with one of his two-storey lock houses, built to the same design as similar houses on the Grand Canal and Lagan Navigation. At Shannonbridge an even shorter canal, formed in the river by creating an artificial island at the eastern end of the bridge, had a similar arrangement with just one set of gates to overcome the fall of about 9in (0.2m) with a similar lock house. Both the Banagher and Shannonbridge lock houses survive today. The work at Shannonbridge coincided with the building of a new bridge here. In 1757 Henry L'Estrange and Willam Talbot were granted £2,000 by the Irish Parliament to enable them to finish this bridge and it was subsequently reported to parliament that the work was completed but considerably more than the grant had been expended.[14]

Banagher: the lock house as it was in the 1960s, built to Thomas Omer's design in the 1750s.

Banagher: Omer's lock house today.

Shannonbridge: Omer's lock house as it was in the 1970s is now used as a tourist information office.

It is known that Omer had turned his attention to Athlone by 18 January 1757 because it was reported in Faulkner's *Dublin Journal*:

Next Saturday the jury of the town of Athlone are to assemble to value the ground through which a canal is to be cut next Spring. Special Commissioners of the Inland Navigation are to assemble to receive the verdict of the jury. A scheme in imitation of the one at Belfast is in negotiation for the benefit of the poor of this town during this severe season which will be of infinite service to many hundreds in and about Athlone.

The same newspaper reported on 23 July 1757: 'Mr Omer arrived in Athlone on Thursday and appointed a spot for erecting a lock on, where contrary to expectation there was a fine foundation. There are thirteen gangs at work of twenty-five men each, which makes in the whole 325 men on the Canal.' This gives an interesting insight into the gang system, which he used, and the large numbers of men involved. The canal was one and a half miles long and to overcome the fall of 4ft 6ins (1.3m) Omer placed the lock measuring 120ft (36.5m) long by 19ft (5.79m) wide, the

Athlone: a detail of the gate recess of the guard lock showing the small ashlars used at that time.

Athlone: the recess for the guard lock on the canal built in the 1760s.

Clondara: the navigation passed through the lock and along the River Camlin to Lough Forbes.

Clondara: the lock dating from the 1760s as it is today, much restored on a number of occasions. (Niall Galway)

same size as the lock at Meelick, about one third of the way up the canal with the same two-storey lock house at the lock. He had to build a bridge to carry the main road to the west, widening out the canal to form a harbour or lay-by above it. He also placed a single set of guard gates to protect the canal in time of flood. These guard locks were sometimes referred to as rymer or rimer locks, although in fact a rymer was the name given to the posts that supported the sluices, enabling them to slide up and down, in early flash locks that did not have conventional gates. Another widening of the canal to form a second lay-by was made at the upper end of the canal, near where it re-entered the river. Again, as at Meelick, there were no plans to construct a weir in the river to regulate the flow.

A strange event was recorded in Faulkner's journal on 17 September 1765 which might have proved very helpful in the carrying out of the works: 'This hath been the driest season ever known in this kingdom in so much that the bed

Clondara: the wall of lock chamber showing the restoration over the years. (Niall Galway)

of that fine river the Shannon was dry at Athlone bridge.'[15] This was a repetition of a similar drought recorded in 1252, mentioned in the Introduction.

The timescale of the remaining works is uncertain, Omer's employment with the commissioners ended in 1768 and a decision seems to have been taken to reduce the scale of the locks on the upper river. In that year John Trail, the Grand Canal Company engineer, had recommended reducing the size of the Grand Canal locks to 80ft (24.3m) by 16ft (4.87m) and the 1st and 2nd locks on the Main Line were built to these dimensions although a further reduction in size was later recommended by Smeaton and adopted. At Lanesborough a similar approach was used as at Shannonbridge, creating a small island to form a short canal on the west side of the river with a single set of gates to overcome the small fall of 1ft (0.4m). Brownrigg said the lock chamber was 87ft 38in (26.5m) by 18ft 6in (5.6m), beginning just below the bridge with a lock house built over the upper part of the canal, partly over the lock itself.[16] From Tarmonbarry to Lough Forbes the river was full of shallows and it was decided because the fall was greater to make a short canal with a conventional lock, 85ft 8ins

Clondara: the lock house built to Omer's design, rather neglected today. (Niall Galway)

Roosky: the early navigation canal is in the line of trees on the left, passing under the road in the village and continuing on to Lough Bofin with the present navigation and lock on the right. (Photograph Kevin Dwyer AIPPA)

Roosky: the flood gate grooves on the canal just downstream of the road bridge. (Niall Galway)

Roosky: the lock wall showing the small ashlars used at that time. (Niall Galway)

(27.5m) by 18ft 4ins (5.6m), to link up with the River Camlin, which was narrow but navigable from there into Lough Forbes.

By 1769 Roosky lock was completed; in that year Patrick Edgar, giving evidence before parliament, had reported that by November of that year 80 miles (130km) of the Shannon would be navigable.[17] At Roosky a longer lateral canal had been needed. The lock, 85ft 10ins (27.5m) by 18ft 69ins (5.6m) to overcome the fall of 3ft 4ins (0.9m), was at the lower end of the canal with flood gates just downstream of the canal road bridge. Further upstream the great bend of the river from Drumsna to Jamestown was bypassed by cutting a canal across the loop with a lock and two bridges. The locks were getting smaller: Jamestown lock was only 66ft 6ins (20.2m) by 14ft 3ins (4.3m) to overcome the fall

of 5ft 3ins (1.6m). It appears to have been completed in the early 1770s because John Cowan made reference to 'the Charleston Canal' in his publication in 1773.[18]

The original parliamentary grant in 1755 allocated to the Shannon works was £17,000. In 1771 it was stated that £38,651 had been expended on the river upstream of Killaloe between 1755 and 1770, which suggests that tillage duties had also to be expended to fund the continuation of the works. In 1785 the first report received for some time on the works from Killaloe upstream was received.[19] Access to coal, to meet the growing demand from the city of Dublin, was uppermost in the minds of the members of parliament. Thomas Riely gave evidence that there was an 'inexhaustible' supply of coals around Lough Allen and iron ore 'in greatest abundance'. Colonel Tarrant, superintendent of works to the Grand Canal Company, reported that there were a great number of falls from Lough Allen to Jamestown and Richard Evans, principal engineer to the same company, appears to have carried out a complete survey of the works for the Navigation Board. He estimated that it would cost £12,000 to make the river navigable from Jamestown into Lough Allen and that £7,000 was needed to carry out works between Jamestown and Killaloe. He reported that the Jamestown Canal was 'open to the Passage of Boats but needs some Repairs'. Colonel Tarrant had recommended the construction of sections of lateral canal on the west side of the river between Battlebridge and Lough Allen, and he appears to have carried out some works in the 1780s

Roosky: the lock on the canal, the only original lock dating back to the 1760s which was not subsequently altered. (Niall Galway)

Roosky: the upper gate recess of the lock giving an indication of the size of the lock. (Niall Galway)

near Battlebridge and also between the Shannon and Arigna rivers at the southern end of Lough Allen.

At Carrick a new bridge had replaced the old one in 1718 financed by Sir George St George of Hatley Manor, Carrick, who was awarded the tolls of the bridge to pay for its maintenance. He had an admirer in Samuel Clifford, who dedicated a poem to him in 1786, 'I beheld with pleasure your beautiful improvements on the banks of the Shannon, and how your happy tenantry, basking in the sunshine of prosperity, see their annual rents returning into their own hands; nor can complain that their landlord is an absentee':[20]

> But above all, may Irish patriots strive
> To make the inland navigation thrive.
> May commerce fill thy stream from shore to shore
> Spread thy broad sail, and ply the well-tuned oar.

The quality of some of the original works was now being called into question. The locks at Roosky and Clondara needed 'very little Repair' as did the single set of gates at Lanesborough. These works had been completed some twenty years earlier, but the works at Athlone, which had been completed even earlier, came in for criticism. The banks of the canal and the lock were said to be 'much out of Repair. At both Shannonbridge and Banagher he said that the single sets of gates were very unsatisfactory requiring a great number of men to haul the boats up against the current. At Meelick the sills and floor of the lock were in bad condition, and 'the Machinery in such bad Order that Boats cannot possibly pass'. He estimated that it would require £350 to put it into repair. Evans suggested that the Grand Juries of the relevant counties along the Shannon should put up funds at the rate of £150 per mile to add to the Navigation Board funding, and he recommended encouraging the setting up of a company to manage the entire navigation.

Roosky: the original road bridge arch which is unaltered on the upstream side. (Niall Galway)

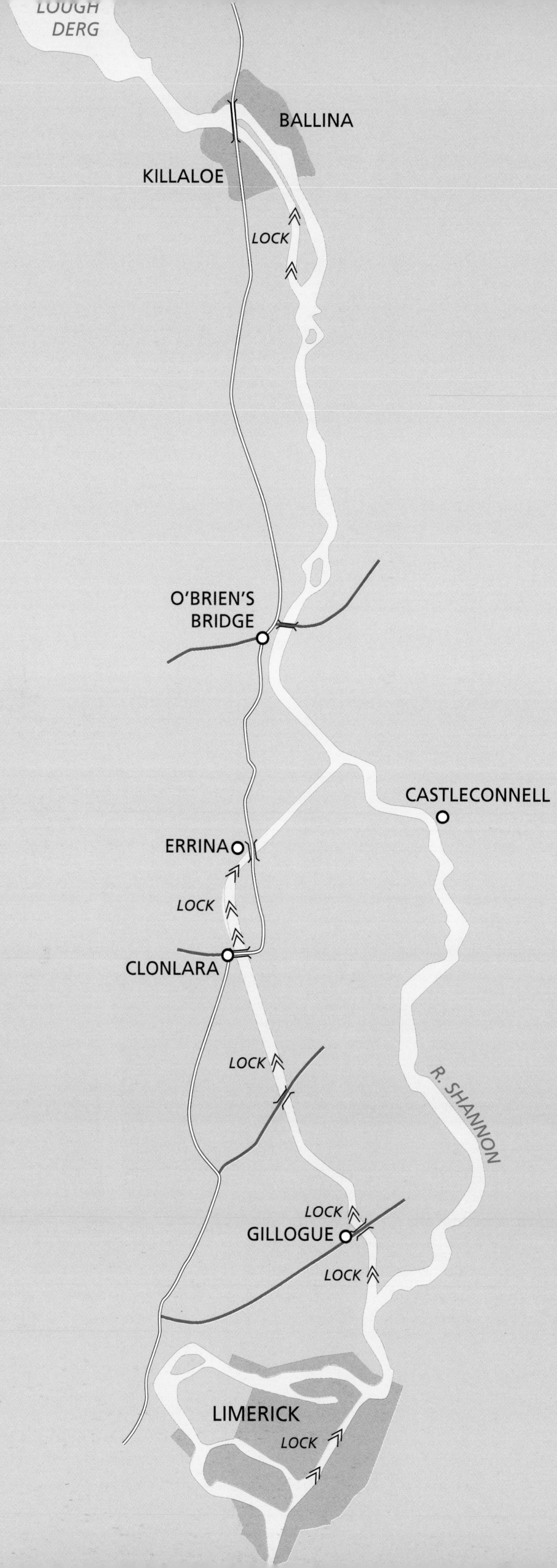

LOUGH DERG

BALLINA

KILLALOE

LOCK

O'BRIEN'S BRIDGE

CASTLECONNELL

ERRINA

LOCK

CLONLARA

LOCK

R. SHANNON

LOCK

GILLOGUE

LOCK

LIMERICK

LOCK

LIMERICK TO KILLALOE 1757–1783

According to Maurice Lenihan, the Limerick historian, Ockenden began work on 13 June 1757.[21] His extremely difficult task was to overcome the fall of some 100ft (30.4m) in the river in the few short miles between Killaloe and Limerick. He was also overseeing works on both the Nore and the Munster Blackwater at the same time, neither of which was to prove successful, which did not augur well for his works on the Shannon. There were three main areas of rapids to overcome, the first just upstream of Limerick, the second the extensive area of the well-known Doonass Falls and the third at Killaloe.[22] He began work in Limerick where the river made a large loop, which he bypassed with a two-mile-long canal. In 1759 he reported to parliament that he had completed two miles of canal to Rebogue with a single lock at the lower end and that he had expended £7,745 of the £8,000 allocated to him.[23] Two years later his deputy engineer, Edward Uzuld, gave detailed accounts of the expenditure of a further £3,713 7s 10d, and stated that Ockenden's salary was £250 p.a. and his own salary was £120 p.a.[24] He said that the first stretch of canal to Rebogue was nearing completion, needing a further expenditure of £401 and that it would require a sum of £19,548 to complete the remaining works to Killaloe, an estimate that, like so many of these early estimates, was to prove greatly inadequate. It was also revealed that these canal works were also supplying water for extensive mills, the Limerick Lock Mills above the 1st lock, in which Edward Uzuld had an interest. In the early 1760s money was also allocated by parliament for a new Custom House quay at Limerick and for works to Baal's Bridge.

Ockenden died in June of that year and, in 1763, a committee appointed to look into expenditure on the works reported that a further grant had not been claimed because work was held up owing to a difference of opinion that had arisen as to which of two courses to adopt.[25] A further report in 1767 accounted for the spending of another £2,994 12s 6½ between 1 November 1766 and 7 April 1767.[26] The report stated: 'very considerable progress had been made during the above Period, in the said Work, which Account was confirmed by several Members of the committee, from their own Knowledge'. As already indicated, public works grants were drying up by this time and parliament gratefully agreed to the incorporation of the Limerick Navigation

Limerick Navigation: the recess in the quay wall for the gate of the proposed lock at the entrance to the Abbey River gives some indication of the size the lock would have been. (Ray Dunne, Waterways Ireland)

Limerick Navigation: attempts were made in the 1780s to make a weir and lock at the entrance to the Abbey River which were uncovered during the drainage and navigation works in 2001. (Ray Dunne, Waterways Ireland)

Company and handed over the concern to them.[27] Under the terms of the Act the new company was to receive a grant of £6,000 to add to the subscriptions it had raised of £10,000. A total of twenty-five subscribers had raised the capital, among them well known Limerick figures such as Sir Lucius O'Brien and Edmond Sexton Pery.[28] These men were all wealthy landowners and merchants of the area but had no engineering or administrative experience in running a navigation company.

In 1783 a parliamentary inquiry into works on the River Shannon came up with some further information.[29] The Limerick Navigation Company's proposal had been to create a wet dock in Limerick by building a weir and lock at the entrance to the Abbey River so that boats could lie in a dock with a fixed water level up to the New Bridge (later renamed Mathew Bridge to honour Father Mathew) that had been erected in 1762. This would also make it easier for smaller boats to pass under Baal's Bridge entering and leaving the 1st lock. However, around 1778 the Mayor of Limerick mounted objections to this scheme because it would 'deaden the flow' and divert much of the water of the Abbey River into the main channel of the Shannon to pass under Thomond Bridge. It was considered that this bridge would be unable to cope because some of its arches were blocked up and it would be costly to remedy this. The result was that the company had to abandon work on this scheme. The inquiry went on to look at the works being carried on by the Limerick Navigation Company. The 1st lock had burst several times because the Lock Mill was demanding too great a head of water. It was stated: 'This company laboured under many Difficulties from the Ignorance and Knavery of the Persons concerned under the first and subsequent Acts.' It was estimated that a further £5,000 would complete the navigation from Limerick to O'Brien's Bridge and another £5,000 from there to Killaloe. Work was also needed at O'Brien's Bridge which may have been a reference to the making of a navigation arch here.

THE END OF THE NAVIGATION BOARD

By this time the inevitable had happened and the parliamentary surplus had turned into a deficit. A letter written to the Duke of Bedford by a Mr Rigby in 1765 reflects the opinions of some people at that time:

Discontent [is] lurking in the breasts of some of the oldest and steadiest supporters in government, owing to the sacrifice which [it] is daily making to popularity, and the profusion of public money given away in jobs, to the amount of £114,000, more than double the sum which your Grace would let them have in your last session. How my Lord Lieutenant could at present prevent it, is indeed another question.[30]

By this time the reign of the 'undertakers' in the Irish Parliament had ended and the English administration had re-imposed its control. A further Act continued the tillage duties until 1779 but stipulated that if a navigation 'at the expence of the Publick may be found in many instances inconveniently burthensome, and attended with great delay' private undertakers could be approved on any of the schemes, who could receive public funding out of the tillage duties up to one sixth of expenditure incurred, payable when the money had been expended.[31] A time limit was to be imposed and the property forfeited if the agreements were broken. In the late 1770s another Act authorized the continuation of the tillage duties but stipulated that no new warrants could be issued by the Navigation Board until those unsatisfied and other debts had been discharged, save salaries, rent and accidental breaches.[32] Thereafter, the commissioners had to rely on the tillage duties with the result that many of the navigation works ground to a halt. In some cases like the Grand Canal, companies were formed, who raised money by subscription and took advantage of the 1771–1772 Act. However, the navigation upstream of Killaloe appears to have had virtually nothing further done, even by way of maintenance, for some years. In actual fact, just under £400,000 was expended on all the navigation works in the country between 1755 and 1769, almost half of which was from tillage duties. However, this so-called 'bonanza', not such a large amount of money, was to kick start the construction of the fine waterways network heritage enjoyed today.

In October 1783 Mr Crofton addressed the Commons. He said that money had been given to Mr Hercules Brown, who undertook to complete work on the Limerick to Killaloe navigation, but 'this gentleman however had done little or nothing'.[33] He lamented the wretched state of the Shannon Navigation in other parts: 'the banks fallen in – locks without gates, requiring fifty men to drag a boat through them – the lock houses, as unnecessary, fallen to decay'. At this stage Parliament directed that the Navigation Board was to account annually to the Commissioners of Imprest Accounts.[34] These five commissioners, who had started out in 1761 as unpaid, had been given a salary of £500 p.a. in 1771 and, subsequently, this had been raised to £800 when their work was increased by taking over the functions of investigations into all accounts by parliamentary committees.[35] Their role was also extended into assessing future navigation schemes, together with the estimated costs, and when the work was completed, examining proof that the money had actually been spent correctly. They also administered the subsequent debenture scheme for public works which was to follow shortly. The weakness in this arrangement was that, while they were in a position to examine accounts, they did not have any technical engineering staff to make judgments about the actual work.

Parliament now began a full inquiry into the activities of the Navigation Board and the insufficiency of the accounts furnished was criticized: 'In reality no more in the Discharge Part than a General Abstract of the Warrants granted to the different Persons to whom Money had been paid subject to Account, unsatisfactory in itself and unattended by any Book, Voucher or Paper whatsoever.'[36] When the commissioners were asked for more details they responded by saying that 'no other Account than the Abstract above mentioned could be expected from the Corporation as a Board'. At this stage it was reported that the debts of the Board stood at £21,952 13s 6d and that this debt had arisen 'from the Anticipation of their Funds, by drawing Warrants on the Vice-Treasurer and raising Money thereon when there was no Fund in the Treasury for that purpose'. It was further identified that a sum of £57,000 and upwards had been issued at various times for which there was no manner of account produced.

A deeper investigation into the affairs of the Navigation Board uncovered even worse practices.[37] A report was received from the Imprest Accounts Commissioners by a parliamentary committee stating that warrants were brought to members' houses to sign and then their names entered as having attended meetings. In order to raise money for the warrants some of the members lent the money at a rate of 6 per cent or more. These amounts were then repaid with the interest, which added to the debt. Even though the practice was queried, the repayments were allowed as were charges for travelling expenses, dinner bills, gunpowder bills, law business and land conveyance bills. The committee said it was their opinion 'that from proceedings of the said Corporation, and the Nature of the Business entrusted to them, they are incompetent to promote the Inland Navigations of this Kingdom agreeable to the Intentions of the Legislature'.

The writing was on the wall for the Navigation Board. Parliament decided that the board would be dissolved on 25 March 1786 and its functions replaced by local commissioners for those navigations that had not been taken over by private companies and were relying solely on the income from tolls.[38] Navigation debentures could be issued at 4 per cent and parliament decided to discontinue the tillage duties and, in future, assistance for navigation works would be given in the form of loans. This was enacted in 1789 when an Act was passed authorizing the payment of debentures at 4 per cent to be issued when double the amount was shown to have been expended.[39] Rules and regulations were also drawn up to be observed by people applying for private funding for waterways: they had to lodge detailed plans and estimates and subscribers were to be compelled to make the payments of the sums subscribed on pain of forfeiting their shares and deposits.

The investigations into the board's affairs continued after its demise. In 1786 it was reported that salaries were owing to Tarrant and Evans for their survey work, that a petition had been received from the Grand Canal Company about money owed to it and the salaries for lock keepers on the Shannon had not been paid. A supplement to this report, detailing the debts, had some of these disallowed, including items for entertainment and quarterly dinners.[40] It was revealed that the secretary, Richard Baggs, not only was receiving a salary from the board but at one time was also treasurer for the Shannon Navigation, treasurer and secretary for the Barrow Navigation and secretary to both the Grand Canal and Kildare Canal companies, giving him a total income at that time of £817.

In the same year both he and the unfortunate accountant, John Mitchell, were told that their salaries for the previous ten years were to be forfeited if satisfactory accounts were not produced by the beginning of August. A plaintive letter was received from the accountant, John Mitchell, asking for more time:

... as an Officer of the Board, acting without their Instructions, and consequently neither Supported nor Protected by anything but a fair Character, that I have no Assistance, but one Hand, to go through so great a labour, no Office to execute it in, no Emolument to be derived from it, and that my office will, I presume, cease with the Navigation Board, 24 inst. I should, in my judgment, rather have a Claim to your Protection than run the risk of your Censure.[41]

As a result of these threats of forfeiture of salaries some accounts were forthcoming, which showed that between 1778 and 1784 only £47,080 had been received in tillage duties and £74,365 paid out. The accounts submitted showed that between 1782 and 1786 a total of £12,621 had been paid out for the Shannon Navigation but it is not clear whether that included the £10,000 paid to the Limerick Navigation Company. The Commissioners of Imprest Accounts were obviously struggling with the accounts submitted:

Notwithstanding much Time has been employed in diligently inspecting the Accounts and Papers delivered by Mr Mitchell, the Commissioners have deemed it expedient to defer reporting upon them for the present, further Investigation being still necessary in Accounts defective in Material and involved in much Perplexity, in order that the Public may derive all the Advantages that the Nature and peculiar Circumstances of the Case will admit.[42]

Limerick Navigation: Errina lock today obscured by dense vegetation.(Brian Goggin)

By this time they were coming to grips with all expenditure of public money on public works: 'But since the Nature of this Office is better understood by those to whom Public Money has been entrusted, the Business of accounting is in a State of Improvement, and most accounts are now brought forward in so regular a Method as to render much Observation unnecessary.'[43] Eventually in 1790 they reported that a total of £587,537 11s 7d had been issued by the Navigation Board, of which £359,868 9s 6d had come from tillage duties and the rest from grants.[44] All of this money had eventually been accounted for, although most of the warrants had been lost, but seventy-seven people had been instructed to deliver accounts of their expenditure, fifty-eight of whom had ignored the precepts.

THE LIMERICK NAVIGATION COMPANY 1784–1800

Early in 1788 a report had been received from the Limerick Navigation Company.[45] The directors said that the work was 'in great Forwardness but not so as to form a Communication with the different Counties intended by Parliament' and they estimated it would require a considerable sum of money to complete the navigation. They said that they had spent £8,524 of their own funds and now needed financial aid, for which they were willing in return to relinquish all rights. Even though they had been unable to pay any dividend, several gentlemen had agreed to subscribe a further £18,000 if granted £6,000 in public funding and they undertook to complete all the work within five years. Parliament agreed that they had fully complied with the conditions and deserved aid.[46] After 1789 the company was able to avail of the 1789 Act to apply for debentures and William Chapman, who had come to Ireland initially as an agent for Boulton and Watt to supervise the erection of a steam engine at the Tyrone collieries and then made a name for himself working with the Kildare Canal Company in 1786 and subsequently as a consultant with the Grand Canal Company, was invited to advise the Limerick Navigation Company about the state of their works. He prepared a report in 1791, which gives some idea of the state of the navigation.[47]

Chapman indicated that many of the locks had been constructed to different dimensions and designs and some of them would have to be rebuilt. The chambers of the triple-lock at the head of the middle Errina section of the navigation were 20ft (6m) shorter than all the other locks and he recommended doing away with the middle chamber and reducing it to two chambers to allow them to be extended. He was invited to join the Limerick Navigation Company as a consultant engineer and he remained with them for about three years, carrying out the rebuilding of the Errina and some of the other locks. He also laid out the line for the final stretch of canal to Killaloe but left the company before it was completed. As far as parliament was concerned work was proceeding and the application accompanied by certified accounts for a draw down of debentures was supported by Chapman's comment: 'They are proceeded upon with all possible Diligence and Attention to Economy, and are in as good a State as the Nature of them will admit.'[48] There was a strong hint in this comment that the undertaking was proving very difficult. In making its next application for a further draw down the 'sub engineer' reported that the works 'are in as good a State as could be expected from the almost continuous Rains which fell during the last season'.[49]

In 1795 Chapman was forced to address a letter to the subscribers of the Limerick Navigation Company in response to accusations that were being made about his conduct of the works by Richard Griffith of the Grand Canal Company.[50] Griffith had pointed to 'the Error of laying out the Line and the Blunders of Execution'. Chapman responded that the line had been laid out long before he joined the company and except for the failure to avoid the deep sinking at Errina, he reckoned it was laid out judiciously. He did criticize the fact that they had not chosen to use the River Blackwater and for the diversity of lock dimensions. He added that the bad workmanship in the use of lime was a matter that should have been reported to the board by those overseeing the work, but he disputed the accusations about the works at Errina and Cussane locks. He said that the Errina lock had to be lengthened to conform with the others and it had not been an option to extend it as a triple-chambered lock because of the lack of foundation so it had been reduced to a double chamber. The method he adopted caused the least

Limerick Navigation: Errina lock as it was in 1974. It was originally constructed with three chambers and subsequently altered to two.

possible alteration to the original structure, requiring only the raising of the lower sill and an adjustment to the next lock down the line. He defended the site chosen for Cussane lock, which Griffith had claimed was on a poor foundation, by saying that winter flooding was a consideration and he was avoiding a long tail canal that would tend to silt up. He claimed that moving it farther up the canal would not have resulted in any better foundation, according to his investigations, and that all that was needed was to build the lower chamber to his plan on a wooden platform secured both by sheeting and bearing piles, with the body of the chamber on an inverted arch. He concluded:

I know that, in all bodies of men, there are some, who from being misinformed or misled, are perpetually accusing of error those who have the charge of public works: - of course, I am not surprised at having experienced this in your Company; but, I trust that, whoever has read the various reports I have, from time to time, given to you, attended with other corroborative proofs, will have seen a sufficient refutation of every charge worthy of notice. At the same time, I am ready to palliate the conduct of those, who have been apparently inimical to me, by attributing it to the want of consideration that all the operative causes in fixing the site, and particular circumstances of great works, can never be known to the casual observer, and, even if known, can only be judged of by those of professional experience. I wish you success in the future measures you may pursue.

Significantly, an N.B. had been written in by someone in long hand: 'Mr Griffith proposed to purchase the Navigation and rather disparaged than exaggerated the value of it.'

After Chapman returned to England the works appear to have dragged on and the closing years of the century saw further statements from the Limerick Navigation Company to the Imprest Accounts Commissioners, but the small amounts certified of payments made to enable further debenture payments to be drawn down would suggest that there was not a great deal of work going on. Reporting on the Limerick Navigation Company in 1799 the commissioners stated that the company had raised £8,300 by subscription and received £16,600 in public funding and debentures and the estimated cost of completing the works amounted to another £6,080. The navigation was now open to small boats; there were ten of these operating restricted to fifteen to twenty tons. In that year over 1,000 tons of corn came down the navigation together with cargoes of slates and turf, and £102 10s was received in tolls, which was almost enough to meet the cost of the small establishment of secretary, treasurer, overseer and nine lock keepers. The navigation

Limerick Navigation: Annabeg lock today, at the lower end of the Errina to Plassy Canal. (Brian Goggin)

William Chapman (1749-1832).

To the SUBSCRIBERS of the
LIMERICK NAVIGATION,

GENTLEMEN,

HAVING been fhewn, by Mr. Griffith, his printed propofals to you, relative to the completion of your Navigation; I was forry to find that he had, from inadvertance, or fome other caufe, expreffed himfelf, in fuch a manner, as might be implied a cenfure on my conduct: and, therefore, in juftice to myfelf, and thofe who have been pleafed to think favourably of me, I feel myfelf called upon to take notice of what he has faid on " the Error of laying out the Line, and the Blunders of Execution."—As to the laying out of the Line, it was done long before I was concerned in it; and, in juftice to my predeceffors, I muft fay that, excepting in not taking meafures to avoid the deep finking of Erinagh, the Line was in general laid out judicioufly.——They erred, however, in turning the courfe of the Blackwater, which might have been paffed over by giving it fufficient width of water-way; and, alfo, in making their Locks a diverfity of different dimenfions.—Blunders of Execution may be of two kinds;—the ill Conftruction, and the bad Pofition of the works.—The firft, will, in general, confift of badnefs of workmanfhip, arifing from ill wrought or infufficient ftones, and bad mortar a long time made, or not made with quick lime:—that fault will lie with the executive perfon, if he did not reprefent thofe things to you and his reprefentations were not attended to.

THE other, as to pofition, I take upon myfelf, and therefore I defired Mr. Griffith to point out, to me, what he conceived to be fuch; which he did, by telling me that he thought the fall of Erinagh Lock ought to have been in three Chambers as before:—and that the Lock at Caflane ought to have been further inland, to have avoided the bad foundation of its lower Chamber.

I SHOULD not have thought it worthy my notice to enter into a juftification of thefe things, were it not that the implied general cenfure is publifhed with the authority of a Gentleman, who defervedly ftands high with the Public, for his encouragement of, and attention to Inland Navigations.

THE Lock of Erinagh, when I took the chief Superintendance, was ftanding firm in the higheft and loweft Chambers, but much broken down and deeply excavated in the middle one, by the Shannon having been permitted to run through.— Each of the three Chambers was 20 feet too fhort; and, at a few yards below the tail of the Lock, there was running clay to a great depth, which had rifen 6 feet above the level of the Sill——Under this predicament, as it was in vain to attempt extending the foundation into the running clay, by lengthening the Lock 60 feet; and, equally fo, to attempt keeping that clay (with high banks on each fide of it) down

down to the depth of the original Sill; I concluded the moft œconomic mode was to avail myfelf of the building, as it ftood, with the leaft poffible alteration; which was to make two Chambers out of the three; which left the exifting building ftanding; and to raife the loweft Sill fo as to be fuitable to a double fall, and above fuch Level as would be attended with material difficulty in keeping down the rifing clay; by doing of which, and raifing of Newton Lock, a confiderable fum was faved, and no more intervening Falls required than were originally intended.

THE Scite of the Lock of Caflane was fixed fo as to avoid deep finking to the tail, and in the lower Chamber of it, further than neceffary to retire out of the Winter-flooded lands, which would have required confiderable embankment at the head of the Lock.—This pofition was the moft eligible, on two grounds; the one the heavy expence of making a long tail cut, 6 feet under the loweft water of the Shannon (which, fhort as it is, the Company have found very expenfive;) and, the other, the difficulty of keeping a long tail Canal from fhoaling, as you may, fufficiently, have experienced in the tail cut of Annabeg.—From thefe caufes, the pofition of the Lock was the beft, independently of foundation, which foft as it is (on marle and other depofits of ftill or flowly moving water) will be fully fufficient, if the tail of the Chamber be built according to my plan, on a wooden platform fecured both by fheeting and bearing piles, and the body of the Chamber on an inverted Arch — Befides this, I am of opinion, that, had the Lock been fet fo much further back, in fearch of a good foundation, as to have incurred as great a charge as is now neceffary for fecuring the prefent, the defired effect would not have been produced; becaufe, I have reafon to believe, from what I faw in the foundation of the middle breaft of that Lock, that the bed of gravel, in which the higher part of the Canal runs, only thinly fuperinduces the bed of marle that the lower Chamber is now upon; and, confequently, that the effect of placing the Lock higher, would have been an additional charge, attended with all the inconveniencies of a long tail Canal

I KNOW that, in all bodies of men, there are fome, who from been mifinformed or mifled, are perpetually accufing of error, thofe who have the charge of public works:—of courfe, I am not furprifed at having experienced this in your Company; but, I truft that, whoever has read the various reports I have, from time to time, given you, attended with other corroborative proofs, will have feen a fufficient refutation of every charge worthy of notice.—At the fame time, I am ready to palliate the conduct of thofe, who have been apparently inimical to me; by attributing it to the want of confideration that all the operative caufes in fixing the Scite, and particular circumftances of great works, can never be known to the cafual obferver; and even, if known, can only be judged of by thofe of profeffional experience.

I WISH you fuccefs in the future meafures you may purfue,

And am,

GENTLEMEN,

Your obedient humble Servant,

WILLIAM CHAPMAN.

Dublin, 26th November, 1795.

N.B. Mr Griffith propofed to purchafe the Navigation, and rather difparaged than exagerated the Value of it.

William Chapman's letter to the subscribers with the handwritten comment.

was, however, still far from satisfactory; there were no towpaths on the river sections and shoals were a hazard in the river when the water was low in the summer, while strong currents made it impassable in places in winter.

THE MIDDLE SHANNON AND UPPER SHANNON 1786–1800

By the 1790s both the Limerick Navigation Company and the Grand Canal Company, who saw their works as moving towards completion, began to show concern about the state of the works on the middle and upper Shannon. In 1791 William Chapman had also been asked to carry out a survey of the Shannon from Killaloe to Lough Allen at the request of the Limerick Navigation Company.[51] Because

of the existence of shallows he recommended using 'Dutch vessels' with shallow draft and lee-boards and masts that could be easily lowered, which could carry a cargo of fifty tons. He confirmed the evidence of Richard Evans's 1784 report about the condition of Meelick lock, bearing out the fact that it had been very badly constructed: 'The present gates are in such a wretched state through want of swing beams, sluices etc., that even with the help of loose boards to stop the openings, and other contrivances, it requires near three hours and a considerable force of men to pass a boat through the lock.' He put forward two schemes for extending the navigation into Lough Allen, both requiring canals. He produced a modest estimate of £7,650 to put the navigation in order, which included fitting new lock

Lough Ree: a drawing of Rindoon by Daniel Grose made in the 1790s illustrating the type of boat used on the lake. (Courtesy of Lord Rossmore and the Irish Architectural Archive)

gates and making a canal into Lough Allen, with a further expenditure of £6,381 for less urgent improvements, which together with expenditure on machinery and other expenses brought it to a total of £14,931 12s.

Chapman also referred to how useful he had found a chart of the river drawn by John Cowan. This had been published as early as 1773, the first of its kind to be produced, and was subsequently republished in 1795 in a slightly different form.[52] Cowan indicated all the works from the Jamestown Canal to Portumna and also showed a shortcut canal across St John's Point at Rindoon on Lough Ree. The following legend is engraved on his second edition:

At the summer Assizes of 1794, the High Sheriffs and Grand Juries of the counties Roscommon, Leitrim, Mayo, Galway, Clare, Limerick, King's County, and Tipperary, resolved that the completing of the navigation of the River Shannon and the great rivers adjoining thereto, from Lough Allen to Limerick, will tend effectively to improve and open the home and foreign markets, to the produce of more than two million acres of land in the heart of the Kingdom; and the execution of this great navigation will effectually advance the commerce, manufactures, agriculture and population of this Kingdom, and the consequent strength of the Empire at Large.

This demonstrates that the Grand Juries were aware that public funding was no longer being allocated to navigation works, but their resolution was not followed by any active attempt to progress the works. Cowan also suggested a scheme to alleviate flooding by diverting the upper reaches of the river from Lough Allen into Sligo Bay. This was commented on many years later in 1859 by Bernard Mullins in a paper to the Institution of Civil Engineers in Ireland, who considered that it was a feasible scheme but impractical 'from the great expense of such an undertaking and its comparative inutility'.[53]

In 1794 the Grand Canal Company proposed to parliament that they should be given a grant to restore the middle Shannon works from Killaloe to Athlone, which they undertook to complete within seven years and to thereafter maintain these works at their own expense, and they received a positive response to this proposal.[54] At the same time the directors instructed John Killaly to survey the river between Killaloe and Athlone. Killaly had carried out some survey work for the canal company and they were about to invite him to join the company and he was to become their principal engineer. The canal company also sought a report on the state of all the Shannon works from their English consultant engineer, William Jessop, who reported in 1794.[55] Jessop began his inspection at Lough Allen and reported that the coalfields here were in urgent need of development and this potential made the extension of the navigation important. He made no reference to the earlier attempts of Colonel Tarrant to make a canal on the west side of the river and suggested diverting the Arigna River into Lough Allen and making a canal to Battlebridge. He recommended improving the Jamestown Canal and he pointed to what he considered the principal problem with the navigation, the lack of towpaths throughout. He suggested the construction of a seven-mile stretch (11km) of canal to bypass the large lakes of Bofin and Boderg rejoining the river above Roosky. Lough Ree also was difficult for the type of boat that could navigate the river sections and canals, and shelter could be provided by planting trees on the islands. Jessop also produced an estimate for the work of £130,000, which included raising embankments to carry a towpath and cutting a navigation channel through the reed beds on one side of the river. His estimates were to influence the negotiations for the company to take over the middle Shannon works. He was later to carry out a further survey of the river in 1801.

CONTEMPORARY ACCOUNTS

The navigation works on the river attracted comments on the potential of inland navigation. C(J), writing in 1778, was enthusiastic about the prospect of making 'communications with every part of the country'.[56] He had an interesting comment to make about the boats in use at that time: 'Their sails are square and hoisted very high; this makes the boat top-heavy and liable to be overset by every sudden squall, whereas my sail having its whole breadth below, and terminating in a cone at the mast head, those dangerous

Killaloe: a print of the original nineteen-arch bridge by Jonathan Fisher in 1792 just before the navigation works were carried out here.

gusts of wind had no effect on my boat.' The well-known traveller and agricultural commentator, Arthur Young, who visited Ireland in the 1770s, referred to the current criticism of the way public funds were being allocated by the Irish Parliament but he pointed to the fact that inland navigation works had been the most favoured and he suggested that the public works were executed 'if not with oeconomy, at least without any dishonourable misapplication; and, as the whole was spent within the kingdom, it certainly was far from being any great national evil'.[57] Young stayed in two places on the shores of Lough Derg, with Peter Holmes of Johnstown, near Dromineer, and Michael Head of Derry Castle at the southern end of the lake. His account gives a very good picture of life around the lake at that time. In addition to his favourable comments and detailed account of how they farmed their estates, Young said that the quantity and size of fish in the lake was 'amazing': pike up to 50lbs, trout of 14lbs, caught by extending a line between two boats lying at anchor, perch, which had appeared on the river for the first time about ten years ago, 'in such plenty that the poor lived on them', bream, eels and gillaroos. He said that Mr Head's grandfather had been the first to use dredged marl from the lake as manure: 'It proved so profitable that the use has much increased since.' The marl is left on the quay to dry for a year before spreading for crops

with all the dung being used for potato growing. J. Fisher in his publication *Scenery of Ireland* in 1792 included an interesting illustration of Killaloe bridge with its nineteen arches and the salmon and eel weirs above it before the navigation lock had been constructed. He commented that the fishery 'gave a degree of employment to the inhabitants of the town' and he added optimistically that a canal was now under construction between Limerick and Killaloe and that all the works on the river were 'at this time considerably advanced' and would soon be completed from Limerick to Carrick. He also included an illustration of Lough Derg from Derry, Michael Head's estate, and remarked that the lake 'for the entire extent is navigable for barks of thirty to forty tons burthen'.

There were also visitors to the river attracted by the historical sites, some of whom left behind some fascinating drawings. Gabriel Beranger and Bigari were rowed down the river from Athlone to Clonmacnois in 1779 and described the trip:

We set out at 5 in the morning in a long narrow boat with Mr Bigari and our interpreter; this vessel was so narrow that the seats held but one person, so that we were sitting one behind the other, with orders of the conductor not to lean to left or right, or that if we did we should be upset and drowned, which not choosing, we kept an erect posture having got only leave to move our head to admire the Shannon and its pleasing banks. [58]

They stopped for something to eat on an island and eventually arrived at Clonmacnois after three hours: 'though the vessel by its structure went fast, one man making it go by two oars or paddles'. In Francis Grose's *Antiquities of Ireland* published in 1791 and subsequent volumes with drawings of Lough Ree by his nephew, Daniel Grose, and other contemporary artists, there are interesting drawings that show sailing boats, small gaff-rigged craft with a bowsprit and a mainsail and two foresails.[59]

A DYING IRISH PARLIAMENT PASSES THE 1800 ACT

In 1799 a resolution was passed by the House:

Resolved that no Money be granted this Session of Parliament for any Pier, Harbour, Quay, Canal, Navigation, Colliery, Road, Bridge, Mill, Mill-work, nor for building or re-building any particular Church or Cathedral, or for any Charity or Public Institution, except Hospitals and Schools, which has not usually and regularly received Parliamentary support. [60]

William Jessop (1745-1814).

Lough Ree: a drawing of Inishbofin by Daniel Grose made in the 1790s illustrating the type of boat used on the lake. (Courtesy of Lord Rossmore and the Irish Architectural Archive)

In the following year, in the closing months of the Irish Parliament before the Act of Union with Westminster, a committee was appointed to investigate the whole state of inland navigation works and operations and its detailed report provides a very clear picture of how things stood at that time.[61] The committee's findings, pointing to the bad superintendence of the expenditure on the works, were very critical:

Your committee find that the period from which the bounty of Parliament for promoting Inland Navigation became conspicuous was that at which there appeared to be a surplus in the Treasury to the amount of nearly half a million, viz about 1755. The avidity with which public grants were from that time sought after for Inland Navigation as well as for other purposes appears from the Journals of the House; the objects of those grants being as various as the interests and inclinations of the Petitioners. . . . It is much to be regretted that great sums of public money have, from time to time, been lavished, without being attended with corresponding advantage to the public. A system of granting public monies, at once so profuse and abortive, was at length exploded.

The disappropriation of the tillage duties, the granting of aid in the form of debentures in proportion to private subscription and the ending of tempting forms of patronage were all moves to create greater accountability. Under the Irish Parliament the only form of accountability had been parliamentary committees, a system that was open to abuse as works and expenditure were often presented in a favourable light to elicit further financial support. The committees met in the Speaker's Chamber, where although minutes were recorded, 'it sometimes happened that three or four friends of a party got together and agree just what they pleased'.[62] However, in considering money spent on public works, including inland navigation, and public funding for manufacturing and other schemes all in the same light, the English Administration made out that they were all subject to 'jobbing'. In fact, the starting up of navigation schemes was to prove critical to the future development of inland navigation in Ireland and any misuse of public funding was due more to bad accounting and faulty estimates and engineering rather than misappropriation. In England navigation schemes were a response to a demand for improved inland transport. If this had been the criteria in Ireland, little would have happened. The total expended in public funding on inland navigations between 1730 and 1790 had only amounted to £857,382 of which over £350,000 had been collected in duties and, considering the impact this was to have on the inland waterway system into the future, it could be said to have been good value for money.

However, the Irish Parliament was encouraged by the comments of both Brownrigg and Chapman about the coalfields at Lough Allen:

It is reasonably presumed that there are many thousand acres; it is good and easy to be worked, and as much of it can be drained without Steam Engines, it may be got at an easy expence; it is found excellent for smelting Iron Stone, of which there are immense Quantities of the best Quality.[63]

Following these investigations and deliberations in 1800, the dying Irish Parliament passed an Act setting up Directors General of Inland Navigation with a fund of £500,000 at their disposal, and for the next thirty years this was to be the body that controlled inland waterway development in Ireland.[64]

CHAPTER TWO
THE EARLY WORKS UNDER THE DIRECTORS GENERAL OF INLAND NAVIGATION 1800–1814

THE DIRECTORS GENERAL OF INLAND NAVIGATION

The appointment of the Directors General of Inland Navigation restored the direct involvement of government in inland waterways.[1] This was a small salaried board of directors with power to set up their own administration including technical advisors, a fund at their disposal and their decisions and accounts subject only to the approval of the Lord Lieutenant, the senior representative of the English Crown in Ireland. It should have been good for the waterways. However, the full potential was not realized for two principal reasons. The appointments, which carried a salary of £500 p.a., were the prerogative of the Lord Lieutenant and inevitably they became political appointments. Instead of choosing men suitably qualified, he was influenced by the fact that promises had been made of rewards in the closing years of the Irish Parliament, at a time when great efforts had to be made to secure a majority during the Union debates to bring about the winding up of the Irish Parliament and achieve a single parliament in Westminster. The second reason was vagueness attached to the future replenishing of the funding of the body when the initial £500,000 ran out. A discussion about this had taken place in the Irish Parliament when a member, Patrick Duigenan, had suggested that the allocation should be doubled, but he was persuaded to withdraw this proposition when he was given a solemn pledge by Lord Castlereagh that further funds would be made available when required.[2]

The Lord Lieutenant, Cornwallis, appointed Sackville Hamilton as chairman together with Hans Blackwood, the Hon. George Cavendish, Francis Trench and William Penefather. Some of them and their successors served for short periods and then moved on to more lucrative positions and others served for longer periods.[3] They were all former members of the Irish Parliament as was the secretary, William Gregory, and one cynic of the time remarked it was 'a new office created by Lord Cornwallis for rewards'. There was also an accountant, three clerks, a messenger and a porter with the total annual outlay in salaries for the establishment of £3,660. A house was rented, 11 Merrion Square, into which Gregory moved while he remained secretary. He was replaced in 1810 by Francis Trench, who was ill for extended periods but served until his death. Engineers were employed when their services were required, but John Brownrigg, who had started out as a surveyor working with Bernard Scale, became their permanent engineer from the outset with assistants appointed as required. Brownrigg had been previously caught up in controversy when he had been pressured by John Binns in the 1780s to comment favourably on the original 'Royal' surveys when the latter was trying to get parliament to agree to the incorporation of a company to construct the Royal Canal.[4] He had also worked under Richard Evans as an assistant engineer on the Boyne Navigation works in the 1790s. His new appointment was to bring him in contact with many of the navigation works.

SHANNONBRIDGE

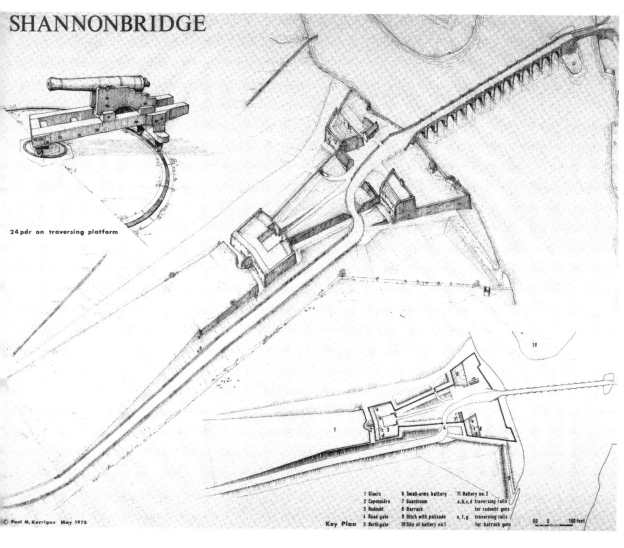

24 pdr on traversing platform

© Paul M. Kerrigan May 1975

Key Plan

1 Glacis	6 Small-arms battery	11 Battery no.2
2 Caponnière	7 Guardroom	a,b,c,d traversing rails
3 Redoubt	8 Barrack	for redoubt guns
4 Road gate	9 Ditch with palisade	e, f, g traversing rails
5 North gate	10 Site of battery no.1	for barrack guns

50   0   100 feet

The Directors General, assuming that the promise of more funding when required in the future would be honoured, allocated sums freely in those early years; they were given a very free hand, with the imperial parliament showing little interest as did the constantly changing administrators in Dublin Castle. They proceeded with their brief, which was to try to bring about the completion of outstanding schemes and generally improve inland navigation throughout the island. The availability of funding prompted the private companies to approach them for financial assistance and they received a number of applications in the early years.

SHANNON FORTIFICATIONS

This was also the period when war was renewed with the French and the administration in the Castle was aware of the support for Napoleon throughout Ireland with the potential threat that he would attempt to invade the unprotected west coast of England by first taking Ireland.[5] As had so often been the case in the past, the strategic importance of the Shannon as a line of defence once again became of importance. A survey of the defensive positions along the Shannon, arising from the events of 1798 and the threat of a French invasion from the west, showed that at the major bridges and fording places the defences consisted largely of earthworks with timber palisades, and a decision was made to make these more substantial. Robert Emmet's rising, which was timed to coincide with a French landing on the west coast, added urgency to the situation. A letter written three days after the rising, on 26 July 1803, relating to the preparation of plans and estimates for the works at Shannonbridge, contained an interesting comment: 'You will also cause levels to be taken to ascertain whether a dam at Shannonbridge would destroy the ford at the Seven Churches [Clonmacnois], and more especially that at the old castle three miles above Shannonbridge, to which there is good access.' Extensive stone fortifications now replaced the earthworks at the two fords at Keelogue and Meelick, at the bridgeheads at Banagher and Shannonbridge and at Athlone, where the Norman castle commanding the bridge had already been repaired and strengthened in the 1790s.

Meelick: the unusual cam-shaped Martello tower built in the early 1800s as part of the defences against an attack by Napoleonic forces from the west.

The importance of defending these crossing places, when there were obviously many other places where the river could be forded, was because it was known that the French forces would have needed the better road approaches to convey their equipment and heavy guns. Although it was also known that Napoleon had made plans to carry portable boats with his army in his plans to invade Ireland, access to the river, except at the bridgeheads, would not have been easy as much of the land was subject to extensive flooding each year and was very marshy. The defensive works were carried out between 1810 and 1816 and the Shannonbridge defences alone cost about £30,000, money that could have made an immense difference if it had been available for navigation works. One result of this was that even after the French threat no longer existed, the garrisons remained on and acted as a support to the police in a law and order role in an increasingly unsettled situation. The works as such had little impact on the navigation, although the plans did include building thirty pontoon boats complete with planks, beams, anchors and cables, which were to be used if any of the bridges had to be destroyed. There was provision for a gun-boat to carry a 'long six-pounder', while the river was also used to convey gunpowder from Athlone, which was the central depot, to the other locations downstream.

THE LIMERICK NAVIGATION 1800–1814

The Limerick Navigation Company had opened the navigation to small boats by 1800 but there appeared to be a reluctance among the directors to invest the necessary money to improve navigation depths and the other improvements necessary to allow larger boats to pass

through. They were, however, quick to get an application in to the Directors General for public funding and negotiations were to prove long and tedious.[6] There was no attempt to sit down together to discuss the matter; it was all carried on by letters passing backwards and forwards.

The Directors General immediately commissioned their engineer, John Brownrigg, to carry out a survey of the works and he reported back in September 1801. He explained the difficulties involved in making river navigations because the canal cuts were vulnerable to flooding, a comment which was to be borne out on the Limerick Navigation over the years. He described the highly unsatisfactory position in Limerick: 'Nothing can equal the inconvenience of the termination of the Navigation in this City of the unnecessary trouble, vexation and want of accommodation experienced without the least redress by the poor boatmen and traders from the country that frequent this port.' He referred to the fact, mentioned in the last chapter, that it had been intended to create a wet dock where vessels could lie at the Custom House quay always afloat in deep water but, he added, 'like all the other works of the Limerick Canal Company it was dropt when almost ready to receive the finishing hand'. This seems a little harsh in the light of the objections about the limitations of Thomond Bridge to cope with the anticipated additional flow created by the plan. It is not easy to establish exactly how much work had been carried out on the scheme before it was abandoned, although during the drainage and navigation works in 2001 some evidence of what may have been an attempt to install the weir and lock was uncovered. Apart from the problem about the tidal nature of the access to and from the Limerick Navigation by way of the Abbey

Banagher: The smaller Martello tower built in the early 1800s.

River, it was also greatly inconvenienced by Baal's Bridge. This was a very old bridge of four arches, the charter for which was issued in 1340, which at one time had rows of houses on both sides obstructing the roadway. Boats wanting to pass under this bridge had to unload on one side, sail through light and then reload.

Brownrigg described 1st lock that had a bridge across the chamber with stores and a navigation house where the company carried out its business. He said the lock was a fine and costly one with much 'needless ornament'. To facilitate Park Mill, which had been erected at the next lock, Park lock, the gates had to be kept open in summer to keep the canal at the same level as the river where the canal joined it upstream: 'The canal is more like the property of the miller than of the Company of Undertakers.' This made the level above Park lock very shallow and Brownrigg reckoned that it had never been sunk to a proper level. He added: 'The boats are tracked by men not by horses up from Limerick to the Shannon side about three quarters of a mile, and then some take to oars and square sail, men jump into the boat and out again to pass places that they can track.'

The lower lock on the next stretch of canal, Annabeg, was leaking badly through the stonework and the next lock, Gillogue, he described as 'very old and built in a strange and unusual figure, a double lock with unequal falls, I can't understand why'. Newtown lock showed signs of having been altered several times and Clonlara, which had a fall of 10ft 4½ins (3.16m), was of a new and improved construction with sluices under the breasts, which was a technique used by William Chapman, who it will be remembered was acting as consultant engineer at the time it was constructed. The next lock, Monaskea, also showed signs of having been pulled down and altered several times and had a similar fall. The locks lately constructed had been built under contract, without the superintendence of a constant inspector. The stonework looked good to the eye but the stones were placed on edge with unconnected rubble behind, a technique well known on the Grand Canal as 'starters', because the water got in behind the stones and, when the lock emptied, it washed out the rubble. The guard lock at Errina, as already stated, at one time had three chambers with the fourth set of lock reveals under the bridge. Above this lock the canal was not properly excavated leading back out into the river. This was due of the neglect of the contractor, the late Mr Browning and his executors: 'loud complaints are constantly heard, but no steps taken to compel the executors or his security to complete the contract, although all the money was paid to him many years since'. His securities were said to be men of rank and influence and members of the canal company, 'and there the canal remains almost impassable'. Brownrigg said that William Chapman had altered the entrance out into the river to make access easier for boats.

Brownrigg referred to the difficulties encountered at O'Brien's Bridge because of the strong current. The history of this bridge is difficult to follow.[7] There was no bridge here in the mid-seventeenth century but there was an extensive shallow and six stone arches were built on the Clare side in the 1690s by a local landowner, John Brown of Clanboy, at his own expense. The agreement by Donal O'Brien to complete the bridge was not carried through and there was a temporary structure erected until the stone bridge was competed by the county. Brownrigg described the unsatisfactory situation:

... there is one arch near the Clare side something loftier than the others, this is called the Navigation Arch [the 4th arch from the Clare side], because the boats pass under it; it may be safe to do so in winter but I would not advise the smallest boat to make the choice of this Arch in Summer, because just close above the bridge and on the west point of the arch, is the remains of an Old Castle, demolished in the war time.

In 1803 Brownrigg installed a cable fixed to a large rock in the river above the bridge marked by a buoy. The cable was led through the navigation arch with another buoy attached to the end enabling boats to warp up against the current and let their boats down more safely. The Grand Canal Company's agent in Limerick was to complain about these difficulties a few years later in 1807. The great difficulties when the river was in flood were reported again to the Directors General: 'a step of sixteen inches almost perpendicular at which time the passage through the bridge occupied half a day, and required the united assistance of all the kindly disposed people in the village'. The suggestion was that 'a cabestan' (capstan) was needed and this must have been subsequently installed because when the canal company appealed for the erection of a lock here in both 1818 and again in 1822, requests that were turned down on the grounds of expense, it was told that the fault lay with the boatmen who 'all think themselves so clever, none of them, or at least very few of them, will make use of the Buoy or of the Capstan to either of which if they make fast they can let themselves down in perfect safety'.

In the four miles (6km) of river up to the final stretch of canal to Killaloe, Chapman had cut a short length of 'running canal' or short stretch of bypass canal without a lock, at Parteen, but had left the company's service before it was completed and it was very shallow. Brownrigg said he witnessed a boat carrying eight tons with slates for Limerick, which had to be lightened using a cot. This had to be repeated three times in the course of her journey: 'can anything exceed such labour, or be more disheartening, dangerous and expensive'. He added: 'In the present state of the navigation it is next to impossible to carry on trade, except in time of flood when the boatmen are obliged in desperate weather to lye bye on the water day and night for a fair wind to bring them up stream, and to depend on their little anchors for safety.'

The final stretch of canal came in for less criticism, which was probably due to the fact that the company now had the expertise of William Chapman. However, he said that Cussane lock, a large double lock, was built on a bad foundation and must have cost a vast sum of money, because even by sinking the lock pit and preparing the mason work, it had to be built on a timber foundation. It will be remembered that Chapman had defended the decision to build the lock on this site and explained his reasons for doing so. Brownrigg added: 'They found several stone weapons and tools, a kind of stone falchon or pattoo pattoo, some like Chizels, wedges or hatchets fixed in wooden handles. Mr Chapman, the engineer, got these things and gave some of them to the present Bishop of Killaloe and brought some to England.'The middle, or Moys lock, had an accommodation bridge over it for the Bishop: 'This part of the canal was a very nice and critical piece of work and attended with more than common expence. It is much to be lamented that Mr Chapman, who laid it out, did not remain to complete his own plan.' This resulted in the canal being unfinished although it was being used. Two of the contractors, Clark and Carroll, had unfinished contracts leaving stone behind: 'in resentment for not being paid some of the contractors say they are unsettled with since 1794, some complain of large sums remaining due to them'.

The last lock at Killaloe was the most recent on the navigation. He described how it had reveals for the gates to open both ways because it was being suggested that the rapids at Killaloe, which produced a fall of about 23ft (7m) should be partly removed with a view to lowering Lough Derg, in which case the Killaloe canal would become a summit level fed by a millstream above the bridge. William Jessop, in his report to the Grand Canal Company in 1794, had also mentioned this idea of lowering Lough Derg and laying dry from 6000 to 8000 acres of land. However, nothing came of this ambitious idea although it did surface again in 1813 when William Vavasour, a landowner, approached the directors of the Grand Canal Company saying that he had a plan to reduce the company's debt by £200,000 but that he would need a payment of £1,000 to reveal his scheme. The board returned his plan to him unopened but a few months later they proposed that they would pay him £500 at the passing of the Act required and £500 if the plan was productive.The plan was then handed over and it is recorded in the minutes that it was then 'locked in the Chairman's private drawer'. Six months later, it was once again returned to him with a note that 'the Directors do not think that it

Killaloe: the lock constructed at the time as a rising or falling lock with double gate recesses to enable this stretch of canal to be used as a summit level if it was decided to lower Lough Derg.

would be advisable for them to embark in a work of such magnitude as the one suggested'. Finally, the details of the plan were revealed in the minutes when it was reported that Vavasour had approached the Chief Secretary, Robert Peel, with the scheme, which was to acquire all the land around Lough Derg, which was currently covered up to a depth of 15ft (4.5m), and then lower the lake by altering the fall at Killaloe.[8]

Brownrigg stated that the intention had been to build a wall to lead the navigation up to Green Island above Killaloe Bridge but only a short section of this had been built and the navigation was then open to the strongly flowing river:

I am at a loss to form an opinion or to conceive any cause for such a respectable and intelligent body of Gentlemen, as compose the Limerick Navigation Company, bringing this great work to above the bridge at Killaloe to within a musket shot of the deep water, and there ceasing their work altogether, one would imagine they were under some baneful influence or blind infatuation.

In three places he found the depth was down to 2ft 6ins (0.75m). Brownrigg described the boats using the navigation: there were flat-bottomed sand boats, raking fore and aft a great part of their length, carrying six to eight tons of cargo, such as sand, turf, lime, brick, stone, timber, coals and dung, and manned by two men, usually the owners. Then there were lighters of twelve to sixteen tons manned by four men, who were hired crew; they had two oars in the stern and no rudder, and were used in Limerick docks for loading and unloading larger boats. There were also a few half-keeled boats but flat in part of the bottom with a dropping mast, square sail and rudder and were crewed by four men, usually the joint owners. Similar boats were used for dredging marl from above Killaloe, carrying eighteen to twenty tons with a square sail and flat bottom, crewed by four men and a skipper. He remarked that boats had to 'lye bye' for a fair wind and carried cargoes such as timber, merchandise, coals and porter. Brownrigg concluded with the following statement:

It must be a matter of Astonishment to an observer to see, from its present State, the poor progress that has been made in half a century, under several descriptions of bodies that have had the management of the work from time to time, and the expenditure of prodigious sums of Money, and how much remains to bring it to anything resembling a perfect Inland Navigation.

The correspondence between the Directors General and the company had begun in January 1802 and a grant of £6,000 was eventually made to it to carry out further works, linked to an agreement to lower tolls. This was an extremely short-sighted policy adopted by the Directors General in their dealings with all the companies. They saw it as their role to try to make the movement of trade easier and cheaper, but in doing so they were depriving the companies of the already small income on which they relied for maintenance. It was agreed that in future the tolls would vary, ranging from 1d per ton on corn, 2d on other goods and 3d per passenger. It is interesting to note that at this early stage passengers were being carried.

An unsatisfactory situation appears to have arisen when in July 1802 it was stated: 'That the Members who compose the Committee for conducting the Limerick Navigation are all absent at present, mostly at the different Watering Places in England.' There was apparently trouble with the appointment of an engineer and the Directors General agreed to arrange to have an inspection carried out but refused to become involved in carrying out any work. Further attempts to contact the company that year produced no response. Eventually, in December, there was a reply saying that they would now need double the amount of funding, to which the Directors General responded by lamenting that an entire season had been lost for the execution of the works and they requested that the secretary, Andrew Watson, should be asked to come to Dublin for consultation. He was requested to report among other things on the current amount of the company's debt, the state of the navigation, an explanation of the need for the increase in expenditure to complete the navigation and the current position about the contract of the late Mr Browning. This he did in February 1803 when it was agreed that Brownrigg would be asked to inspect the works to look into the estimated costs. Watson advised the board that Browning's contract was for £8,000 of which he had been paid £7,000 before he died although the work was incomplete.

Emphasizing the problems he had raised in his earlier report, Brownrigg reported back in May 1803. He stressed that were four places where the navigation was obstructed. There was a long shallow where the Park Canal terminated; the upper end of the Errina Canal, 'Browning's contact' had never been sunk to more than 2ft 6ins; the short running canal at Parteen was through very difficult ground which had baffled the contractors: 'by which I understand two of them were broke and left the work unfinished' and, finally, there was a need for a protecting wall at Killaloe. He reported that at present boats carrying fifteen to sixteen tons could pass through in winter dropping to five to six tons in summer:

'and even these sometimes were obliged to shift their Cargoes twice or thrice'. What was even more disturbing was that the mason work on the locks and bridges required repairs and all the gates were in a state of decay. His estimate for the works amounted to £13,157 4s 7d, paying labourers 1s 1d per day. The company's engineer, Daniel Corneille, advised strongly against the Grand Canal Company's idea of the removal of the shoals at Killaloe to lower Lough Derg. He had reported earlier that he had witnessed thirty men there hauling a boat up the navigation in winter.

Acting on Brownrigg's report and estimated costs, the Directors General reluctantly decided to inform the company that they would take on the execution of the works themselves, 'which they think should more properly be done by the Proprietors but that they have reason to apprehend that unless they undertake it, there is not much Probability of the completing of this very important Navigation'. Surprisingly, in the circumstances, almost immediately, a further letter from the company was received in which they 'intimate their Astonishment that no Attempt has yet been made to forward their works, that the season is so much advanced'. The board resolved not to reply to this letter: 'not being in the Habit of using such a Stile, not disposed to adopt it'.

Brownrigg commenced work in July; a supply of lock gates was ordered from James Murphy and he put in place an establishment. Michael Dillon and Daniel Elliott were appointed as overseers, Andrew Watson as pay clerk (which seems a strange decision in the light of his previous role with the Limerick Navigation Company) and Timothy Mackey as inspector. Almost immediately work was held up by locals who alleged they were not receiving payments. A decision was made to suspend attempts to continue the works through the winter until the following May, and the navigation was temporarily reopened with seven boats reported to have arrived down in Limerick with cargoes of slates, ash, oak, elm and potatoes.

By May 1804 Brownrigg reported that boats had been cautiously passed up and down through Cussane lock but then the lock had to be closed and a dam erected above it, which involved goods having to be carried by land some 150 yards (137m). Maybe the Limerick Navigation Company was beginning to realize how lucky they were because they wrote to the Board in October praising Brownrigg's work. He listed further operations undertaken during that year as follows: work at the Limerick end of the Park Canal to improve facilities there; rebuilding the upper chamber at Cussane lock; the building of a lock house at Killaloe above the bridge, work on a canal wall there and general work on other locks as required. Boats continued to use the navigation, portaging around the dam, and there was a depth of 4ft 6ins (1.35m) throughout with the exception of below Cloonlara and Cussane locks. He was scheduling work to continue through 1805 on Cussane lock, works at Clonlara lock and completing the wall from the lock to Green Island at Killaloe.

Brownrigg reported that he was having trouble with the local landowner, Lord Eyremount, over the cutting of the stretch of canal at Clonfadda. At Illanamandra there was a violent current with great difficulty for boats if the wind was in the east or west:

… and in this place heavy loaded vessels were delayed for several days at a time, and it generally happened that the miserable boatmen were obliged to get out and haul the vessel with the greatest Slavery and Danger, up to their wastes [sic], nay often up to their necks, in water in the depth of winter, in floods, and dark nights, where lives have been lost, and many through fatigue and cold have got their deaths.

There were only two acres of land that had to be acquired for the work and the Jury had awarded £4 11s per acre for this piece of land, isolated by the new canal, when the normal price varied from £3 10s to £2 8s. The work continued over the summer months of 1805 and once again the directors of the Limerick Navigation Company conveyed their 'Approbation of Mr Brownrigg's conduct of the Prosecution of the Works'. They decided to present him with a piece of plate worth £100: 'as Testimony of the high Opinion which they entertain of his important Services and Exertions in forwarding the works of their Navigation'. The Board, however, would not allow him to accept it. The company now put in a memorial for assistance in making a harbour at the Limerick end of the navigation.

In the summer of 1805 Francis Trench, one of the Board of the Directors General, reported on the progress of the work. He gave a detailed description voicing concern about the dangers of the narrow arches of Baal's Bridge and also the difficulties for the boatmen in crossing the river to and from the Park Canal to the Errina Canal. He felt that putting a chain down to draw themselves over and back was an unsatisfactory suggestion. He described how seventeen arches had to be cut under the towpaths on the Errina Canal to allow farmers access to water for their cattle. Passage through O'Brien's Bridge was extremely hazardous and Brownrigg had fixed up a system of using a chain attached to a buoy in the river for the boatmen to let themselves up and down. The excavation works on the Parteen running canal was still causing great problems and the bottom had to be blasted out to deepen it.

Killaloe: Cussane lock (later known as Pigeon's lock) at the lower end of the Killaloe stretch of canal later to be submerged as part of the hydro-electric works. (Courtesy of the National Library of Ireland)

By December 1805 it was reported that the 'great double lock at Cussane' was finished, retaining Chapman's design of the sluice tunnel opening out into the lock through the middle of the sill. The new running canal across the peninsula of Clonfadda at Illanamandra was finished and also across the peninsula of Ardclony at Bunown, and the navigation was now opened for the winter. In September 1806 it was reported that the navigation was opened to trade but that it would have to be closed again for two or three weeks to allow repairs to Annabeg lock, a new floor and sill for Newtown lock and the lowering of the sill of Moys lock. By the end of 1806 Brownrigg was exceeding his estimates by £2,500, which he explained was due to the fact that his estimates had been made in time of peace and 'the price of materials and of labour rose immediately upon the War [with France] and was further increased by the Number of Men entering the Land and Sea Service'. The costs had also risen because of 'the Combination of Workmen and the Advantages taken by Interested People'. He recorded, as Trench had done, that they were experiencing difficulty in completing the Parteen cut; pumping was necessary day and night, gunpowder had to be used: 'In our presence one of the Blasters was desperately torn and bruised by two or three pieces of stone which struck him in the Body and Thigh'. The situation was made worse by 'storms, Floods, and prodigious Rise of the Shannon' during December. However, he added that work would all be completed by the promised date of 1 December 1807.

This promise came under threat in May 1807 when he repeated his difficulties in getting labour: 'because of the late tillage, which together with the Experience and Knowledge of them being wanted for the Works give Rise to such Scheming and Combining as distresses him greatly and, if he submits to them, there will be no End to it'. He said that he was going to have to place a dam across the Errina Canal to sink out the hard bottom with shovels and barrows instead of using dredgers. He also recommended rebuilding the wall of Annabeg lock. The Limerick Navigation Company suggested extending the completion date to 1 December 1809 in order to defeat the combinations for higher wages because the men knew that the Directors General had to compete the work by a specified date. The snags list continued: there was a leak reported in Annabeg lock; shoals on the Newtown level and repairs needed to Newtown and Monaskea locks. Brownrigg also reported that he was encountering difficulties at Errina because of the nature of the soil, which was running sand and soft blue clay together with the added problem of the steep nature of the banks. He emphasized that a capstan and pier was needed at O'Brien's Bridge where the boatmen were continually reporting difficulties in time of flood. The navigation company, still trying to push their luck, asked for two new locks, one at O'Brien's Bridge and the other at Parteen, to which they received a sharp reply that 'these were entirely new ideas'.

The fates were working against Brownrigg. By late September he had to report that there had been damage caused by floods and it would be impossible to remedy this damage in the current season to which the Directors General voiced their concern about such damage occurring 'so near the Close of Business'. In October it was reported that the Shannon was continuing to rise one, two or three inches each day.

It must be remembered that all this time the Limerick navigation works were just one of many being tackled or supported by the Directors General, and in May 1808 the first signs of future trouble about their funding position was voiced to Westminster when they indicated that parliamentary grants were going to be needed if their work was to continue. Flooding was again hitting the Limerick navigation works. On 24 October Brownrigg said that floods 'as were scarcely ever known in one day' had caused more damage, 'and that he feels this the more severely as he had gone on that day to speak to Mr Watson about resigning the Navigation into the Company's hands'. He did try to hand over the works on the 14 November: 'upon which they resolved unanimously that having examined Evidence on Oath and from our local Knowledge, we are decidedly of Opinion that the works are not complete'. Brownrigg told his Board that 'the long continuance of very bad weather has not only done considerable mischief to such of the works as were within the Reach of the Mountain Rivers but has swelled the River Shannon to within one foot of the highest point of last winter'. He said that some control of the boats on the navigation was needed as they were damaging the works and he considered that the company, which was in receipt of tolls at this time, should be made to take steps to stop this. The company complained about the collapse of the banks between Newtown lock and Clonlara Bridge and were told in no uncertain terms that they were enjoying the 'Emoluments of the Navigation without contributing even the smallest Repairs of the constant Depredations which such works must suffer from time and weather and from the carelessness of those who use the navigation'.

Worse was to follow in the following February 1809 when the rising river 'made a Breach in the canal Bank at the South Side above Errina Lock, entered the canal below the Lock, broke out again and re-entered and out again . . . that the great Height of the Shannon and the rapidity of the Water removes it out of the Power of any Person there to stop its Progress', placing three locks in danger. A new bridge would have to be built at Errina to replace the one swept away and a dam constructed to act as a temporary bridge. The handing over of the navigation was now extended to 1 December 1811. The frustration of the Directors General can almost be felt emanating from the pages of the minute book. The costs of the repairs at Errina were estimated to run to £8,112 2s 6d and the dam remained in place, used as a bridge, with the boats having to unload there and carry by road to Limerick. Bad weather through the winter held up the work but it was reported to be nearly complete by June 1810 together with further repair works at Monaskea and Clonlara locks. In October the navigation company was asked to inspect the works, which would be ready to hand over in about one month. The stone dam at Errina could be removed but no boats were to be allowed to pass until further notice except those employed in the works. It was winter again and heavy rain was reported with men standing by to repair damage and in January 1811 the navigation company passed a resolution:

We are convinced the Canal Works are in many essential Parts very incomplete, that some of the Erections, and particularly the Foundations thereof are far from being durable, and that considering the Necessity of every Attention being directed to the Support and Permanency of such a great National Object, we are satisfied we would be extremely culpable were we to take up the Works of their Magnitude without there being in a sufficient and lasting State, and without such Improvements being made as are requisite according to the Intention of the Legislature and the Deed executed to us by the Directors General. [9]

It was decided to run off the levels to allow for an inspection. Brownrigg reported that the Limerick Navigation was now complete 'in a superior Stile of Execution, that there was not on 1 December last a nail wanting'. A rumour was now circulating that the company had made up its mind not to take the navigation off the board's hands 'in any Event', despite the fact that 25 March had been appointed as the day for the handover.

The Mayor of Limerick complained that: 'the number of Poor in that extensive Country are destitute of Fuel of which vast Quantities lie ready for Delivery on the Banks of the Canal'. The company arranged in February 1811 for Mr J. Donnell to inspect the works on its behalf but he was delayed by 'the long continuance of rainy and stormy weather'. Brownrigg suggested that some improvements could be carried out such as repairs to the lock houses, lengthening the piers of Gillogue lock, which was forty-five years old and a very strange shape, repairing the trackway and deepening the canals. It was suggested that the banks of the canals were being damaged by 'cars and pigs rooting' and the lock keepers should prevent this. Five letters to the company went unanswered and it was told that the lock keepers were 'seldom seen'. The handover date came and went.

The fates were working against the board. In February 1812 it was reported: 'Rain has fallen incessantly, in greater quantities than has ever been remembered for many years.' There was a breach in the canal at Clonlara and another above Gillogue lock and further damage reported. Brownrigg was instructed to consult with John Killaly, who had now joined the establishment, as to how to secure the canal against future flooding. Killaly reported: 'Though it has been unquestionably a very arduous and difficult Undertaking to bring that Work to its present State of Perfection, he apprehended something further must be done before the Board can reasonably expect the Limerick Navigation Company to take it off their Hands.' He produced a long list of suggestions which does cast some doubt on Brownrigg's ability: dredging; repairs to the trackway; backing and repairing bridges; pointing Annabeg and Cussane locks, enlarging back drains. He also claimed that Chapman had laid the line of the canal too near the river below Killaloe to save a row of the Bishop's fir trees.

The stand off with the navigation company continued because the company directors would not reply to letters or help to protect the navigation, and finally they were asked 'whether they intend to assert and secure their Rights or to abandon them'. All this time the navigation was still closed by the dam at Errina but the board now agreed they would reopen the navigation if the company agreed to forfeit their tolls towards keeping the works in repair. The company was told 'to speak out and say distinctly and explicitly what are the Expectations, and what is their final Determination'. In May 1812 the Mayor of Limerick appealed to the Lord Lieutenant to do something about the re-opening of the canal, which had now been closed for three years. The directors of the navigation company now came up with some figures about the financial state of the company and offered to sell it to the Directors General for the price of their original share subscriptions plus interest and expenses. This offer, which involved a payment of some £73,500, was turned down and the Directors General said that they were about to re-open the canal and would keep the tolls towards repairs. The Attorney General was consulted as to how the company could be made to accept its responsibilities and there was even a suggestion that the Grand Canal Company might take it over.

Finally, in December 1812 a meeting between the two sides was arranged and the board stated its position to the navigation company but this did nothing to break the stalemate. The company was looking for further works, that had not been originally specified, and the board said that if they allowed it to be reopened the tolls must be kept for repairs: 'The Navigation should then be opened by which its Deficiencies, if any, upon the Contract, would be shewn or its Efficiency be proved in Practice.'

The Lord Lieutenant intervened in October 1813 and suggested that the navigation should be purchased from the company. The company directors agreed to drop their request for interest on their original investment, which brought the purchase price down to £26,500. The Board, with the support of the Lord Lieutenant, made an offer of £17,666. It was pointed out that the company had little hope of ever providing a dividend 'after providing faithfully for its necessary Expenses and therefore that should it be permitted to remain with the Company it would again inevitably fall into Ruin and Decay'. The company accepted this offer, trying to reserve the right to receive or sell rents of £150 p.a. for redundant water or pass this on to the board for an additional £30,000, which was refused. Eventually in 1813 the company accepted the offer and, in June 1814, the long saga came to an end, the dam was removed and the navigation reopened under the management of the Directors General.[10] The navigation, which had been commenced in 1757, could at last be said to be complete, although damage from flooding was to continue to cause problems.

THE MIDDLE SHANNON 1800 – 1810

It is recorded in the Grand Canal Company minutes in 1794, the year in which William Jessop had reported to the board on the state of the Shannon navigation, that one of its directors, Richard Griffith, together with some others, had made a petition to the Irish Parliament to be allowed to take over the Shannon Navigation. This was resisted by his fellow board members and, after discussion, Griffith agreed to withdraw his request in order to allow the canal company to prepare a bill.[11] Nothing came of the Grand Canal Company's subsequent approach to the Irish Parliament and, with the canal to the Shannon nearing completion, they anxiously submitted an offer to the Directors General to carry out works on the middle Shannon for which they would be reimbursed. At the same time they entered into negotiations for a purchase of a percentage of their existing toll income in return for receiving a lump sum for reducing their tolls on the Grand Canal.[12] The Directors General had then asked their own engineer, John Brownrigg, about the state of the middle river and he reported back in October 1801.

Brownrigg reported that although Meelick lock was a fine piece of mason work: 'the lower gates gave way two years ago. The timbers of the upper gates are in their place, shut and fixed, the swing beams gone, the sluices broke and demolished, the sheeting rotten and sticking in pieces, the gates stopped with sods and bundles of potato stalks to retain some water in the upper level of the canal. What a grievous sight.' He praised the plan of the lock house, which unlike the other two-storey lock houses designed by Omer had the rooms on one floor. Of the canal he said:

'it must have been a beautiful and complete thing from the hands of the Engineer, but now, what a scene of ruin and depredation'. He praised Mr Omer's work at Banagher with its profusion of cut stone, 'all now disordered and partly hastening to ruin'. The gates in the lock were gone with boats experiencing difficulty coming up against the stream. The same problem existed at Shannonbridge, with the gates gone in the single-gated lock, but 'it is however in constant use'. Here the lock keeper endeavoured to pick up a miserable livelihood by catching eels, having received no salary for many years past.

The Athlone works were 'designed on so magnificent a scale, and executed in so masterly a manner, and at such prodigious expense that I am almost at a loss to describe it'. They were said to have cost upwards of £30,000 but now the gates of the lock were gone and the walls warped but still sound and were said to have been like this for thirty to forty years. He added that 'everything of iron not only taken from the wood but wrenched out of the stone work even under water, the cramps of iron are dug out of the table of the breast and the clay and gravel that backed the lock up to the level of the coping is actually dug away and carried into an adjoining field to manure the ground'. The banks of the canal had been torn away by the free passage of water, the gates of the 'rymer' lock further up the canal having failed soon after their erection. They had been originally piled with timber but now the earth was washed away and the piles were standing some distance from the bank so that he actually moored his boat between them and the shore.

This misfortune is much increased by the Publick, here they drive all their cattle to water, here the Artillery horses of the Cavalry have been permitted to ride into the canal, trampling down the banks in a lamentable manner. I saw a man sitting on his horse, drive his car into the Canal through one breach and come out at another . . . An attempt was made to make a green walk for inhabitants but now the gates are gone and those beautiful banks are consigned to the pigs of Athlone, horses exercised and Artillery men exercise with great guns, firing at targets.

Despite this gloomy picture, the Directors General were slow to act on the Grand Canal Company's offer. Their policy of getting involved in trying to bring about a reduction in tolls came into play with an offer to purchase two-thirds of the canal tolls for a period of twenty-five years. The Grand Canal directors were not prepared to bring the tolls on their canal into the discussion but were prepared to negotiate the tolls that would be charged on the Shannon if they took it over. It would seem that the canal company was still thinking in terms of taking over the entire Shannon navigation. During 1801, while these negotiations were continuing with long letters passing back and forth, it was agreed that the company should spend 'a few hundred pounds' on temporary repairs on some of the middle Shannon locks.

The canal company also asked their consultant engineer, William Jessop, to carry out further surveys of the river in December 1801.[13] This time he said he had been instructed:

to consider this work as a great National concern unfettered by local considerations or parsimonious frugality, and that it was to be fitted to embrace and accommodate all Collateral Canals which may hereafter communicate with it, and be adapted to the largest size of vessels which can Navigate on any such Canal, now made or making. I therefore must look on the River Shannon as the great Artery of Ireland, destined by future Ramifications to circulate its commerce and give animation to the Country.

We have seen that his earlier survey had identified the importance of providing towpaths and he had indicated which bank of the river sections would have to be used, necessitating the use of horse ferries where they would have to change sides. He also had gone into some detail about the actual difficulties involved in making towpaths and had suggested lowering stretches of river by removing obstructing eel weirs because of the problem caused by reed beds in order to build up trackways. Now, aware of the funding that could be available for navigations, he recommended making the canals and locks of a much larger dimension. He reckoned that without towpaths 'any other improvements would hardly be worth the cost of them', and he suggested raising the proposed trackways higher, with gaps spanned by timber bridges, 'as I am told that the landowners would rather have the flat lands overflowed than have the Waters of the Shannon excluded'. This comment indicates that drainage issues were deliberately not being linked to navigation plans at this time. All these changes involved almost doubling his earlier estimates to £119,454 for the river north of Lough Ree and £55,821 for the middle Shannon including towpaths for all the river sections, and so in 1802 the canal company asked its own engineer, Israel Rhodes, to carry out a more detailed study of the middle Shannon. He recommended lowering the sill of the lock at Athlone by 3ft (0.9m), also lowering Meelick lock sill and constructing conventional locks at Shannonbridge and Banagher to replace these single-gated locks.

In the same year, frustrated by the delay, with the completion date for the canal to Shannon Harbour drawing ever closer and with plans in preparation for a grand opening ceremony, the canal directors appear to have continued work at Meelick. Instead of making the Shannon locks larger, they decided to make the middle Shannon locks conform with the size of the upper Shannon locks, 80ft (24.3m) by 16ft (4.8m), and the last two locks on the Grand Canal, leading down to the Shannon from Shannon Harbour, were also constructed to this size at this time. It is recorded that they had paid the travelling expenses and engaged a carpenter, Thomas Lancaster, from England to build the lock gates for Meelick. Some idea of the problems involved in undertakings of this kind at that time can be seen from a report of Richard Griffith, who had been given an official role by his fellow directors to supervise the completion of the canal to the Shannon and the works on the river. Of the works at Meelick he reported:

I fear we are proceeding on a very expensive and unwise system in our preparation for the Shannon – I found Thomas Lancaster, who had sawyers, carpenters and smiths at work by the day in the Company's account, stupidly drunk at 11 o'clock on Wednesday morning last. We have also fourteen stone cutters at work by the day in the fields near Cloninogue [Cloonaheenogue] lock superintended by one of their own party from Limerick, Mr Jones, who in the absence of Mr Rhodes, had charge of the business having been by your orders sent on a survey from Philipstown.[14]

Griffith imposed a new, less costly, system whereby the stone for the locks at Meelick and Banagher was prepared on site near Clonmacnois using the English stonecutters, Woodcock and Turner. He said that he and Killaly had looked at the lock at Meelick in an attempt to preserve as much of the old lock as possible, consistent with permanent safety, but subsequently he said that the lock had to be almost rebuilt.

The canal company directors wrote again to the Directors General in October 1803:

We desire however to have it remembered, that the great work, which thirty one years increasing perseverance and an expenditure of upwards of a million of private property, have now accomplished, was undertaken by the Grand Canal Company under the full confidence that they should find the river Shannon made completely navigable and free from toll, from Lough Allen to the sea, long before this company could expect to form a junction with it; a confidence founded on the avowed intention of Parliament, proceeded on to a considerable extent. . . If the reductions of our tolls, which however high they may be considered on the part of the public, are certainly too low for our reimbursement, be an object with government, we are still ready to dispose of

Meelick: Hamilton lock, the site of Thomas Omer's original lock built in 1755, which was rebuilt as a smaller lock by the Grand Canal Company in the early 1800s.

a portion of them on fair and equitable terms, but we will never intermix the sale of them with any proposition for undertaking a new work.[15]

They added that they were still prepared to enter into negotiations regarding the work on the Shannon and reminded the Directors General that they were already working at Meelick and hoped to complete this work shortly, adding that unless they were reimbursed the £10,000 they had already spent they were not prepared to expend 'another guinea in this work'. They added that they would also undertake to make the Suck navigable to Ballinasloe if allowed to proceed with this work while their other works were in progress, an offer that unfortunately was not accepted.

In the summer of 1804, with matters still unresolved and with the first trade boat having passed through the canal from the Shannon to Dublin, the Directors General were informed that the navigation would have to be closed until November in order to carry out works at Meelick, Shannonbridge, Banagher and Athlone. Some idea of how difficult the works were can be seen in a further report from Griffith to his Board:

From the open and gravely soil at Shannon Bridge in consequence of which a horse mill had been added to the water wheel and I have reason to believe that we shall have occasion for both to keep the foundations dry while the inverted arch which is to be turned under the walls of the old

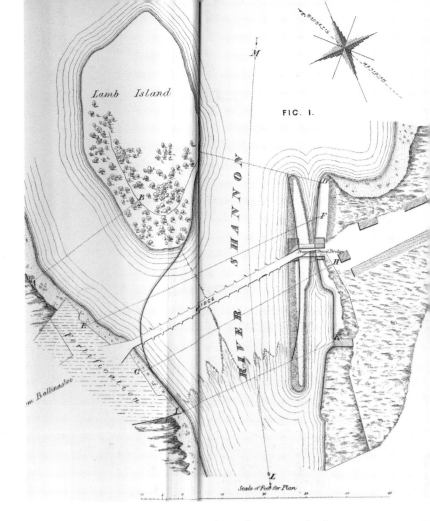

Shannonbridge: Omer's flash lock with a single set of gates was replaced by the Grand Canal Company in the early 1800s which in turn was removed by the Shannon Commission in the 1840s leaving one gate recess still visible.

Banagher: the lock built by the Grand Canal Company in the early 1800s to replace the single set of gates in Omer's original flash lock. Some of the ashlars have been taken and replaced by bricks.

lock shall be building. Everything is in a state of preparation to begin this work, and on Monday morning we agreed to give the labourers one and half pence per cubic yard for pumping the water out of the hole in the river where a dam had been formed for the purpose of laying the platform on which the water wheel is to be erected. We had three of Mallet's copper pumps and one wooden pump with about nine scoops at work and thirty three men, who relieved each other in turns. In the first hour they have sunk the water nine inches, but after that the progress became much slower as they had to contend with the leakage through the dam. I could not however wait to see the job completed.[16]

A few months later Griffith reported that they were having great difficulty controlling the water at Shannonbridge because of the closeness of the river to the canal with high water in the river. At the end of the summer the work at Banagher was 'very little advanced' and work at Meelick was proving very difficult because of considerable slippage in the canal bank and the bottom was very hard, yielding 'but slowly to the heaviest pickaxes'.

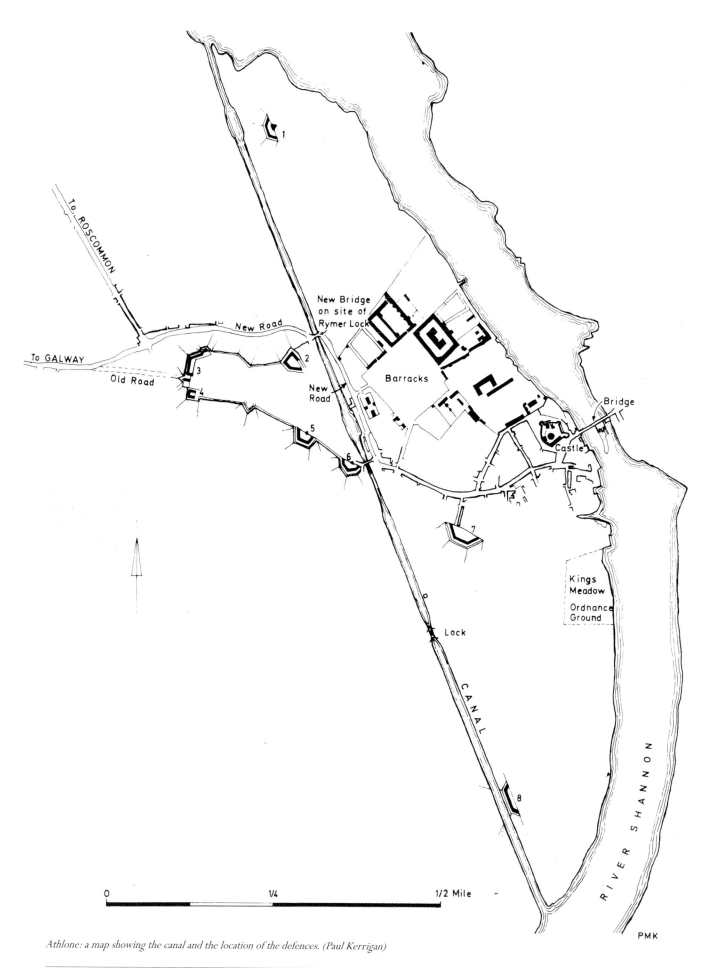

Athlone: a map showing the canal and the location of the defences. (Paul Kerrigan)

A report was received from Killaly that it had been agreed to re-site the bridge over the canal at Athlone at the government's expense, because the military deemed it necessary to take over the present bridge and defray the expense of the new one to correspond with the line of the new road to the west. The canal was considered as an important outer line of defence together with earthwork batteries. There were eight of these batteries and the military authorities agreed to the dismantling of No. 8 battery to facilitate the work on rebuilding the lock with the proviso that it was to be replaced when the work was completed, a condition that was subsequently never carried out. The large old lock here had to be rebuilt to the smaller scale and Killaly said he had to increase the number of men there, paying them 2s 6d per 'solid yard' for taking down the old lock and 10d per 'superficial foot' for setting cut stone and 3s 6d a perch for masonry. Facing into the winter Killaly recommended ceasing work at Meelick until next spring but he said the Banagher lock was nearly ready and work on the canal could be left until the spring, allowing boats of up to forty tons to ply over the winter.

Having eventually successfully managed to separate the negotiations about lowering tolls on the Grand Canal from the issue of payment for the works on the Shannon, the canal company now said that it would have to increase the original estimate from £40,634 18s 7d to £65,195 7s 6d because of additional costs incurred. Work ceased over the winter and the company told the Lords of the Treasury that it intended to seek repayment of expenses already

Athlone: remains of the lower gate on Athlone lock. (Niall Galway)

incurred and cease any further work. The Directors General insisted that they had given no undertaking to reimburse the company if negotiations failed. To this the canal board replied that they wished to 'put an end to this tedious and (to us) painful negotiation . . . the period for recommencing the work is at hand – on you alone depends whether the navigation of the River Shannon shall languish or whether it shall be completed within the ensuing year, which great work we are capable of effecting if immediately favoured with a decisive answer'.[17]

Finally, having been supplied with details of the works already carried out and still to be completed, an agreement was reached on 25 March 1806 that the company would take over the middle Shannon and be paid the original estimated amount plus two-thirds of the additional expenditure, up

Athlone: the lock built by the Grand Canal Company in the early 1800s replacing Omer's large lock. (Niall Galway)

GRAND CANAL.

Regular Parcel Boats to Athlone.

SAMUEL ROBINSON informs the Public that Goods sent to

THOMAS OLDHAM'S STORES,

Letter C.

NEW STORE YARD, GRAND CANAL HARBOUR,

JAMES's-STREET,

Will be regularly forwarded every Fortnight to *Samuel Robinson's* Stores in ATHLONE, by his Boats, which are provided with experienced, careful and respectable Captains; and the smallest damage immediately paid for, without litigation or unnecessary trouble.

S. ROBINSON will have the Goods carefully forwarded from Athlone, or stored there, (free of expense,) until sent for; any Goods sent to his Stores in ATHLONE for DUBLIN, will be forwarded in like manner.

NOV. 1807.

to £14,000, making a total of £54,634, which included payment towards the maintenance of the works. The rate of tolls charged by the canal company on this part of the river was also agreed. The chairman of the Directors General, the Rt Hon. Sackville Hamilton, visited the river in August and inspected the works from Athlone to Portumna, and to mark the occasion the canal company named the lock at Meelick, Hamilton lock. It is worth noting that this would seem to have been one of the few occasions when such an inspection was carried out by any of the Directors General, who normally seemed to rely heavily on reports from their engineers.

The canal company recommenced work and during that summer Killaly reported that the earthworks at Athlone had nearly been completed, they were still having difficulty keeping the water out to complete the works at Shannonbridge, the gates were being fitted at Banagher and work at Meelick had been completed. A memorial was received from Patrick Branagan to be allowed to replace his father, who was now blind and helpless, as lock keeper at Meelick. He added that his father had been the first lock keeper to be established by the former Navigation Board and that 'when the lock gates failed and there was no way for the boats to pass except up the falls at Meelick and Keelogue, he being a very strong man was found of very great use in affording assistance to the boatmen'. He was taken on with a salary of 6s 6d per week, which was an improvement on the treatment his father had received, who had had to appeal to the Directors General for twenty-three years arrears of wages.

The work continued over the next few summers. The Bishop of Clonfert complained that a channel had been cut through an island owned by him without his permission, which should have been purchased by inquisition. A soothing reply was sent to him and Killaly reported: 'I waited on the Bishop of Clonfert yesterday and have settled with him in the most amicable manner.' The directors reported to the shareholders in September 1807 that the Shannon works had been completed. The company also erected a large number of beacons, which were needed to mark the channel when the river was in flood. Killaly reported a brisk trade at Athlone mostly in small craft carrying turf, bricks and potatoes. The lock keeper's widow was living in the lock house with her son-in-law helping with the lock. The trade gradually expanded with thirty new boats being built to operate between Dublin, Athlone and Limerick. Having had their offer to make the Suck navigable turned down by the Directors General, the canal company began to consider making a canal to Ballinsloe from Shannon Harbour, which would

BOAT for LIMERICK,

BY THE

Grand Canal and River Shannon.

A Boat is now ready to take in Goods for Limerick, Killaloe, &c.

At THOMAS OLDHAM's

General Accommodation Stores and Parcel Office,

NEW STORE YARD,

GRAND CANAL HARBOUR, JAMES'S-STREET,

And will proceed early next Week.

Portumna, Loughrea, &c.

In consequence of the Resolution of the Directors of the Grand Canal of the 7th Inst. THOMAS OLDHAM, will now undertake to forward Goods direct to PORTUMNA, without delay of transhipping, &c. and will have them carefully forwarded from thence, on arrival, to LOUGHREA, GORT, BURRISAKANE, &c.

Goods forwarded from these Stores to every part of the Line, the Rivers Barrow, Shannon, &c. daily.——Nov. 1807.

PRINTED BY J. & J. CARRICK, BACHELOR's-WALK.

Grand Canal Company notices. (Goodbody Archives)

GRAND CANAL

AND

RIVER SHANNON.

AT a Meeting of the Court of Directors, for the ordering, managing and directing the Affairs of THE COMPANY OF UNDERTAKERS OF THE GRAND CANAL, The 19th Day of *October*, 1808:

IN Order to promote a more extensive Inland Water Carriage of Goods, between Dublin and LIMERICK, and also between Dublin and LANESBOROUGH, &c.

RESOLVED that, for one Year, to be computed from the first Day of November next, and until further Order, a Drawback of Tolls payable, outwards, to the Grand Canal Company, (as well on the Grand Canal, as on the River Shannon) be allowed on all Goods, Merchandize, and other Articles whatever, that shall (without breaking Bulk) be conveyed, by the Grand Canal and the River Shannon, from the City of Dublin, to any Place to the Southward of, or lower down the Shannon than, the Island of Ilanmore, in Lough Derg; or to any Place to the Northward of, or higher up the Shannon than, the Island of Ilanmore, in Lough Rhee: provided that such Drawback shall be allowed, for no greater Number of Tons than shall have been brought from or beyond the above-mentioned Points on the Shannon, to Dublin, by each Boat, on her next preceding Voyage; and that any excess of each Cargo outwards, beyond the Quantity of the next preceding Cargo inwards, shall be liable to the Payment of the ordinary Toll, without such Drawback.

RESOLVED, that the Directors do not deem the Transhipping of the whole Cargo, from one Boat to another, at Shannon Harbour, under the Inspection of their Collector at that Place, as breaking Bulk, within the Intent of the foregoing Resolution.

BY ORDER,

DANIEL BAGOT, Sec.

N. B. The former Regulations, concerning the Trade from Ilanmore in Lough Derg, are to continue in Force, until the said first Day of November next.

Printed by *William Porter, Grafton-street, Printer and Stationer to the Grand Canal Company.*

GRAND CANAL

AND

RIVER SHANNON.—

At a Meeting of the Court of Directors for the ordering, managing and directing the Affairs of THE COMPANY OF UNDERTAKERS OF THE GRAND CANAL, the 4th Day of *October*, 1806.

RESOLVED, that from the Tenth Day of *October* Instant, until further Order, the Toll on all Goods, Merchandize and other Articles, to be brought from any Part of the River Shannon, at or below the Bridge of PORTUMNA, by the River Shannon and Grand Canal, to or towards Dublin, be no more than One Penny Halfpenny per Ton per Mile on the Grand Canal.

In order to promote a more extensive internal Commerce, between the Cities of DUBLIN and LIMERICK:

RESOLVED, that for Two Years, from the Tenth Day of *October* Instant, and until further Order, a Drawback of the whole of the Tolls payable Outwards to the Grand Canal Company, (as well on the Grand Canal as on the River Shannon) be allowed on all Goods, Merchandize and other Articles whatever, that shall (without breaking Bulk) be conveyed, by the Grand Canal and the River Shannon, from the City of Dublin to the City of Limerick.

By order of the 16th of 1807 the above mentioned Draw... is extended to goods conveyed to any place to the southward of or lower down the Shannon than the Island of Ilanmore in Lough Derg

17th October, 1806.

RESOLVED, that the Directors do not deem the trans-shipping of the whole Cargo from one Boat to another, at Shannon Harbour, under the Inspection of their Collector at that Place, as breaking Bulk, within the Intent of the Resolution of the 4th Instant.

By Order,

DANIEL BAGOT, SECRETARY.

CARRICKS,' PRINTERS, BACHELOR'S-WALK, DUBLIN.

14 Tons

---

solve the difficulty of the lack of towpaths on the Shannon and up the River Suck.

In 1810 John Killaly resigned from the Grand Canal Company and joined the Directors General of Inland Navigation remaining as their engineer until his death in 1832. Killaly now reported that he had made an inspection of the works accompanied by John Brownrigg on board a boat drawing 5ft 9ins (1.7m), carrying sixty tons, from north of Athlone to Lough Derg. This was confirmation that the contract had been fully completed and the final balance was paid over. Although now responsible for running and maintaining this part of the Shannon Navigation, the company was later shown not to have taken this role sufficiently seriously.

While very little appears to have been done by the Directors General to make navigation easier on the two large lakes, Ree and Derg, they did decide to have charts drawn up in 1804 and Messrs Longfield and Murray, surveyors, were commissioned to carry out this work. Longfield, who subsequently was one of those involved carrying out bog surveys, did the surveying and the arrangement was that he was to be paid by the day. It appears to have become a very lengthy operation as he still had not finished Lough Derg in the following year. It was not until 1808 that Longfield finally reported that he had completed both charts. Brownrigg was very critical, not only about the length of time it had taken but also because he found the charts very deficient.

Lough Ree: the legend from Longfield's chart of 1808 showing the original sailing course approaching Lanesborough. (Athlone Branch IWAI)

THE UPPER SHANNON 1800–1814

The incentive for improving navigation on the upper Shannon had always been to make access easier to the Lough Allen coalfields because of the increasing demand for coal in Dublin and the high price being paid for coal coming across the Irish Sea. The surveys carried out in the closing years of the Irish Parliament had shown that the works carried out by the Navigation Board at Lanesborough, Clondara, Roosky and Jamestown had received little in the way of maintenance since they were constructed and Colonel Tarrant's efforts to make a canal into Lough Allen had come to nothing. Inundated with applications from all sides, the Directors General gave little time initially to the upper Shannon.

John Brownrigg had carried out a survey of the upper river in the summer of 1794 and his report is recorded in the first report book of the Directors General dated 2 December 1800.[18] It is not clear on whose behalf this survey was carried out but Brownrigg pointed out that it was 'an authentic copy' and added that 'very uncommon

pains were taken with the Survey. It was done I believe in a manner never practised before in this Kingdom, the river was carefully surveyed first on one side and then on the other from Lough Allen to Lough Ree and I took all the soundings with my own hand'. His account gives a good insight into the condition of the upper Shannon. His comments on Lough Allen are interesting: he said that the lake was 3ft to 4ft (0.9m to 1.2m) higher than a century ago, many acres of the lake were full of oak roots in shallow water, up to 10ft (3m) deep, and about forty years ago the island of 'Gurbnacuna' was part of the mainland. He added: 'I have no doubt but at some early Period of Time, Lough Allen and the Shannon below the Island of Ballintrave were upon one Level and I am inclined to think they will be so again'. He reported that torrents pour down the Arigna River, which strike the Shannon and push the water back into the lake, and thousands of tons of gravel fill the mouth of the lake with shoals and the bed of the river with islands, bars, banks and shallows, dam up the mouth of the lake and annually raise its surface. He described how Colonel Charles Tarrant proposed making a cut to turn the waters of the Arigna River into Lough Allen, and that he had begun to excavate a canal on the west side of the river, which was to have two locks, one at Drumherriff and the other at Battlebridge. Tarrant was another of the military engineers becoming involved in civil works at the time and had supervised work on the construction of the Grand Canal in the 1770s. Brownrigg added that local people claimed they were not paid for work

t suffer the Works

ck of Port', near
ch allowed boats
gh with difficulty.
bridge at Carrick
weirs from there
e lock here were
ches in the canal:
done here in the
hree or four feet
ered to lay out a
rd at Derrycarne

*n in the narrows
sed my surprise,
they are entirely
remote Ages of
ses were among
g from a savage*

ys waiting for a
ere were seven
the lock house
ome repair. The
repair and 'like
dfully as to be
here had been
k was good but
l iron work for
the gates. It had originally been built too low: 'all above the lower gates was raised, but below these gates remain as first built'. At Lanesborough 'the Labour and Straining the Gates of this absurd lock soon demolished the wooden Work and there is now a rapid free stream through the Canal, very difficult to bring a Boat against particularly under the Bridge'. The lock house was in exceedingly bad order, built on an arch over the upper part of the lock: 'a mere whim and is a great Inconvenience in passing Boats up and down as there is no tackway under it'.

Other than Brownrigg's 1798 report, the Directors General's first encounter with the affairs of this part of

the navigation was a complaint from Richard Griffith of the Grand Canal Company who sent in a diary of a voyage of three boats from Carrick to Shannon Harbour during the winter of 1803 when they were stopped by a wall in the Roosky Canal erected by the local miller, Galbraith Tredennick. He claimed that because the floodgates at the upper end of the canal were out of repair, he had 'rolled in some stones to confine the water' to operate his mill. It is not recorded what they did about this but five years later they received a letter from Henry Percy, a trader on the river, enclosing a letter from John Hewitt, who had formerly been lock keeper at Roosky, saying that 'the lock house was destroyed and converted to private purposes, and the Banks of the Canal set for grazing to different tenants'. This was followed by a further letter from Percy saying that promised work on the river had not been undertaken and he would be forced to give up trading.

In 1805 they instructed Brownrigg to update his report on the upper Shannon and he presented a very gloomy picture. He said that there were breaches in the Jamestown Canal and the lock house needed repairing. He confirmed the previous reports of the problems caused by the miller Tredennick in the canal at Roosky. He reported that the gates of the lock at Lanesborough were gone and boats had to be hauled up against the current, but it was however in constant use. He added: 'the lock keeper endeavours to pick up a miserable livelihood by catching eels having received no salary for many years past'. The weir wall here protecting the canal had been taken down to build an eel weir: 'that below the Bridge there was a dry wall in the rear and parallel to the lock which is greatly injured and much of the stones gone, that from the tail of the lock there ran another weir wall between the Canal and the River, 550ft in length which is almost entirely demolished being carried away by Boatmen as Ballast upon discharging their cargoes of slates from Killaloe'. It was decided that the navigation of the upper river should be put into 'sufficient order that it may be made use of until it can be fully completed'. Brownrigg estimated that £1,677 9s 5d was needed to put it into working order and an application was made to the Lord Lieutenant and the Lords of the Treasury to authorize this expenditure.

However, nothing much seems to have happened and in the first six years only £551 was recorded as having been spent by the Directors General on the upper river. No attempt was made to collect tolls from the few traders who endeavoured to use the navigation and no local conductors were appointed as had been intended. In the summer of 1809 there were complaints that shoals had built up caused by the winter floods at the mouth of the Lanesborough and Clondara canals. This time there was some response, the work on the upper river was begun and overseers appointed. Brownrigg reported that when the water was let out of Clondara lock it was found to be very defective below water, built of rubble masonry with scarcely any mortar. When finished there he intended moving the timbers for forming the dams to Roosky to remove the offending wall, advising against taking Tredennick to law. He was told in no uncertain terms: 'only to repair the present navigation that he is not to construct any Works beyond what may be necessary for the Purpose'.

Towards the end of the summer, having become more familiar with the upper river and its limitations as a navigation, Brownrigg suggested to his board that it would be beneficial to remove some of the ancient fording places and dredge some of the 'running canals' constructed in the river by the Navigation Board. His supervision of the works was brought into question by a report from Terence McCormick of Roosky who complained of: 'flagrant Abuse and Imposition practised at Roosky for the last eleven weeks. John Nesbitt, an overseer, removes men to his harvest, with the sanction of Mr Murphy but they are still returned against the Board. . . that several others are returned by Murphy who hardly worked at all, that the Carpenters do but very little, and that no Public Business was ever carried on with less Attention'. The board's reaction was to dismiss Nesbitt. The lock and canal were operational before the winter and John Hewitt was appointed lock keeper.

The trader, Henry Percy, complained about the total absence of marks and that there were many shallows between Roosky and Clondara and also below Tarmon at Kiluacarra. In one place he said there was an annual Patron, probably to do with St Barry, and in the summer when the water is low 'the country people regularly on that occasion refill the place to make a fordable passage'. At Lanesborough it had been reported that boatmen were using the stones in the wall separating the canal from the river as ballast and, initially, the Directors General decided that because there was such a small fall there was no need to replace the gates as boats could be hauled through. However, over the summer of 1810 the lock gates were replaced at Lanesborough. They were also replaced at Jamestown and Brownrigg was given permission to raise the lock here by about 9ins (0.2m) and the banks of the canal by about a foot because of constant trouble with flooding. Brownrigg complained that the workmen and materials were being taken from the works to get boats off shallows. He was told: 'Persons desirous of using the Navigation must employ Boats of Dimensions suited to the Navigation with proper and sufficient Crews to navigate them, upon whose Exertions they must depend.' The complaints about shoals continued but nothing seems to have been done about it.

THE DIRECTORS GENERAL UNDER SCRUTINY

There had been some public criticism of the board's activities. In 1812 Edward Wakefield in his statistical and political survey had made reference to the current suggestions that they were 'one of the Union jobs' and were deliberately procrastinating the works to eek out their continued existence.[19] There was some justification in this accusation. Wakefield had however defended the members of the board saying they 'were qualified in every respect for their situations'. Another contemporary commentator, Anthony Marmion, accused them of deliberate misappropriation of funds saying 'they did nothing but receive their salaries and squander a large portion of the amount in selfish and corrupt practices'.[20] While it would be fair to suggest that the cost of the establishment was hardly justified by the amount of work achieved, there is no evidence to support Marmion's accusations of corruption but it was rather a case of a lack of expertise. However, their accountability was also in question because for the first five years no accounts had been presented to the Lord Lieutenant as prescribed by the 1800 Act. After that annual accounts were presented to the Commissioners of Imprest Accounts with periodic statements laid before parliament on the state of their fund.

By 1812 the balance remaining to the Directors General of the original fund of £500,000 was dwindling fast and there were many demands on them from all quarters. From 1800 up to March 1811, £18,6973 had been expended directly by them, about one third of this on running the establishment and the rest on navigations under their direct control. In addition, they had approved the issuing of £209,409 to navigation companies, which left only £103,618 of their original allocation of £500,000 to be drawn down.[21] By this time the Royal Canal Company was in deep trouble.[22] Having completed the canal to Coolnahay, west of Mullingar, its debt had risen to an alarming level. Despite grants of public funding through the Directors General and the re-organization of the company, it was finding it impossible to raise further loans from private sources. It was a time of great unrest throughout the country and there were attacks on the canals. The directors of the Royal Canal tried to shorten the proposed line of the canal by dropping down via the River Inny into Lough Ree, which was sharply resisted by the Grand Canal Company.

At this stage the Westminster Parliament, which had shown very little interest in the way in which inland navigation was being managed in Ireland since 1800, was forced to intervene. A parliamentary committee carried out investigations not only into the Royal Canal affairs but also into the Grand Canal Company, which was also in financial difficulties.[23] As a result of these investigations the Royal

Canal Company was dissolved in 1813 and the Directors General were instructed to complete the canal at a cost of £198,110 5s 4d, based on John Killaly's estimate, with the funding being made available as a special parliamentary grant. The contract to carry out the work of extending the canal from Coolnahay to the Shannon, under the supervision of Killaly, was awarded to an Irish firm, Henry, Mullins & MacMahon, and work began in May 1814. The prospect of the completion of the Royal Canal to its original destination at Clondara was to put significant pressure on achieving a more satisfactory navigation on the upper Shannon and re-opened the issue of bringing about an extension of the navigation into Lough Allen.

The 1812 inquiries into the affairs of the canal companies had led inevitably at the same time to an investigation into the affairs of the Directors General. While acknowledging their 'zeal and anxiety', the investigating committee was very critical of their reliance on their officers: 'this mode of expending the public money is objectionable on general principles and consequently should not be recurred to unless under unavoidable circumstances'.[24] The committee had added that there was a case to be made for continuing the board but with considerably reduced functions. This criticism had led to a tightening up on the rather casual attitude of the board to the committee meetings; the weekly attendance now had to be reported to the Lord Lieutenant and meetings had to begin no later than 11 am. The parliamentary committee also recommended that the earlier short-sighted decision to insist on the lowering of toll charges when awarding grants should be reversed. The appointment of new members to the board with greater expertise led to the full acceptance of all these recommendations, but the gradual reduction in funding was going to have a considerable impact on what could be achieved.

CHAPTER THREE
THE DIRECTORS GENERAL 1814–1831

FUNDING PROBLEMS

In 1814 the Directors General were in control of the Limerick Killaloe Navigation, Lough Derg and the upper Shannon upstream of the Athlone Canal, with the Grand Canal Company in charge of the middle Shannon from Portumna to Athlone. The government was now keeping a closer eye on the affairs of the board and becoming more actively involved in inland waterway affairs. When further vacancies occurred on the board, the appointments were no longer motivated politically. In 1813 Captain Daniel Corneille, a military-trained engineer who had carried out investigations for the Directors General, was appointed and, in the following year, John Armit filled the vacancy left by one of the early directors. He had risen from the ranks of junior engineer in the ordnance department to serve as secretary of that body. When a further vacancy occurred in 1818, it was not filled, reducing the number of directors to four and when George Bouverie, who had hardly ever attended, resigned in 1820 his place was given to Henry Paine. Paine had joined the establishment back in 1800 as clerk of the minutes with a salary of £160 p.a. but had gradually assumed more responsibility during the frequent absences of the secretary Francis Trench. Trench had actually originally been appointed as a Director General, a 'Union Job', but resigned in 1810 to become secretary, thereby increasing his salary. His frequent periods of absence led to Paine being appointed assistant secretary in 1813 and by the time of his appointment to the board he was, in fact, acting secretary. The final vacancy on the board was filled in 1825 when John Radcliffe was appointed. He was only thirty years old at the time and had received training as a military engineer.[1]

The board consequently had become much better equipped to carry out its functions but this coincided with the ultimate exhaustion of the original funding. Approximately one fifth of the original funds had been expended on the Shannon with only a small percentage of this on the upper Shannon works. After 1817, until 1831, the board had to rely on annual government funding together with parliamentary grants for specific works such as the completion of the Royal Canal. It really became like a part of a government department, dependent on receiving funding based on the estimate of expenditure for the coming year. The official change-over from Irish currency to sterling (£13 Irish equal to £12 sterling) occurred in January 1826 and until then most transactions in Ireland appear to have been in Irish currency, but sums issued by parliament in Westminster were quoted in sterling and it is not easy to establish whether amounts were in Irish currency or sterling in this period.

Between 1817 and 1831 the annual issues amounted to a total sum of only £66,932 (stg) together with three small additional grants: a small extra allowance for the chairman, a grant to construct the Lough Allen Canal and a small grant to complete work on the River Suir. In the 1820s the board was forced to cut back on its establishment to reduce expenditure. In fact, the total issued for inland navigation in Ireland between 1800 and 1831 amounted to a small amount compared with the expenditure of £516,799 issued for a single waterway in Canada, the Rideau Canal, which had strategic military purposes.

By Order of the Directors of all Works relating to Inland Navigation in Ireland.

By authority of an Act passed in the 40th Year of His late Majesty King George the III.

Schedule of TOLLS *to be charged upon the* UPPER SHANNON NAVIGATION, *between Lough Allen and Lough Ree, from and after the 1st of March, 1821, until further Orders :------*

Every Boat navigating either upwards or downwards between Lough Allen and the Camlin River, shall pay Five Shillings per Lock, for each Lock through which such Boat shall pass.

And every Boat navigating either upwards or downwards, between the Camlin and Lough Ree, shall pay Ten Shillings per Lock, for each lock through which such Boat shall pass.

Empty Boats, or Vessels laden with *Corn, Meal, Malt, Flour, Potatoes, Turf, Manure, Lime, Lime-Stone, Iron and Iron Stone, Native Coal, Culm, Killaloe Slates,* or *Cut Stone* from the Quarries at Lanesborough, to pay *no more* than Two Shillings and Six-pence for every Lock through which such Vessel shall pass on any part of the Navigation. Vessels lying or discharging at the Harbours of Lanesborough, Drumsna, or Battle-bridge, to pay Two Shillings and Six-pence each.

By Order,

FRANCIS TRENCH,

Secretary.

N. B. By a subsequent Order of the Board, *Native Coal* and *Culm* are permitted to pass free of Toll for one year, from 1st December, 1823.

Navigation Office.
Jan. 26th 1824.

J. Carrick & Son, Printers.

A notice issued by the Directors General of Inland Navigation in 1824.

The economic depression, which spread through the whole of Great Britain and Ireland following the end of hostilities with France, coupled with bad harvests in Ireland in 1816 and 1817, had led to a deterioration in conditions in the poorer districts and the people's plight gradually became known through accounts of travellers and parliamentary investigations. The government's response was to issue loans, which had worked well in England, but failed to a large extent to address the destitution and unemployment in Ireland because of the stringent repayment conditions and demands for security. In 1817 a new loan scheme set aside a sum of £300,000 to be administered by the Exchequer Loan Commissioners for promoting public works in general and canal companies were able to avail of this fund for extensions.[2] In 1820 authorization was given to the Lord Lieutenant to advance a moiety of the amounts in the form of grants, involving him directly in the allocation of grants, but even this failed to encourage works in the poorer districts. The failure of the potato crop in 1821 and 1822 saw famine conditions beginning to prevail in these districts but, apart from involving the Grand Juries in sanctioning some road works and setting up relief committees, the system of loans persisted. The funding of the Loan Commissioners was very inadequate although the issue from the consolidated fund was increased to £500,000 and subsequently increased by another £100,000. From 1822 direct funding to carry out public works, mostly road works, for the employment and relief of the poor was made available up to £300,000.

As far as the Shannon was concerned it was largely left in the hands of the Directors General to do what they could on the upper Shannon and there was little attempt to put pressure on the Limerick Navigation Company or the Grand Canal Company either to maintain the works under their control or do anything to improve them. A gesture had been made by the government in 1821 when it directed John Rennie to make a survey of the river with a view to effecting the drainage of the flooded areas to promote more cultivation and create employment, but with no reference to improving the navigation.[3] He appointed John Grantham to carry out the work and Grantham produced a detailed report and charts of the river. It was estimated that two million acres could be drained for the expenditure of £300,000. Any attempt to follow through on this scheme was abandoned on Rennie's death but the fact that Grantham had been made aware of the potential of the navigation in the course of his survey work was to bear fruit later when he was one of the pioneers to bring steamers to the river. Alexander Nimmo, another well-known engineer, also pointed to the potential of the Shannon in 1824, giving evidence before a committee appointed by the House of Lords, when he drew attention to the lack of landing places, quays or road access except at the bridge crossings, and he added: 'I should suppose that four or five thousand pounds will accomplish all that is wanted in making roads and landing places.'[4]

THE SHANNON ESTUARY

The Directors General did not assume responsibility for the port of Limerick or the estuary except for the River Maigue, which had some small improvements carried out to improve navigation to Adare as a result of the 1715 Act. In 1815 they began to take action to carry out further improvements and arranged a meeting to agree a valuation of the ground that would be required where the original little dock and quay were located. It was reported that this was 'a mere Rut in the Mud and which he did not consider to be of the smallest consideration or value, but had it been part of the Custom House Quay, there could not have been more Noise made about it'. A price was agreed and work began to install a turning bridge, which was supplied from Newry. A toll-keeper's house was built 'with a strong small porch with loopholes because of the particular lawlessness of the Part of the Country'. Work was held up by a strike with the men refusing an offer of 13d per day. It continued to be a troubled area and Brownrigg reported in 1818: 'The Rudeness, Wickedness, love of Mischief and inclination to destroy or injure Public Works is so strongly imbued in almost every creature of the lower class, that it will require the utmost Care in the Bridge keeper to protect his Charge.'

THE LIMERICK KILLALOE NAVIGATION 1814–1831

Having purchased the navigation from the company and finally opened it to navigation, the Directors General must have hoped that this troublesome waterway would take up less of their time as they faced into other problems including the major works to complete the Royal Canal.[5] It is interesting that Brownrigg reported that the former Limerick Navigation Company had measured the navigation for the purpose of tolls as fifteen statute miles when it was only eleven Irish miles, but he recommended the erection of milestones in Irish miles. This is an indication of the widespread use of Irish mileage at this time, which unlike Irish currency did not have an official change-over date and continued in widespread use, causing much confusion. By November the bad weather had set in, flood damage was reported and boats were experiencing problems at O'Brien's Bridge. The tolls collected for that month amounted to just over £104.

Their troubles were just beginning and it was not just the weather. In December Brownrigg reported that 'an outrage' had occurred. The bank at Gillogue lock had been cut with spades: 'that this is the third Time the People in that Part of the Country have cut the Canal Banks across; that on one occasion the Mischief cost above thirty pounds to repair and he thinks the Board would do well to take notice of the Conduct and put a stop to such Villainous Practice'. The board decided to put up a reward of £100 for information leading to the arrest of those responsible. Further storms and floods followed and a subsequent inspection stated: 'no Boat or Horse can get near the River owing to the great Surge, but that a great deal of Damage must have occurred'.

In January 1815 the board received a request, a portent of a significant change that was about to take place for the entire Shannon Navigation. Ringrose Watson from Limerick said he wanted to establish a steamboat on the river to use for towing boats. He said that often boats were held up for many weeks waiting for a fair wind. He claimed that he had seen steamboats operating successfully on the River Clyde near Greenock in a high sea. He sought 'fair encouragement' from the board in the form of a sharing of the costs and he submitted plans and estimates. His request was turned down, the board saying that they needed to complete the works on the upper Shannon first. They failed to realize what a revolution in trading on the river was about to take place and, in fact, it was to be over ten years before the first steamer actually arrived on the river.

The troubled state of the country led eventually to the need for military escorts for boats passing between Limerick and Killaloe. In June 1817 a convoy system was introduced with a sergeant and twelve men escorting boats in both directions once a week. Turning down the Grand Canal Company's urgent request for a lock at O'Brien's Bridge, referred to in the last chapter, the board said it did not have any funding for such work; it was pointed out that the receipts from this navigation amounted to £560 p.a. and the expenditure £1,400. Even when the canal company repeated this request some years later, saying that winching the boats through the bridge with a capstan was considered to be dangerous and time-consuming, again the request was turned down as too costly. The reluctance of the board to incur further expenditure on the navigation was confirmed in the summer of 1819 when it stated that repairs were to be limited to 'what shall appear to be indispensable for maintaining the Navigation against the Floods and Storms of the Winter'.

The unsatisfactory way in which works had been undertaken in the past began to become apparent as early as 1820 when Errina lock, which Chapman had earlier lengthened and converted from a triple to a double chamber, was reported to be in a bad state of decay. When the repairs had been completed and the water was let back into the canal a breach occurred that then had to be repaired. During the following years continuing work was required on the locks, and the high levels and floods that occurred in most winters were a constant cause for concern. Some of the arches of

the bridge at Killaloe were swept away. There is evidence that there was a timber bridge here in the eleventh century but it is also recorded that the river had to be forded here in the fourteenth century. The nineteen-arch stone bridge had been erected in the early eighteenth century. It remained impassable from 1821 to 1824 until Dr Arbuthnot, Bishop of Killaloe, finding it very inconvenient, intervened and insisted on repairs being carried out and five new arches were constructed to replace the seven carried away. A rather gloomy picture of Killaloe emerges from T. Crofton Croker's *Researches* published in 1824:

> [Killaloe] wears a poor appearance and seems to be little frequented by strangers, as the inn, if it deserves the name, included the business of publican, linen draper, hosier, and chandler, under the same roof: one room was appropriated for a table d'hote, where my companion and myself joined a noisy good humoured clerical party, none of whom could be accused of fastidiousness.

The hazardous condition of the bridge at Portumna at the northern end of Lough Derg did not help matters. John Cowan had found a ferry boat operating here in 1795 but said that there were the remains of an old bridge: 'whole arches survive on the island in the middle'.[6] One year later a new bridge on timber piles had been constructed, designed by Lemuel Cox, with a drawbridge near the west side of the island and a toll house.

The early 1820s were years of increasing distress among the people and there were appeals to the board to give employment from committees set up for relief of the poor. The policy of *laissez faire* operated by the administration precluded giving direct handouts of relief. The distress led to boats being robbed that were carrying provisions such as potatoes. In July 1822 the unfortunate lock keeper at Gillogue lock was dismissed because he refused to name the perpetrators of an attack; the board felt it was unsafe to replace him and had to make a request for the police to operate the lock 'until the country shall be tranquillised'. Further disturbances were reported with crowds turning up looking for employment when any work was being carried on.

The board must have been beginning to regret that they had turned down the request to help to bring steamboats to the river because it was becoming clear that they would have a dramatic effect, particularly for towing boats across the large lakes. They asked for a meeting with the Grand Canal Company to discuss the issue but, when they sounded out what the cost of a vessel would be, they found that it was estimated that it would cost over £1,400 (stg) to have a steamer built and the running costs would be high. When John Grantham approached them about encouragement to

Limerick: the new Baal's Bridge erected by the Limerick Navigation Company in the 1830s. (ESB Archives)

bring a steamer to the river, they willingly agreed to lease him land to build a store at Limerick and they even asked him where he would like more beacons erected on Lough Derg and gave him the job of supplying and installing them with a contract for their maintenance. When his steamer did arrive on the river in 1826 he was offered permission to pass toll-free through the Limerick Navigation for one year although he did not avail of this initially, fearing the passage through O'Brien's Bridge and the poor state of some of the locks. He subsequently negotiated good terms to operate a lighter passenger boat. The steamers had arrived and this was to become an important incentive to the government to improve the entire Shannon Navigation.

Traffic was gradually increasing and by 1829 receipts from tolls had risen to nearly £1,000 p.a. and half this sum was sufficient to meet the wages and routine maintenance. The government agreed to the transfer of the navigation to a newly formed Limerick Navigation Company on condition that the company would rebuild Baal's Bridge in Limerick.[7]

It has already been shown that this ancient structure was a great obstruction to the navigation. The new Limerick Navigation Company had to agree to expend £3,000 on the rebuilding and to complete the work within two years, but the new single arch bridge over the tidal Abbey River would still limit both headroom and draught right up to recent years. Once again a navigation was being transferred to a private company with all the expenses of improving it paid for from public funds. The new company's reign, however, was to prove short lived as it was to be taken over again in 1836 although the directors were to do well out of the episode, receiving compensation of £12,227. Consequently, in the end the navigation was actually purchased twice by the State within a thirty-year period at a total cost to public funds of £28,539 in addition to the money expended on its works. However, despite the introduction of steamboats, the opportunity for the company to make profits was somewhat limited. By 1831 it was recorded that 14,600 passengers were carried and 30,018 tons of goods yielding a gross profit of £1,154.

By this time a new bridge, Wellesley Bridge, had been constructed across the Shannon downstream of the junction with the Abbey River. The bridge, which was designed by Alexander Nimmo, was authorized by an Act in 1823 that allocated £60,000 for its construction and for a new dock.[8] It is said that Nimmo was influenced in his design by the famous Port Neuilly bridge in Paris. The first stone was laid on 25 October 1824 but because of the death of Nimmo it

had to be finished by John Grantham and was not opened until August 1833. Because the bridge would cut off access from the sea to the Custom House quay, Nimmo designed it with five arches and at the south end he made a lie by and entrance channel to a lock chamber with a twin-span swivel bridge intending to erect a weir above the lock to create a dock. Grantham shows this intended weir running from the lock to the upper corner of the Custom House quay, leaving the access into the Abbey River tidal. In fact, lock gates were not fitted and the weir and dock were not built; new docks were later constructed farther downstream. The result was that the approach remained tidal; boats wanting to access the Custom House quay and inland navigation now had to pass through the open lock chamber and the bridge had to be opened if they required headroom. The opening spans were later replaced by a steel box single-span swivel in 1923, which was electrified in 1926 and permanently closed in 1963. The drainage and navigation scheme completed in 2001 was to see the ultimate completion of the tidal lock and the building of a weir but, unlike Nimmo's plan, the weir extended across to Curragour Point to include the entrance to the Abbey River.

THE MIDDLE SHANNON 1814–1831

The Grand Canal Company had finally managed to do a deal about payment for works on the middle Shannon but it was later to establish that it had spent £30,000 over and above the agreed grant of £54,634 for the works. Independently of this deal, arising out of the investigations into both the Royal and the Grand canal companies in 1812, the company had received a grant of £150,000 to help to liquidate its debts.[9] It had managed to avoid any reduction in tolls as a condition of the awarding of this grant, but the company did have to agree to suspend dividends, except out of clear profits, which had been running the company deeper and

deeper into debt, and to build up a sinking fund of £30,000, representing one third of the grant.

The Directors General showed little interest in the management of the middle Shannon and the company was left to adhere to its commitment to maintain it. The works completed by the company enabled trade to build up particularly between Shannon Harbour and Limerick with a more limited trade with Athlone. By 1817 it was reported that there were twenty-six boats operating on the river and through the canal to Dublin. Because of the lack of any towpaths, trading was very difficult and weather-dependent

Limerick: from Grantham's chart showing his proposed design for a dock.

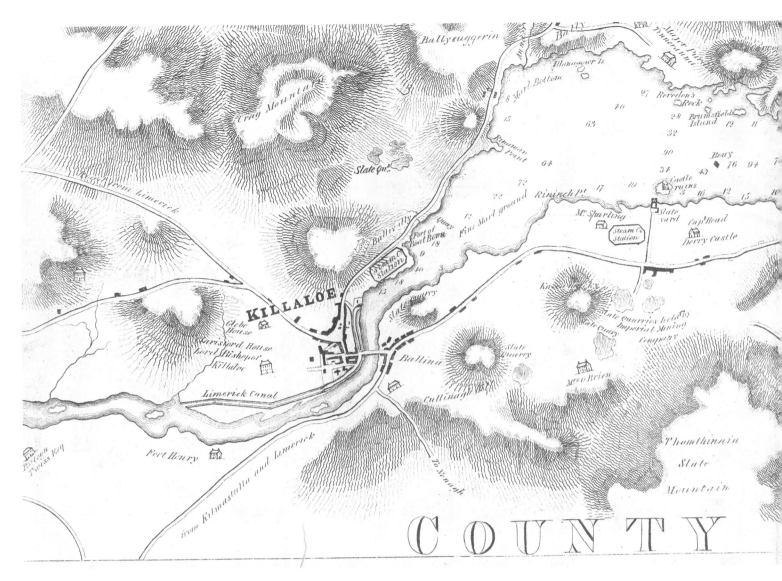

Killaloe: from Grantham's chart later adapted by him to show the Steam Company's stations.

with the boats having to be sailed or poled, although the arrival of the steamers was about to change this. There is also a reference in 1823 to a boat called *The Speed of Banagher* with 'John Fahy and Francis Molloy, owners of the celebrated passage boat' in a book called *Inhabitants of Banagher*.[10] While there were passengers carried on both the Grand Canal and Limerick Navigation, it is hard to see how a passage boat could have operated satisfactorily on the river before the arrival of the steamers.

In the meantime the canal company's agreement about maintenance appears to have fallen short and in the 1820s complaints had begun to be made. The same severe weather and floods that had plagued the Limerick Navigation from time to time also caused problems on the middle river; some of the swinging buoys had to be replaced by stone beacons and the company subsequently had to resort to driving in metal piles. Just as the Directors General had done, the canal company directors set up a small group to investigate the

possibility of introducing steamers on the Shannon, which entered into correspondence with Christopher Owens in Cork. He said that he was using a Boulton & Watt engine, which, although more expensive, costing £1,100, could produce more horse power than locally made engines; in a passage of ten miles (16km) he could give the local boat a four-mile (6km) start and still get there before it. The steamers began to arrive and trade increased but so did the complaints and soon the company was to find itself in trouble with the government about its failure to abide by its maintenance contract.

With the arrival of the steamers the Directors General had to look to improving navigation on Lough Derg and they followed up the agreement with John Grantham to provide buoys and beacons with an annual fee of £25 for their maintenance. The local landowner, Ringrose Drew, offered to build a quay at Tuamgraney on the Scarriff River and quays were also proposed for Dromineer and Youghal.

THE UPPER SHANNON 1814–1831

Unlike the rest of the Shannon Navigation, the upper Shannon remained under the control of the Directors General at all times. John Brownrigg was asked to send in a report on the condition of the navigation, which he completed in November 1814. He said that all the locks and canals were in full working order, but that at Lanesborough the 'very handsome lock house built a long time since by Mr Omer', which was built astride the canal, needed to be re-roofed and re-floored and the Jamestown lock house needed to be virtually rebuilt. One of the bridges over the Jamestown Canal needed raising by four to five feet (1.20 to 1.50m). Following winter floods over the next two years further extensive work was needed on the Jamestown Canal, closing the canal with a dam, and it was eventually reported that the dams would be removed and the canal re-opened in the spring of 1816. The shoals upstream of Lough Forbes were marked to indicate the channel, which had been made some years previously 'by dredging with considerable difficulty'. The river was considered to be sufficiently navigable to ask the Lord Lieutenant for permission to begin charging tolls in the summer of 1817, and these were fixed at ½d on corn, coal and iron, 1d on other goods and 2d per passenger. Once again this reference to passengers is puzzling unless they just travelled on the trade boats as it is hard to see how any regular service could have operated.

In 1818, with the Royal Canal now completed to the Shannon and the New Royal Canal Company established, the issue of extending the navigation into Lough Allen was raised once more. Killaly carried out a new survey of a line to the east of the river with an estimate of £20,623 and permission was authorized to proceed. Dennis Hayes and Patrick Kelly won the contract, with Killaly as directing engineer, to construct the canal from Battlebridge to Lough Allen, with two locks, passing through Acres Lake. Their contract included a twelve-month maintenance clause following completion, which was probably because some problems had arisen with contractors following completion of the Royal Canal extension. With the prospect of Lough Allen being opened up, the board was now looking for 4ft (1.2m) throughout the navigation at all seasons but this was going to require considerable dredging of shoals and also a short running canal was needed to avoid the shallows at Port just downstream of Battlebridge.

Hayes and Kelly reported that the canal to Lough Allen had been completed in December 1820 and it was opened to traffic the following February. Killaly praised the contractors and reported that the work had been completed 'in a Manner highly creditable to their Character'. They were subsequently to become embroiled in bitter controversies both about the awarding by the Grand Canal Company of the contract to construct the Ballinasloe Line and by the Royal Canal Company to construct the Longford Line to Henry, Mullins & MacMahon. They accused John Killaly, who was the father-in-law of John MacMahon, of exercising undue influence in the awarding of both these contracts.[11]

In the 1820s the receipts from tolls for the entire upper Shannon only amounted to £3 17s 6d for one quarter year and the salaries for that quarter were £9 5s. The same floods, that had made work on the Limerick Navigation difficult in December 1821, also made it difficult to carry out dredging on the upper river. Complaints began to come in from the proprietor of the Leitrim collieries about continuing problems with shoals and shallows, particularly in the Jamestown Canal. The sill of the lock was lowered and the canal was dredged with the intention of giving the required 4ft (1.2m) but this involved closing the canal for almost a year. Great difficulty was experienced in raising the banks of the canal, which had been 'originally formed on a treacherous foundation'. The Mining Company of Ireland, which was not only mining in the Lough Allen coalfields but had also opened extensive slate quarries near Killaloe, were told in response to their complaints that 'the Board are ready to afford every Assistance in their Power towards the Extension and Application of the Capital of Ireland and of affording employment to the People consistent with due Attention to the Public Economy which is periodically and strictly enjoined them'. The board was relying on the government for its annual expenditure and was under great pressure to reduce the costs of both its works and its establishment.

Through the 1820s the navigation continued to suffer problems during the summers when levels were low and it was reported that the river was obstructed in seven places between Drumsna and the Royal Canal at Richmond Harbour. The objective of achieving a 4ft (1.2m) navigation at all seasons was as far away as ever. To make matters worse it was proving very difficult to get contractors to undertake the work and they were forced to carry out works themselves by 'day's work'. To encourage trade, coal boats of thirty tons or upwards from Lough Allen were allowed to pass toll free for a period of three years and the production of coal was increased; this encouraged the Directors General to continue to have shoals removed. In 1825 the board of the Royal Canal Company complained to the Lord Lieutenant about the difficulties that were being experienced with the navigation on the upper Shannon: 'the experience of the last thirty years has fully proved that no Art or Expenditure can render [them] effective'. An example was quoted of a boat loaded with twenty-five tons of coal leaving Lough Allen, which had to be lightened at twelve different places with eight rapids to be overcome and which arrived at Richmond Harbour to enter the canal with only five tons aboard.[12]

A Royal Canal advertisement of its services in 1828.

The increase in trade is also reflected in a letter to the Royal Canal directors from Thomas Duggan Hall saying that he had 'at great expence opened the Boyle Water, a River which leads from the Shannon into the interior of the country about nine miles'. He said he had brought a loading of pig iron from the Arigna works to the Royal Canal.[13] The Directors General were also looking at the opening up of the Boyle Water and suggested that an expenditure of £2000 was needed to make two short canals to bypass shallows. They assisted with the construction of harbours. In most cases the local landowner gave the land free and contributed to the cost. A harbour was made at Drumsna in 1817 and at Lanesborough in 1819. In 1828 St George gave the land and subscribed a third of the cost of £312 for a harbour at Carrick and in the same year Lord Forbes and Francis Nesbitt provided land and paid one third of the cost of £139 for a habour at Drumod and a quay was provided at Carnadoe Bridge at a cost of £348 assisted by the landowner Molloy McDermott. Early in 1830 further problems were reported at Clondara lock where the sill had disintegrated, which meant that the canal would have to be closed to erect a dam to effect repairs.

THE END OF THE DIRECTORS GENERAL

In their final years other functions had been added to be carried out by the Directors General. They assumed responsibility for the repairing and maintenance of certain roads and bridges in 1825 and of the Fisheries Commissioners in 1830, which involved completing some fishery piers and collecting repayments to the Fishery Loan Fund.[14] At this stage the government was turning down any unnecessary expenditure on navigation works and had intimated its intention to establish a new Board of Works, which would take over all the functions of the Directors General. In 1829 a select committee had questioned the usefulness of continuing the board for which the cost of the establishment was now accounting for nearly half the annual expenditure.[15] The members of the board issued a long reply in their own defence in which they questioned 'the principle that the weight of business must be proportionate to the amount of the disbursements'. They pointed out that they also acted in an advisory capacity to the government in matters of inland waterway policy in addition to the other functions that had been added, including acting as the Board of Control to the new Royal Canal Company.

However, by the end of 1830 their navigational responsibilities had been reduced to the uneconomic Tyrone and upper Shannon navigations and the opening bridge on the Maigue with a total income from tolls of under £400 and an average outlay of £800, while the establishment was costing about £4,000. Then in 1831 the government decided to carry through its intention to co-ordinate all public works under a single body in order to provide employment for the increasing numbers of distressed poor. The Directors General were dissolved and their existing functions were transferred to form the nucleus of the new Office of Public Works.[16] One of the Directors General, John Radcliffe, was nominated as one of three new Commissioners of Public Works together with Colonel John Burgoyne as chairman and Brooke Taylor Ottley.[17] The Act giving assent to this was passed on 15 October 1831 and the three new Commissioners of Public Works assumed control. The thirty-one year period of the Directors General may have been accompanied by controversy but, overall, positive progress had been made with the expenditure of a relatively small amount of public funds.

Dromod: the harbour built here in the 1820s – the harbour walls were set back and lowered to facilitate modern cruisers in recent times.

CHAPTER FOUR
THE WINDS OF CHANGE IN THE 1830s

PRESSURE ON THE GOVERNMENT

There is very little doubt that, just as inland waterways benefitted in the 1750s as appropriate public works at that time on which to spend the financial surplus and laid the foundation for the extensive waterway system we enjoy today, so in the middle of the nineteenth century they once again were to prove to be convenient public works, this time to create employment for the destitute population. In 1830 a series of select committees was set up to examine the state of the poor in Ireland and it was recommended that a fund of £500,000 should be established to promote public works in Ireland in order to provide employment but, once again, this was to be issued in the form of loans.[1] It is significant that these exhaustive inquiries did not even bother hearing evidence from the Directors General, relying for inland-waterways information amongst others on the testimony of Bernard Mullins, a contractor and director of the Royal Canal Company, and Charles Wye Williams. Williams was the son of Thomas Williams, secretary of the Bank of Ireland, and was to have a lifelong interest in steam boats both on the Shannon and on the Irish Sea.

The parliamentary inquiries on the state of the country continued to reveal a very disturbing picture.[2] The list of unlawful groups roaming the countryside levying sums of money from farmers was extensive: Peep O'Day Boys, Thrashers, Whiteboys, Righters, Carders, Shanavats, Caravats, Rockites, Black-hens, Riskavallas, Ribbonmen, Lady Clares, Terry-alts and Whitefeet. The situation was not helped by the lack of employment and the 'immoderate use of spirituous liquors'. Thomas Bermingham, who was a landowner in Queen's County (Laois), said in evidence that efforts should be made to avoid the evils of the English Poor Law system. He claimed that the answer was to give employment to the able-bodied on public works, suggesting a number of productive inland navigation schemes, and there was much evidence in a similar vein. There was, however, an element of doubt creeping in about the policy

of *laissez faire*, making people work for their living rather than providing hand-outs, as demonstrated in a comment at one parliamentary inquiry:

The committee are aware how nearly allied a remedy for this evil [the plight of the poor] is with a Poor-law system, but it appears to them that a partial remedy may be applied, even if the apprehensions of the consequences of Poor-laws should deter the Legislature from introducing them to Ireland.[3]

In order to administer public-works schemes, the government had decided to establish the new Board of Works so that all the works could be co-ordinated. Little did it realize that it had established a department that essentially was going to run the country through the difficult famine years and for many years to come.

As already indicated, in 1794 Jessop had highlighted the problems in developing trade on the river when boats were dependent on sails and poles. At that time he had advocated the need to create trackways and had even suggested making a parallel canal to bypass Lough Bofin and Boderg, which would have involved making an aqueduct over the Carnadoe Water. Steam power had now dramatically altered all this. It has been shown that neither the Directors General nor the Grand or Royal canal companies had responded positively to approaches for support, failing to appreciate what a difference steamers would make, and it had been left to individuals to take the initiative. Back in 1715 the original Act promoting navigation had also included the improving of 'the bogs and other lost grounds'. Year by year the Shannon flooded out onto the surrounding countryside for many months and nothing had been done to improve the situation. Now the concept of arterial drainage as a useful form of public works surfaced again and the idea of linking navigation and drainage works became popular.

Charles Wye Williams, who had been one of the pioneers in bringing steamers to the Shannon, was quick to seize on the opportunity to make the suggestion that the extension of inland navigations would be a useful form of public works to promote employment.[4] In 1831 he set out in vehement terms the shortcomings of the Shannon as a navigation. He pointed out that the measures he was urging were 'practical in their nature and would be permanent in their beneficial results'. Alluding to the tendency in the past for public works to follow political agendas, he stated: 'My politics are – trade and commerce. These are the great pioneers of civilization, and will continue to be so in all ages and in all countries.' He drew attention to the fact that one million pounds had been spent on the Rideau Canal in Canada whereas the Shannon was 'a lamentable picture of great neglect'. He added that the callows annually submerged could produce good crops and 'for nearly one hundred miles not a sail or a boat to be met with'. He quoted the fact that a trader from Limerick with a cargo of timber and wheat had taken three months and five days to reach Lough Allen and return to Limerick with a cargo of coals and produce. The Lough Allen Canal, which the Directors General had praised the contractors for their work in constructing, 'remained unfinished and the locks and works fast verging to decay'.

The condition of the navigation upstream of Athlone was detailed by Williams in a vivid description of a journey made by three trade boats towed by a steamer from Killaloe to Jamestown described in a letter written by Lieutenant John Tully dated 27 June 1831:

On 7th inst., three boats started from Killaloe with about thirty tons of wheat each, for Jamestown, which was only two thirds of what they could have taken, provided there was no want of water . . . On our journey upwards (having accompanied them myself) we encountered some difficulties between Shannon Harbour and Athlone. We however got to Athlone after a long passage from the state of the river. On our arrival at Athlone, the three boats (although not drawing more than 3ft 6ins) stuck fast in the canal; suffice it to say, we had to lighten them considerably to get them through the canal into Lough Ree. The steamer had to lighten also. We crossed the lake with three boats in tow of the steamer; such a sight was never before witnessed on that lake, although there are a few beacons and buoys wanted on some bad rocks and islands which could be done at little or no expense. On our arrival at Lanesborough, our troubles only commenced, which induced me to stay with the boats to see it out. I lightened two of the boats to 2ft 6ins and 2ft 8ins and put the cargo into the third, being obliged to use some stratagem, not having any boat to spare. The canal is filling up fast; the very walls on its banks are falling into it. We had to take almost the whole cargo out before we could get the

OBSERVATIONS

ON THE

INLAND NAVIGATION OF IRELAND

AND THE

WANT OF EMPLOYMENT FOR ITS POPULATION,

WITH A DESCRIPTION OF

THE RIVER SHANNON.

SUGGESTED BY THE REPORT OF THE SELECT COMMITTEE OF THE
HOUSE OF COMMONS IN 1830,

ON THE STATE OF IRELAND, AND THE REMEDIAL MEASURES
PROPOSED BY THEM.

BY C. W. WILLIAMS, ESQ.

SECOND EDITION,

COMPRISING AN EXAMINATION OF THE APPLICATION

OF

MONEY GRANTS IN AID OF PUBLIC WORKS.

LONDON:
VACHER & SON, 29, PARLIAMENT STREET;
AND
R. FENN, CHARING-CROSS.
W. CURRY, DUBLIN;
T. KAYE, LIVERPOOL.
1833.

Frontispiece of C. W. Williams's book which contributed to the call for improving the Shannon Navigation.

boats through. Although the Board of the Directors General must have known very little of the state of the navigation when that part of the regulation was framed, and which was rigidly enforced, that I should not be allowed to discharge a single sack of wheat either in the lock or any part of the canal, though it was the shameful state of their navigation which rendered it necessary. We were obliged to haul out into the lake to tranship, with the greatest difficulty and danger, and after six days' hard labour, I got the two boats to Drumsna. I had there to hire two boats of a man named Blanchfield to take forty tons out of the boat, which was left behind at Lanesborough, to Jamestown . . . Altogether it was a most vexatious trip that could possibly be. The Government or Directors General should be called on to pay the expenses incurred. They had a dredge-boat at work last January, when the water was high; now they have none, when it is low, and when it might be useful. The beacons are all washed away or stolen, and a parcel of stones and rocks are left behind in their place, which increases the danger considerably. No person to look after or take the least care *of anything; and although they exact their tolls, the lock keepers throwing every obstacle in the way; I, however, persevered, and accomplished the voyage.[5]*

The government responded in 1831 by establishing a special commission to report on the condition of the River Shannon, from Limerick to the source, also to include the tidal estuary. C.W. Williams' tirade may have helped, but it was possibly more in response to many factors including the need to carry out drainage to produce profitable agricultural ground and to address the growing problems of lawlessness and destitution.

THE SHANNON COMMISSION 1831

This was a very workmanlike commission. There were just three members appointed: Colonel Burgoyne, Captain Mudge RN and Thomas Rhodes. Colonel John Fox Burgoyne was born in Ireland in 1782, son of General John Burgoyne, Commander-in-Chief of the army in Ireland. After a career in the army, including serving under Wellington at Waterloo, he had been appointed chairman of the new Board of Works and was now appointed chairman of the Commissioners of the Shannon Navigation; he was also president of the Institute of Civil Engineers in Ireland.[6] The Board of Works had offices in the Custom House and he remained in Dublin to co-ordinate the work. Captain Mudge was described as 'a practical navigator and naval surveyor' and he was instructed to survey the Shannon Estuary. The third member, Thomas Rhodes, had become a member of the Institution of Civil Engineers in 1827 and had worked as an assistant with both Thomas Telford and William Jessop.[7] The son of James Rhodes, an engineer who had superintended the construction of lock gates, bridges and other works on the Leeds & Liverpool Canal, he followed his father and elder brother, William, into the profession. He gained wide experience on navigation and harbour works in England and Scotland and showed considerable initiative. In 1816 he had been responsible for the erection of an early steam bucket-dredger, designed by Bryan Donkin. In 1822 he had worked on the chain for the Menai Bridge across the Menai Straits to Anglesey for the Holyhead Road Commissioners, which he was the first to cross on 30 January 1826. In that year Telford selected him as his resident engineer in the building of St Katherine's Dock beside Tower Bridge in London, where he was responsible for designing an interlocking swivel bridge, which he was afterwards to use on the Shannon. Rhodes was instructed to survey the river from Limerick to the source.

The commission was set up by directive in October 1831 and the various stages of the work can be followed through the entries in one of the commission's letter books and subsequently in printed reports for parliament.[8] They started work almost immediately. The first letter from

Colonel John Fox Burgoyne (1782–1871). (Courtesy of Engineers Ireland)

Rhodes to Burgoyne was dated 1 December, and the initial survey was finished and the first reports completed by May 1832. The preparation of further reports, plans and estimates extended into the summer of 1833 because Rhodes was also subsequently asked to continue his investigations to cover how the situation in Limerick port could be improved. Apart from providing a record of the state of the estuary and of the river, the reports also give a very good idea of the poor condition of the people in these parts of the country.

THE ESTUARY AND LIMERICK PORT

Mudge recommended that a boat should be built specifically for the survey work which he estimated would cost £350, and this was agreed to by Burgoyne. In mid-December he sent a long report to Dublin on the works that would be needed in the estuary, clearing rocks and shoals and placing buoys to mark the channel. Rhodes had also begun work at Limerick and his first comments on the Limerick Navigation were not very positive: 'The masonry of the locks, bridges, towing paths, side drains and every other thing, I find in a grossly neglected state.' He and Mudge reported together on the Wellesley Bridge and dock area in Limerick, which they found unfinished and 'far from a state of completion'. As already indicated the opening bridge and lock chamber were built but the rest of the work in developing a dock had not been carried out. This meant that the Abbey River, which linked the Limerick Navigation with the main channel of the Shannon, remained tidal and Rhodes said that 'a considerable quantity of stones, Rubbish and other matter having accumulated near Baal's Bridge which causes the Current to flow with great velocity and it is with considerable difficulty that a Canal Boat can get up at the present time even at high water'.

Letters were received from the Rev. Duggan, parish priest, and Magistrate at Carrigaholt, in which he recommended extending the pier 'like an arrow to give an oblique angle to the surge'. Boats were able only to come alongside at spring tides and the people could not get their produce to the markets at Limerick. The drought the previous summer had destroyed their corn crops: 'The People are in actual despair from the pressure on them from a double levy which is now demanded, three Tythe claims and from one to three years rent which the People in general owe, never was there a blessing hailed with such joy by the People as employment would be.' A second letter from him said that Carrigaholt was like an island the roads into it were so bad: 'People are obliged to put their Corn into Canoes in some parts and convey it to Kilrush.' However, there was widespread distrust and want of public confidence among the people who said: 'Everything you wrote to that Engineer will get into the hands of the Government – the Government will betray us to the Landlords and the Landlords will then burn us.'

In January Mudge recommended to Burgoyne that Foynes should be developed as a harbour, and not Grass Island as had been originally suggested. The survey boat was duly launched for fitting out and named *The Investigator* but Rhodes was called away to London where he was detained for longer than he had anticipated. The list of equipment needed gives a good indication of how the surveying was carried out:

A land chain and arrow etc. @ 15s, a cross staff with jointed sights and mahogany legs @ £2 6s 6d, best finished Theodolite with one telescope @ £51 10s, 20 inch improved level to adapt to the Theodolite staff £11 11s, ditto with legs @ £10 10s, 6 inch Circular Protractor @ £4 14s 6d, Schmalcalder Compass with cover etc. @ £2 15s, Gunters chain and Arrows @ 15s, Station Staff divided decimally @ £1 8s.

Mudge's detailed report of the Fergus said that boats drawing up to 16ft (4.8m) could get up to Clarecastle on the tide and he recommended building wharfs for five or six boats so that grain could be shipped to Liverpool to save expensive land carriage. He did not think it would be worth making a canal to Ennis but instead the road could be improved. He added: 'Clare is a small wretched Village and

owes its existence to its Proximity to the River; it consists of a few Miserable and poor Hovels, some without even thatch, you may here and there see a slated Cabin but the whole is a picture of misery and distress.'

The difficulties in navigating the channel up to Limerick had also been described by Thomas Steele in 1828.[9] He said that pilots told him that they would often tremble below Limerick where 'the channel is so narrow and such a rapid tide'. Steele had carried out experiments at that time on a new diving bell. He had come up with an improvement on existing diving bells. He designed one with two compartments, one with the usual open bottom and the other 'a communicating chamber' with a window for observation fed by an air pipe large enough to allow men up and down to it. This allowed conversations to be held under water and also permitted 'artificial submarine illumination'.

Things did not always go as planned with the commission's work: Mudge reported that one of their cutters was set adrift by some of the men demanding higher wages. The fitting out of *The Investigator* was still not finished: 'The Tradesmen in this part of the Country are so very slow in their movements that time is quite out of their calculation.' The cost had risen to £500, which met with a frosty response from Burgoyne in Dublin:

As the Government is always extremely particular as to the Estimates not being exceeded without authority grounded on circumstances that could not have been foreseen, and as our attention was in this very case called to that point, any excess of expense will I fear not be approved.

THE LIMERICK NAVIGATION AND LOUGH DERG

By March 1832 Rhodes was reporting from on board *The Investigator* in Killaloe. It appears that the charts, which had been prepared by John Grantham back in 1822, had apparently gone missing. Grantham had already put forward his opinion at that time on the issue of drainage, which was to prove very accurate, by suggesting that the only way to achieve this was to improve the run-off by taking away the shoals and enlarging the arches of the bridges. He held that what was needed was a government scheme 'under a specific law', and he added: 'I only regret that I am not twenty years younger and had time to promote to so useful an object.' Grantham now said he would reproduce the charts for a fee of £450, an offer which was not taken up, and he made a reference to the earlier scheme to reduce the level of Lough Derg by changing the falls at Killaloe: 'I think the reclaiming land on the lake with a view, that by its sale, the Expense may be covered, is in the present state of Ireland a mistaken feeling.'

Reference has already been made to charts of the river published by John Cowan as early as 1773 and republished in 1795. Lough Ree and Lough Derg had been charted for the Directors General of Inland Navigation by John Longfield, which were now used by Rhodes. Grantham's work was not to be wasted as he was to subsequently make use of his own charts in a publication *The Traveller's Map of the River Shannon* in 1830 when he was acting as manager and superintendent of the Inland Steam Navigation Company. However, for the first time detailed drawings of the entire navigation, apart from Lough Ree and Lough Derg, were drawn up and the Admiralty was later to send Commander Wolfe and Lieutenant Beechey to chart the two lakes in 1837–1839.[10]

Rhodes now produced a detailed report on the Limerick Navigation. It is hard to believe that he was describing the same navigation that the Directors General had done so much to try to improve some twenty years earlier. Rhodes said that 'from various appearances and the dilapidated, neglected or unfinished state of the works that it would be necessary to make a particular examination'. In places it was as shallow as 2ft (0.6m) and boats frequently had to be lightened. The list was long and revealing: a bridge over the first lock in Limerick was so low that the level had to be lowered to pass the boats under it, many repairs were needed to the locks and lock houses, the channel needed deepening in many places, the banks were so steep that they were slipping. A ferry boat had to be used to bring the horses across from Plassy to the next stretch of canal at Annabeg and when the river was running hard passengers had to be ferried in small boats using a buoy anchored in the middle of the river to haul them across. A bridge was badly needed here. He gave the dimensions of the locks, which were all different, reflecting the piecemeal way in which the navigation had been constructed. The variation in length was extraordinary from the 2nd lock on the Park Canal, which was only 72ft 3ins (22m), to Newtown lock, which was 101ft 7ins (31m).

At O'Brien's Bridge, where the velocity of the water was about 5mph, Rhodes wrote: 'vessels laden with merchandize are obliged to stop here for a considerable time for the purpose of being warped up through the arches by a capstan placed upon a pier projecting into the river fifty feet', adding that there was not even a towpath under the bridge. He suggested the number of navigation arches in the bridge needed to be reduced from four to two, made of iron to give better headroom, and a weir was needed here to control the flow of water. Based on his comments about the towpath, it is not clear whether proposals by the Directors General in 1829 to make the first arch on the Clare side a navigable arch had actually been carried through, as when Rhodes surveyed the bridge in 1833 he showed an elevation with fourteen arches indicating eleven arches on the Limerick side, ranging from 18ft (5.5m) to 26ft (7.9m), with three remaining segment arches on the Clare side ranging from 19ft (5.8m) to 23ft 6in (7.1m), and the fourth arch from the Clare side, which had been used as the navigation arch, the widest with a dip in the parapet.

At Parteen rapid, Rhodes reported that boats also had to be warped through taking thirty to forty minutes. On the final stretch of canal at Killaloe, the locks again varied in size. At Cussane lock the lower chamber was in a very bad state and likely to fall down. It needed immediate attention or the navigation would be stopped, the gates were so hard to shut because of rubbish behind them and the leakage of the gates so bad that it was scarcely possible to pass boats through. He described the eel weirs at Killaloe:

They are formed on the bed of the river and are composed of oak stakes about three inches in diameter set vertically in the river, their length varying to suit the irregularities of the bed of the River and rising to a height somewhat above the surface of the medium water. They are placed at small distances apart and strongly wattled together with smaller material in the form of hurdles or basket work from top to bottom, and for the purpose of giving strength to oppose the current, large stone and coarse gravel are thrown in against them to the depth of several feet, small openings about four to five feet wide are left at the lower end of the weirs to fix the nets.

He said that a stone weir of solid masonry was needed here to deepen the river to the bridge and although five of the old arches had been rebuilt, some of the other arches on the east side needed enlarging. The construction of weirs in the river farther upstream would help to control flooding and would enable vast tracts of bog to be reclaimed which would afford employment 'to large and populous districts which are at present in a state of idleness and want'. This would lead to the production of much arable land, but he did refer to the fact that there were some landowners who might object because they were setting their land at high rates to produce grass that grew so abundantly because of the rich deposits provided by nature during the flooded state of the river, which in turn led to much smaller numbers being employed. Burgoyne also commented about this: 'It would appear that there is a difference of opinion amongst the proprietors of the lands subject to inundation regarding the extent of the evil. Many would object to being deprived altogether of the effects of the floods, which they describe as being in some respects beneficial.'

Of Lough Derg he noted the want of beacons and he investigated the potential of the various rivers coming into it. The river to Scarriff would need deepening; there was already a quay at Tuamgraney and he recommended using the island nearer the town of Scarriff by closing off one side to form a harbour. The Rossmore river would also need dredging but the dredgings could be disposed of to the farmers as it was a marl that made excellent manure. He also looked at the Cappagh and Ballyshrule rivers. He said there was a landing pier at Cow Island (Williamstown) and by connecting the island to the mainland a good harbour could be formed where the Steam Navigation Company was planning to build a hotel and establish stores. The Board of Works was constructing a public harbour at Garrykennedy to facilitate the Slate Company. He noted that the bar at the northern end of the lake was causing problems for the steamers in bad weather when there was too great a swell, and that sometimes the passengers had to be discharged into small boats when it was unsafe to cross.

He gave a vivid description of the bridge at Portumna, which had been erected in 1796.[11] John Cowan had described the situation here prior to the erection of this bridge.[12] He said that there was a ferry in operation and there were remains of an old bridge of which 'whole arches survive' on the island in the middle of the river and on the Tipperary side. The new bridge was a wooden toll bridge erected in two halves using Hayes' Island in the middle with a drawbridge to the west of the island. Lemuel Cox designed it along the same lines as similar bridges erected at Derry and Waterford. It was administered as a toll bridge by commissioners, whose registrar was aptly named Mr Shrewbridge, and there was frequent trouble with the

operation of the lifting spans. The Galway end had been carried away by floods in 1814 and was rebuilt by Nimmo in 1818 together with repairs to the Tipperary end by means of a loan. The loan was not repaid and a receiver was appointed and the bridge allowed to become ruinous. He went on to describe its present state: 'It is in a state of great dilapidation and neglect and almost impassable rendering it dangerous to foot passengers let alone horses, cattle and wheel carriages, and its general state reflects no credit on those who have charge and maintenance of its repairs.' He described the small bascule bridge as 'suitable to allow the Canal Vessels to pass without lowering their Masts'. The width had originally been 18ft (5.5m) and this was widened to 40ft (12m) to allow the new steam boats pass through but using the same mechanism which was too light for the purpose. A new swivel bridge was urgently needed and because the commissioners in charge of the bridge were heavily in debt an Act was subsequently passed dissolving them and leaving the way open for a new bridge to be constructed.[13]

THE MIDDLE SHANNON

Of Meelick Rhodes said his investigations had proved interesting and needed a good deal of consideration, which he would have to return to. Banagher Bridge was 'in a falling and dangerous state. . . The Canal and River Navigation now under the charge of the Grand Canal Company as far as I have gone, I find in a very neglected state, and from what I can learn they have not laid out a Penny in improvements or repairs since it was given over to them but what was

Banagher: an engraving of the old bridge in 1820 by Thomas Cromwell.

Garrakennedy Castle

Garrykennedy: from a drawing by Paul Gauci before the harbour was constructed.

merely necessary to make Vessels to pass and this at times with considerable difficulty.' The Steam Company had contributed to having the bridge over the Banagher canal raised to allow the steamers to pass through when the river was high in winter, but the lock gates were so rotten that they had fallen to pieces when lifted out for repair. With regard to making the Brosna navigable to Birr, he suggested that a parallel canal would be cheaper than the cost of dredging and deepening the river. He revised this on closer inspection because by widening and deepening the river it would also help the flooding problems: 'The deposits of silicious matter in the hay and grass render it useless and destructive to the cattle by the disease called murrain.' He estimated that it would cost just under £23,000 to make the river navigable to Birr with four locks.

Burgoyne was very critical of the expenses involved in crewing *The Investigator.* A boat master, mate, carpenter and five men all at high wages were employed 'while many a much larger vessel crosses the Atlantic with a smaller establishment'. Rhodes was also experiencing trouble with his crew. He wrote to Burgoyne: 'I consider it my duty to inform you that I have parted with the Captain of the boat for getting intoxicated and disorderly conduct, and three others have left in a sort of a Panic thro' the dreadful epidemic, the cholera that is now making such ravage in this quarter.' He had managed to replace some of them, 'although getting fresh men so frequently and not accustomed to the work is attended with some trouble to bring them under proper discipline'. Rhodes described making 'a diving machine', which was made of timber and a square bag, making it airtight by caulking, which he suspended from the boat, using an air pump.

Burgoyne communicated with the Chief Secretary, Stanley, with reference to the great advantages of the steamers: 'This trade is yet in its infancy and well worthy of encouragement. The facilities afforded by the tributary waters of the Shannon and its lakes for extended communication with the interior have been so little required and consequently so little understood and

developed that what may almost be called "Discoveries" are now making daily of great existing capabilities.' The Grand Canal Company had availed of an Exchequer Commission loan to build an extension of its line to Ballinasloe in the 1820s; this meant that any works that might be considered on the Suck would be purely drainage works. There was the usual problem of eel weirs, mill dams and shoals holding up the flow in the Suck and causing flooding. He described the large area of surrounding bog as 'unproductive and the atmosphere unsalubrious and present a miserable appearance rendered so by the winter floods being upon them during upwards of seven months in the year'. He considered that there was a case for making the Suck navigable, which would require only three locks and weirs and would also act as a drainage scheme: 'the means would be obtained for restoring tranquillity and peace to a district rent asunder by factions and acts of disorder'.

John Stokes, the Grand Canal Company engineer, had given a vivid description of the bad state of the Athlone Canal and chaotic scenes there in 1833.[14] He described how large crowds assembled around the turf cots and there was a need for a military or strong force of police to be stationed at the lock to enforce proper regulation: 'I am principally induced to recommend this measure by the insubordination of the people employed in those turf cots, over whom there is no control as their party is no numerous . . . they arbitrarily govern the trade, admitting only such boats as they please to pass.' At least the Revenue Police were patrolling the river because the Excise Office in London asked the canal company for free passage for their boat through the lock, but the response to this request does not seem to have been recorded.[15]

Rhodes described the Athlone Canal, which would need to be widened and the lock enlarged: 'the whole of which is in a very dilapidated and neglected state, and from its banks having slipped in various parts along its entire length, has rendered it impassable during the summer season for vessels drawing more than from 2ft 9ins to 3ft, the lock gates, bridges etc. are much out of order'. In places the banks had been cut through to allow drainage of the adjoining land and the banks had been let for grazing. There were people drawing water, washing clothes, unloading turf boats, making it appear as if it belonged to no one. It is little wonder that Commander Wolfe in describing its neglected state described how boatmen used to shoot the main river bridge even during floods with empty boats to avoid paying tolls.[16]

Rhodes said that a weir would be needed in the main river channel and he said the town bridge was built of rubble masonry and with its ten arches was reducing the waterway considerably. This bridge had been erected in 1566–1567 on instructions from Sir Henry Sydney and supervised by

Sir Peter Lewys, proctor of Christ Church Cathedral.[17] The piers had been formed by heaping stones into the river retained in place by wooden piles. Four of the centre arches fell down and had to be replaced in 1731 and other repairs carried out from time to time. The whole structure was:

... inconvenient and extremely narrow, not exceeding fourteen feet in breadth of roadway, without footpaths, and this confined passage is very much obstructed on market days, by persons attending for the purchase of meal and flour at the three mills which have been erected in the river course and open on to the bridge. Owing to these inconveniences, accidents are of frequent occurrence, and occasionally, after fairs or market days, the general passage for carriages and carts is altogether interrupted for a considerable time by large droves of cattle.

Below the bridge there were many eel weirs on the shallows and an island with a garden on it that formed the tailrace for the mills. There were three mills on Athlone Bridge, which were obstructing the flow through four of the arches. Isaac Weld had made similar comments in 1832 in his statistical survey for the Royal Dublin Society when he said that the bridge was 'not merely a discredit to the town alone, but a positive stigma on the nation'.[18] This description of the bridge is also supported by Henry Inglis's comments in 1834: 'the carriage road is so narrow that on a market day, it frequently happens that one can pass in no other way than by jumping from cart to car and from car to cart'.[19]

Inglis had stressed the importance of supporting the efforts of the Inland Steam Navigation Company and had made a number of trips on the steamers. He said that the company's objectives were 'too important and too vast to be left in the present infamy of the Establishment to private exertions or even to public patronage'. At this time the company had not yet extended its passenger service upstream of Athlone, but they placed a steamer at his disposal for a tour of Lough Ree. He was struck by the fact that 'not one prow clove the waters of the lough but my own' and he added: 'In place of being in the very heart of a fruitful and civilized country, we might have been navigating a lake in the interior of New Holland'. Isaac Weld had also commented on the lack of trading boats on Lough Ree and the fact that there was not 'a single public quay for boats of burthen'. He said that there was no steady trade 'except it be for the few cargoes of native coal brought down from Lough Allen; and the coal is neither in request for the distilleries and breweries of Athlone, nor for the steamboats on the lower lakes of the Shannon; the former chiefly consume turf, the latter sea borne coal'.

THE UPPER SHANNON

Upstream of Athlone the condition of the navigation was steadily getting worse. At Lanesborough, where Lieutenant Tully had experienced so much trouble, Rhodes said that the single pair of lock gates were twenty years old and dilapidated and the lock house, built over the upper end of the lock, prevented boats passing through without lowering their masts and even prevented laden boats passing under when the river was in flood. The bridge here erected in 1706 needed a great deal of underpinning. Writing from the Camlin at Clondara he said that the lock would need to be reconstructed because the sills were the wrong height: 'the whole is in a very imperfect state of repairs, some parts of the walls bulged out and the mortar washed out of the joints'. Parts of the Camlin River were impassable in summer. Tarmon Bridge over the main channel 'has a neglected and unsafe appearance', and there were eel weirs 'of stone of the most imaginable description which choke up the passage' and a mill dam obstructing the flow: 'These encroachments appear to be done with impunity as there does not appear to be any Conservators of the River.'

Eventually, having grounded in a number of places where there were fords and the boat had to be warped off with a double-purchase windlass and six men, he reached the Roosky canal. The walls of the lock here needed to be racked out and pointed, the gates were dilapidated and the canal barely sufficiently deep for an empty boat: 'Our vessel was aground three times in passing this short channel and was obliged to be forced all the way through by warping.' The difficulties, he added 'present almost an entire prohibition of the navigation'. He had to lighten the boat and managed to get through with twenty men hauling with a warp ahead applied to the double-purchase windlass. They met a boat in the canal stuck fast laden with machinery from Lough Allen bound for Killaloe. The boat had left Clondara on 20 July, had taken nine days to get to Lough Allen and returning downstream had to partly unload and lighten at several places, then was held up for twelve days at Lanesborough with contrary winds, eight days sheltering at Rindoon on Lough Ree and eleven days getting across Lough Derg, and did not get back to Clondara until 1 October. There was little profit to be made with a crew of three men and lock charges to be met. The eel weirs in the river above and below the bridge at Roosky were 'as bad as any on the river' and there was a ridge of rock right across the river with only 4 to 6ins (10 to 15cm) on it in the middle of August.

Of the Jamestown lock he reported that the sills were the wrong height, the walls were 'battering', the upper and lower sills leaking. Two upper courses had been added about thirteen years ago to stop the water overflowing in time of flood and the lock gates were dilapidated, the canal was too narrow and less than 4ft (1.2m) deep, the accommodation bridges too small and too low and would need to be rebuilt, rocks had been left in the canal and there were sharp bends in it. He added: 'This part of the Navigation presents a very bad appearance, indeed the worst that I have yet met with. It was with the greatest difficulty imaginable that we got the vessel through it although not drawing 2ft 6ins water, and it appears the next to a prohibition of any trade being carried on it in the present state.' The obstructions in the river, between the shoals, eel weirs and bridge piers were causing the water to rise up in the canal and back up the main channel: 'lands on each side submerged to a great extent and for a long period. The farmers frequently lose their crops by floods that happen early in July.' The eel weirs, which were the property of Sir Gilbert King and Admiral Rowley, were responsible for obstructing about four-fifths of the flow of the river. All the obstructions would have to be removed and a weir would be essential here to control the water level.

Carrick Bridge was more recently built but it had eleven arches of different sizes and the piers were in a loose and dilapidated state. The bridge caused flood waters to be impeded and back up. Of Carrick itself, he said it 'appears to be a respectable and thriving little town with a good market well supplied and is conveniently situated for commanding the trade which is chiefly agricultural'. There were four main areas of shoal upstream of Carrick and at Port, near Leitrim, there had been a narrow cut made in the shoal, which the water was being forced through, making it difficult to bring boats up against the stream. At Battlebridge three of the six aches had been totally washed away on the Leinster side and were rebuilt and eel weirs were also obstructing the flow. He noted that the sill of the lock at Battlebridge was too high and the walls of the harbour too low, and he asked the question: 'Was the canal ever executed to the proper scale?'

Isaac Weld had made some interesting comments about the coal trade, remarking on how little the new Lough Allen Canal was being used; in 1831 only 47 boats had passed through the canal.[20] Only a small amount of Arigna coal was making its way to Carrick and Athlone. The cost of a ton at the pit head was 7s 6d but delivered in Carrick was 15s. There was an increasing use being made of road transport and Arigna coal was unable to compete with the coal coming into Ireland from England at very cheap rates. The entire tonnage of goods on the Shannon north of Athlone in the 1830s averaged under 10,000 tons per year, of which more than half was coming in or out through the Royal Canal, and the tolls collected were under £100. Rhodes reckoned that there was a good case to be made for opening up the Boyle Water. This was an area of rich agricultural land and the only outlet for produce was through Sligo over very bad roads. A lock and weir would be needed at Knockvicar and both

Cootehall Bridge, with its eight arches, and Knockvicar Bridge, with ten arches, were holding up the flow of the river and would need to be replaced with larger arches.

THE COMPLETION OF THE SURVEY

At this stage Rhodes left the boat at Carrick and returned to Limerick where endless discussion about the expenses of the survey had begun with the administration in Dublin. It would appear that the total cost of the survey was not to exceed £2,000 and Burgoyne now wrote to Stanley that it was estimated that this would have to be exceeded by over £600. Rhodes was obviously getting frustrated by all this and explained he would need another forty-four days at 15s per day to complete his reports and draw up the plans. Burgoyne wrote to Mudge saying: 'He is certainly an able man . . . well worth even the rather costly working of his Establishment.' It was estimated that ultimately some saving could be made by handing over the boat when they were finished to the Ordnance Survey, also a small 26ft cutter and 16ft gig. An inventory was carefully drawn up of the material on the *Investigator*. Burgoyne sensed the impatience felt by Rhodes and he wrote to him: 'from the judgement, industry and ability that you have shown during the investigation, I shall at all times be happy to encourage or to hear of your future employment on objects worthy of you'. But in March 1833 Burgoyne wrote to Rhodes: 'I feel some anxiety about the length of time occupied in completing your Shannon Survey business, not because I have any doubt about the utility of your operations or your activity in pursuing them, but on account of the excess of expense beyond the Estimate which always creates much embarrassment to Government.' In the final analysis the total cost of the survey was to amount to £3,463 7s 2d. of which Rhodes's salary for the 413 days he had given to the survey amounted to £1,300 19s.

He had been requested to carry out further investigations to solve the inefficient accommodation for shipping in the port of Limerick. Currently ships of 300 to 400 tons had to discharge in a pool about a quarter of a mile below the city to lighten their loads before coming alongside because the quays were too shallow. He recommended that the proposed dock to complete the Wellesley Bridge scheme would not be sufficient and would only cater for about one tenth of the shipping. He recommended a more ambitious scheme to build a circular weir with sluices to regulate the flow farther downstream with locks giving access on both sides of the river, one for larger boats and the other for the canal trade. This would provide continuous quays from Kelly's Quay to the Custom House and graving docks and slips would also be needed. This scheme would also provide power to pump drinking water up to a reservoir near the barracks for filtration as the water was currently 'of an unwholesome quality, being strongly impregnated with sulphate of lime,

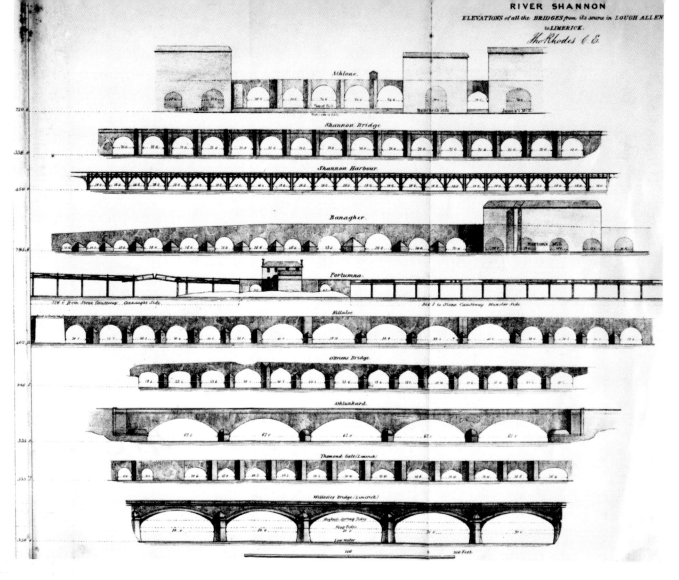

Thomas Rhodes's drawings of the lower Shannon bridges as they were in the 1830s.

this is particularly unhealthful to strangers visiting the city, and I understand is frequently the cause of much suffering to the troops stationed here'. His estimate for this scheme came to £82,756 10s from which could be deducted the original cost of making the smaller dock which would reduce the cost to £53,730 10s.

Some further interesting comments appeared in Rhodes's reports. He described the 'cotters' as 'living in a miserable state, the principal food of potatoes, scantily supplied and in many cases of an inferior quality'. An extensive and valuable fishery in Limerick had been almost completely annihilated by the practice of collecting and selling the eel fry, reckoned to amount to nearly 400 million in a season and in retaliation the salmon fry were being destroyed. He saw signs that agriculture was improving but although there were some ploughs being used, work was usually carried out with a spade 'of rude description . . . and like all other machinery to facilitate labour, there is a prejudice to using it'. The want of improved roads was evident everywhere; limestone, lime and manure had to be carried in creels on horses' backs because the roads were so bad. The cattle,

sheep and pigs, supplied extensively to the English market, were losing their value through the difficulty and expense of transport. He added:

Having purposely visited some of the towns upon Market Days, I am unable to state that there is much business transacted in the sale of native produce and the various necessities of life . . . By adopting the proposed improvements and rendering the Shannon permanently navigable, it would open a great thoroughfare and line of intercourse from the far extremities of the Kingdom.

He went on to suggest that promoting habits of industry among the people would be the most effectual means of dissipating the present feelings of discontent and of preventing the increase of those lawless acts that were so much to be regretted throughout this part of the country. This would require government intervention: it was too great a work otherwise. The plans suggested would not only give much manual labour in their execution but the improvements to the land would give employment, 'a

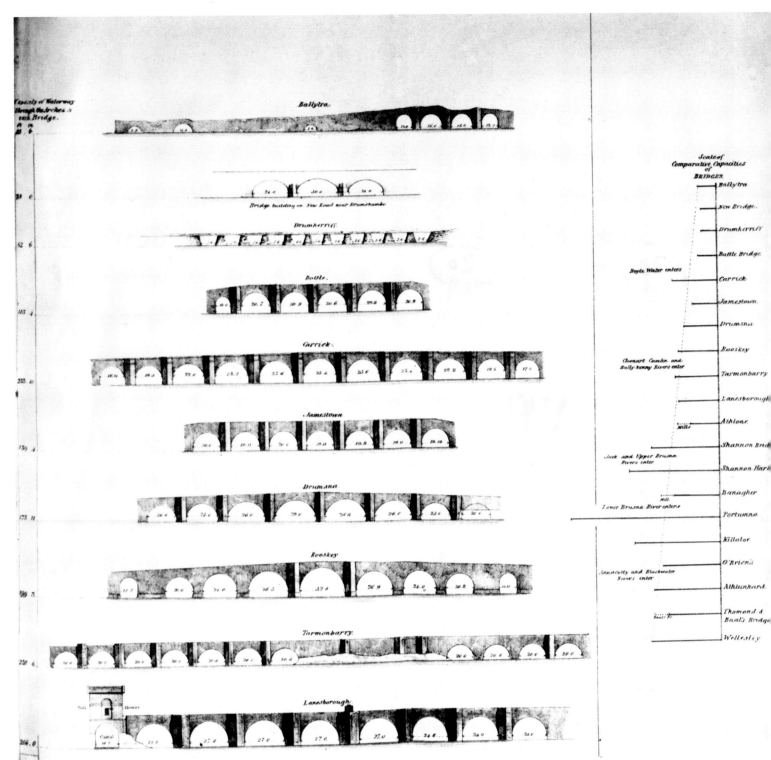

Thomas Rhodes's drawings of the upper Shannon bridges as they were in the 1830s.

most salutary relief to numbers of distressed inhabitants'. Improving the flow in the river would help to drain the bogs: 'By drains made in the first instance (I was informed by the Bishop of Clonfert), and huts having been built at convenient distances and the bog allotted out to the peasantry which shows what may be done by perseverance towards reclaiming them.' But flooding in winter 'produces a desolate and miserable appearance and renders them unproductive, and during this period the peasantry live in a state of idleness attended by its concomitant evils'.

Rhodes, who spoke of the river as being 'superior to any in the Empire', was now in a position to point to what needed to be done to make it a working navigation and fit for the new generation of steamers and which would also improve the flow and reduce flooding. Overall he identified fifteen areas of shoals that would have to be removed between Portumna and Athlone and twenty-one between Lanesborough and Lough Allen; these were holding up the flow of water and reducing the depth of the navigation, and he listed the works required at each of the sites. In addition, the piers of the existing bridges together with the many eel weirs were seriously holding up the flow of water. Mill dams had been built across the river with impunity. For example at Banagher Bridge five of the seventeen arches were blocked by a mill dam causing a head of water of over 2ft (0.6m) in winter. Some of the bridges also badly needed to be replaced and weirs would be needed to control the flow of water on each of the levels. Accommodating the new steamers was essential, which meant that the locks would have to be considerably enlarged and the side canals widened and deepened or alternatively the river at these places dredged, doing away with the canals where the fall was insignificant. He estimated that all this work could be accomplished in two years and he produced a detailed estimate of the cost of the work at each of the locations, which came to a grand total of £153,163 2s 10d or, if it was decided not to have a wide navigation upstream of Lanesborough, £20,329 5s 4d could be deducted from this figure.

In a note accompanying the final report to the Chief Secretary in April 1833, Burgoyne said that with Rhodes's report on Limerick completed, he was now finally closing down the duties of the commission. He suggested that the large locks might be limited to the middle Shannon between Meelick and Athlone. He also said that sluices should be fitted to the proposed weirs so that the water levels could be controlled in winter, adding significantly 'Many would object to being deprived altogether of the effects of the floods, which they describe as being in some respects beneficial.'

THE GOVERNMENT RESPONSE

The findings of the commission were unequivocally saying that it was decision time for the Shannon Navigation. The frequent use of words such as 'impassable' and 'dilapidated' had made it clear that the navigation was useless in its current state. Extensive works were needed to make it viable, particularly in the light of the arrival of the steamers, and the extent of winter flooding had been clearly spelt out. C.W. Williams brought out a new edition of his *Observations on the Inland Navigation of Ireland* in 1833, with a new section in which he pointed out that since 1831 £500,000 had been appropriated for public works in the form of loans and only £50,000 in grants, nearly half of which had been paid out, but only £8,910 of this was for inland navigation works. The stringent requirements for securities and repayments had meant that the works carried out had not reached into the areas where the greatest deprivation existed. He pointed

to the fact that one and a half million had been given to America for inland navigation alone and only half a million to Ireland for all public works. He called for the issuing of public funding in the form of grants not loans for public works, which would have continuing advantages in giving employment. In drawing attention to some of the neglect and dilapidation reported by Rhodes on the Shannon, he added: 'Government have now the materials before them for making the Shannon what it ought to be. It remains with them to give animation to this hitherto unavailable navigation, and to make it the instrument of improved agriculture, extensive inland trade, intercourse and amelioration.'

When the Steam Navigation Company was seeking an extension of its powers to erect small piers and landing places and to increase its capital, which received the Royal Assent in July 1833, evidence was heard from both Colonel Burgoyne and Thomas Rhodes.[21] Burgoyne, when asked what the findings of the Shannon Commission had been with regard to the Shannon Navigation, said: 'It was found to be in a most deserted and disgraceful state. I must say generally a disgraceful state.' Burgoyne, in his role as chairman of the Board of Works, had responded to criticism about its selection of public works in its second report in 1834, stating that under the Act they did not have the power to either select or originate schemes, that all they had was a negative authority to refuse aid to any schemes which were not conducive to public utility or which could not provide security of repayments.[22] It was pointed out that expenditure on public works 'would be to a considerable extent repaid by the indirect returns made to the Revenue, arising from an increased general prosperity'. Attention was drawn to the fact that, unlike in Ireland, investment in England was easy to obtain because direct profits were apparent. There was a need to examine what was happening when, for example, the cost of improving the entire Shannon could end up amounting to the same as one major harbour scheme in an influential area. At the very least grants of one half of the costs should be available where there was no obvious direct return. It was also advised that, if public grants were made, the works should be vested in a government department.

The sequel to all this was the setting up of a select committee of the House of Commons in June 1834 'to inquire into the present state of the navigation of the River Shannon and its tributaries and the best means of improving the same'.[23] The committee heard evidence from among others Colonel Burgoyne, C.W. Williams and Nicholas Fanning, a director of the Grand Canal Company. Williams said that he disagreed with Rhodes about the necessity to construct locks big enough to fit the larger steamers. He maintained that most of the trade was to and from Dublin by the Grand Canal in canal boats (or 'lumber boats' as they were called), that there was no point in making the locks larger than the small steamers used to tow these boats and that the larger steamers were only used on the lakes. He recorded that on one occasion two of his lumber boats had broken adrift on Lough Derg and blown ashore but because they were made of iron instead of wood they were not damaged. He was very critical about the failure of the Grand Canal Company to provide beacons and piles on the middle Shannon: only thirteen existed of the one hundred and ten that were supposed to be in position. Nicholas Fanning defended this by explaining that the country people used to cut them down to use as axles for carts and when they used lighter posts the steamers knocked them down.[24] Williams gave evidence that before the steamers arrived traders were taking a month to six weeks to make the journey from Dublin to Limerick. When questioned about the potential of the navigation of the upper river he said that his company would extend its steamer service if the navigation was to be improved. He reported that Faraday & Co. were trading between the Royal Canal and Drumsna but they were only able to carry small loads because of the 'imperfect' navigation. Lieutenant Tully's letter, which had

been such a damning illustration of the conditions on the upper river, was repeated as supporting evidence.

The committee made the recommendation that as a first step the entire river should be placed under the control of a single body, which would have power to carry out the works and implement the scheme put forward by the Shannon Commission, on which it considered 'any really beneficial improvement of the Shannon must be grounded'. It reprimanded the Grand Canal Company and said it should be compelled to keep the agreement of 1806 to maintain the middle Shannon. The Limerick Navigation Company was also criticized for failing to ensure that the money received in tolls was laid out on improving the navigation. This was followed by the passing of the Shannon Navigation Act in 1834, appointing 'Commissioners for the Improvement of the River Shannon' and authorizing them to prepare plans, survey lands and do everything necessary to carry out the extensive works envisaged; their terms of reference also included drainage concerns as well as navigation.[25] The winds of change had finally brought about a positive decision for the future of the navigation.

CHAPTER FIVE
A NEW ERA BEGINS

THE SHANNON NAVIGATION ACT 1834

The passing of the Shannon Navigation Act in 1834 marked the beginning of a new era for the navigation, rescuing it from almost certain demise. There were five commissioners appointed to oversee the carrying out of the works, all of whom had engineering expertise: Colonel Burgoyne, who was a Royal Engineer and was chairman of the new Board of Works and who had chaired the previous commission that carried out the preliminary survey, Captain Henry Jones, Royal Engineer, Richard Griffith, William Cubitt and Thomas Rhodes. Richard Griffith had been born in Dublin in 1784, the son of Richard Griffith senior, who had been a leading ascendancy figure and who had played an active role as a director of the Grand Canal Company.[1] Richard junior had a very brief military career before becoming an influential civil and mining engineer. He had worked with Colonel Burgoyne on surveying several of the bogs as one of the commissioners appointed to 'enquire into the nature and extent of the several bogs of Ireland and the practicability of draining and cultivating them', work that must have been useful in the light of the combined navigation and drainage brief of the new commissioners. William Cubitt was a civil engineer, who was later to take over the work on the Ulster Canal following the death of Thomas Telford and was also to become active as a railway engineer. Thomas Rhodes was a civil engineer whose detailed knowledge of the river acquired in the preliminary survey was now to be the foundation on which the detailed survey would be based, which in turn would determine the actual works to be carried out.

The Act was very specific: the works were to provide a navigation 'for the free passage of an appropriate class of steam vessels' and also combine this with useful drainage works; the works would be financed by public funding with one half of this expenditure afterwards to be repaid by the relevant districts. The commissioners were to establish what works were necessary and to estimate the costs, and this would then go before parliament for approval. They were to determine which counties would benefit directly from the improvements and apportion the repayments accordingly, and they were to set the appropriate tolls to be applied towards the maintenance of the navigation and finally to ascertain appropriate places for harbours, piers, wharfs and landing places and decide which of these should be part of the works and which left to private enterprise. They would also be responsible for adjudicating and making awards on compensation claims in relation to eel weirs, water power to mills and land acquisition. In addition they were to examine the liabilities entered into by the Grand Canal Company in relation to the middle Shannon and what steps should be taken to fulfil the recommendation that the whole navigation be placed under a single authority for its future maintenance and management. It is important to look at the reports of the survey in some detail so that they can be compared with Rhodes's earlier suggestions and with the works that were ultimately carried out.

A drawing by Edward Jones which it is thought might depict the Shannon Commission's survey in progress at an unidentified location possibly down the Shannon Estuary. (Courtesy of the Society of Antiquaries of London)

THE 1ST & 2ND REPORTS

The commissioners divided the river up into five divisions: the estuary up to Limerick, Limerick to Killaloe, Killaloe to Tarmonbarry, Tarmonbarry to Leitrim and Leitrim to Lough Allen. They delivered their 1st Report to parliament in March in which they said that it would require at least one season to complete the investigation and they drew attention to the reports already submitted by Captain Mudge and Thomas Rhodes.[2] They undertook to tackle at least one division in detail in the present session of parliament. They attached to this report some figures showing the rapid increase in the shipments of flour and oatmeal from the interior of the country to Liverpool and also showing an increase in tolls paid on the Grand Canal and Shannon by the City of Dublin Steam Packet Company's boats, which had risen from £2,439 in 1830 to £9,587 in 1835, with the tonnage rising from 11,270 tons to 40,733 tons. For the first time a scheduled passenger service was in operation and in 1834 22,295 passengers had been carried by the steam company, rising to 31,562 in 1835. These figures, which just reflect the movement on the middle Shannon, show the considerable impact the steamers were having.

THE FIRST DIVISION—THE ESTUARY

True to their word, the commissioners issued a second report, dated December 1837, in which they dealt with the first three divisions from the estuary up to Tarmonbarry.[3]

Dealing first with the estuary and relying on Captain Mudge's 1832 report, which had highlighted the need to provide transport to the Limerick markets for the produce of the area because of the poor condition of the roads, they provided detailed plans for harbour works at Kilrush, Tarbert and Foynes. In addition they looked at the potential of other sites and produced plans for them showing smaller developments of moderate expense for Carrigaholt, Querrin, Cahercon, Ballylongford, Glynn and Kilteery.

Plans for the rivers Fergus, Deel and Maigue were produced. In particular it was recommended that a wharf was badly needed up the Fergus at Clare, which was fully navigable on the tide to this point. They agreed with Mudge that the considerable expense of extending the navigation to Ennis was not warranted. They suggested moving the site of the quay on the Deel at Askeaton to a better location. As already indicated in Chapter 3, the Maigue had some minor works carried out on it as a direct result of the 1715 Act and had also had some works carried out by the Directors General in 1817 when a short canal with an opening bridge was installed at Court Bridge to make it easier for boats to continue upstream to Adare. The commissioners now noted that Adare was only ten miles from Limerick with a very good road whereas the journey by water would take much longer and that only turf boats used the river; consequently, they were only recommending minor works.

Some of the local landed proprietors and the Inland Steam Navigation Company were prepared to contribute to these works around the estuary because of the advantages that would follow, and the commissioners estimated what proportion should be paid by them, with a low toll levied to meet maintenance costs in the future. With regard to the upper reaches of the estuary, they referred to Captain Mudge's report, which had drawn attention to the need to remove some shoals and to place buoys on some of the other shallows. The actual development of Limerick Port they appear to have considered a separate issue, presently under consideration by government based on Rhodes's earlier report.

THE SECOND DIVISION–THE LIMERICK NAVIGATION TO KILLALOE

Moving to the second division the commissioners reported on the Limerick Navigation to Killaloe. They recommended that the navigation be taken over and the shareholders fully compensated to the value of their stock. This was despite the fact that C.W. Williams, as one of the managing directors of that company, remonstrated with them against this action. Until the arrival of the steamers the large expanse of Lough Derg had prevented regular traffic but now there was evidence of an improved trade and the prospect that this would increase. Williams pointed out that, since the navigation had been handed back to it, the company had spent over £20,000 on improvements and it was now in

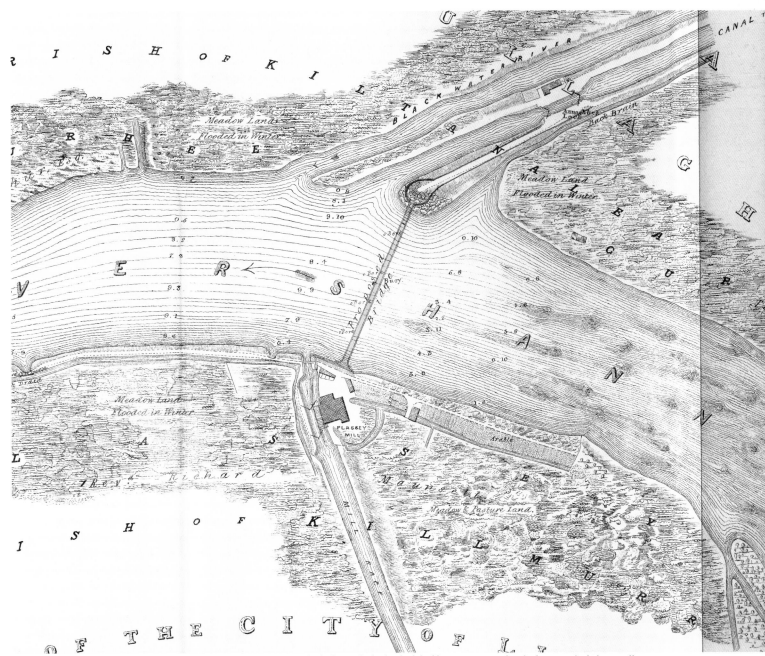

Limerick Navigation: Thomas Rhodes's proposals for the Plassy area which shows the lock which had been constructed at the lower end of Plassy millrace to serve the mill which was built in 1824. The water wheel was replaced by a turbine in the 1860s but the mill closed a few years later.

Plassy: the lock at Plassy millrace today with the ruin of the mill on the right. The lock curved around with another set of gates before reaching the river (Neil Arlidge)

'a nearly complete state', a fact which the commissioners acknowledged. They recommended a limited amount of works to improve the navigation that was already capable of accommodating boats of sufficient size. Two weirs would be needed to exercise control over the water, one above Illaanaron, just downstream of the upper end of the Park Canal and one at World's End, downstream of the exit from the Errina Canal. In addition, a wooden footbridge was needed at Plassy, where it is necessary to cross the river to gain access to the Errina Canal together with the clearing away of some shoals to improve the flow in the river. The plans showed that a lock had been constructed at the downstream end of Plassy millrace, which entered the river almost opposite the entrance to the canal and which would have enabled boats to load and unload at the mill out of the strong current in the river. The millwheel operated in a channel alongside the lock with a wall above and below the lock protecting boats from the flow.

Plassy: the Shannon Commissioners footbridge, which replaced the ferry in the 1840s, was reconstructed in 1949. (Brian Goggin)

Plassy: a replica sand cot (right) and a gandelow, examples of the shallow draft boats used in the tidal and estuary waters for transporting sand and for fishing. (Brian Goggin)

At Killaloe, Rhodes's plan was followed to erect a long L-shaped weir above the bridge, extending right across to the canal above the lock, which would regulate the water level of Lough Derg and up the river to Meelick and would be of sufficient length to allow for runoff of heavy floods in winter. In addition the wall and island forming the canal would be removed.

THE THIRD DIVISION - KILLALOE TO TARMONBARRY

Apart from increasing the number of buoys and beacons on Lough Derg and possibly removing a few rocks surrounded by deep water, which formed a hazard in stormy weather, no further works were proposed for the lake because the steamers appeared to be navigating it without experiencing problems. There was, however, a great lack of landing places and places of shelter, which it was considered was largely a matter for local people to remedy. The Derry Island ford at the northern end of the lake needed to have a dredged channel opened through it.

Dealing with the middle Shannon, under the control of the Grand Canal Company, there had been widespread criticism of its management since the 1806 agreement. In the same way as they had done with the Limerick company,

the commissioners notified the company that they were recommending its takeover and were looking into what compensation, if any, should be paid. They judged that the company stood to lose no revenue on this transfer but stood to gain considerably from any improvement works, which would facilitate the trade to and from the canal. The company complained that it had expended £30,000 of its own funds in addition to the grant of £54,884 it had received for the works and maintenance of the river, but the commissioners side-stepped this and said it was an old claim, that their role was to assess the immediate and existing value of the property. They did, however, suggest that the government should give the company encouragement because it was performing a very important national work.

The locks at Meelick and Athlone would have to be retained but because there was only a difference in level of 16ft (4.8m) between Lough Derg and Lough Ree, it would be possible to do away with the need for locks at Banagher and Shannonbridge. At Meelick they were proposing the construction of a new canal and lock, rather than enlarging the existing one, with a weir at Keelogue and the removal of the shoals and eel weirs to provide a navigation over the shallows. They said they had no hesitation in recommending that the locks at Meelick and Athlone should be increased

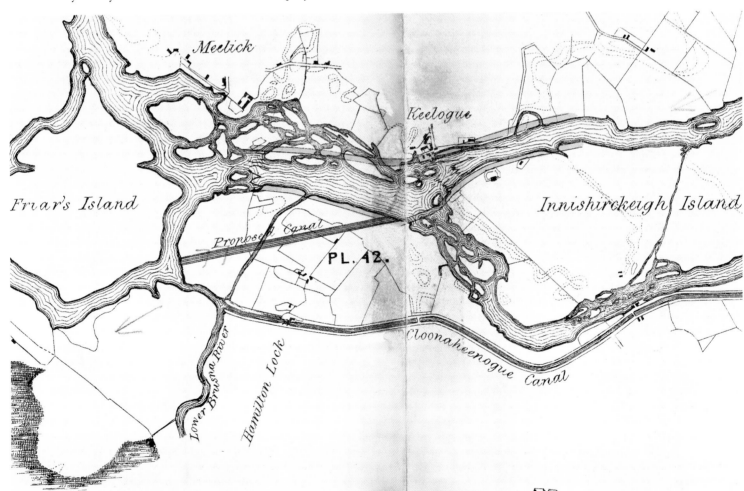

Meelick: Thomas Rhodes's proposed works to create a new canal and weir and excavate the shoal at Keelogue.

in size, to 140ft (42.6m) long by 40ft (12m) wide, so that the larger steamers needed to navigate the lakes could pass through, which was actually reverting to nearer the size of Omer's early work. At Banagher the medieval bridge of twenty-seven arches had been replaced in the late seventeenth century by a seventeen-arch structure and a new bridge was needed here that would have wider arches to improve the flow.[4] The canal would be widened to form a running canal without a lock and a swivel bridge inserted. At Shannonbridge the exisiting sixteen-arch bridge erected in the 1750s would need some underpinning, the short canal would be enlarged and the lock removed to create a running canal.

At Athlone the canal would need to be considerably widened and the new enlarged lock moved to a site with better foundations. A new bridge was needed to replace the existing one and upstream of this a u-shaped weir would span the river. The present old bridge at Athlone had come in for sharp criticism from writers such as Isaac Weld and Henry Inglis and the commissioners now endorsed this. They recognized that the erection of a new bridge here because of its strategic importance had now become a priority.

Below Lanesborough there was a very awkward sailing course at the head of Lough Ree and they proposed cutting a wider and straighter course here. Lanesborough Bridge would require considerable underpinning and they now

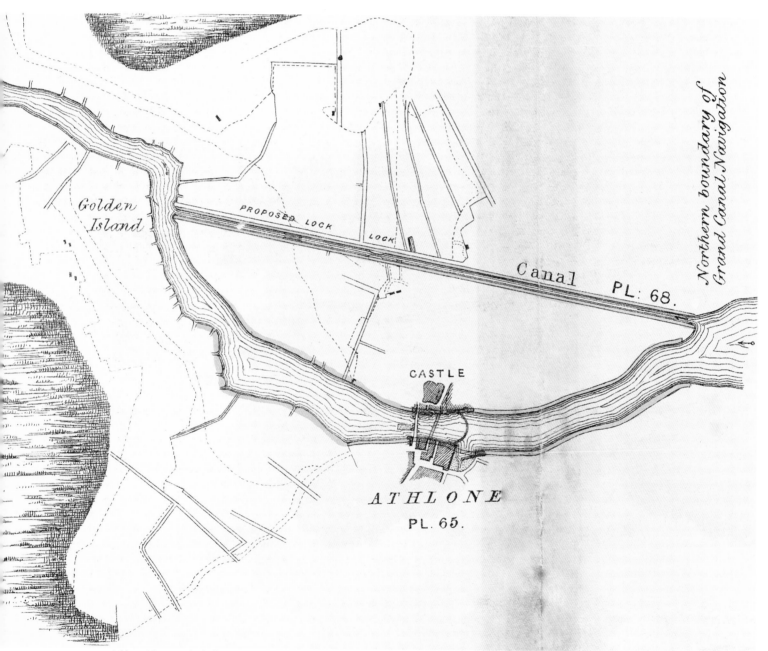

Athlone: Thomas Rhodes's proposed works to widen the canal and construct a weir across the river.

recommended removing the eel weirs and completely removing the river side of the canal wall and the lock and lock house and inserting an opening bridge. All the shoals between Lanesborough and Tarmonbarry were identified and fully surveyed with detailed plans of the work required. At the Lodge Cut just below Tarmonbarry a new wider sailing course would be provided, by removing the embankment of the old cut and the extensive eel weirs.

The plan was to insert swivel bridges the whole way up the river from Killaloe to accommodate boats with masts. The weirs recommended at Killaloe, Meelick and Athlone would bring about an improvement in the widespread flooding along this stretch of river. The removal of some shoals and eel weirs would also help the flow of the river. There was considerable detail provided in the accompanying plans of all the works including the plans for the new locks, weirs and bridges with a detailed drawing of the proposed cast-iron swivel bridges designed by Thomas Rhodes. There were detailed soundings given of all the major shoal areas to be removed. At Bishop's Islands, where a short running canal had provided the course to the west of the islands, the navigation channel would be moved to the east of the islands and the river dredged. At Long Island the navigation channel to the west of the island would be retained and widened. No attempt was made to survey the large lakes, Derg, Ree or Allen. The chart of Lough Ree, which made up the final plan in this report, was reduced from Longfield's original chart produced for the Directors General.

The estimates for the works were given as follows:

The estuary	£52,070
Limerick to Killaloe	£22,200
Killaloe to Tarmonbarry	£188,507
Steam engine, vessels and machinery for dredging shoals	£4,000
Total	£266,777

According to the Act, one half of this would be by free grant of public funds and the rest would be refunded by twelve half-yearly instalments; some of this, as in the case of the estuary by individual landlords, some by tolls, after defraying the maintenance, and the rest by assessments on the relevant counties.

With regard to the new bridges, again half would be provided by the counties that would benefit directly from them. All the milldams and eel weirs, which were interrupting the flow, would have to be removed but new mill sites would in turn be created by the new weirs. The hardship created by the removal of the many eel weirs could be overcome by 'other modes of fishing for this prolific article'. Finally, the commissioners pointed out the importance of improving the Shannon, convinced that it would be a wise use of public funding leading to great advantages.

THE 3RD & 4TH REPORTS

The 3rd Report followed in 1838 in which the commissioners detailed the valuation of the lands and rights that would have to be purchased, and also recommended that the Government should assume control of the middle Shannon from the Grand Canal Company.[5] The company had been looking for from £50,000 to £100,000 compensation for the loss of tolls, which, because of the introduction of the steamers had risen from £1,699 in 1822 to £5,669 in 1837, with the tonnage carried rising from 3,120 tons in 1822 to 20,534 tons in 1837. The commissioners, however, suggested an award of a nominal compensation of £5, not only because of the fact that the company had failed to keep the agreement to maintain the navigation in good repair but also because they were actually showing a loss on their administration of it despite the increase in trade. The company strongly defended its position and requested that it be reconsidered, but the most the commissioners would do was to suggest that the company had a strong claim on the public finances 'for every concession that can reasonably be made to it'. The fact that the Limerick Navigation Company was to be awarded compensation of £12,227, based on the criteria of ownership of property, even though it had only been in control of the navigation since 1829 must have made matters worse. However, the government did subsequently, in 1844, agree to commute outstanding loans of just under £100,000 on the construction costs of the Ballinasloe, Mountmellick and Kilbeggan branches to £10,000.

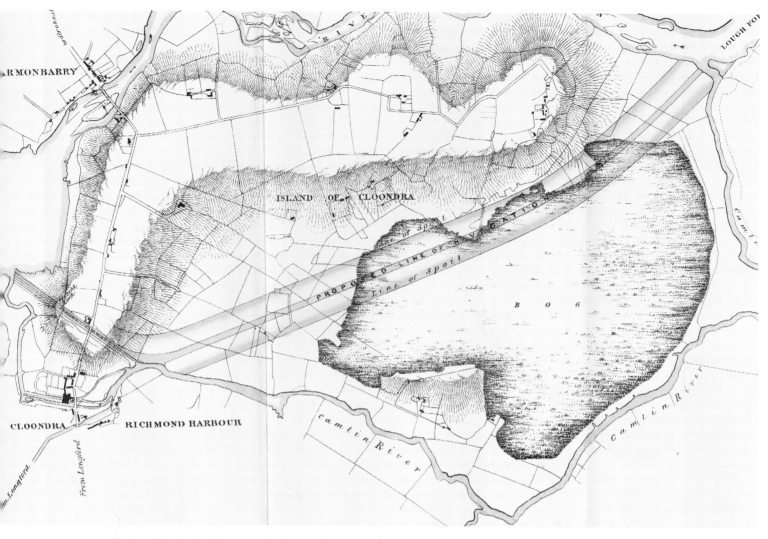

Clondara: Thomas Rhodes's proposed works to make a new canal to bypass Tarmonbarry.

THE 4th AND 5th DIVISIONS— TARMONBARRY TO LEITRIM AND LOUGH ALLEN

The 4th report, with detailed plans of the remaining two divisions and the suggested works on the main tributaries, was completed in February 1839.[6] The division from Tarmonbarry to Leitrim had falls amounting to only 18ft (5.4m) but there were significant shoals and eel weirs that would have to be removed and a mill dam at Jamestown that was responsible for much of the flooding. In the appendices tables were provided to show how serious this flooding was, based on the heights recorded at the locks, also tables illustrating the fluctuations in rise and fall of levels and extremely detailed lists of borings to show the nature of the soil. Also included were details of the tonnage on the upper Shannon in the years 1835, 1836 and 1837, with a breakdown of what was being carried. The tonnage remained at approximately the same levels, averaging 8,220

tons each year, roughly twice the amount, mostly grain and sundries, being carried upstream, with only comparatively small amounts of coal and iron being carried downstream.

The navigation was, in fact, only passable in some places when the waters were above the normal summer levels. The commissioners added that 'having long and attentively considered the scale of the works' on the upper river, they saw no reason to alter the view already expressed that the locks and side-cuts be constructed suitable for smaller steamers than on the middle river, the locks to have chambers 130ft (39.6m) long and 30ft (9.1m) wide. Weirs of sufficient extent to allow for the rapid discharge of floodwaters would be needed and these would retain 6ft (1.8m) on each of the levels in summer. The bridges would need to be underpinned, or where enlarging the waterway was necessary, larger arches constructed and also swivel opening spans for the navigation channel.

They proposed erecting a weir above the bridge at Tarmonbarry and removing many of the obstructions from there to Lough Forbes to improve runoff, while making a completely new side canal from Clondara to Lough Forbes, replacing the River Camlin route, with a new enlarged lock replacing the present lock at Clondara. They added, as was in fact subsequently found to be the case, that it was possible to use a cleared river channel instead of having to make this new canal, which was largely through bog and callows. A wide navigation channel would need to be made through Lough Forbes. Extensive removal of shoals was needed at Clooneen Cox, where a short running canal had been made in the past on the east side of the river. This would be replaced by a navigation channel provided by removing the eel weirs and shoals in the river here and upstream at Cloonfad and Clooneen Kennedy. Below Roosky they proposed removing

two islands, Bird Island and Rabbit Island. The existing canal and lock at Roosky, which lay to the west of the river, would be widened and an opening bridge inserted. The nine-arch bridge would be replaced by a seven-arch bridge to improve the flow, a large u-shaped weir built above this bridge and three extensive areas of eel weirs removed.

Some deepening would be required at Derrycarne in the narrows between Lough Bofin and Boderg and also in the middle of Lough Tap. At Drumsna new quays along the river would supplement the existing small harbour and the river would need to be deepened to allow steamers to approach throughout the year. In the loop of the river extensive eel weirs would have to be removed and, in particular, the mill dam and other works that were causing such flooding upstream. A new large curved regulating weir would be erected downstream of the mill site. The Jamestown Canal

Roosky: Thomas Rhodes's proposed works to enlarge the lock and widen the canal.

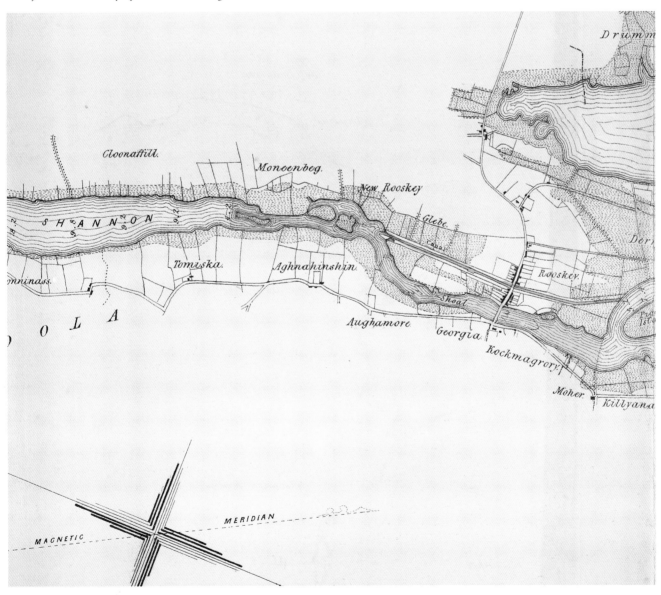

would need to be widened and the two bends taken out of it, with the new enlarged lock located nearer the lower end and the bridges replaced by opening spans.

Five more shoal areas were identified where the river was so shallow in summer that laden boats could not pass; at Grose's Islands, now called Rosebank, it was proposed to remove the entire downstream island and use the spoil to build up the upper island, moving the navigation to the west side of the island. At Carrick they proposed replacing three of the arches of the bridge on the Leitrim side with

an opening span and widening out the mouth of the existing harbour. The bed of the river under the other arches of the bridge would need to be deepened to allow for run-off.

The fords at Hartley and Port would need to be widened and deepened. While the ford at Hartley was described as 'a shoal of small extent', the position at Port was more complicated. Here a short running canal had been made to bypass the shoal and eel weirs, which extended right across the river, considerably obstructing the flow. They proposed abandoning the canal and removing all the obstructions

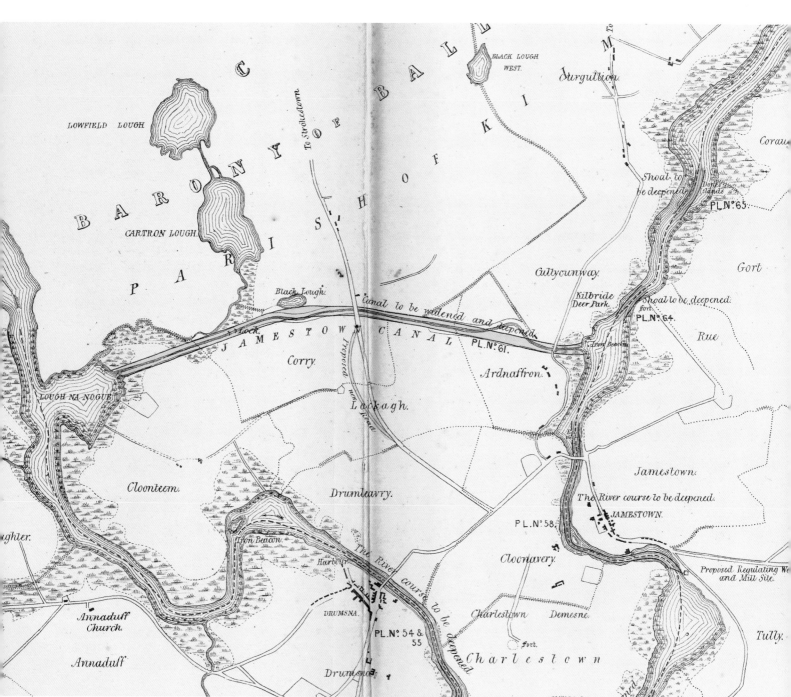

Jamestown Canal: Thomas Rhodes's proposed works to widen the canal and relocate and widen the lock.

from the main channel, which would both provide a navigation course and also improve the run-off. The river would need to be deepened in places up to the junction with the Leitrim River. Upstream of this, they proposed making a short cut for the navigation to bypass the sharp bend in the river where they had identified a site for a wharf and stores, which would become the terminus for the steamers. From here a towpath would be made to Battlebridge lock. The intention to end the steamer navigation at this point was because they were recommending that the traffic on the Lough Allen Canal was so limited that it was not necessary at present to widen the canal, but the two locks in the canal would require a total reconstruction. In the future, when the ironworks and the Arigna coalfields were worked more extensively, a larger scheme for the canal could be undertaken.

They understood that the local counties intended to pull down the 'dilapidated bridge' at Battlebridge which they said was 'in a ruinous state'. Part of the current bridge over the canal was too low and they proposed erecting a new bridge at a site downstream of the present entrance to the canal. This entrance to the canal was on an extremely bad bend in the river and they were proposing to make a new entrance downstream of the new bridge. The lower sill of the current lock was too high and the lock would not accommodate the boats from the Royal Canal because it was shorter than the size of the locks on that canal. In creating a new entrance to the canal, the present lock would be abandoned and two new locks made, removing the lock house and enlarging the current harbour as an intervening basin between them. The eel weirs and old mill and mill dams at the existing bridge would all be removed to improve the flow. Some limited improvements were also needed to the canal: raising the banks, widening it and increasing the water level. The second lock at Drumleague would also need to be lengthened, thus bringing the canal up to the dimensions of the boats using the Royal Canal. The rather unfinished nature of the Lough Allen works was indicated by the fact that they said it would be necessary to make proper 'formed and gravelled' towpaths along the canal with an embankment to carry the towpath through Acres Lake on the west side.

Where the canal entered Lough Allen they were proposing a harbour and stores, as the site most suited for access to Drumshanbo, and the channel out into the lake would need deepening. The Arigna River, which was carrying down a great deal of alluvial deposits, discharged into the Shannon close to where it left Lough Allen causing silting. A cut had been made many years before to try to divert the Arigna directly into Lough Allen and they proposed widening this cut and building an embankment across its present course to ensure that its waters would be diverted. A regulating weir would then be constructed and the river to Battlebridge deepened and cleared of obstructions to improve the flow. A harbour on O'Reilly's Island in Lough Allen was also needed. An interesting plan was included of the river from the junction with the Boyle Water to Lough Allen, which clearly shows the extensive flooding of lands that occurred in this area. It is noted on this plan that it had been reduced from the Ordnance Survey of the area. It shows considerable flooded lands particularly from the Leitrim area downstream, much of which was attributed to all the obstructions in the form of bridges, shoals and eel weirs and, in particular, the mill dams at Jamestown.

The Railway Commissioners were also busy surveying the country in the 1830s, although the full implication of the impact the spread of railways would have on the inland waterways had not been realized. Their comments about the potential of coal mining in the Lough Allen area are of interest:

The coal occurs in detached basins near the summits of some of the hills; it has never been wrought extensively, and there is but one workable bed which, in some localities, is three feet in thickness, and in others less than two feet, it is not probable that many extensive collieries or manufactures can be successfully established in that district; and consequently we cannot expect it will at any period produce an abundant supply of fuel for distant markets.[7]

Of the Arigna Ironworks they said they had been lately at work and the local coal was well adapted to their use. They added: 'cast iron of the best quality can be made at a moderate expense. . . public expectation has been so often raised and as often disappointed. [It] will at length become profitable to the speculators, as well as advantageous to the labouring population of the surrounding district'.

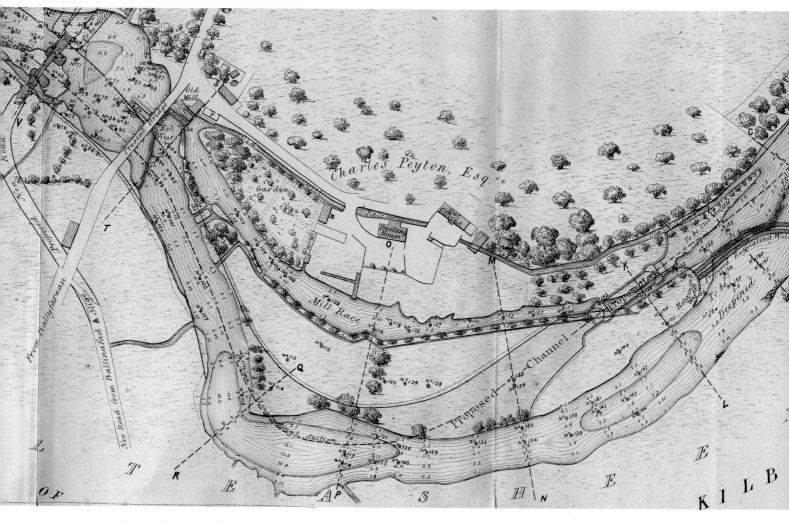

Boyle River: Thomas Rhodes's design for a new lock and weir at Knockvicar.

THE TRIBUTARIES

Because of the importance of the town of Boyle, the Shannon Commissioners estimated that the Boyle Waters would become one of the chief feeders to the upper Shannon. A shoal area at Tumna, at the entrance into Lough Drumharlow, would need to be deepened and at Annalecky and the Doctor's Weir, upstream of the lake further removal of shoals was required. These shoals were substantial ledges of solid rock, which would make creating a navigation channel difficult. It would also be necessary to take away some of the sharp bends in order to straighten the channel. The removal of eel weirs and more deepening would be needed in the vicinity of Cootehall Bridge. This eight-arch bridge was obstructing the flow of water and would need to be replaced by a three-arch bridge a short distance downstream with an opening arch in the middle. They were recommending extensive works at Knockvicar to provide access to Lough Key. The nine-arch bridge would be replaced by a similar three-arch bridge to the one at Cootehall, again at a new location downstream. A good deal of excavation would be needed to form a channel where much gravel had

formed against the bridge. The navigation channel would then cut across through the west bank to the head of the old millrace where a lock would be needed 130ft (40m) long. A regulating weir would span the river at this point and more deepening would be needed to give access to Lough Key.

Having crossed Lough Key, in order to bring the navigation up as far as Boat House Ford, within a mile and a half of the town of Boyle, certain improvements would be needed. The Boyle River would have to be straightened up to the ford where a turning place could be made and there was a site for a wharf and stores. From there a new road needed to be made to Boyle. A further drawing was added illustrating the possibility of a canal from Lough Key to Lough Arrow showing the height that would have to be overcome to make the canal through the high ground to Lough Arrow, from where the waters discharged by the River Arrow into the sea at Ballisodare near Sligo. It showed the distance between the two loughs at 1,613 yards (1,475m) and Lough Arrow's water level at 41ft 8ins (12.7m) higher than Lough Key with only a height of some 40ft (12m) to overcome up to the summit level of the canal.

They recommended the opening up of the Carnadoe Waters to give access for steamers over a distance of six miles to within two miles of Strokestown. This would require a limited amount of work: improving the line of the navigation from Lough Boderg up to Carnadoe Bridge; replacing this bridge with an opening span and two new arches; and making quays here on both sides of the river. There was currently a narrow winding natural channel linking Carnadoe and Kilglass lakes, and they proposed making a new channel to bypass this.

A detailed plan for the River Scarriff from Lough Derg was also included showing the proposed channel and excavation required, based on the anticipated lowering of the lake by the regulating weir at Killaloe. At this stage they were only proposing extending the river to near Tuamgraney, where there was already a quay, Reddin's Quay, at right angles to the river. The current position was stated to be very difficult: boats of up to 50 tons could get up the river only when the level was high, but they could not make way up the river when it was in flood when the banks were covered and the course to be steered uncertain. The plan for the extension of the River Fergus from the proposed wharves at Clarecastle to Lifford near Ennis on the Shannon Estuary had not been completed for the 2nd report and these were included in the 4th report. This would require a short canal, to avoid the rocky shoals in the vicinity of the bridge at Clarecastle with a lock, a swivel bridge and a weir.

THE PLANS ARE COMPLETED

The final plans included in the 4th report were drawings of a bascule bridge designed by William Cubitt with two lifting leaves. It was stated that this design had been used on the River Wensum at Norwich. It was operated by wheels and pinions, which 'from the leaves being accurately balanced, can be worked with a very small force, even by a woman or boy in the space of one minute'. However, it was the swivel bridge designed by Thomas Rhodes with two leaves opening horizontally, similar to one designed by him for St Katherine's Dock, which had appeared in the 2nd report, which was the design eventually adopted. The 5th and final report followed in 1839 tying up further loose ends and the whole issue of the controversy with the Grand Canal Company was addressed in detail.[8]

The detailed plans had been prepared throughout by Thomas Barton, Charles Tarrant and William T. Mulvany, civil engineers, and Thomas White, John Tully, George Tarrant, and John Long, surveyors. Some of these engineers and surveyors were subsequently to be employed on the works. They showed clearly the depths found and where dredging and removal of shoals and eel weirs would be needed and also the extent of the lands flooded in winter. Each of the planned works was accompanied by a breakdown of the estimated costs and a detailed abstract provided. The grand total for all five districts and all the tributaries amounted to £584,805 17s 9½ d, which included £40,000 for new bridges and £74,054 for compensation claims. Of this total

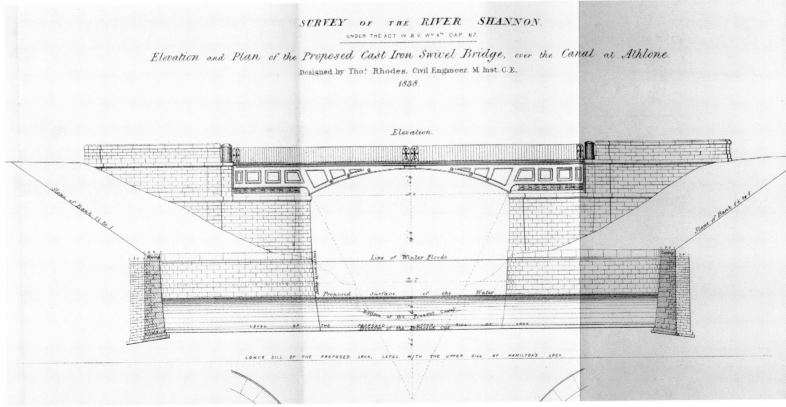

Thomas Rhodes's design for the new opening swivel bridges.

they were recommending that £290,716 1s 4d would come from public funding, £266,334 6s 2¼d from the counties and baronies and £27,775 10s 3¾d from proprietors of the relevant districts.

There must have been wide interest in all this activity on the Shannon. It is recorded that a public meeting was held in Nenagh in the summer of 1838 to seek interest in setting up a company to construct a canal from Nenagh to Dromineer using the line of the Nenagh River.[9] It was to be six and a half miles (ten and a half km) long with eight locks and was estimated to cost £58,000. Others were suggesting as an alternative that a canal should be made from Nenagh to Youghal Bay and yet others suggested a rail link to Garrykennedy. Henry Buck was the engineer who was involved in the Youghal Bay scheme for the proposed Nenagh & River Shannon Canal Company. He estimated it would cost £33,000 and 6,000 shares would be issued at £5 each. Buck had served under William Chapman on the Sheffield Canal in 1816– 1819 and was described as 'a gentleman of a very respectable family in Ireland, who since quitting his employment at Carlisle, obtained it elsewhere in this kingdom, and has now (January 1823) an important situation in his own profession in his native country'.[10] He was subsequently employed on the Shannon navigation works. It was suggested at the meeting that 'canals were the best and the safest of all speculations' but others warned: 'If the repeal of the Corn Laws be carried, the farmers will all be broken.' An editorial in the same issue supported the scheme: 'Above all, let us impress upon the minds of everyone the necessity for employment. How much better

will the money be bestowed upon useful works than giving it away in alms from which we can derive no profitable return'. However, there was insufficient interest in promoting the scheme and nothing came of it.

There is an interesting glimpse of the lack of activity on the river upstream of Shannon Harbour in Caesar Otway's comment about the stretch of river below Athlone in 1839.[11] He was brought on a trip from Athlone to Clonmacnois by the vicar of St Mary's in what he described as 'a little cot'. Comparing the river with the Thames and Severn he wrote:

here no trade except that carried on one steam barge, no timber, no smiling lawns, no cultivation, the solitary hopelessness of the bog is all around and nothing interrupts the silence of the waste but the wild pipe of the curlew or shriek of the heron'. They only met one boat returning from the pattern at Clonmacnois the previous day with 'a square sail composed for the nonce of blankets and quilts, the coverings of yesterday's tents.

It was full of drunken publicans who had been catering for the pilgrims and they were relieved when they passed by safely.

The government responded quickly to the detailed plans and estimates, passing an Act in 1839 setting up Shannon Commissioners to carry out the proposed works and giving them the entire control of the river.[12] The problem was now going to be whether they could accomplish what they had planned within the stated estimate.

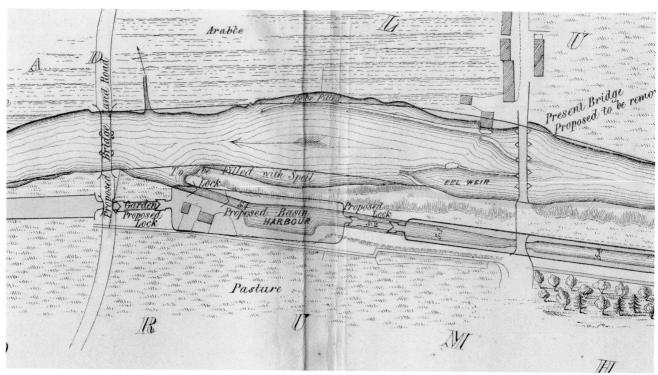

Lough Allen Canal: Rhodes planned to carry out extensive work on the canal including creating a new entrance with locks and a harbour at Battlebridge but this work was never done because of lack of funds.

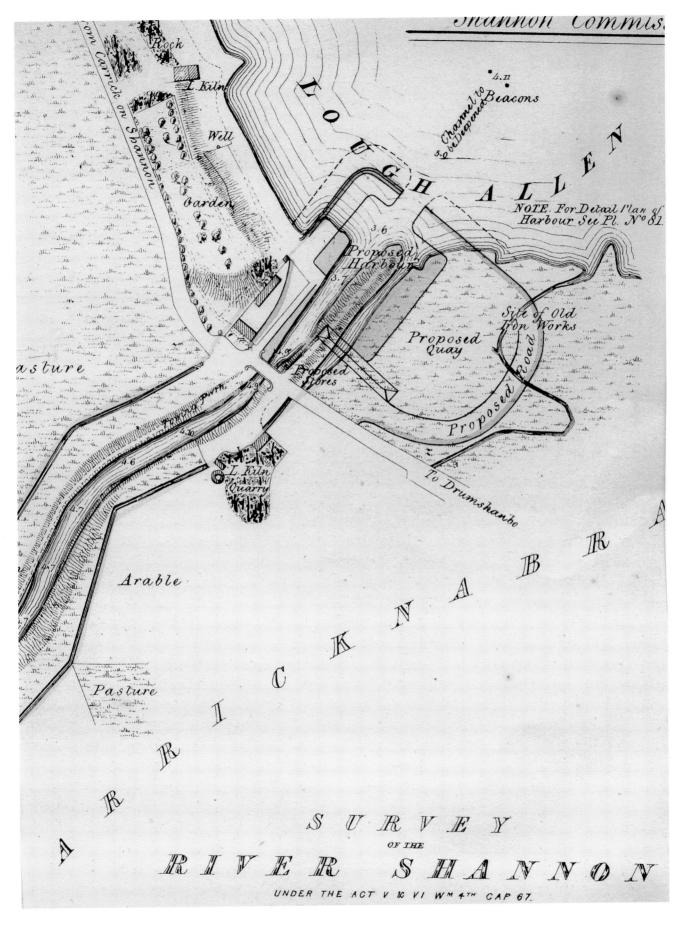

Lough Allen Canal: Rhodes planned to construct a harbour where the canal entered Lough Allen but this work was not done because of lack of funds.

CHAPTER SIX
WORK BEGINS: THE ESTUARY AND
LIMERICK NAVIGATION 1840–1850

WORK BEGINS

It was a formidable task that was about to be undertaken, made more difficult because they were going to have to keep the navigation open for as much of the time as possible during the works. The Act establishing Commissioners for Improving the Navigation of the River Shannon appointed three of the original five commissioners to carry out the works: Colonel Burgoyne, Harry Jones and Richard Griffith. Thomas Rhodes was no longer a commissioner but was offered the appointment of principal engineer.[1] He undertook to make Ireland his principal residence for the duration of the works, spending a minimum of six months here each year and not being absent for more than three months consecutively without the consent of the commissioners. His salary was to be £200 per quarter plus £50 per quarter travelling expenses. The engineers to work under Rhodes were put in place: W.T. Mulvany was placed in charge of the works from Lough Derg to the sea and Henry Buck of the upstream works; working under them there were to be resident engineers, John Long, Henry Renton, William Owen and Thomas Barton.

William Thomas Mulvany was born in County Dublin in 1806.[2] It is said that the home he grew up in was the rendezvous for many Dublin intellectuals including the architects Gandon, Johnston and Temple. He studied architectural drawing and then joined the Army Engineering Corps. In 1827 he joined the boundary survey under Richard Griffith and in 1835 transferred to the Shannon Commission. His maps and sectional drawings are examples of his exceptional draughtsmanship. He was later to serve a controversial period with the Board of Works on arterial drainage and left Ireland to carry out mining works in Germany. His younger brother, Thomas John Mulvany, also joined the Shannon works. Henry Buck as already noted had been involved in the proposed Nenagh canal plans and also previously in road works in the 1820s. John Long, a surveyor, had been involved in preparing the recent plans and subsequently designed Limerick Docks.[3]

The works were divided into five divisions and the commissioners were told they would be limited to the expenditure of £100,000 in any one year. The total funding allocated for the works would be based entirely on the proposed works and estimates as recommended by the previous commission, amounting to £584,805, and they were directed to make detailed accounts of their proceedings up to 31 December each year and present these to parliament. This meant that any deviation from the original plans had to be approved and it will be seen that a number of significant changes were in fact to occur and the reporting of these would be a matter of controversy. However, the great detail included in the original surveys would now become of immense assistance, with some of the engineers and surveyors who had worked on them becoming an important part of the establishment.

Killaloe: Thomas Rhodes's drawing of the river showing the extensive eel weirs above and below the bridge which were obstructing the flow.

The commissioners furnished their first annual report on 24 January 1840.[4] They said they had assembled in Dublin on the previous 9 October and proceeded to set up the establishment that would be required. This was divided into two sections, an office establishment and a works establishment. The office establishment had a secretary, accountant, clerks, office keepers, messengers etc.; these would be based in a Shannon Commission Office in the Custom House in Dublin where the Office of Public Works was located. The Dublin section would cost £3,000 per year, including the payment of £600 plus expenses of £200 to each of the commissioners. The works establishment was made up of the engineers and draughtsmen. Having taken over the administration of the upper Shannon from the Office of Public Works, they also put in place an inspector for this part of the river. William Mulvany was also placed in charge of the valuation office and in October, November and December court sittings were held in Limerick, Banagher, Athlone, Longford and Carrick-on-Shannon to deal with issues of compensation. This was to prove a far from straightforward procedure: 'in consequence of the confused state of the titles and the number of persons interested in each case'. The awards were then paid out, including those agreed to the Limerick Navigation Company and the Grand Canal Company, so that possession could be taken of these parts of the river and full ownership of all the properties could be established before commencing the works.

In some cases mills were let back to the original owners for a period until they would be required but in the case of Jamestown they proceeded at once to lower the mill dam about 4ft (1.2m) giving immediate relief to lands for many miles upstream which had been flooded for as much as six months in each year. With regard to the eel fishing all the eel weirs on the upper river were to be removed as soon as possible and, as the season had just ended, it was a good time to terminate this fishery, giving the people concerned time to resort to other types of fishing or other employment. They were determined to put an end to all illegal fishing and took a number of prosecutions with fines of £2 or twenty-nine days in prison.

They also had to work towards building up a fleet of steam-dredging vessels and lighters and an order was placed with Messrs Perry & Mallett for ten of these iron lighters. Two dredger hulls were ordered from Grantham Page of Liverpool at a cost of £1,000 each and these came down the Grand Canal for fitting out at Shannon Harbour; they later were to add a third dredger. They were referred to as A, B and C, but they were actually named *Victoria, Albert,* and *Prince.* The dredgers were insured with the London Union Assurance; the premium of dredgers A and B for one year was quoted as £45. This was a wise precaution as there was a fire subsequently on board Dredger A in the engine room, destroying the engine and forepart of the vessel; this was judged to have been accidental and the damage was paid for immediately.

The commissioners also had a boat built for inspections, the *Isabella,* and in a letter to Captain Tully from one of the commissioners, Harry Jones, he was told: 'This boat is not intended for yachting and it is the express orders of the Commissioners that she is not to be used by the gentlemen employed on the river for amusement. . . the sails are to be easily operated by people with little boat sailing experience and easily stowed to leave maximum space.' They also had two smaller sailing boats, the *Gertrude* and the *Edith.* They were looking in the first instance at the major works needed at Killaloe and Athlone and particularly at the latter place because the existing bridge was in such a bad state they felt it would be necessary to add a wooden footway as a temporary expedient.

The Shannon Commission letter books of Henry Renton 1841-1842 who was resident engineer at Banagher in charge of the works between Meelick and Shannon Harbour, give a very good idea of the day-to-day affairs in these early years of the works.[5] For example he was instructed that marl was to be pounded, burned and then mixed with two parts of sand to one of marl which, when immersed in water, 'sets as hard as any Welsh lime'. A less hard mixture could be used to make good mortar. Water cement could also be formed by mixing quick lime fresh from the kiln with twice its own weight of blue clay fresh from the river. The quick lime after being weighed had to be slaked with water to make it into a paste and allowed to stand for twenty-four hours before mixing with the clay. He was frequently criticized for failing to furnish the many returns he was supposed to send to Dublin. Weekly returns were needed of the number of men employed, the dredging returns, the nature of the work executed and the water bailiffs' fishery reports. Monthly returns had to indicate if any extra work was carried out or if there were any reductions in the contract. In addition certificates of work had to be completed and returned quarterly signed by both the resident and district engineers. At one stage his salary was stopped because of his failure to furnish lists of maps as had been requested. The returns of men showed that while most of the labourers were Irish, there were some English and Scottish men acting as gangers and stonecutters; it was recorded that there were thirty-two men and seventeen women, all Irish, employed cutting turf. He also had to record on a daily basis the height of water on the lock sill of the Hamilton lock at Meelick, the state of the weather and the materials being used or delivered to the works.

THE 2ND REPORT

The 2nd Report was issued on 22 February 1841 and it showed that a great deal of progress had been made.[6] They were finding the system set up to award compensation was working extremely well to everyone's satisfaction 'with justice and fairness'. The engineers were busy preparing plans and specifications and works would begin in the spring, starting with the most urgent places. They intended carrying out a number of the major works simultaneously and they had already entered into contracts for works at Killaloe, Meelick, Banagher, Shannon Harbour (work on the horse bridge over the river), and for the new bridge at Athlone. In addition they had contracted for all the dredging and minor clearance works on the middle river. The two powerful steam dredgers had already been fitted out and were ready to be handed over to the contractors.

On the estuary, proprietors from Querrin, Kilrush, Kildysart and Kilteery had notified the commissioners of their interest in co-operating with the improvement works, and tenders were being sought by public advertisement. They were also turning their attention to seeking contractors for the upper Shannon works and also for the Limerick Navigation where there had been some work needed on the banks and towpaths because of flood damage. As 'stone-pitching' was being used instead of the former use of sods and was being carried up much higher, these works could be considered as part of the permanent improvement works. Overall the works needing the most immediate attention were the removal of all the impediments to improve the flow in the river, including looking at the security of the bridges. This had to be done in a regulated way so that the increased flow did not cause problems farther downriver; already these works were showing results in reducing flooding.

Looking at the principal fisheries of eel and salmon, they found that these could be an important source of food and commerce 'if habitual, unlawful, and very injudicious practices could be prevented', which was a reference to the wholesale destruction of both eel and salmon fry out of season. By appointing their own water bailiffs and bringing some of the offenders before the courts they had greatly reduced these practices and there was a noticeable

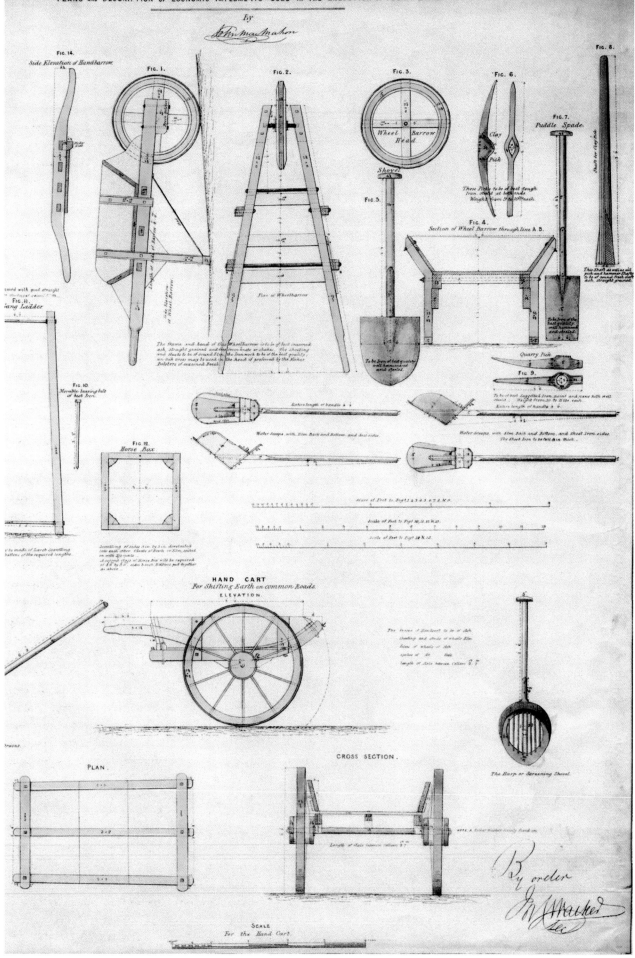

A drawing by John MacMahon, OPW engineer, of tools and implements used in the 1840s on public works.
(Department of the Environment, Heritage & Local Government)

improvement in the stocks. In a few cases some of the eel weirs were being left in particular places to help regulate the water and these were let on a temporary basis. Once the eel weirs were removed the commissioners:

... are of the opinion that Angling or Line Fishing or Cross Fishing with Lines and Flies only or spearing of Eels should not be interfered with. Neither do they recommend the Seizure of Nets in the open Season during the Existing State of the Law, excepting those used for taking fry, or set in Mill Races of course, and the Commissioners direct that those Places be constantly visited by the Bailiffs and others protecting the Fisheries.

Different systems of tolls and wharfage were being charged on the river, ranging from 1d per ton per Irish mile on corn on the Limerick Navigation to less then this on the middle Shannon and a charge per boat-load on the upper river, with general merchandise slightly dearer and turf usually charged by the boat-load. They endeavoured to reduce this charge to a uniform rate, based on the distance travelled and the quantity carried, keeping a higher rate for the Limerick Navigation, which had higher maintenance needs. They found that wharfage was seldom charged except at private quays and they were proposing to establish low uniform rates 'more with a view to establish order and regularity at the several landing places, than as a source of revenue'. When the works had all been completed the issues of tolls and wharfage would need to be reviewed.

With regard to an accounting system, they had established seven headings: Office, Works, Loans repayable by the Grand Juries, Rents & Tolls, Upper Shannon Navigation, Lough Derg buoys and beacons, together with a General Abstract of each of these accounts. Full details were supplied for each of these accounts as required under the Act. The amounts expended at each of the ninety-four locations on works and awards were shown, together with details of the sums advanced as loans to the counties. Rents, tolls and wharfage received in 1840 amounted to just under £4,000, which just about met the expenditure on salaries and maintenance. The greatest amounts had been spent on works at Meelick and Athlone: in total they had expended £99,623 in that year, 1840, keeping within the maximum allowed of £100,000.

Beginning with this report, each of the next nine annual reports, ending with the final report in 1850, included schedules of trade figures, showing the cargoes carried, the amount of tonnage entering and leaving the Grand and Royal canals, and the number of passengers being carried.[7] For the next nine years until they issued their eleventh and final report in 1850, the annual reports now became progress reports on the works.

THE SHANNON ESTUARY

The Shannon Commissioners were authorized to construct only certain piers and landing quays, subject to contributions being received from local landowners, the estuary being under the control of the Limerick Harbour Commissioners, whose role it was to place buoys and beacons to mark the channel. Works commenced in 1842 on the extension of Kilrush pier by the contractor Charles Flaviell, but because of the exposed position of the works a diving bell had to be used to lay the foundations; it is not clear whether they used the one recently designed by Thomas Steele already referred to. Steele's practical suggestions for the estuary were 'more particularly of that part of it named by Pilots "The Narrows" with some remarks intended to create a doubt of the fairness of not keeping faith with the Irish Roman Catholics after they had been lured into a Surrender of Limerick by a Treaty'. Through the winter months preparation were made so that work could commence in the spring but the pier at Kilrush was not finally completed for another year. The extension ran in a new direction to give better shelter and, when the work was completed, the commissioners were able to report that Kilrush had become an important station both for the export and import trade: 'Large sea-going vessels constantly line the wharf and powerful steamers, belonging to the City of Dublin Steam Company, carry on a daily traffic in goods and passengers with the port of Limerick.'

At Kilteery work on the new pier was held up by a succession of gales and high tides but was completed by the middle of the summer in 1843. It was not built to the length originally planned because of the difficulty in finding good foundations; the Earl of Clare had already paid his contribution to the works. At Cahircon (Kildysart) the pier was also operational as was the one at Querrin which had been carried out by the contractors, Sykes & Brookfield, 'in a very satisfactory manner'. Large limestone ashlars from a quarry at Foynes were being used to construct the piers, so that maintenance on them would be minimal, and it was estimated that the small charge for wharfage would be sufficient to cover the expense of employing someone to take charge of them. A quay was also completed at Saleen, in Ballylongford Creek, where considerable traffic was reported, consisting chiefly in corn for the market in Limerick and also 'latterly in pipe draining tiles, from the valuable and extensive tile manufactory established in the neighbourhood within the last two years by Mr St John Blacker'. Work was carried out on the quay at Clarecastle on the River Fergus together with dredging of the river to give access to it. The old quay here was used while the work was in progress so as not to interrupt the trade and then, subsequently, it was pulled down and rebuilt.

At the same time with regard to the proposed works at Carrigaholt, Tarbert, Glynn, Foynes, and at Askeaton, and widening and deepening the River Maigue at Adare, the commissioners recommended that unless the local proprietors declared their intentions to contribute to these work within one year, the money allocated should be 'otherwise appropriated'. This produced answers from the proprietors at Glynn, Askeaton and Adare and, subsequently at Foynes but, apart from works at Foynes, there is no record of any sums expended on any of these places. At Foynes a change was made with regard to the site of the quay so that a large harbour area could be enclosed to give shelter. The commissioners decided to carry out the work here under their own superintendence by day's work instead of by contract. They explained that 'owing to the increased prices which contractors were looking for, by reason of the numerous railways and other large works going on through the country . . . Tide works are subject to so many casualties . . . which is taken advantage of by a contractor, who founds upon them a bill of extras, frequently difficult to be dealt with. Such having been the case on all the Lower Shannon works.' At Foynes a dam had to be formed to enable the foundations of the quay wall to be laid, which on one or two occasions slipped causing delays and additional expense. When completed, sea-going vessels could lie alongside at all states of the tide. By 1850 most, but not all, of the works recommended by Captain Mudge had been finished and the contributions promised by the proprietors paid.

THE LIMERICK NAVIGATION

In order to give employment to the poor in the vicinity and in the city of Limerick work on the navigation was accelerated, beginning at once in May 1841 with work on a shoal at Illaanaroon downstream of Plassy, which was impeding the flow in the river and causing the water to back up at the mill and also leading to much flooding. The system used for removing shoals was to erect dams around the areas and pump them dry. This work lasted for six months until stopped by floodwaters and was completed in the following year; it employed an average of one hundred men per day. Work on the abutments for the Plassy footbridge was completed, all the iron-work for the bridge delivered and it was finished in the following year. Not only was it of great use to the traders to bring across their towing horses but was also used by many people who used to have to be ferried across by barge at Arthur's Ferry. Work was also carried out on improving the towpaths throughout the navigation.

In 1842 work began on deepening the river at Athlunkard Bridge and at Castle Troy but at both these places the work was not finished on schedule and the areas laid dry by the dams were inundated when the floodwaters came down. There were problems with the workmen not being paid their wages and the work had to be removed from the hands of the contractors, Burke & Smith, when it was revealed that they also owed money for machinery, which was then seized under warrant from the magistrates. Eventually, in the following year, the work had to be taken on

Limerick Navigation: by comparing O'Brien's Bridge today with Thomas Rhodes's drawings in the 1830s the further alterations can be seen.(Brian Goggin)

The capstan at O'Brian's Bridge. The short tunnel beside it was probably the access to the original capstan which was sited on an arm projecting out into the river before the new navigation arch and towpath were constructed in the 1840s. (Brian Goggin)

by the commissioners' own engineers but was subsequently given to new contractors. The labourers then assembled at the works at Corbally, because their former claims against the contractors had not been settled and this held up the work there. The contractors, Sykes & Brookfield, who had done such good work at Kildysart and Querrin, undertook to remove a shoal at World's End and the stone taken out of the excavation was used to make a landing quay for the people of 'the interesting village' of Castleconnell. While this was purely flood-relief work and not part of the navigation works, it did make access for boats possible; an average of 270 men were employed during the six months. Works continued on towpaths, clearing out back-drains and repairing lock gates on the canal sections and an unforeseen problem arose with Gillogue lock when the south wall of the chamber was forced forward and threatened to fall in, and the wall had to be taken down and rebuilt. When the navigation was stopped for this work, the Killaloe to Cussane stretch of canal was also cleaned out.

Work began on the new regulating weirs at Corbally, just downstream of the head of the Park Canal and at World's End, Castleconnell, which were designed to keep up the level of water for the navigation in summer. Work had

begun to deepen the river at Parteen but the contractor ran into difficulties and all his plant and stores were seized and once again the commissioners had to instruct their resident engineer to take over the works. Work went on day and night to try to complete them before the winter floods; an eight-horse steam engine with two 14-inch (35cm) pumps was used, assisted by two chain pumps, and two additional 10-inch (25cm) pumps had also to be added to keep the water down. When completed, the lowering of the head of water here was a great improvement where formerly the traders had had to use a capstan to make headway up this stretch of river over the shallows.

In 1844-1845 the commissioners tackled the 'old and badly-constructed' O'Brien's Bridge referred to in Rhodes's original survey in Chapter Four. This bridge had been erected on a shoal across the river and was greatly obstructing the flow.[8] The pier and capstan suggested earlier by Brownrigg had eventually been put in place by the time Rhodes carried out his survey. Boats had to be winched through the fourth arch from the Clare side by means of the capstan placed on a pier projecting out 50ft (15m) into the river. The rope was then led to a floating buoy and dropped down through the arch and eight or ten men then worked the capstan.

Because of the force of the current this was obviously an unsatisfactory and dangerous operation. The commissioners now used excavated material from the river to build up the bank to create a lay-by and quay, and work was carried out to improve the towpath to the Errina Canal. Seven arches were taken down at the eastern end and replaced by six wider arches, and the bed of the river deepened to improve the flow. A new navigation arch and towpath replaced the two nearest arches at the west end, producing the twelve-arch bridge as it is today with the present arches two to six from the west end remaining of the pre-1833 bridge. Keeping the stanks (as the areas created by the dams were called) dry while rebuilding the foundations for the new arches proved very difficult. Messrs Sykes & Brookfield also had this contract and here again there were problems with the workmen being owed money when it was reported that they had not received wages for five or six weeks. The traders,

however, immediately reported the great improvement they experienced when coming upstream because of the diminished head of water as a result of the new weirs.

So many interruptions to trade were happening because of low water on the Park Canal during the dry summer of 1845 that the commissioners decided to dry out the level between the two locks and deepen it. It was reported that this 'was a work of some labour' employing 450 men per day, affording great relief at a period in July when it was most needed. Maintenance contracts were entered into for the upkeep of the towpaths and, apart from continuing maintenance works in the canal sections to the locks and lock houses, no further works were carried out by the commissioners; the revenue from tolls was just about meeting the maintenance costs. In their eleventh and final report the commissioners summed up what they had set out to achieve:

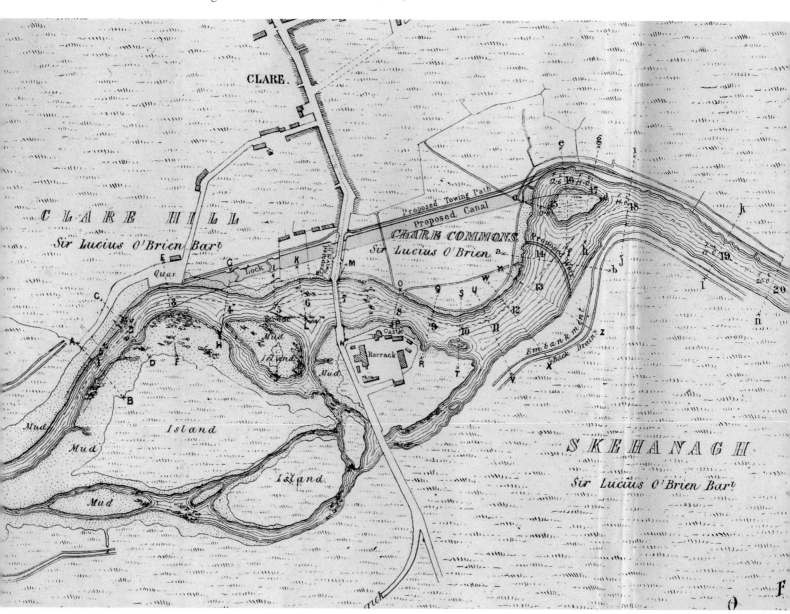

Shannon Estuary: Captain Mudge planned to create a short canal with a lock and opening bridge at Clarecastle on the River Fergus to bypass the shallows and extend the navigation to Ennis but this work was not carried out.

Finding it to be impossible, owing to the rapidity of the fall, to render this portion of the Shannon navigable for large steam-vessels, we limited our views to render it, as an ordinary barge navigation, as perfect as local circumstances would permit; but to guard against the rapidity of floods in the portions in which the river-course had been adopted, and to preserve a sufficient depth of water in dry weather, we found it necessary to construct two extensive regulating weirs; viz. one at Corbally and one at World's End.

They pointed out that the lock at Clonlara was 5ins (13cm) too narrow for the Grand Canal Company steamer but short of rebuilding the lock nothing could be done about this. They listed the other works, which they said had all been completed, including the new arches at O'Brien's Bridge, and all within a timeframe of five years.

Killaloe: only five arches of the original nineteen-arch bridge remain today, seven of the central arches were replaced by five in 1825, then four on the east side were replaced by three in the 1840s to further improve the flow.(Shannon Development)

CHAPTER SEVEN
THE MIDDLE SHANNON
KILLALOE TO ATHLONE 1840–1850

KILLALOE AND LOUGH DERG

The commissioners had already drawn attention to the fact that the works at Killaloe were going to be extensive. Preparatory work began in the summer of 1840 but there were problems with the workmen who complained they were not getting their wages and of 'the harsh conduct of the overseer'.[1] The response was to suggest that 'the men were inclined not to do more work than what was agreeable to themselves' and Colonel Jones told them if they were not satisfied with their employment 'they might quit'. In order to clear away the eel weirs and shoals above and below the bridge on the east side of the river, a clay-dam was made the whole way down the middle of the river, which enabled a space of about six acres to be laid dry. This was a big operation. A length of railway was laid down and the excavated material was removed to wagons in wheelbarrows to deposit the spoil, some of it was used to build up the Cussane embankment. Double gangs of men, with 380 men in each gang, worked through the summer of 1841 from 3 am to 10 pm removing up to 500 cubic yards a day.

The middle five arches of Killaloe Bridge had replaced seven original arches swept away in the 1820s. Now the four original older arches of the bridge on the east side were taken down and three new arches erected. The piers of the five remaining arches of the early eighteenth-century bridge on the west side were underpinned to a depth of 5ft (1.5m) below the original foundations, and a temporary wooden structure erected to enable pedestrians to cross during the works. The cross dams, which increased the velocity of the water, caused problems for the boats between the Pierhead and the lock; piles and booms had to the erected but eventually a retaining wall had to be built the whole way up along the canal. At the west end of the bridge a new lock keeper and collector's house was built on the site widened by the filling in of one of the old arches. Then on 3 September a breach took place in the dam because of a rise in the river, but as the work was sufficiently far advanced no injury to the works occurred, and the bridge was re-opened on 1 December.

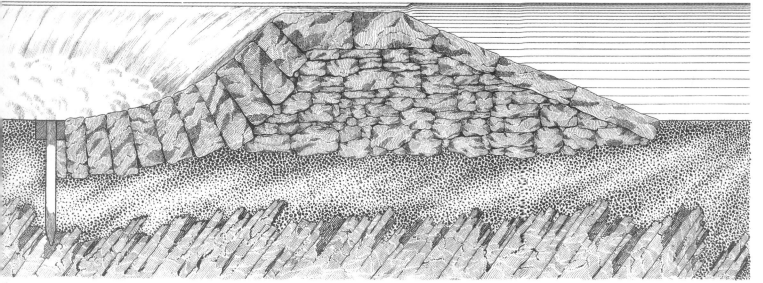

STRATA.

Thomas Rhodes's design for the new weirs.

The major work on the construction of the weir was started in 1844 and completed by August of the following year although once again there were problems with the dams being breached by summer floods. Having completely finished all the excavation work above and below the bridge, the water was allowed to flow over the new weir, all 1,100ft (335.5m) of it, which was fitted with a salmon gap and eel-inclined plane. The weir, which was designed to hold Lough Derg at about 1ft (0.3m) lower than before, did its work well. Despite the great falls of rain during that winter, Lough Derg, which had sometimes risen for long periods in winter by as much as 9ft (2.7m), never exceeded a rise of 2ft 6ins (0.75m) and that only for a few days. Finally eel weirs and shoals and two tiny islands, Insha Islands, a short

Killaloe: the new L-shaped weir constructed to Thomas Rhodes's design. (Courtesy of the National Library of Ireland)

Killaloe: the lock keeper and collector's house built as part of the works in the 1840s which was later enlarged and more recently demolished.

distance above the weir at Killaloe, had to be removed in order to improve the run-off over the weir even more.

In July 1842 the commissioners responded to an appeal from the guardians of the Scarriff Union Workhouse 'praying for some employment for the poor of that Union in consequence of the distress and the crowded state of the Workhouse'. One hundred men were employed under the contractor Flaviell. The works here consisted in dredging the river, building up the banks and making quays at Tuamgraney and at Scarriff. At Tuamgraney the former cut known as Reddin's Quay, which was at right angles to the river, was replaced by a new quay and at Scarriff a harbour was formed by closing off one channel around an island. Here a temporary side cut was made to divert the river and dams erected but on several occasions floods caused the works to be suspended. Mr Maunsell, in charge of the works there, was asked to explain anonymous remarks that appeared on the envelopes of two letters received from him with 'very serious imputations of intoxication' and his response was considered 'anything but satisfactory'. They seemed to be

a troublesome group because in 1843 there was a further disturbance among the workmen over the hours the various gangs worked.

A channel with a depth of 4ft 6ins (1.35m) was also made up the Ballyshrule River to Kelly's mills; the lowering of the level of the lake by the construction of the weir had made it impossible for boats to reach the mills and Kelly had previously spent a great deal of money fitting up his mills and deepening the river. A bar was removed from the entrance to the Woodford River using the dredging vessel, *Prince*. Some work was also done to remove some of the large stones in the approach to the wooden jetty at Williamstown erected by the City of Dublin Steam Company, which had to be blasted before they could be removed. Similar work was carried out at Dromineer. In 1845 a site for a pier was identified at Mountshannon in a sheltered bay. It was intended that this pier would not only improve conditions for shipping of corn but would also serve to make easier the landing of the rich marl found in the lake, which was 'much prized as a manure in the surrounding country'.

Work began in 1842 removing the shoal at Derry Castle at the narrows at the north end of Lough Derg. In bad weather the swell on the shoal was preventing the large steamers getting over it and passengers had to be transhipped to smaller steamers to reach Portumna, which was a dangerous operation. As no dredger was available, an experienced diver 'with Dean's apparatus' was employed, who surveyed the shoal and passed chains around the large boulders, which were raised on to the deck of a boat by derrick. The success of this method for removing shoals prompted the commissioners to order a 'diving dress' from Mr Liebe, the patentee.

PORTUMNA TO MEELICK

At Portumna a new bridge had to be erected urgently. This new bridge was once again a wooden structure but much stronger, with cross ties linking the piles. The opening span was moved to the west side of the river with one of Mallet's bridges mounted on solid stone piers. There were already two harbours above the bridge approached by short canals, Connaught Harbour on the west shore and Munster Harbour on the east side, which needed some dredging. The commissioners also erected a new quay above the bridge to facilitate the steamers.

The takeover of the middle Shannon from the Grand Canal Company had been carried through in January 1840. The £5 was handed over to John Stokes, the canal company's engineer, in the lock house in Athlone and he was instructed by his board to avoid 'any act which could on the one hand be construed into or have the appearance of a voluntary surrender or abandonment of the company's rights in respect of the Navigation or on the other of any opposition or interruption to the proceedings of the commissioners'.[2]

Portumna: the toll gate from the earlier bridge.

Apart from the shoal at White's Ford, which had to be removed by divers using Liebe's diving apparatus, there were no further works needed up to Meelick. In the first year of the works at Meelick, in 1841, some of the islands, which the commissioners had taken over in the area, were leased back to people for a limited period, including one island that was let to the friars. The plan for Meelick involved making the new canal and damming the original east channel at the head of the new canal. This closed off this channel except for some water passing down a pipe to below the new lock and confined most of the flow of water to the main river; this was to lead to problems when the river was in flood and created a situation that had to be remedied later. The excavation of the proposed new canal was begun in 1841 by the contractor, William Mackenzie. Particularly good quality limestone rock was excavated while digging the canal and the large ashlars proved very suitable for the formation of the new lock, while the smaller stones were burned in the kiln to make hydraulic lime. This meant that stone from other quarries was not needed.

The letter books of Henry Renton, the resident engineer for this division, show the sort of problems he had to deal with in the course of overseeing the works.[3] It was his role to keep a careful account of the work carried out by the contractors and report to the commissioners. He received a report in connection with damage caused by the man in charge to one of the dredgers, who it was alleged was not paying attention. He added: 'if you think my observations on the Dredging master too severe in the report, will you have the goodness to mollify them to your own satisfaction, leaving the same to your Superior Judgement'. When he had to go to Athlone to report to the district engineer, he was criticized for wasting time going up the river by water and

Old Bridge, Portumna

1909.

Portumna: the bridge erected by the Shannon Commissioners.
(Molloy, Portumna)

taking one of the water bailiffs with him instead of going by land. They accused him of making it 'a mere pleasure trip', which could have taken him away from his duties for a week if the wind had been contrary. An irritable letter arrived from Dublin from the secretary, Hornsby:

The Commissioners having received Complaints from the Tenant of Cloonaheenoge Farm that he is subjected to great inconvenience from the Trespasses committed by the Workmen employed by the Contractor on the Canal, and that proper places for the Men to answer the Calls of Nature have not been provided which proves a very great nuisance. ... decency and propriety required upon commencing any work that suitable premises should be immediately constructed.

In April 1841 there was a strike at the Meelick works with the men seeking 1s 3d per day. James Sutcliffe, Renton's assistant, informed him: 'a Notice appeared at White's Gate this morning threatening Death to anyone that should continue to work. There is a funeral coming from Banagher to Meelick this evening and the men at work are afraid that they will beat them when they come down'. Next a notice appeared at the chapel gate 'with the figure of a Coffin at the Bottom threatening anyone with Death that shall go to Work'. The pile drivers agreed to continue working and others 'would go to work if they durst but are afraid of the rest'. Renton was instructed that 'no unreasonable or extravagant demand should be given into'. It was eventually sorted out but there was further trouble and he was criticized in the following year for failing to report a riot when the police had to interfere between some of the contractor's men and some locals, but he claimed that it was just caused by the locals being intoxicated, who were in no way connected with the works, and it was not important enough to report.

Meelick: the new lock was named Victoria lock.

In August 1842, following an inspection by Rhodes, Renton was told he needed to push the contractor to speed up the works at Meelick lock, 'otherwise the floods will be down on us'. It was good advice because in November it was reported that the water was rising fast in the lock and the pumps could not keep it dry. The exceptionally dry summer was causing problems in the old canal for the steamers and the boats were actually grounding on the sill of the Hamilton lock and on a shallow of loose stones below the lock. Renton was told by his district engineer, Buck, that he needed to exert himself more. Clearing the shallow was not easy; because of the low water the dredger could not be brought into the canal and he had to clear it 'by spoon and bag'. This seems to have been done with a canal boat and a bag over one side of the boat, which was dragged along the bottom with a crab using a chain mounted on a derrick on the deck.

The commissioners learnt that the contractor's steward had sown potatoes on the east bank of the canal and Renton was told that the banks were exclusively for the use of the works. In November 1842 Henry Renton was severely censured for allowing the quarrying to endanger the embankments of the canal. He was dismissed in May 1843 for 'studied disregard of numerous communications' but it would appear that he was subsequently reinstated. In 1843 the Inspector General of Constabulary threatened to withdraw a party of police who had been stationed at Meelick. They were there because of the large numbers of men employed so that their presence prevented breaches of the peace 'which are very likely to occur where so many workmen are assembled together'. The commissioners were concerned and requested that they remain for about another six months.

Meelick: the inscription on a bollard.

Meelick: the inscription on one of the sluice housings.

The excavation of the canal and paving of the banks was all completed in these first years and a large amount of work was also carried out on the foundations, chain and sluice tunnels for the new lock. There was an extraordinary amount of indecision about the dimensions of the new locks at Meelick and Athlone. Rhodes had originally included a plan for Athlone lock in the 2nd Report, which was 140ft (42.6m) long from mitre to mitre. This would accommodate a boat approximately 8ft (2.4m) less than this to allow for the upper sill. The largest steamer on the river at this time was the *Lady Lansdowne*, which was 135ft (41.1m) long, and so a decision was made to increase the proposed size of Meelick and Athlone to 175ft (53.3m), mitre to mitre, by 40ft (12m) wide at the hollow quoins, with a rise of 8ft (2.4m) giving 7ft (2.1m) on the sills at summer levels. A decision was made in 1842 to lengthen both Athlone and Meelick by 25ft (7.6m) to cater for the anticipated larger steamers, but then it was decided to reduce this and finally it was agreed that Meelick would be increased to 170ft (51.8m) with Athlone staying at 155ft (47m). In fact Meelick lock was actually constructed 142ft (43.4m), from lower mitre to upper sill and Athlone lock, for some reason, was reduced to 127ft (38.7m), which would not accommodate the larger steamers, and the locks above Athlone were made only 102ft (31m) long.

The east end of the new weir was also finished quite quickly. The methodology used to make the weir appears to have been to drive in an outer and inner line of piles and then planks or 'wales' were screwed to the tops of these piles, to stabilize the construction, which was then faced with squared ashlars. It was completed to nearly half the required length by 1843. It was not easy work; James Sutcliffe reported, 'the piles in the weir cannot be drove close together until the stones are removed'. In 1844 all but the last 50ft (15m) was completed when the work was overtaken by the winter floods, and it was not finally finished until 1845.

At the same time work was being carried on deepening the Keelogue shallows and this was done by erecting dams to create stanks, as they called them, formed with wooden planks, first on one side of the river and then on the other. Coffer dams had been used by Robert Semple many years earlier in 1751 in the rebuilding of Essex Bridge in Dublin, but during the works on the Shannon much experience was gained in using a method of drying out areas of the river bed for excavation. The clay and gravel in the river bed at Keelogue had become so compacted that gunpowder had to be used to break it up, which was slow and costly for the contractor. This material proved as difficult to excavate as solid rock and made the commissioners worried that similar problems would occur at some of the other shoals, which they soon learnt was to prove the case. That Keelogue had been an important fording place in the past was borne out by the discovery of 'antiquities'. Richard Griffith wrote to Renton: 'The very interesting antiquities lately transmitted to Dublin from the excavations at Keelogue have created much interest and many inquiries have been made as to the relative positions in which the bronze swords were found and also the stone hatchets'.

The masonry of the lock was completed and the gates hung in 1843. French oak had to be used for the gates because English oak was not available, and they were planked with memel. Northern pine *(pinus sylvestris)* was often named after the port of shipment – in this case Memel at the mouth of the River Niemen on the Baltic. It was recorded that each pair of gates could be opened and shut in one and a half minutes and the lock filled or emptied in three minutes so that a vessel could be passed through the lock in five minutes. The lock house was finished and occupied by 1844. Only the final excavations of Keelogue shoal remained to be finished, section by section having to be enclosed with stanks, before the new navigation could be opened. Repeated summer floods from April to August interrupted the work despite working twenty hours a day from 2 am to 10 pm, with two gangs of men. A railway had been laid and the excavated material was conveyed by wagons to form an embankment to close off the back river channel on the east bank at the head of the new canal and also to link up islands to create banks on the west side of the river. A new quay wall was also made above the weir for the village of Meelick. The work was slow because of the 'hard indurated clay and gravel mixed with large boulder stones' and again gunpowder had to be used to break it up. At the same time, using the steam dredger *Victoria* with the 'pentagraph shears', shoals were being removed at eight further places in the channel up to

Banagher: a drawing of the opening of the new bridge on 12 August 1843 drawn by the contractor William Mackenzie.(James Scully)

Banagher, including Counsellor's Ford and Shannon Grove. The removal of all these shoals proved very difficult and was much more costly than originally estimated, just as the commissioners had feared.

Eventually the dam at the head of the new canal was removed and the trade boats began to use it on 14 November 1844. C.W. Williams of the City of Dublin Steam Company asked to see the commissioners to explain that because of the very exposed nature of this part of the river, the steamers were experiencing difficulty when waiting to pass up through the lock. Colonel Jones, having watched the difficulties experienced by the *Lady Burgoyne* below the lock, arranged for two sheltered lay-bys to be made, using piles to secure the boats while waiting. The entire contract had now been finished here and the workshops were removed.

MEELICK TO ATHLONE

The work originally planned at Banagher by Rhodes was to do away with the lock, make a wider running canal with a swivel bridge. It was intended to construct a weir across the river and replace the old bridge, with its many arches, together with removing the eel weirs and shoals. This would improve the flow and remove the need for the lock. The decision seems to have been made at an early stage to abandon the canal completely and to make the navigation channel in the river, with an opening span in the new bridge on the east side. This made more sense because the river was going to have to be deepened to improve the flow and a navigation channel could be made at the same time and there would be no need for a weir. In the meantime, in order to keep the traffic moving, some repairs had to be carried out to the old lock gates on the canal and tolls continued to be charged.

The works here were commenced early in 1841 by the same contractor as at Killaloe and Meelick, William Mackenzie, who employed George Woodhouse as his resident engineer in Banagher. Mackenzie also took over two of the steam dredgers, some hoppers and close-bottomed barges. The first task was to try to identify a quarry within a short distance of the town and this was found at Gurtagown, less than a mile away. Large limestone ashlars were prepared at the quarry and then transported to the work sites. A coffer dam was erected on the east side of the river at the site of the new bridge, steam engines extracted the water and the first stone of the first abutment was laid in August 1841. A railway was laid to bring the stone across the river and the first stone of the west abutment was laid by the end of September. Renton had to keep a meticulous account of all the works; for example there was an extra claim because the piles for the dam had to be driven deeper than specified and therefore had to be longer, and the number of piles had to be increased because the bases of the piers were enlarged.

All work in the river had to be suspended for the winter months and Renton had to deal with a strike for higher wages among the stonecutters, who continued to work preparing stone through the winter. In 1842 all the remaining piers were put in, using coffer dams, and the swivel bridge put in place. In order to remove the shoal above the bridge, part of the old bridge had to be removed to allow the steam dredger to pass down and a temporary wooden length was put in. The new bridge was opened on 12 August 1843, having taken just two years to build. The commissioners agreed to a request from the 'Body of Free and Accepted Masons' to be allowed to walk in procession at the opening ceremony, having received a dispensation from the Grand Lodge to do this. The new quay was also completed below the bridge.

The removal of the old bridge now had to be carried out and there is a vivid description of this in the 5th Annual Report of 1844:

Upon the opening of the new bridge an experimental charge of 50lbs of powder was placed in one of the piers of the old bridge, which, when exploded, succeeded perfectly as to the effect desired; it was then decided to destroy the remaining portions by simultaneous explosions; every alternate pier was then charged as above, and fired; the effect was admirable; the entire length (550ft) of the old bridge was gently thrown up and fell in a mass of rubbish.

The river bed was then dried out, using a longitudinal dam closed off at both ends, so that the spoil could be removed from each side, with loaded wagons working right down in the bed of the river. The shoal in the bed of the river beneath the old bridge was found to contain immense rounded blocks of limestone, which had to be blasted before they could be removed. While all this was happening, on two occasions during the summer, the dams gave way and had to be repaired and the area unwatered yet again. Finally, when the winter floods came down, the dams had to be removed and the remaining clearing was carried out by the *Victoria* steam dredger. So by early 1844 the new navigation was open to the steamers from Killaloe to the entrance to the Grand Canal at Shannon Harbour, although some work continued clearing the channel in places. Work had also been completed by then on the remaining shoals between Meelick and Shannon Harbour with the intention of achieving a navigation channel 150ft (45.6m) wide by 7ft (2.1m) deep at summer level to correspond with the sill of the new lock at Meelick.

A new bascule bridge had to be erected at the junction with the Grand Canal at Shannon Harbour of 40ft (12m) span to give greater accommodation to the steamers and this was opened by November 1841. Once again there had been problems with the contractor, Burgess, who at one stage was given a week to get on with it or it would be completed at his expense. Because of the exposed nature of the river here, there were frequent accidents reported. The bridge keeper was threatened with dismissal because the steamers were constantly held waiting for the bridge to be lifted, but he claimed that a heavy fall of snow had caused the recent delay. The captain of the *Avonmore* steamer said he wished the bridge had been made wider 'as there will be damage done, we have had two very narrow escapes'. The

Banagher: the inscription on the new bridge.

steam company was subsequently fined for damage to the bridge. Battens had to be placed across the new decking to prevent the horses slipping and there were also complaints about the decking on the rest of the bridge because the horses were putting their feet through the rotten planking. In the end, after all this work, it was eventually decided to remove the bridge completely and substitute a ferry-boat to bring across the horses used for towing.

The shoals in the river were proving much more difficult to remove than anticipated. There were often large boulders, or rolled masses of limestone, enveloped in indurated clay and limestone gravel. There were a number of places where extensive widening and deepening had to be carried out. At Derryholmes the old sailing course had twisted its way through to find the deeper water. There had been an ancient ford here and stanks had to be used to dam off each section to provide a straight and deep channel. There were great problems keeping the water low enough for the men to work because it was percolating and boiling up through fissures in the bottom. The original steam engine was pumping insufficient water and a larger one was brought in and then a second and a third so that in the end they were operating twelve large pumps. Eventually a substantial cross dam was made and this enabled the work to proceed better; some of the work was also done by the steam dredger at the head of the shoal. The work was almost finished by the time the winter floods came down in 1845 and it was

eventually all completed by the end of 1846 but not without much hardship and trouble with the pumps and not without causing problems to traffic trying to get through. At the lower of the Bishop's Islands a short running canal had been made to the west of the main river. This was now abandoned and a navigable channel dredged in the main river to the east of the islands. Many of the large boulders lifted from the river were used to form beacons. Extensive work was also carried out at Garrymore at the upstream end of the Bishop's Islands and this continued into 1847 when divers had to be brought in to help pass chains around the large boulders which once again were then used to form beacons. Gunpowder was used to break up the larger boulders:

... by means of boring holes into them with long jumpers worked by men in barges moored immediately over them; the holes being bored from two to three feet in depth, the canisters of powder, with patent fuze attached, were inserted and fired ... the fragments were raised in some instances by the pentagraph shears and by means of Lewis bolts and chains worked by crab winches.

At Shannonbridge it was decided to underpin nine of the arches, remove the lock and embankment, which had formed the short canal, build the new abutments, install the swivel bridge, and deepen the river to improve the flow. Work began in early 1843 to remove the embankments and

Shannon Harbour: the remains of part of the bridge for bringing horses across the river to the Ballinasloe Line the main part of which was removed by the Shannon Commissioners.

place coffer dams around the piers to be underpinned. The summer floods, which had caused trouble elsewhere, flooded the dams and held up the work. All this time every effort was made to keep the navigation open but it was completely closed for a period in 1844. Despite a strike by the men the work had almost been completed in 1844, when the winter floods came down. A temporary bridge was erected over the old lock, the bridge works were completed and it was open to the public in March 1845. In the following year all that remained to be finished was the removal of the stanks and some further deepening on the west side of the river to improve flow.

In 1845 work began on one of the most difficult shoals of them all, at Clerhaun Ford, near Clonmacnois, where stone was being quarried. Two stanks were created, a navigation channel was left between them and the pumps were brought in to de-water them. It was then discovered that an extension of the quarry of solid rock ran out under the river in addition to the usual large boulders. To make matters worse, water was springing up through the bottom and eight steam engines had to be used to provide enough pumps. In the middle of August 1846 unusually heavy rain caused the river to rise, as much as 12ins (0.3m) at Shannonbridge, and it came in over the tops of the dams. Most of the men had to be discharged but the contractor, Mackenzie, decided to try to continue work: 'the men had not been at work a week, however, when a second and even greater flood occurred, which caused the river to rise at Shannonbridge in the space of 24 hours not less than 2ft and in 48 hours from its commencement nearly 4ft, delaying all work for a fortnight'. Work began again to dry out the stanks and a little more was achieved until the middle of October when all work had to cease for the winter. In the following spring work recommenced and the men worked double shifts but it was once again slowed down by heavy rain and also by the fact that wet turf was being used to fuel the steam engines and coal had to be brought in. Towards the end of June there were 300 to 400 men working in

Many of the large markers in the river were made out of the large boulders raised during the excavation of the navigation channel.

double shifts from 2 am until 10 pm. An enormous quantity of solid rock had to be taken from the river to make a navigation channel. Work was going on at the same time at Tullymore upstream of Clonmacnois and at Rann (Wren) Island, a short distance downstream of Athlone. Here once again the shoal was made of very hard material and two of the dredgers had to be used for periods until one of them struck a rock with such force that she was holed and had to be sent to Killaloe for repairs.

The 11th and Final Report of the Commissioners recorded that, despite the erection of the regulating weirs and all the work done to deepen the river and remove obstructions, 'the present channel is found to be insufficient to discharge the great accumulation of water with sufficient rapidity to prevent partial floods'. This they added was because of the narrowness of the river channel on the main river course between Athlone and Meelick together with the added water of the Suck coming in below Shannonbridge: 'the volume of water discharged by the Suck during the prevalence of wet weather being nearly equal to that of the Shannon'. They added that, therefore, at some time in the future further works would be necessary to widen the confined channels and they were rash enough to add: 'Fortunately such works, though probably indispensable, will not be very expensive.' These comments were to prove highly significant in the years that followed when severe flooding was to once again make this a very controversial issue.

Shannon Harbour: the ferry which replaced the horse bridge in the 1840s. (Shackleton Archives)

ATHLONE

The most urgent work to get underway at Athlone was the building of the new bridge because the old one was in such bad condition. The owners of the mills on the old ten-arch bridge had to receive compensation, which amounted in all to £10,287 11s 11d. Jones's mill at the east end of the bridge had enjoyed 61ft (18m) of frontage on the bridge, occupying a single arch, one arch separated it from Steele's mill (referred to as Bracken's mill in the 1833 report), which had 34ft (9.2m) frontage, and there were then five arches between them and Mullins's mill (referred to as Dawson's mill in the 1833 report), which had 26ft (6.2m) occupying two arches. The five middle arches were the ones that had been swept away and rebuilt about seventy years earlier, and all these obstructions together with extensive eel weirs were greatly obstructing the flow of the river.

A number of important decisions were made about the works at Athlone early in 1841. Rhodes, Mulvany and Buck attended the board in Dublin with a proposal to abandon the canal and to use the river instead as they were doing at Banagher. Having carried out a more detailed examination of the river bed, they suggested moving the site of the proposed weir to a location below the new bridge and erecting a new, large lock at the west end of the weir. Buck produced detailed drawings and estimates which showed that less compensation would be required and it would have greater advantages for the town. It also had the advantage that the old canal could continue to be used while the work was in progress. This major change in the plans was accepted by the government and in the meantime the erection of the new bridge was in progress. John MacMahon's tender of

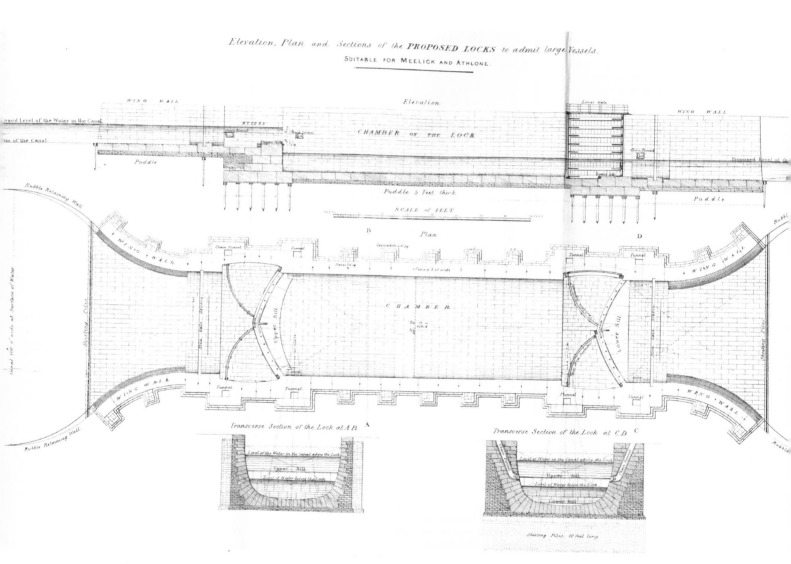

Athlone: Thomas Rhodes's design for the new large lock on the navigation; some reductions in the sizes of the locks were eventually made.

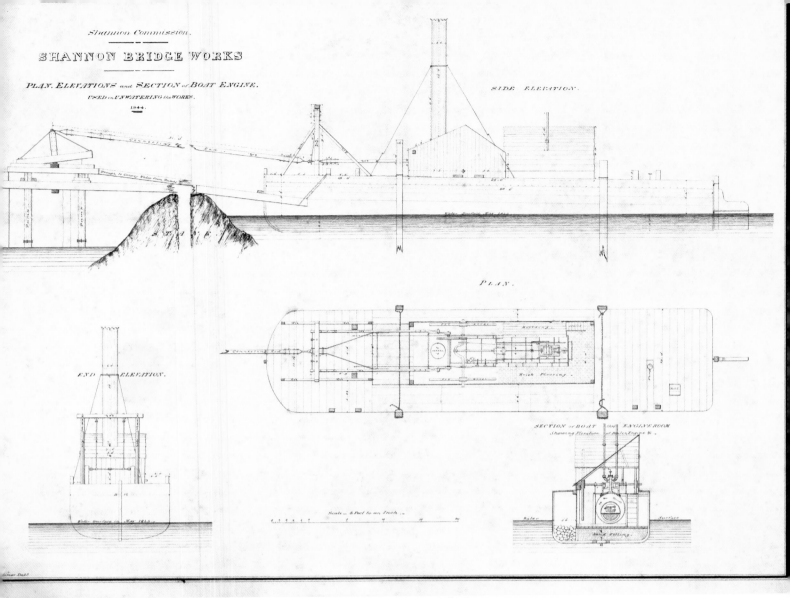

Shannon Commission.

SHANNON BRIDGE WORKS

PLAN, ELEVATIONS and SECTION of BOAT ENGINE.
USED in UNWATERING the WORKS.
1844.

SIDE ELEVATION.

Shannonbridge: the 'Boat Engine' constructed to assist with unwatering the works. (Waterways Ireland)

£23,000 to build the new bridge was accepted and in May 1841 work had begun. John MacMahon had been involved in waterway engineering for many years and had formed the partnership of Henry, Mullins and MacMahon, which had earlier won the contract for completing the Royal Canal. He subsequently resigned from this partnership so that he could apply for the contract to construct the Longford Line of the Royal Canal. With his two former partners, Henry and Mullins, now directors of this company, he had won that contract and he now undertook to build the new bridge at Athlone.

Two quarries had been identified, one at Cashel on the east shore of Lough Ree where a 'tramroad' was laid to bring the ashlars the 300 yards to the lakeshore, and the other at Clerhaun, just below Clonmacnois, where the deepening of the river was causing such problems. Subsequently quarries at Lecarrow and Ballyhuran were also used. The contractor set about erecting workshops and taking down some houses on the approaches to the new bridge, which was located just upstream of the old one, and laying down the usual temporary railways for handling the ashlars. Coffer dams were then put in place for the construction of the abutments.

Although the annual report to parliament sounded positive, the first signs of problems with MacMahon's contract began to appear in the minutes of the commissioners in May 1841 when he was asked why he had not yet started opening up the quarries and was not getting on with the works, and a similar letter went to him in August. In October it was reported that there was a danger of Charles Dillon's malt house falling into the river because of a problem with the eastern abutment. He tried to negotiate some changes in his contract, which he said would save time and expense, but without success. Matters deteriorated further when his two sureties, McCarthy and Mullins, the latter probably his former partner in the firm of Henry, Mullins and MacMahon, refused to sign the bond of security and the commissioners suspended all payments to him until the deed was executed.

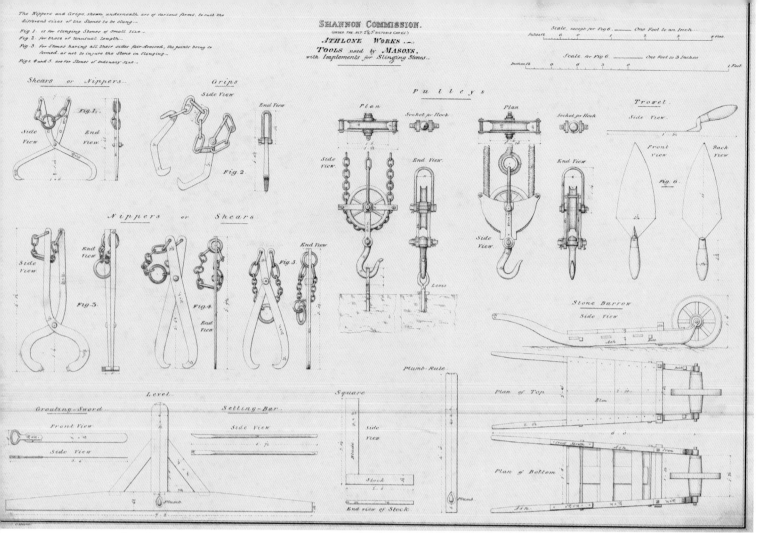

Tools used by the masons. (Waterways Ireland)

The problems continued and in April 1842 there was a strike because the men objected to the fact that they were only being paid monthly and by 'the truck system', based on work done. The strike was settled but a letter was sent to MacMahon in May complaining of 'the tardy and dilatory manner in which the works at Athlone are being carried on'. He was told in no uncertain terms that more energy and vigour was required and that he must employ more men. In their next report to parliament, dated February 1843, the commissioners did mention these problems. They said that although they had no reason to find fault with the quality of the works, their own engineers had suggested that there should have been more progress. They added that despite a good summer the contractor had failed to maximize on this, but they were confident that he could still meet the terms of the completion date in his contract. There was some

Athlone: an early drawing showing the new bridge looking downstream.

disagreement between MacMahon and Rhodes towards the end of 1843 when the latter expressed disapproval of the way the arches were being centred, and his doubts about their stability. MacMahon's response was uncompromising. He said he was 'acting on his own risk in following his own Plan for the Centres as the Commissioners hold him responsible for any expense that may be occasioned by his having so acted'.[4]

Their next parliamentary report was a bit more encouraging. It was stated:

The works of this contract are now in a forward state; the great difficulties experienced from the water boiling up in great force within the dams, which were constructed according to his own designs, and approved by us, were perfectly water-tight, and sufficiently strong to resist the great pressure of the water outside, during the winter floods.

All the piers and abutments had been completed and the 70 tons of metal castings for the swivel bridge had been delivered. Finally, on 9 November 1844, the new bridge was opened to the public but with some dredging under the arches and some pointing still to be completed. All the earlier problems seem to have been forgotten. The bridge works were said to reflect the greatest credit on MacMahon, and Rhodes added; 'This bridge has been built in a most substantial manner, both as regards the workmanship and the materials used, which were of the best description of their respective kinds.' Although he was in his seventies MacMahon now joined the drainage division of the Office of Public Works and played a significant role in the survey work for the navigation and drainage schemes on the Corrib, River Bann and the Ballinamore and Ballyconnell canals. He died in 1851.[5]

In the meantime advertisements were placed in fourteen Irish, eight English and two Scottish papers for tenders for the building of the lock and weir. Messrs Anderson & Wardsopp of Lanarkshire won the contract with the lowest estimate of £22,904 5s 7d. Before long they too were falling behind with the work. In 1843 it was reported that the contractors had set up their workshops and commenced the piling for the coffer dam for the weir and lock on which about 35,000 cubic feet of timber was used. They recorded that a Mr John Davis, who had just returned from Pesth in Hungary, where he had been engaged in forming coffer dams for a suspension bridge over the Danube, was entrusted with the piling. Over the following summer, 1844, there was a constant struggle to keep the water out using water wheels for power for the pumps, against the advice of the commissioners who said they should use a steam engine. In June Rhodes reported that the work on the new weir and lock was 'at a stand', that the labourers at Lecarrow quarry had not been paid for seven weeks 'and consequently reduced to a state of great

Athlone.

The Castle.

The Wrench Series, No. 1969.

Athlone: A later postcard looking upstream.

destitution'. The position worsened and in July the workers were 'clamourously assembled and demanded a settlement'. They said that they were owed money for food and lodging and the commissioners had to agree to settle with them. The contractors resorted to 'bad expedients, which invariably failed' and finally the commissioners decided to take the work out of their hands. Mackenzie was now asked if he would like to take over the works; Sykes & Brookfield were also asked and Bernard Mullins, MacMahon's former partner, showed an interest. When new tenders were sought Mullins won the contract to finish the works and the commissioners said he was 'a person whose reputation as a builder of work of this description stands high, and from his great experience we entertain the best hopes that, however much we were disappointed in the original contractors, the delay occasioned by their mode of proceeding will be redeemed by him'. They also drew attention to the fact that all the clearing of obstructions in the river resulted in a total absence of flooding that winter: 'such as never before was witnessed at that season of the year'.

However, in January of the following year, 1845, Mullins was being written to for failing to show enough action and again at the end of March there was still no progress and the old bridge, which he was to demolish, was still there. In April he was told that he must get the steam engine in operation at the lock, employ more masons and work longer hours. In May he was told the commissioners were very surprised to learn that he had only thirty men working 'on a contract of such magnitude and importance as the Athlone lock and weir, and as nothing is doing towards building the lock, the working of the wheels to pump out the dam is both useless and mischievous, disturbing every part of the foundations' and they asked why the remains of the old bridge had not been cleared. The depth of these difficulties was not really reflected in the parliamentary report, which stated that the first stone of the lock had been laid on 2 April. The water wheels, which became useless when the water was low, were at last supplemented by a 10-horse steam engine. The contractor had reached terms with the men, following a strike and work had proceeded until the winter floods came down.

A lengthy parliamentary report was made covering the works during 1846. No work could be undertaken with the lock until the end of April and even then it was a continuing struggle to keep the level of the water down and 'progress made with all parts of the work was on the whole very unsatisfactory'. Work continued through the autumn on both the lock and quay walls but there was constant trouble with the piles in the dam, some of which were not entered down into the bed of the river or were broken off or twisted out of direction by meeting with boulders. Severe weather next spring delayed restarting the work but over the summer

progress was made and three of the gates of the lock were hung. Progress was also made with the weir, the piling was completed and about 10,000ft (3,050m) of masonry put in place. 1847 saw much of the work on the lock and weir completed but very little progress had been made with clearing out the bed of the river and the contractor was criticized for not making more use of the fine season during the summer.

During 1848 very little more progress had been made with the extensive clearing of the bed of the river. The 11th and Final Report issued in 1850 announced the completion of all the navigation works but gave no indication of the fact that great difficulties had been encountered with the Athlone works during 1849. Details of these events were subsequently revealed in a parliamentary inquiry into drainage problems held in the 1860s.[6] Giving evidence in 1866, Mr Kelly, the county surveyor for County Roscommon, criticized the fact that the commissioners had laid dry the entire bed of the river at Athlone in 1849 having already built the new bridge and the lock with caissons and a coffer dam. W. Forsyth, an OPW engineer, also gave evidence. He explained that the river had been laid dry by erecting a dam farther up the river 'nearly opposite the Royal School at the narrow part of the river'. He said that this was an emergency measure to cope with a difficult situation. It would not have been practical to have tried to hold back the waters of the river for sufficiently long to carry out all the works on the bridge, lock and weir, during which time the waters had to be diverted down the old canal. This would have meant suspending the considerable trade that had continued to use the canal.

Forsyth explained how the emergency had arisen. The river bed was sandy and gravelly in the area where the new weir was being constructed. A double row of piles had been driven in with planks bolted to them and the masonry inserted, the method which had been used at Killaloe and Meelick. However, water had worked its way into the masonry, undermining it in one place, and it had been found impossible to remedy the situation. There was still excavation to be carried out to the bed of the river, eel weirs had to be removed as well as shoals and the remains of the old bridge. So it was decided to try to hold back the river for a limited period. While the river was dry the weir was completed and work was carried out clearing the bed of the river. He gave a vivid description of what happened next:

'During the execution of the work they were troubled with water because the bottom was so low it would scarcely run out, so they opened the gates of the new lock to allow the drainage water to pass it there. However, the water rose until it burst the dam and the whole flood and damming up of Lough Ree came down upon us. I was sent down from

Dublin to get the gates of the new lock shut, and with a good deal of difficulty we got them shut at last'.

A report in *The Westmeath Independent* of 30 June 1849 confirms these events.[7] It records the arrival of the promised period of employment: 'In consequence of a report which had been spread through the country, some thousands of poor creatures crowded into the town.' On 14 July the same newspaper said that nearly one thousand men were at work in the bed of the river, 'which is completely dry, and which as far as the eye can reach is filled with workmen, horses, miners and engineers etc'. At the same time divers were at work on the new weir repairing the damage caused underwater by the previous winter floods. There is no record of whether there were fatalities when the dam burst; it is possible that there were some warning signs of the impending surge of water and, as the last entry in the surviving minute books of the commissioners is on 4 October 1847, there is no contemporary account of the event in these records.

Mr Kelly was also very critical of the decision to abandon widening the old canal as he reckoned that the original plan to build a u-shaped weir upstream of the bridge would have allowed much more water to run off in time of flood. He drew attention to the fact that the original estimate for the Athlone works had been £60,000 and he quoted a figure of £104,276 as the actual cost, which made up about 18 per cent of the total expenditure on the entire works of £584,806. This was the total figure within which the commissioners had to stay and there is little doubt that the extra costs of the Athlone works forced savings elsewhere, most of which were at the expense of the drainage works, carrying out further excavation to increase the width and depth of the channel to improve the flow. Other savings also had to be made on the works on the upper river, including reducing the size of the locks and erecting fixed bridges instead of providing opening spans upstream of Roosky.

CHAPTER EIGHT
THE UPPER SHANNON
WORKS 1840–1850

LOUGH REE

From the evidence of Rhodes's survey and other accounts it was clear that the upper Shannon works were in a very bad state and, in fact, had really never been very satisfactory. Apart from the construction of a number of bypass canals and locks, very little else had been done. The river suffered from shallow water in summer because of the many shoals and the flow of floodwater was seriously impeded at other times by these shallows, extensive eel weirs and narrow-arched bridges. While the major effort went into the lower and middle river in the first years of the new works, some work did begin on the river upstream of Athlone in 1841.[1]

One of the first works undertaken on Lough Ree was the opening up of a small stream up to near Lecarrow Mills, on the west shore in 1841. This work was done in the first instance to facilitate the transport of oatmeal and corn from the mills down river to the Grand Canal and it immediately encouraged trade. It was reported that steamboats arrived twice a week to tow the trade boats down river and it was anticipated that it would become an important point of shipment for all kinds of agricultural produce. In the following year it was said that 'an advantageous offer' from R.W. Bond to improve the short canal had been made, which gave employment to 'a great number of men of the poorest class at a distressing season, when most required to save themselves and families from starvation'. His suggestion that the canal be extended farther with the installation of a lock was turned down. The canal was dredged and subsequently, at Bond's request, the quay wall and harbour were formed. Bond also opened up a nearby quarry, which was to become one of the important sources of stone for the Athlone works, although there was a continuing row about payment for the stone. During the work the 'fossil remains of a Moose deer of a large size' was found and the commissioners were very angry because they were not informed about this. They instructed that 'every portion of these remains [to be] carefully collected, packed and forwarded to this office'.

Because of the increasing use of the lake with the steamers in operation it was also found necessary to mark the channel, 'which is now defined by 32 buoys, 6 of sheet-iron and 26 ordinary casks'. The only other work on Lough Ree was at Curreen Ford at the northern end of the lake where the navigation course twisted around an island and a new straight channel was made by excavating the shoal.

While there is little evidence of the troubled state of the country during the 1840s in the minutes of the commissioners or the reports to parliament, some indication of this can be seen in a report in the *Illustrated London News* on 29 July 1843:

Six gunboats arrived in Athlone harbour on Saturday, guarded by six men and a second mate named Brown. The boats are to be stationed between here and Hare Island for the purpose of preventing our garrison being surprised by water. Forty gunboats are, we understand, in preparation for the Shannon.

LANESBOROUGH TO ROOSKY

Work began at Lanesborough in 1843 to remove the lock, lock house, canal embankment and shoal at the bridge and underpin the piers. A longitudinal dam was made down the middle of the river the entire length of the shoal, which was connected to the Longford shore by cross dams. During an exceptionally wet spring and summer work was interrupted three times by high water and suspended for the winter in November when the water again came over the tops of the dams. As soon as the piers of the bridge had been laid dry it was found that they were in such a bad state that underpinning them threatened to bring down the whole structure and so a new bridge was recommended, which it was estimated would cost just over £2,000 more than underpinning the old bridge. It was proposed to replace the eight arches and navigation arch of the 1706 bridge with five arches and an opening swivel bridge. This was sanctioned, Sykes & Brookfield won the contract, the first stone was laid on 17 July 1843 and by the end of December five of the six arches had been keyed in. The bridge was completed, the swivel bridge installed and it was opened to traffic within a year on 25 July. It is interesting that the contractors asked to be allowed to substitute 'teak wood or African oak' for Irish oak for the planking of the opening bridge. A small amount of money was allowed to deepen the old harbour, the final works completed to remove the dams and finish the surrounding area. The country was in an increasingly troubled state with partial failures of the potato crop in 1817 and 1822 even before the Great Famine struck in 1846, and there was much unemployment, destitution and distress. There had been trouble here from people looking for work, which led to police protection being needed for the works and this was not withdrawn until 1844 when the

works were finished. Sykes was reprimanded for blasting 'in a very incautious and improper manner' and for keeping powder in the blacksmith's forge.

To facilitate all the work on the upper river, the commissioners closed the navigation completely from March 1845 each year for the summer months and it was not declared officially open to boats drawing 4ft (1.20m) until August 1848. Excavation of shoals had to be carried out at Kilnacarrow, Crompawn, Erra, Cloonberlaw and the Lodge Cut between Lanesborough and Tarmonbarry. This work was started in 1844 and again stanks had to be created at most of these places and at Crompawn the steam dredger was able to excavate a navigable channel. The work was more extensive at the Lodge Cut where a longitudinal dam had to be put in to close off the areas to be deepened. In addition to the pumps operated by horses, steam engines also had to be used here to keep the pits dry. The work was still going on in 1846 after three years of struggling with the continual battle to keep the pits dry and, eventually, it was completed and the dredger was brought in to remove the dams.

The decision had been made as early as December 1839 to abandon Rhodes's original idea of creating a new canal from Tarmonbarry to Lough Forbes and to use the river instead, because they realized they were going to have to remove shoals and deepen the river up to Lough Forbes in any case to improve the run-off in the river to lessen the impact of flooding. This change of plan now involved building a weir downstream of the bridge, with the new lock at one end, similar to the method used at Athlone, and it was estimated that this would bring about a saving of £19,000 over the original plan of the new canal. Work did not begin at once but, owing to the increasing destitution of the people in the spring and summer of 1842, some work was begun in clearing shoals upstream of Tarmonbarry Bridge. There was a temporary strike with the men seeking wages higher than the 10d per day offered but the men were told the work was only being undertaken at this time to relieve their distress 'and if dissatisfied with their payment it is quite optional with them to leave'. However, the commissioners did add that there would be the promise of constant employment for a considerable number of people for some years.

Sykes & Brookfield won the contract and when the river bed around the piers of the bridge was laid dry, this bridge, as had happened at Lanesborough, was also considered too dangerous to underpin and a new bridge was authorized. The existing bridge between the island and the Longford shore was considered to be sufficiently sound, because the river did not need to be deepened on that side and the piers could be safely underpinned and so it was proposed that the western seven arches should be replaced by four arches and a new swivel bridge; the increased cost of this was just under £1,600. A contract was entered into and work began in 1843, and the piers and abutments were built so that the bridge and swivel bridge could be completed in the following year.

The fact that the upper river broadened out into lakes in places meant that towing by steamer was going to be needed but, when work on the lock began, C.W. Williams agreed with the decision to make the upper Shannon locks of a smaller scale because he said that the invention of the screw propellor meant that the same width was not now required as was needed for paddle wheelers and the dimensions agreed were 110ft (33.5m) by 30ft (9m) mitre to mitre.

The commissioners had in fact written to Messrs Grantham & Page in June 1843 seeking information about 'a new discipline of steam propellor' so that they could judge whether it could be adapted to steam navigation on the Shannon. Some indication of the troubled state of the country, just prior of the onset of the famine years, is apparent in the fact that Sykes & Brookfield received a threatening notice that their magazine of gunpowder at Tarmonbarry was going to be blown up. They were advised that they must store the minimum quantity at all times and that four barrels was the absolute maximum allowed.

Most of the work on the lock was completed by 1844 even though it had been hampered by rising water bursting over the dams from time to time. The work on the weir had also begun together with making an embanked road down to the lock. To ease the flow of water when the river was in flood, the lock gates on the old canal at Clondara were thrown open but this created problems for Fleming's mill. Because this lock was still needed as access to the Royal Canal and was in a very bad condition and needed considerable repairs, some of chamber walls had to be taken down and rebuilt. The greater portion of the Tarmonbarry contract was completed by the end of 1845 with just the coping stones on the new lock and quay wall, closing off the weir and further excavation of the river bed, to be completed in 1846.

An immense amount of hard rock had to be excavated from the river bed to make a channel up to Lough Forbes, enclosing each area with stanks as before. Some of the excavated material was used to form the dams and the remainder was wheeled into spoil to form embankments along the river edge with the rock laid on the outer edge as rough pitching. The banks had to be built up and a back drain made to prevent flooding, because of the higher level of the water in the river due to the new weir. There appear to have been problems with the contractors who did not complete their contracts in the same satisfactory manner as their earlier ones and it was mutually agreed that Mackenzie

would take over and complete the work at the Curlew shoal and Gannon's Island. He was the contractor for the works upstream at Roosky and he was depending on the completion of the works at Tarmonbarry, the opening of the weir and the clearing of all the shoals in the river up to Lough Forbes, to bring down the level of water upstream. However, when the dams were finally removed, the water in the Camlin River fell so much that the headrace to Fleming's mill at Clondara had insufficient water. The commissioners had to accept responsibility for the changes in levels caused by the new navigation works and agreed to deepen the head and tail races, pay for alterations required to the machinery and put in a new regulating weir. They were able to put in a dam and divert the water down the short Clondara canal through the lock and dry out the water course to the mill to carry out the work. The men were paid 'by task' and while they objected at first, they soon found that they could earn more if they worked hard, and the work actually cost less to achieve. Over one hundred men were employed; this work was carried out in 1846-1848, at a time when the ravages of the famine were making matters considerably worse and the commissioners drew attention to how important it was to give employment to the able-bodied.

Some dredging work was needed in the passage between the upper and lower parts of Lough Forbes and an extensive amount of work was needed on the river between Lough Forbes and Roosky in two places, between Clooneen Cox and Clooneen Kennedy and at Bird Island. The situation was made more difficult in April 1845 when threatening notices appeared and, because there was no police presence, the men would not work. Eventually a police presence was created and a temporary footbridge erected so that they could patrol both sides of the river.

Rhodes's original plans for Roosky, to widen the old canal and build a new lock on it, had been changed at the same time as the other changes downstream at Tarmonbarry had been made in December 1839. This now involved abandoning the old canal and using the main river channel. The works were advertised, with a two-year period to complete them and security of 15 per cent of the tender price, and William Mackenzie won the contract with his estimate of £18,502. Because the work of underpinning the bridge was so expensive and there was only an increase of just over £2,000 to build a new bridge, this was agreed. The old bridge had nine arches one of which was a larger central arch and two of them small pedestrian arches at either end. It was proposed to replace these with six arches. Work on the lock began in 1844, the old bridge was blown up and a temporary one installed with the first stone of the new bridge laid in August of that year. The possibility of making the centre arch high enough to pass steamers was considered but the Marquis of Westmeath protested that this would exclude pleasure craft with masts from coming up the river and that it was an area that was very desirable for gentlemen's residences and 'every owner of such would naturally wish for a sailing vessel'. In response they did agree to put in a swivel bridge on the east side in this case but the need to keep costs down was to make them abandon installing any further opening bridges in the Jamestown canal and farther upstream.

There were about 700 men on average employed and Mackenzie was forced to complain when the police protection was removed. In one week the number employed reached a peak of 2,865 men. Controlling these large numbers became a problem over the next few years. Mackenzie said that the men were 'composed of different factions and come from different counties' and that large sums of money were being distributed once a fortnight,

which made the men vulnerable and there were a number of bad characters among the workmen. An appeal was made to the Lord Lieutenant and the situation worsened with gunpowder being stolen from the contractors. The problems resurfaced in the following year: 'Here have been combinations among the workmen in the district alluded to near Roosky, attended with more organisation and violence than usual.' A military force was offered which the commissioners welcomed as a precautionary measure. Eventually a case against some of the men was heard at Roosky and nine of them were convicted, which usually meant transportation. It was agreed that workers would be dismissed for concealing any antiquities found in the course of the works at former fording places but, to encourage them to produce them, they would receive some payment.

In the meantime the work was progressing; longitudinal

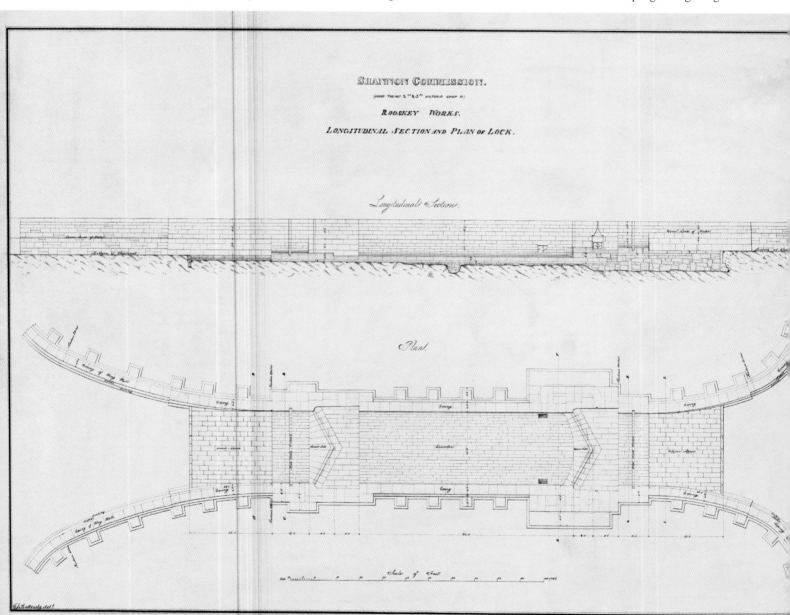

Roosky: Thomas Rhodes's design for the new lock. (Waterways Ireland)

and cross dams were made to dry out sections for the removal of the shoals and eel weirs and work on the bridge and lock was proceeding. By the end of 1844, the lock was nearly finished together with the quay wall above it. The foundations for the new lock were found to be sufficiently sound of hard gravel clay and boulder stones to dispense with the proposed puddle and timber platforms. All the arches of the new bridge were keyed in and work was nearing completion on fitting the swivel bridge. Ironically, in 1846 it was reported that the works were held up because it was becoming difficult to get labourers during the harvest period; the famine and emigration had reduced the available workforce. The foundations for the new weir were laid and work began on the new lock house. In 1847, because of the difficulties involved in keeping the enclosures dry enough to remove the shoals, the contractor made a dam right across the river and diverted the water down the old canal. The riverbed was laid dry and he was just about to start work in August when the dam burst and had to be repaired. For the next weeks the men worked night and day and they had scarcely managed to complete what had to be done and remove their tools when the dam burst in three places and the whole river was flooded. Another large shoal still had to be removed at Pigeon Island, near the entrance into Lough Bofin, which was done in 1848.

ROOSKY TO JAMESTOWN AND THE CARNADOE WATERS

Tenders were sought for the works in the Carnadoe Waters in 1844 and three were received: Mackenzie, Samuel Gamble and Richard Gray. Mackenzie's was accepted and the works were all achieved in 1845. The potential of opening up these lakes had been realized back in 1830 when a local landowner, Molloy McDermott, had approached the Royal Canal Company indicating that he intended to rebuild Carnadoe Bridge and Grange Bridge, put in a lock and bring the navigation up to within a mile of Elphin.[2] He was looking for the company's help with the stonework involved but, as he did not get any assistance, he appears to have dropped the idea. In December an armed gang attacked the workers and four police were allocated to guard them. The commissioners had to deepen and straighten the channel from Lough Boderg, a new bridge and quay were built at Carnadoe and the winding channel between Carnadoe and Kilglass loughs was replaced by a short canal.

There were also three extensive areas to be cleared between Lough Bofin and the Jamestown canal, at Derrycarne between Lough Bofin and Boderg, at a place known as The Dancing Stone, at the head of Lough Boderg and in Lough Tap. At Derrycarne three and a half acres were laid dry by dams and double shifts of men were used through the summer of 1848. As this was in the narrow neck between the two lakes, the dams were exposed to waves from the lakes and special measures had to be taken to protect them. By this time many lessons had been learnt and two rows of iron piles were driven in about 4ft (1.2m) apart, in cross section and properly stayed. Each pair was about 12ft (3.6m) distant and the intersecting space was filled with puddle, protected by planks set on edge and supported by the piles, thus forming a watertight enclosure. The report added: 'This plan was found very efficacious, and to it may be greatly attributed the rapidity and success with which this shoal was removed.' The Dancing Stone obstruction was caused by an old causeway, known as Skeagh Causeway, which had been formed leading from the ancient monastery of Kilmore; it had been the cause of many problems for boats when the

Jamestown: a new bridge and quay were constructed in the 1840s. (Walter Borner)

water was low. In Lough Tap much soft boggy material was removed and deposited in the deep water outside the shoal. There is no island shown on the drawings and the island that is there today was probably formed from these dredgings.

The possibility of using the river instead of the Jamestown Canal had been considered back in 1839 but the option of straightening the canal, widening it and building a new lock was considered more practical for this location. Rhodes had intended to put in swivel bridges over the canal and now this time the commissioners stuck to their decision to have fixed bridges from here on up the river to try to keep down costs. The stone-arched bridges would have to be skew bridges to allow for the approaches. In 1844 seven

tenders were received for the Jamestown works, a contract was entered into with Jeffs & Sons and work began at once and carried on through the winter excavating the canal. They erected a small steam engine to draw the loaded wagons up an inclined plane from the bottom of the old canal and one fatal accident was reported from the banks falling in. The two old accommodation bridges were taken down and abutments for the new bridges erected. Work continued through 1845 to complete the bridges and continue the excavation, and at one stage Messrs Jeffs were made to take down and rebuild the retaining walls at one of the bridges. The part of the old canal between the site of the old lock and the new one caused much difficulty because it was soft, wet bog to a great depth and it kept rising up and slipping. They had to resort to digging it out and filling it in with heavy rubble.

The excavation was sufficiently completed to start work on the lock in 1846. The lock dimensions were the same as Tarmonbarry and Roosky. The site proved better than expected with a gravel formation located between boggy ground above it, which might have been an old river course, and another below the lock site. This meant that they were able to dispense with the intended puddling under the lock. In the meantime there were constant problems with the canal banks from subsidence particularly near the Black Lough where the bank had to be re-formed and widened. During 1848, while the coping of the lock was being finished, they were still having problems with the bottom of the canal rising in the boggy sections. They had to wait until

Jamestown Canal: in this instance Thomas Rhodes's original plan to widen and straighten the old canal was carried out.

Jamestown Canal: the new lock was re-sited and enlarged and a lock house built.

the embankments settled and consolidated, which were the cause of the bottom rising, and more and more clay had to be added to the section of embankment at the Black Lough. Eventually, the work was completed and the lock was named the Albert Lock to honour the Prince Consort.

Work also began on making coffer dams for the new Jamestown Bridge in 1844. This work was completed in 1846, the new bridge was opened and the old seven-arched one was removed. A new quay was also constructed above the bridge. Much of the masonry for the new bridge was provided by the excavated rock from the canal as well as good hydraulic lime from the boulder stones. In the loop of the river the shoals, eel weirs and the old mill works, which had been responsible for a great deal of the flooding upstream, were all removed. While this work was in progress the river was diverted down the canal and around the lock works by erecting dams at the new bridge and above the lock. This led to legal action being taken against Jeffs by Mr Lawder of Lowfield for flooding of his land caused by the diversion. The weir was built quickly, founded on rock and much of it formed out of the same rock before the rising water flooded the river. A temporary gap was left in the weir so as to keep the level down to facilitate the works farther upstream. While the river was dried out, Drumsna Bridge was examined and some of the shoals and eel weirs removed. The bridge was not replaced and instead the

piers, which were found to be 'nothing more than common rubble-stone, loosely bedded together', were cased in cut-stone pointed with Roman cement, as underpinning was considered to be too dangerous.

Drumsna: the old bridge here was retained and underpinned.

JAMESTOWN TO CARRICK-ON-SHANNON

Five areas of shoal had to be removed between the Jamestown canal and Carrick: at Kilbride Deer Park, Doyle's Islands, Cornacorrow, Inishmucker and Grose's Islands. Sykes & Brookfield won the contract for this work. There were several problems with the works at Doyle's Islands. In 1844 the works were interrupted by the 'lawless conduct of a large body of men' and an appeal was made for more police. A few days later the dams around the excavation gave way because of the rise in the river. The material excavated was heaped on the islands to provide better shelter. At Cornacorrow, while removing the shoal, the very sharp bend in the river was improved and work continued through 1845 until stopped by the winter floods. At Grose's Islands the deepest channel was to the east of the islands but the lower island was dredged away and the spoil from it together with that removed from the shoal was deposited on the larger island with the navigation channel changing to the west of it.

Tenders were sought for the works at Carrick in December 1844 in ten Irish newspapers, the London *Times* and the *Liverpool Courier*. Tenders were received from some of the usual people: Mackenzie, Sykes and Jeffs and also from Samuel Gamble, Williams and Richard Gray. Gray's tender, which was the lowest, was accepted. At Carrick the eleven-arch bridge had to be taken down and replaced by a five-arch bridge and the river channel deepened in the vicinity of the bridge; some houses had to be demolished to alter the angle of the road approach. A temporary wooden bridge was erected and when it was ready the old bridge was removed, which was done using gunpowder. A shaft in the centre of each pier was sunk and wadded with 125lbs of powder: 'when fired the explosion was most successful, throwing down the part required, and without injuring in the slightest degree the temporary wooden bridge'. The

Carrick-on-Shannon: the bridge here was replaced reducing the number of arches to improve the flow.

first stone of the new bridge was laid in July 1845 with work beginning on the land arch on the Leitrim side. An attempt was made to unwater the stanks by putting in a cross dam without success. However, work went ahead simultaneously on the bridge, the quay wall and the harbour and the centres of the next two arches were fixed by October 1845. Work on the harbour and bridge was going well when floods came down and burst the dams, 'and it was with great difficulty the workmen were able to escape'.

Work continued through 1846 and considerable difficulty was experienced in keeping the coffer dams at the bridge works free from water. It continued to boil up through the bottom and they had to use sods and even wooden hurdles to try to keep it out. The four-horse engine working six wooden pumps had to be operated continuously, 'besides a considerable number of men scooping day and night'. There were problems as well with the downstream quay, which had to be taken down and rebuilt because it sank down into the soft bog. The new bridge was opened to the public early in 1847 and all the other work was completed except the harbour which, because of the softness of the material, continued to suffer from slipping.

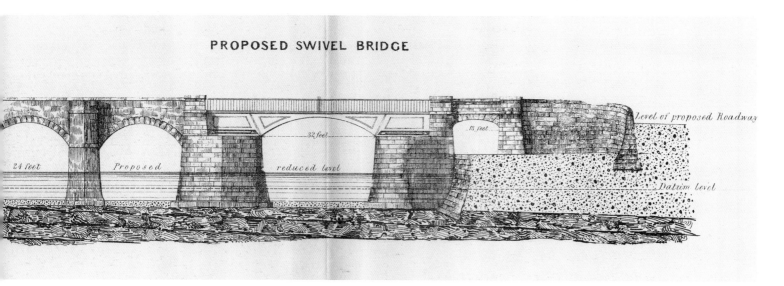

PROPOSED SWIVEL BRIDGE

Carrick-on-Shannon: Thomas Rhodes's original plan for an opening span in the new bridge which was not carried out.

CARRICK-ON-SHANNON TO LOUGH ALLEN

To improve the navigation in the River Shannon up to the Lough Allen Canal, further excavation of shoals and eel weirs was needed in a number of places. At Hartley, which had been a fording place in the past, a channel was made on one side by the steam dredger. Farther up river, at Port, the short running canal was abandoned and a navigation channel made on the other side of the island by excavating through the shoal and eel weirs using dams to create stanks. The final stretch of river up to Battlebridge was both shallow and winding. Short cuts were made across the worst bends and the river was deepened with the aim of achieving a five-foot navigation.

Battlebridge: the old bridge was retained and undepinned.

It had already been decided at an early stage that works on the Lough Allen Canal would be limited to very basic improvements and any question of lengthening the locks was abandoned. In 1847-1848 the canal was dammed off and laid dry so that the planned remedial works on this 'narrow and somewhat imperfect still-water navigation' could be carried out, which included underpinning Battlebridge lock and altering the sills to adjust to the new water levels caused by the excavations. In addition, at Mount Allen, work took place in making the new cut to divert the waters of the Arigna River directly into Lough Allen, which had formerly joined the Shannon where it exited from the lake, bringing down much silt in flood waters from the mountains. This also involved changing the road layout, which was negotiated with the local authority, and work on the cut began in 1842. A list of some of the tools to be sent to the works are a useful indication of the methods used: 3 dozen wheelbarrows, 4 dozen shovels, 4 dozen spades, 1 dozen clay picks, 50 12-ft wheeling planks. The eel weirs and other obstructions had to be removed from the Shannon at its place of exit to further improve the run-off from the lake.

There was a very interesting bridge at Bellantra, Drumherriff Bridge, the only bridge between Battlebridge

and Lough Allen, located about halfway down the main river. It was known locally as 'the wooden bridge' and was a good example of the traditional early form of bridge used in Ireland to span large rivers. John Long who surveyed this part of the river,[3] described it as follows:

... it was built of loose stone piers, such as a common labourer would build, placed close to each other; some rough black oak logs thrown across from pier to pier, and these covered with wicker work in several layers, and gravel etc. strewn on these. It was very frail, and the horse was unyoked from the cart, and the latter pulled across by men.

Rhodes included an elevation of this bridge with the other existing Shannon bridges in the 1833 report with ten piers 7ft 6in (2.2m) apart with 'hurdles' and 'wicker mats' indicated and a 'road surface of gravel'. This bridge was subsequently superseded by a five-span stone-arch bridge in the 1890s at the time when further excavation work was being carried out, but the old bridge remained for some time a short distance upstream and the new bridge became known as 'the wooden bridge'.

THE BOYLE WATER

Tenders were received from four contractors for the opening up of these waters and Jeffs of Killester won the contract. There were a number of small shallows and two major areas of shoal to be removed: one at Tumna, at the entrance to Lough Drumharlow, and a longer stretch at Annaleckey and the Doctor's Weir, upstream of Lough Drumharlow. In addition shoals and eel weirs had to be removed at Cootehall and Knockvicar and this included a long stretch of river at Knockvicar where a new lock was to be built and a weir. As Rhodes had already indicated, the old eight-arch bridge at Cootehall and the nine-arch one at Knockvicar were in a bad condition and the narrow arches were impeding the flow and would have to be replaced by new three-arch bridges. The Boyle River also had to be straightened, widened and deepened up to Boat House Ford.

Cootehall: the Shannon Commissioners' new bridge.

Work began in 1845 but Rhodes's plan to locate the new bridges downstream of the old ones was not followed and they were built on the original sites. At Cootehall longitudinal dams were used to create coffer dams and work was carried out on one side of the river at a time. The shoals to be removed were of rock, which lay in thick beds and this was then used for the piers of the new bridge. Work continued excavating the shoals and putting in the piers for the new bridge and it was opened to the public in November 1848.

Knockvicar: the Shannon Commissioners' new bridge.(Walter Borner)

At Knockvicar, some changes were also made in Rhodes's original siting of the lock as well as the bridge. He had intended diverting out of the river above the bridge by excavating a channel into the existing millrace, with the proposed weir extending right across the river. It was now decided to deepen the river and keep the navigation in it with the lock sited at the east end of the weir. The same method was used to build the new bridge as at Cootehall but keeping the enclosed areas dry was very difficult and 126 men worked day and night manning the pumps. It was possible to remove some of the pressure by diverting the water down the millrace. They erected a 'gangtree' of 45ft (13.7m) span, which traversed over the site of the new bridge.

Messrs Jeffs were praised for the exemplary conduct of the workmen, 'they have been throughout industrious and peaceable'. Work on the new bridge was nearly completed by the end of 1846 and the lock pit was also nearly finished although there had been constant problems with the dams bursting. The stone excavated for the lock was suitable to use to make the ashlars for the chamber. The clearing of all the shoals above and below the lock was also ongoing and a stank created to start work on one end of the weir. Work also was carried out on the Boyle River up to Boathouse Ford but the 'spoon and bag' system proved very slow and it was decided to wait until one of the steam dredgers could pass through into Lough Key, which was all achieved by 1849.

Robert Edward King (Lord Lorton) engaged John Nash to design his mansion at Rockingham in 1810 and had carried out extensive improvements to the estate. Amongst other

Knockvicar: the Shannon Commissioners' new weir which remains unaltered. (Walter Borner)

things he had two short ornamental canals cut through the isthmus, creating Drumman's island, one of them spanned by a bridge constructed with stones of strange shapes from the lake, which had been eaten away by the acidic waters of Lough Key. He also made a canal for a number of miles into the nearby bog so that fuel could be brought to the house, which was carried up an underground passage from the quay so as not to impinge on the view from the house. This private canal had a lock and an attractive ornamental bridge constructed over it. Although the estate owned all the foreshore and islands, the navigation through to the Boyle River was a public facility, a fact which was to become an issue one hundred years later.

COSTS & ACCOUNTS

It has been shown that there were many major changes made in Rhodes's original plans for the works. The estimates, based on the original plans, had amounted to £584,805, represented by £510,751 for the works and £74,154 for acquisition of property and compensation. Half of the total was to be repaid by the counties together with contributions from individual landowners for piers and harbours in the estuary, who were to pay £27,755. The commissioners had to work within this original estimate and were not allowed to exceed a draw down of more than £100,000 in any year. In most cases, where changes were made, the works proved more expensive and inevitably cutbacks had to be made elsewhere to compensate. Their accounts were further complicated by the fact that they had to advance half the expenditure in the form of loans to the counties and individuals, which then had to be repaid over a period of ten years in twenty half-yearly instalments, together with 4 per cent interest. Apart from a dispute about the Limerick repayments due to changes in the boundaries between the county and city and a small amount due from John Scott for a pier at Kildysart in the estuary, the Grand Juries kept up the payments as required.

The commissioners adopted a system of dividing their accounting into seven divisions in their annual reports: Establishment, Boundary Survey, Works, Repayments by Counties and Individuals, Advances as Loans, Rents & Tolls and a General Abstract. They imposed a very strict system of reporting expenditure on their district and resident engineers. The expenditure on the establishment worked out at an average of £3,500 p.a., which included payments to the commissioners and staff in the Custom House and the engineers and others on the river, whose role was to supervise the contractors. The account handling the largest amounts of money was the one for the actual works, which was averaging at about £80,000 p.a. The Rents & Tolls account, which initially was just breaking even, began to produce a reasonable profit with an increase in traffic,

Lough Key: the lock and bridge constructed for Lord Lorton about 1810 for his private canal to bring turf down from his nearby bog to Rockingham House.

despite the obstructions caused by the works, so that by 1848 there was a surplus in this account of over £1,000.

As time went on and it became clear that they were going to run into difficulty keeping down costs, cuts were made in the establishment to try to save money and more and more savings had to be effected in the works. By the end of 1845 a summary of the position shows why these cutbacks had to happen:

Year	Total	Grant	Loans	Repayments
1840	100,000	50,000	50,000	nil
1841	52,500	26,250	26,250	8,601
1842	78,000	39,000	39,000	16,187
1843	80,000	40,000	40,000	18,636
1844	70,000	35,000	35,000	27,256
1845	60,000	30,000	30,000	30,382
Total	440,500	220,250	220,250	101,064

In 1846 a further £55,000 was issued and the final £89,305 was drawn down to complete the final outstanding works by 1849.

In early 1847 it is recorded in the minutes that the accounts were in arrear and had not been submitted for audit. This was blamed on the pressure caused by 'the relief business' caused by the famine years; this was now diminishing, so more attention could be devoted to the accounts. However, in November of that year the commissioners reported that they had taken proceedings against their Chief Accountant, Henry John Mason for embezzlement and forgery.[4] This had only come to light because Mason had an accident and was off work for a period during which time the fraud was discovered. It would appear that he had been embezzling money and moving sums backwards and forwards between the accounts to cover this up; the Tolls & Rents account was now found to be short by £8,018. The secretary, Hornsby, was in the habit of leaving blank signed sheets with Mason, which he could then countersign without supervision.

Mason was also altering the amounts on cheques for 'relief works' by carefully inserting figures to alter the total. He was able to obtain further money when paying out on contracts by adding subsistence and then cancelling this out by making adjustments against payments of actual works. He was convicted of embezzlement and larceny but acquitted of forgery and sentenced to seven years' transportation.

In their summing up in the 11th and Final Report in 1850, the commissioners reported that the works had been completed within budget and had been 'effectively carried out, as far as contingent circumstances would permit'. They claimed that any variations from the original plans had been approved. The building of the regulating weirs and the removal of the many obstructions caused by shoals, eel weirs and the old many-arched bridges had greatly reduced flooding 'except during heavy and continued falls of rain, and the prevalence of high winds from the west and south-west, which have the effect of backing up the water above its natural levels'. All these claims were to be disputed in the 1860s when major flooding occurred. The commissioners were also able to point to the increasing traffic on the river revealed in the trade figures. An Act in 1846 had transferred the powers of the Shannon Commissioners to the Board of Works but as the three commissioners were also the commissioners of the Board of Works this seemed to make little difference, with Harry Jones as the chairman of both, and both establishments based in the Custom House.[5] The last entry in the minute books of the commission was in October 1847 but they continued to produce annual reports to parliament until 1850. At this stage, with the works officially completed, the Shannon Commission ceased to exist and the navigation passed de facto into the hands of the Office of Public Works without any actual change in the administration.

THE EMERGENCE OF THE CIVIL ENGINEER

Back in 1771 Smeaton had been involved in establishing the Smeatonian Society of Civil Engineers in England, creating a clear distinction between military and civil engineering. Some of these early engineers had emerged from craftsmen. Smeaton had been a watchmaker and moved from an interest in developing instrumentation into civil engineering.[6] In Ireland the early engineers were largely from military backgrounds but the Bogs Commission from 1807 – 1812 marks the beginning of a gradual transition to civil engineering. It was the Board of Works engineers, Burgoyne, Radcliffe and others, including the mechanical engineer and metallurgist Robert Mallett, who had been involved in public works such as the Bogs Commission, the Shannon Navigation and arterial drainage schemes, who were responsible for coming together in 1835 to establishing the Civil Engineers Society of Ireland.[7] In 1842 Trinity College Dublin had established its first chair in Engineering 'recognising that nature was both an ally and an adversary'.[8] Then in 1844 this society was reorganized as the Institution of Civil Engineers of Ireland 'for the promotion of mechanical science and more particularly for the acquisition of that species of knowledge which constitutes the profession of Civil Engineer'. It was initially based in the Custom House in accommodation provided by the Board of Works until the administration of relief measures as a result of the famine years led to their rooms being required for emergency staff in 1853.

THE IMPACT ON RELIEVING DISTRESS

The navigation and drainage works on the Shannon had been undertaken as one of the government's schemes to create employment and thereby relieve distress, in addition to the longer-term contribution to the economy by providing improved means of transport and increasing the availability of agricultural land by relieving flooding. It was just a coincidence that the years of the works were to partly coincide with the famine years and, looking at the records written at the time, there is little doubt that the full implications of these events in the history of Ireland were not fully realized. Reading the official reports to parliament there is little to point to what was occurring other than occasional references to general unrest, the distress of the people and strikes for more money.

However, the minutes of the commissioners did reflect the worsening situation by 1846. There is a reference in the Shannon Commission's minutes to a visit in February 1846 from Randolph Routh and Mr Coffin of the Scarcity Commission to ascertain what the position was about movement of boats on the river. Requests were also coming in from magistrates and clergy for providing additional employment who were told that the commissioners 'only had power under the Act to execute works provided for' and the requests were sent on to the Scarcity Committee. The collector in County Clare was instructed to pay the customary wages, 'and if the committee appointed for the purpose consider it necessary, he will pay them every evening, not exacting too much work from those whose distress may have rendered them incapable of hard work'.

By the middle of 1846, the commissioners were receiving requests for funding from Poor Relief committees. They replied that they could not give funding but were endeavouring to increase employment wherever possible 'consistent with the proper discharge of the duties entrusted to them'. They did do their best to keep the navigation operational to help with the movement of supplies; tolls were remitted on all supplies forwarded by the government. The desperate situation is reflected in the fact that permission was also being given for occasional relief works. The Banagher Poor Relief Committee was allowed to have men break stones on the river bank and in Athlone permission was given to dig out a sewer and open it into the river. Already by the autumn of 1846 there was a reference to 'the difficulty of obtaining labourers in some districts'. Death and emigration were beginning to have an effect.

It has to be remembered as well that the three Shannon Commissioners, Jones, who had replaced Burgoyne as chairman, Griffith and Radcliffe, were also commissioners of Public Works and the annual reports of the Office of Public Works, which was the government department that took the brunt for coping with the increasing crisis, do reflect what was happening on the ground. In 1846 giving employment to the destitute poor became a priority. There is a reference to the 'disease again appearing, and much more general, required that greater aid should be afforded to meet the distress this continued calamity would produce'.[9] In their 1847 report they referred to 'The deranging effect which the famine and distress arising from the failure of the potato crop in 1845-6-7 had upon all the proceedings and all relations of life, whether social, physical or moral, in this country.'[10] Large amounts of money were made available in the form of loans to the counties and to individuals to promote works. Many of the schemes were to improve land through drainage and the counties also promoted road schemes. The issue of whether direct relief was required was mentioned in this report. The utility of some of the works was questioned and whether the money could have been 'more judiciously spent in food'. During the nine months from October 1846 until June 1847, 100,000 people were employed on schemes but direct relief was only used in the April to June period. Allocations of funding after these years were towards schemes of 'a more permanent and reproductive character now that the immense operations carried on during the late period of distress have happily come to a close'. The need for a large military and police presence continued and in 1847 it was reported that a gunboat, a sailing boat called the *Pluto,* had arrived on Lough Ree to forestall raids on grain boats.[11]

By 1848, as far as drainage works were concerned, it became a question of limiting funding to the completion of existing works.[12] The situation was assessed in the 1849 report:

The third year in succession of the agricultural crisis under which this country has been suffering, has now passed away, and all persons capable of reflection perceive at length, that they must rely on their own exertions, and not further depend on external aid to help them out of the difficulties by which they are surrounded.[13]

Some of the reports coming in expressed difficulty in getting men, particularly in harvest time and 'some parts of the country are quite deserted'. By 1850 there are references to the 'vast flow of emigration still in active progress. . . where formerly two thousand men could with ease be daily procured, as many as a hundred are now with difficulty to be got'.[14] Thus it may be seen that the records of the time did not really fully reflect the vast changes the events of these years in the 1840s were going to bring about in Ireland's troubled history.

CHAPTER NINE
'DRAIN THE SHANNON'

FLOODING ISSUES

Back in the 1820s John Grantham had used the expression 'draining the Shannon' in his report and this was to become a perennial phrase down the years. Even before the early navigation works Bishop Bolton of Clonfert was said to have made twelve miles of drains in the callows in the 1720s, work which was continued by Bishop Whitcombe in 1735.[1] Right from the start, in the early eighteenth century, work on navigations had always been linked to the beneficial effects such works would have on drainage, hence the 'tillage' duties at that time. In the case of the early works on the Shannon, improving the navigation had been the objective and flooding had remained a problem. This is borne out by a description of the callows in 1801: 'richly clothed in meadow, but all insulated and, of a wet season, in a very precarious state'.[2] At this time the callows were all parts of large estates. The 5th Report of the Shannon Commission in 1839 contained S. Nicholson's valuation of the callow lands, complete with useful maps, following his comprehensive survey of the soil and land conditions.[3] A distinction has to be made between the annual winter flooding, which enriched the land leaving behind silt, which Nicholson said created 'rich dark clayey loam suitable for meadow' when the floods subsided, and summer flooding, which caused major problems in trying to save the hay. There are frequent references to frantic efforts to save the hay when the summer flood waters began to rise. Nicholson estimated their value as hay meadows as they were subject to periodic flooding and also what their value would be if drained. In addition to the middle Shannon callows, he showed extensive lands where flooding occurred along the upper river and also between Meelick and Portumna.

The major works under the Shannon Commissioners were ostensibly addressing both navigation and drainage issues. However, their upbeat 11th and Final Report, issued in March 1850, had included a note of warning.[4] Referring to the fact that they estimated that the works had relieved 18,750 acres from 'lengthened or occasional flooding' of land that previously had been inundated for six months a year, they did report that there were places where the river channel was too narrow to allow great flood waters to discharge rapidly. They added:

It is therefore probable that at some future period, when works of arterial drainage have been executed through the great catchment basin of the Suck and other tributaries of the Shannon, that it may become necessary to make additional excavation at some of the comparatively confined channels of the Shannon above and below Shannonbridge, and immediately above the weir at Meelick. Fortunately such works, though probably indispensable, will not be very expensive.

There is no doubt that the need to stay within the overall estimate for the works had led in many cases to achieving a sufficient navigation channel, rather than the widening and deepening originally planned to improve the run-off in the river.

The emphasis was now beginning to shift; drainage issues were to receive more attention and for a number of reasons the works carried out by the commissioners were to come under scrutiny almost immediately. Arterial drainage works had become an important element of government relief schemes leading up to and during the famine years.[5] In 1842 responsibility had rested with a board of commissioners with the Board of Works commissioners acting in an ex-officio capacity.[6] William T. Mulvany, who had been one of the engineers engaged in the Shannon works in the 1840s, became the engineer responsible for these works in addition to fishery works. The 1842 Act had laid down that landowners were responsible for carrying out preliminary surveys. Two-thirds of the relevant owners then had to agree to the works and they were then undertaken, paid for by means of loans charged on the lands. In 1846, because of the need for famine relief works, Mulvany's hand had been strengthened by the Summary Proceedings Act, which enabled him to proceed with cursory surveys and initiate works with only half the landowners assenting to the costs involved.[7] In his efforts to promote as much employment as possible, Mulvany soon had over 17,000 men working on arterial drainage schemes throughout the country. When the landowners were subsequently charged for these works, there was a storm of protest and he was later found to have exceeded estimates for specific works without the landowners' agreement.

Early in 1847 the government had been forced to introduce a change in policy by offering direct relief and from 1850 the Treasury control in the public economy was more intensive and effective. Mulvany continued to oversee arterial drainage works and make awards for payment until 1852 when a House of Lords inquiry was pursued by Lord Rosse.[8] He put forward two grounds of complaint: that the proprietors had insufficient control over which schemes would be initiated and secondly that the works were carried out by contract and were open to abuse through the employment of direct labour. Mulvany was made a scapegoat as a result of the inquiry, although the accusations of 'mismanagement and jobbery' were largely unproven.[9] The rights of the landowners were what was at issue and it was alleged that the case was heard by a 'committee of complainants and interested parties as accusers, judges and jurors'. There was no attempt made to examine specific cases of abuse or to determine whether half measures or a more thorough approach should have been adopted. It was suggested that in some cases plans and estimates were incorrect and changes were made in them under the stress of famine relief. The outstanding debts amounting to £106,616 were remitted and Mulvany was sacrificed unfairly; he resigned and retired on pension. He subsequently went to Germany where he made a considerable name for himself, becoming involved in coal mining and the development of rail and water transport.

As a result of the proceedings of the inquiry, no new arterial drainage works were undertaken by the Board of Works and responsibility for initiating, surveying, costing and carrying out future schemes reverted to the landowners. The Board of Works still retained the power to offer technical advice, approve schemes, appoint drainage boards and make loans available. This brought about a change of emphasis from draining bogs to opening up and improving channels of discharge. An interesting and far-seeing comment had been made by Sir Charles Edward Trevelyan, assistant secretary to the Treasury, in the course of the inquiry, with reference to the works by the Shannon commissioners in improving the run-off in the river by clearing and deepening of the channel: 'but the complete drainage of the bogs extends far into the future and a great proportion of them will be more valuable as peat than for any other purpose to supply fuel to future generations'. He also identified the difference in the way in which public works were tackled between England and Ireland: 'In England for the business of private society to be done by private society is the rule and for government to do it is the exception. In Ireland for the government to do this class of work is the rule, for individuals the exception.' The difference was that the English Board of Works had deliberative powers only whereas the Irish Board of Works as set up in 1831 had deliberative and executive powers and became the principal dynamic of government action in famine relief.

The development of the railways had an enormous impact both on passenger traffic and trade on the inland waterways and none more so than on the Shannon Navigation, as shown in the previous chapter, which was to lead directly to drainage issues receiving new emphasis. This coupled with unusually severe rainfalls in the early years of the 1850s immediately called into question whether the works had achieved anything to relieve flooding or had, in fact, added to the problems. By clearing away the eel weirs and shoals and enlarging the arches at the bridges, the flow of water had been increased and this had led to sudden rapid discharges of water in times of heavy rainfall, which caused unexpected summer and autumn flooding. In addition, because the proprietors had been assisted in carrying out arterial drainage schemes as famine relief works, land around tributaries such as the Brosna, the Inny, the Camlin and the Rinn had been involved, adding to the sudden increase in the quantity of water entering the Shannon from exceptional falls of rain; schemes for the Suck had not yet received approval, which would add considerably to the problem.

FLOODING IN THE 1850s

Following heavy rainfall in the summer of 1852 severe flooding was experienced between Banagher and Meelick. Summer floods led to the destruction of the hay crop; the suddenness of the rise in the water prevented the hay being saved, creating a serious situation. The inhabitants of the lands along the river, who had just seen their counties levied for large amounts of money to pay for the major Shannon navigation and drainage works, presented a memorial to the Lord Lieutenant setting out their grievances.[10] The commissioners had rightly drawn attention to the constrictions in the channel, which they had not been able to address fully because of financial constraints, but it was the construction of the great embankments, or so-called 'regulating weirs', which were now immediately singled out as the cause of the problem. They cited the weir at Meelick as being the direct reason for their plight, pointing to the fact that a mistake was made in its construction relative to the sills of the new lock. They said that the 200-horse-power steamer had been found to have insufficient navigation depth and wooden planks had had to be added to the weir raising it

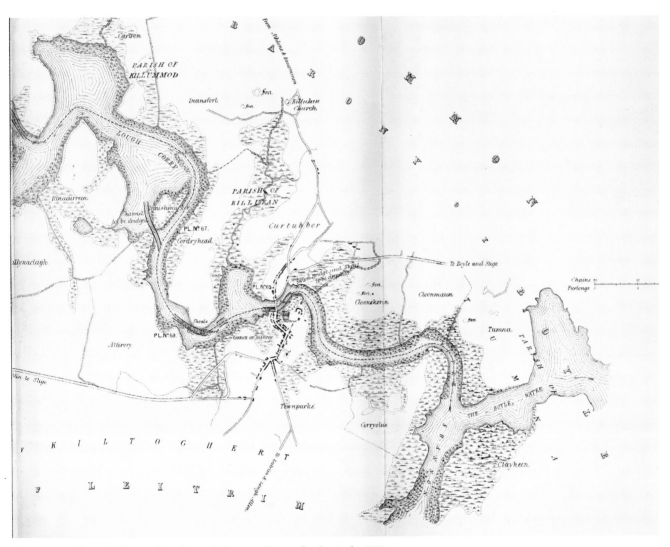

The area around Carrick showing the callows which were subject to flooding in the 1830s.

The middle Shannon at Clonmacnois in summer showing the flat land on either side which is subject to flooding. (Photograph Kevin Dwyer AIPPA)

even higher and obstructing the run-off. They called on the Lord Lieutenant to appoint an independent person to carry out an inquiry into the 'misnamed improvements' carried out by the commissioners.

Further flooding occurred in the summer of 1853 and the Board of Works responded to the memorial by pointing out that removing the former obstructions in the river had increased the flow, leading to the need to regulate it by erecting weirs. They denied that any mistakes had been made and said that the weir at Meelick had been deliberately made one foot lower to allow for a better run off and the wooden planks were needed to achieve navigation depth in summer when the river levels were low. They explained that no specific charge for drainage had been placed on the proprietors of the lands relieved by the works but instead a general charge had been levied for the improvement of the navigation and drainage of the river.

While the Board of Works accepted that the expectations of the commissioners had not been fully realized with regard to relief from flooding it was pointed out that lands, which were formerly covered for periods of six months, were now rarely covered for more than a few weeks. It was intended to carry our further excavation at the old ford above Meelick when funds became available. However, as the likelihood of surplus funds being at their disposal was not very great, this promise did not carry much weight. Although the Board of Works had insisted that much benefit had been derived from the works in the upper river, there was also correspondence from proprietors relating to problems with the Jamestown canal, with calls for the sluices on the new lock to be left open and a similar request for the sluices to be raised at the other locks down the river. The problem in this part of the river was that, trusting that the works would reduce the flooding, land had been tilled and planted that never had been before, resulting in large losses; 'many gardens covered with water, which could not be got at without a boat, the cabbage nearly covered, and the clamps of turf'.

Not surprisingly, funds did not become available, no action was taken and it was suggested that 'a mere delusion was intended'. It was not until further exceptional flooding occurred in the spring of 1857 that the whole issue escalated again. In the vicinity of Carrick many acres of potatoes and oats were destroyed and permission was given to open the sluices of Jamestown lock. In December 1858 there were further letters from the Banagher area about flooding 'adjacent to the great rampart wall at Meelick'. The sluices in both Hamilton and Victoria lock were left permanently open that winter. The correspondence went back and forth with claim and counter claim.[11] The suggestion that the *Lady Burgoyne* needed a draught of 8ft (2.4m) was stoutly denied and it was stated that when fully loaded the maximum she needed was 6ft (1.8m). In June 1860 letters were received

by the Board of Works from both Carrick and Banagher reporting serious flooding and the loss of summer crops. The Carrick letter was signed by over one hundred people and blame for the flooding was attributed to the new weir at Jamestown and they sought permission to make a breach in it. They were told that this was not possible as it would cause problems to the reach below. One of the Banagher letters complained that the summer floods did much harm making the hay crop wholly unfit for use: 'The most experienced persons in this locality know it to be fact, that floods at this season totally destroy the nutritious matter in meadow grass, that it produces sourness and bitterness in the soil, thereby rendering it poisonously destructive for fodder.' They were told that the floods were of a 'most unprecedented character, the Board can, in no degree, hold themselves responsible'. It was suggested that the commissioners had acted illegally in not leaving a 'King's gap' in the weir and the Board of Works was accused of replying with a 'Jesuitical evasive statement'. A further memorial was received from thirty proprietors bordering the river between Athlone and Meelick raising seventeen points detailing issues connected with the way the works had been carried out. The eleventh point reflected their frustration:

Your memorialists humbly submit, that besides the immense damage annually caused to private property, there is also a serious public evil resulting from these works; they exhibit striking evidence of the ignorance and negligence with which Government works are designed and executed in this country; they impress the public with the idea that everything done by Government officers is badly done: they are an outrage on common sense, and a disgrace to the engineering knowledge of the age.

A detailed memorial was submitted to the Lords Commissioners of Her Majesty's Treasury signed by thirty proprietors setting out their complaints and pointing to three great faults in the works. Firstly, the lack of sluices in the weir at Meelick even though the chairman, Colonel Burgoyne, at the time had suggested that sluices would be needed. Secondly, the failure to widen the river channel above the weir as shown in the original plans, and thirdly the blocking up of the eastern channel at Meelick that had carried off some of the flow and was now blocked up by an embankment. This channel had been blocked off because it re-entered the main channel above the weir. It was a narrow and much obstructed channel, which did not account for much of the run-off, and a pipe had been laid to take off water from it to a point below the lock. The memorialists called for immediate action to place sluices in the weir to regulate the water. The memorial was immediately passed on to the Board of Works who replied that they stood by their former statements, which admitted that the relief from flooding had not been as complete as anticipated. They explained yet again that the channel had not been widened as planned because of the hard material encountered and the insufficiency of funds. They disputed the fact that the position had been worsened by the works and believed that to lay out further money would be to employ public funds for the improvement of private property. They pointed out that they did not have the authority to carry out additional works nor did they have the funds beyond those accruing from tolls and wharfage and that their role and responsibility was simply the maintenance of the works and the regulation of the navigation as handed over to them.

The Lord Lieutenant had also received a memorial and passed it on to the Treasury in January 1862, which repeated the accusations that the works had not adhered to the plans and called for the removal of the obstructions caused by the weirs by lowering them and fitting them with sluices to allow for additional, controlled run-off. It was suggested that parliament 'will hardly condemn a large portion of the centre of Ireland to remain in perpetuity a vast swamp, discreditable and injurious to the people and to the Government'. The Treasury responded that they had also received documents from the Chamber of Commerce in Limerick and the Grand Canal Company stressing the importance of maintaining the navigation and that they did not consider that the flooding had been made worse by the works. However, they did consent to the appointment of two engineers to report whether anything could be done to lessen the problem of flooding without injuring the navigation. They imposed three conditions: that the proprietors would pay for half the cost of the inquiry, that nothing would be proposed to injure the navigation on which so much public money had been expended, and that if works were to be carried out they would be at the expense of the proprietors and executed under the superintendence of the Board of Works. A return was included of the money handed over to the Board of Works on the completion of the works amounting to £8,565, which together with receipts for the years 1851 to 1861 (averaging about £3,000 p.a.) amounted to £44,535. For the same period the expenditure on maintenance and works amounted to £43,072, leaving a balance of just £1,462. It was also stated that one of the items included in the expenditure was the sum of £8,144, which was the money 'defalcified' by the accountant that had been disallowed by the Audit Board, an issue which was to be questioned at a later date.

THE BATEMAN STUDY AND FURTHER FLOODING IN THE 1860s

J.F. Bateman, one of the engineers appointed to carry out the investigation, received his instructions in July 1862 and reported in May 1863.[12] In the meantime there had also been further exceptional floods in the summer of 1861. He heard evidence at Limerick, Banagher, Athlone, Longford and Carrick over a period of two weeks in December 1862.[13] Lord Clanricarde referred to the fact that Lough Derg should be lowered by 2ft (0.6m) as there was only 'one miserable steam-boat' operating drawing 5ft 6ins (1.7m). There were many suggestions made such as that the Meelick weir should be moved to above Shannonbridge, upstream of the confluence with the Suck. There were constant disputes about whether the commissioners had altered the levels from the original plans for the weirs and the lock sills. Bateman referred to this as 'the battle of the sills'. James Lynam, who had been engaged by the proprietors to investigate what should be done, sent in some written statements about each stretch of the river. He claimed that the original plan to enlarge the old canal at Athlone would have been a much better option from the point of view of drainage and would have allowed the weir to be placed upstream of the bridge nearer to Lough Ree. He claimed that in none of the instances where deviations from the original plans were made did this result in an advantage to drainage. Roosky weir he described as a 'submerged weir' because of the backwater caused by the eel weir below it and he criticised the fact that Bird Island and Rabbit Island below Roosky lock had not been removed as intended.

Having listened to all the evidence, Bateman examined the tables of water heights compiled for before and after the works and found that these clearly showed that, despite the years of exceptional summer floods, not only had the flooding not been aggravated by the works, the flooding had been materially mitigated. This mitigation had tempted proprietors into a false sense of security to make the decision to plant their lands, which had led to the losses from the subsequent summer inundations. He then set about estimating the quantity of water that would have to be dealt with in these exceptional years together with additional water from drainage schemes that were now underway on tributaries such as the Suck.

Accepting the fact that even a rise of a few inches led to the water spreading out over the low-lying land, he came up with plans and estimates to prevent 'injurious flooding'. He sensibly started with Lough Allen, which he said needed to be used as an impounding reservoir and the outlet controlled by a weir regulated by sluices. He proposed improving the flow by cutting a short new channel as far as Lough Nagalliagh, to bypass the first tortuous course of the river, and carrying out a small amount of excavation at an old mill site. The levels in the next stretch of river were controlled by the Jamestown weir, which he proposed removing and erecting a new weir regulated by sluices upstream of Jamestown Bridge and deepening the channel here. Roosky and Tarmon

Meelick: the present weir, short canal and lock with the new drainage channel to the right of it and the old navigation canal in the line of trees on the extreme right.(Photograph Kevin Dwyer AIPPA)

weirs controlled the next two levels and the small amount of fall between these two meant that the Tarmon weir was throwing the Roosky weir into backwater. Sufficient sluices would be required on these two weirs and considerable widening of the channel. Similarly a sufficient discharge of water through sluices was vital at Athlone weir.

The next level to Meelick was the one that was causing the greatest inundation of the land. The most relief was needed between Banagher and Meelick where the fall was the greatest. The master of the *Shannon*, which brought him up the river, told him that in the year 1852, with a load of only 50 tons on board, it took him seven hours to get up the 200 yards against the current above Meelick with all steam on and with all the men he could collect to haul. Bateman had also heard evidence that frequently the current here was found to be so strong that the steamers towing boats had to use the old Hamilton lock and canal. Some widening would be required at all the places where the excavating works had been curtailed by lack of funding, but he thought that the expense of the proposal to divert some of the rain-basin waters of the Suck directly into Lough Ree would exceed any benefit. He put forward two possible schemes for Meelick. The first involved placing a weir and sluices at the head of the old easterly channel, which had been closed

off by the embankment near the head of the new canal, enlarging this channel and carrying off the water by a new cut alongside the new canal to discharge below the Victoria lock. Sluices would also be needed in the existing weir to pass a portion of the flood-waters. The second and more radical plan involved making a new weir regulated by sluices and a new canal and lock a short distance downstream of Banagher to link in with the old Meelick canal and join the new canal above Victoria lock, removing the embankment across the easterly channel and the existing weir. Under this scheme the navigation would be in still water and the flood-water would pass down the river channel regulated by the new weir.

He recommended keeping Lough Derg at a level two feet lower, which would necessitate some excavation of shallows to keep a navigation depth of 8ft (2.4m), putting sluices in the weir at Killaloe and replacing the embankment wall from Killaloe lock to the Pierhead. He pointed to the fact that the planned excavations below the weir and in the vicinity of the bridge had not been completed and suggested that further excavation was needed here. Between Killaloe and Limerick some deepening of the channel would be needed, and sluices put in to the weir at World's End. Five of the narrow arches at O'Brien's Bridge should be replaced

Banagher: a recent photograph of winter flooding. (John Kenny)

together with some embankment work and changes in the channels at Limerick. He estimated the total cost of all these recommended works on this stretch of the navigation would be £283,000 and he added: 'It is not part of my duty to inquire whether it is worth the while of the proprietors to incur this expenditure.'

Appended to Bateman's report was a response on behalf of the Board of Works from Richard Griffith in which he stated that the recommended works 'appear to be well designed and would probably be effective in each case, and as such the board could not offer any objection'. He said that the board would favour the second plan for Meelick, the new canal option. Nothing happened until April 1865, probably because there were no exceptional summer floods reported in the meantime, when a letter was sent from the Treasury to the government 'on the Works left unfinished on the River Shannon as reported by Mr Bateman'.[14] The letter stated that a memorial had been received from Lord Clanricarde and other proprietors of the middle Shannon requesting yet again the removal of obstructions leading to flooding caused by the failure of the Shannon Commissioners to fully execute the works on which the counties had been heavily taxed. They disputed the large expenditure indicated by Mr Bateman and said that the work to relieve flooding could be accomplished for as little as £40,000 to £50,000 and that this money could be raised by the sale of lands and mills, which had been unnecessarily purchased by the commissioners, and by adding the sum of £8,000 embezzled by the former treasurer, which should not properly be treated as a debt to the proprietors. The carrying out of these works they believed was due to them and they recited yet again the history of events and their expectations that had not been realized.

The government was satisfied that the situation of the proprietors had been improved by the works but that the navigation works had to some degree made improving the drainage more difficult. It was suggested, therefore, that a detailed survey be made of all the injured lands by the proprietors using their own surveyor and valuator, which would then be examined by the government, and that the proprietors should come together and agree a course of action based on the valuations. In the meantime the government would ask Mr Bateman to work with the board's engineer, Mr Forsyth, and the proprietors' surveyor, Mr Beardmore, to investigate what would be the cost of works deemed absolutely necessary and, if these costs were not commensurate with costs of the works of relief, the government would make good the deficiency by means of a public grant.

FURTHER PARLIAMENTARY COMMITTEES

At the end of May 1865 a select committee of the House of Lords was appointed to inquire into the whole affair taking into consideration the reports of Bateman and Beardmore.[15] The committee heard evidence from a number of witnesses over the month of June. Much of this was a repetition of the same accusations about the incomplete works: that the weirs had been made without sluices, that the channel had not been widened sufficiently and that the sites of some of the weirs were in the wrong places. Jamestown weir was not only in the wrong place but was 'the worst contrivance which the mind of man could conceive or construct for the purpose'. Contradictory evidence was also heard about the impact of the flooding before and after the works. J.G. McKerlie, chairman of the Board of Works, stoutly defended the works and pointed out that the average depths were 15ins (38cm) lower than before the works in winter and 2 to 3ins (5 to 8cm) lower in summer. It was clear that these averages did nothing to explain the sudden summer inundations. It was claimed that the board did try to carry out some excavation work at Killaloe in 1863 but there was insufficient funds arising from any small surplus. Accusations were made about the weirs being constructed without sluices and with the levels being held higher than they should be. James Lynam, an engineer who had been employed by the proprietors, suggested that Killaloe weir was holding Lough Derg higher than originally planned to save costs on further excavation and, with the withdrawal of the large steamers, this navigation level was no longer needed. It was also suggested that as there was virtually no traffic on the upper river, the lock gates should be left open and the locks used as powerful sluices, an idea that was to resurface later.

Having heard all the evidence and studied the reports and statistics, the select committee said that the works had not been as successful as they should have been considering the amount of money expended on them, that insufficiency of funds prevented them being completed as projected and in some cases there had been 'errors of judgment on the part of the Commissioners entrusted with the execution of the works'. Further drainage works could be carried out but must not injure the navigation. Because of the widely differing views on what further works were needed another survey was essential. The Treasury should fund this to be repaid eventually out of the increased annual value of the land to be drained. They also recommended that the works should not be carried out by the Board of Works but by a Board of Trustees made up of representatives of the proprietors, the canal companies and with a representative of government.

This was followed by yet another select committee, this time of the House of Commons, which reported in June 1865.[16] It said that owing to the late period at which the inquiry began, it had insufficient time to hear all the evidence to enable it to report on the questions put to it, and it would resume taking evidence in the next session of Parliament, which was to be another nine months away. It did hear evidence from a number of people about the original estimates and the actual costs of the Shannon Commissioners' works. Again the same ground was covered with claim and counter claim. John Kelly, the county surveyor for Roscommon was very critical; because of its long shoreline it had been assessed with 30 per cent of the original repayments, much higher than any of the other eleven counties. He claimed that there had been nothing but injury caused by the works instead of the anticipated advantage. He pointed as an example to the 'ridiculous' fact that the commissioners had leased fishing rights immediately below Roosky weir, that a wickerwork obstruction had been erected there and the country people gathered en masse to take it away but were prevented from doing so on the advice of the magistrate and that they had broken down part of one of the lock gates. He was particularly critical about Jamestown weir, which he claimed was longer than Roosky weir and consequently discharged more water, causing backwater at Roosky and resulting in flooding, a claim that was later contradicted.

The select committee reconvened as promised in April 1866.[17] It heard more evidence from Kelly, who said that there was now only one steamer operating on the upper Shannon travelling from Limerick to Boyle with flour once a month. Some idea of how some of the information was not based on what had actually happened is shown by the fact that he questioned why the commissioners had built the bridge in Athlone, working in deep water when they subsequently were able to dry out the river bed. This was countered by the evidence of Forsyth who explained, as already mentioned, that the river bed had been temporarily laid dry to complete the work on the weir, which was built on an insecure foundation, but that the water could only be kept out for a very limited time. Kelly described how, when the river was in flood, boats rowed over Athlone weir as there was no fall because of backwater and there was consequently no power for the new mill. He cited the work at Clerhaun shoal near Clonmacnois, where the estimate for the work had been £170 but because of the hard nature of the rock encountered, the actual cost was £8,000. This was due to the nature of the cavernous rock with cracks through which water flooded the caissons so that seven steam engines were needed to keep the water down. The work extended over four years involving 87,675 man-days at 1s 3d per day. Having completed some further inquiries, the committee

reported that they were aware that, following the inquiry of the House of Lords, Bateman, for the government, and Lynam, for the landed proprietors, were carrying out further surveys to consider the engineering, valuation and cost issues and that they felt that they should wait until these results had been received before completing their investigations and making their report.

James Lynam's report was received in April 1867.[18] He estimated that the total cost involved in preventing ordinary autumn flooding would be £92,597 but to prevent exceptional flooding the cost would be £143,920. He produced a great deal of statistical evidence about the flooding and pointed to the fact that there were great winter floods every year, which subside slowly in the spring and bring useful silt on to the land but that exceptional floods occurred less often. He reckoned these occurred every twenty years for a five-year period. He drew attention to what he termed 'the Parliamentary Level of the Shannon', that approved by the government based on Rhodes's original plans, and pointed to the deviations that had been made with injurious effect. The works he recommended were putting sluices in the weirs, excavating to widen the channel over a period of years in the now well-known places and removing the eel weir below Roosky weir. By deepening the river at Killaloe, inserting sluices in the weir and replacing the canal wall, the navigation would not be affected by the greater flow through the weir. At Meelick, putting sluices in the weir would regulate the flow and, as rarely more than two steamers passed in a day, the Hamilton lock and canal could be used when the river was in flood. He pointed to the fact that 1,690,000 acres had been drained along the tributaries of the Shannon but nothing was done to allow for this additional discharge into the main river as the outlet. Reed growth was greatly obstructing the river and 'a very curious foreign plant, called by botanists *Anacharis Alcynastrum*, is extending its growth to a wonderful extent'.

Bateman's second report followed in June 1867.[19] He referred back to his first survey and said that he had once again concentrated on working out the volume of floodwater to be relieved, which confirmed his previous results. He saw no reason to alter his original plans and pointed to the fact that putting in sluices would only help the flooding for a limited distance above the weirs. What was needed was to increase the declivity which involved widening and deepening the channel in places. In response to the question as to whether it would be possible to undertake limited works to reduce the costs, he said that although one part of the river was dependent on the rest, there were places where partial improvements might be undertaken. However, he pointed out that this would only work during shorter periods of rain while continuous rain would still overpower the means of control. He set the costs

Killaloe: the weir with the new sluices installed in 1880–1882.

for the work he recommended at £290,605, which was slightly higher than his earlier estimate.

Eventually the select committee considered the Bateman and Lynam reports, heard some further evidence and presented its report in May 1868.[20] Again, this inquiry, before a new group of people, had gone over the same ground as before with little new information coming to light. McKerlie, the Board of Works chairman, was still praising the works: 'The Shannon works afford a rare instance of an undertaking of so vast an extent being carried out, in an element so difficult to contend with, so near to perfect completion for the sum estimated.' He pointed to the need to start in the lower reaches of the river and work upstream in any channel widening and added that even if the works had been completed in full, it would not have prevented the problems of the years of exceptional floods. William Forsyth, the Board of Works engineer, was questioned further and he clarified some of the issues and misconceptions that had arisen. For example he said

that to underpin the five bridges that were actually replaced was estimated to have cost £18,823, whereas replacing them with new bridges only cost £16,942. He defended the use of fixed bridges on the upper river instead of opening spans because the steamers were all fitted with funnels that could be lowered. He again gave a full explanation of the laying-dry of the river at the Athlone works, explaining that these works were built on an esker that had led to the problem when completing the weir. Any suggestion that all the work in Athlone could have been done with the river

Killaloe: deepening the river bed in the vicinity of the bridge to improve the run off in 1887–1890.

dry was quite wrong: 'it would have been impossible to dam up Lough Ree for a sufficient length of time'. He drew attention to the sharp rise in wages during the works, which led to cost overruns. With reference to the fitting of sluices on the weirs he added wisely: 'a change in the dams would not be attended with the anticipated effect unless you made the channels sufficient to bring the water to them'.

Lynam and Bateman were both questioned at length about their reports. Lynam was very critical about the blocking up of the eastern channel at Meelick and he questioned whether this had been done just to make an access passage for the landowner. The first of the two options that had been proposed, making a new channel parallel to the navigation canal to discharge below Victoria lock, was considered the best because it would enable the water from this east channel, which had been blocked off except for a pipe, to flow freely. Bateman underlined the fact that putting sluices in the weirs would only give relief for a limited distance upstream. The fact was that the 'river itself is not equal to the conveyance of the flood waters' and relief would have to be given to the whole basin.

The conclusions reached by the committee after all these inquiries were very critical of the Shannon Commissioners. The low banks of the river were very exposed to floods, no sanctions had been given for many of the deviations, particularly the changes in levels, and the commissioners had undertaken some of the works themselves instead of using contractors and supervising the work, thus making them the judges of their own works. The committee recommended that an Act should be passed to bring about relief from flooding and for 'levying off the lands to be improved a sum equivalent to the increase on the annual letting value of the lands to be improved by this drainage'.

In addition the navigation depths should be lowered and, as the former levy was unjust, no further levy for navigation works should be charged. They added that there was no case for the government granting more money except for navigation works and they admitted that it did not appear that 'any complete drainage of the basin of the Shannon can be effected except at a cost far exceeding the value of the improvement which could be realised'.

After all these years of inquiries, accusations and endless surveys and reports, the government did agree to a free grant of half the costs of a drainage scheme in 1874.[21] This offer was based on Bateman's plans, but not enough assents were received from the proprietors and the powers under the Act lapsed. Only sixteen of the proprietors had assented, seventy-six dissented and one hundred and twenty did not even bother to reply. Further evidence was heard by Board of Works inquiries at various towns and in 1879 more bad summer flooding and destruction of harvests once again focussed attention on flood control.[22] There were descriptions of men having to move haycocks by boat to higher ground.[23] The Board of Works instructed Forsyth to prepare plans and estimates for putting sluices in the weirs, enlarging the old east channel at Meelick to discharge below the lock and carrying out further excavation at Killaloe.

THE MONCK COMMISSION

The government decided to carry out the works on a reduced scale and in 1882 a Royal Commission, with Viscount Monck as chairman, was set up to inquire into the system of navigation linking Coleraine, Belfast and Limerick, and in particular to investigate whether the future success of this route should be weighed against the immediate and continuous loss to agriculture caused by flooding.[24] The

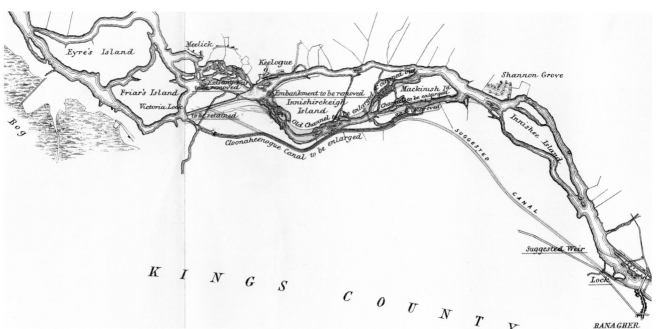

Meelick: Bateman's suggestions for improving the situation at Meelick by making a new channel.

commission reported that the work on the sluices was nearing completion, a grant of £58,757 had been made available and they recommended that the navigation should remain under the control of the Board of Works. Their chief engineer, Robert Manning, was placed in charge with James Lynam as overseer of the works and it was reported that 600 men were at work digging the new Meelick channel. Messrs Brettell of Worcester provided the metalwork for the sluices and all these work were completed by 1882. When the works were almost finished high floods held up the completion and the Board of Works report stated: 'It is almost needless to repeat what has so often been stated before, that during the height of this flood the sluices were incapable of mitigating its effect.'[25] However, in the following year it was reported that the sluices were working well in controlling any lesser floods.

THE ALLPORT COMMISSION AND FURTHER DRAINAGE WORKS

In 1886 a Royal Commission on Irish Public Works had been established under Lord Allport.[26] Part of its brief was to examine arterial drainage schemes but a section of the report dealt with the Shannon Navigation. It drew attention to the fact that the income was not even meeting the expenditure on the river and had to be supported by an annual parliamentary vote of about £300. They recommended the setting up of a Conservancy Board. They also pointed out, what was clearly obvious from all the surveys and reports, that the new sluices without further excavation had only provided a partial solution. They recommended reducing the level of Lough Derg to 5ft (1.5m), carrying out excavation at Killaloe and putting in sluices to control Lough Allen, using the lake as an impounding reservoir. They also drew attention to the fact that in 1886 of the total of 40,220 tons carried on the river, only 629 tons was conveyed to and from Athlone and 2,131 tons upstream of Athlone, bringing in only £81 in tolls. In the light of this they recommended abandoning the navigation above Athlone, removing the lock gates and using the lock cuts to discharge the floods. They added:

If at any future time it be found desirable to restore the navigation above Athlone, which in our opinion is in the highest degree improbable, it would be feasible at a comparatively small cost to replace the lock gates, and to make those improvements of the river channel, which the utilisation of the canals leading to the locks, for the discharge of floods, would for the present render unnecessary . . . It seems reasonable therefore, in the future to treat the Shannon as a channel rather for arterial drainage than for navigation.

This suggestion had been put forward earlier but it was significant that it was now being proposed by a government commission.

In 1887 the Board of Works was funded to carry out limited works in line with suggestions made in the Allport Commission report. These works involved deepening the channel in the river below Lough Allen, work on the wall of the navigation canal at Killaloe, and excavation of the river bed above and below the new sluices and in the vicinity of the bridge. The work was carried out by laying dry one side of the river bed and putting in railway tracks to load the excavated material on to trucks for tipping on the Ballina side of the river; this work was not completed until 1890.

Work continued on the new channel to bypass the tortuous river leading from Lough Allen and to install regulating sluices at Bellantra to permit the level of the lake to be controlled. It could be held at 5ft (1.5m) above the normal summer level or dropped by 12ft (3.6m), which meant that at times the Lough Allen canal could no longer be used. This work, based on the earlier plans suggested by Bateman, was completed by 1893, bringing the total cost of these drainage works from 1880 to £68,355. Fortunately, the government did not proceed to implement the wider recommendation to abandon the upper navigation. It is possible that the large amount of money expended by the Shannon Commission to develop the navigation made the idea of abandoning it now unthinkable. It was estimated by the Allport Commission that the total expenditure on the flood relief schemes up to 1893 had brought the total capital expenditure on the navigation and drainage of the River Shannon from the 1750s to £869,598 of which £582,598 was in grants from public funding. When it is considered that £953,638 was spent on the Caledonian Canal in Scotland and £977,300 on the Rideau Canal in Canada, this would seem to suggest that good value for money had been achieved.

Athlone: sluices were installed on the weir in the 1880s.

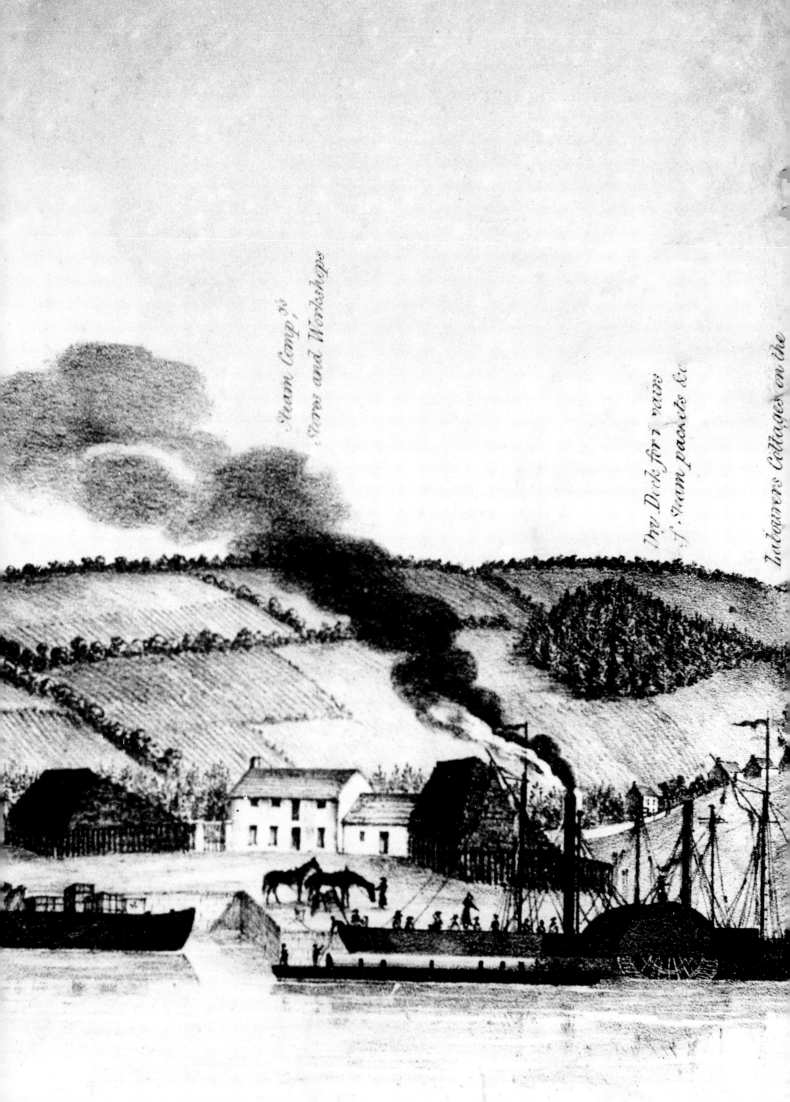

Steam Comp.ꭞ
'ores and Workshops

The Dock for rows
f Steam packets &c

Labourers Cottages on the

CHAPTER TEN
THE STEAMERS AND TRADE 1826–1860s

THE STEAM AGE ARRIVES

The lead-up to the arrival of the steamers on the Shannon took some time. As early as 1816 the Grand Canal Company was in correspondence with Captain Owens of Cove for information about his steamboat with a view to using steamers to tow canal boats and, when a steamer visited Dublin in November of that year, a trial was arranged to see how successfully she would tow a canal boat.[1] The board appointed a committee of five to investigate the possibility of bringing a steamer to the Shannon and Captain Owens was asked for more information about the possibility of getting Mr Hennessy of Passage West to build a steamer of 16hp. Hennessy was asked for an estimate to Mr Hazeldine's plans and Owens replied that his steamer was powered by a Boulton & Watt engine, which cost £1,100 but had proved much faster than locally made engines.

The board of the canal company was approached by C.W. Williams in January 1822 with a proposal for propelling the passenger boats on the canal by steam. In the same year the chairman, James Dawson, was asked to submit an estimate of his planned steamer, which had a double keel with the paddle wheel between the hulls, which was 70ft (21m) long by 15ft (4.5m) beam. At this stage the canal company asked for a meeting with the Directors General of Inland Navigation to discuss introducing steamers on the Shannon to increase trade between Dublin and Limerick. The initial emphasis was on the idea of introducing steamers to tow the canal boats across Lough Derg. Mr McCleery of the Lough Neagh Steam Boat Company was approached for information. He said that his vessel cost £1,000 (stg.) and the engine a futher £1,400. The initiative was not followed up and the Lord Lieutenant turned down the suggestion that the government should support a steamers on the Shannon. The failure of the Directors General or the government to encourage the introduction of steamers by offering financial help is hard to comprehend in the light of the obvious difference they would have made to a navigation such as the Shannon, made up of lakes and river sections without towpaths.

Initially there was not so much emphasis on developing passenger services. Up to this time there does not appear to have been much passenger traffic but some were carried, in particular on the Limerick Navigation. John Grantham, who had become familiar with the river when carrying out his survey in the 1820s, saw the potential in carrying passengers as well as freight and entered into an agreement with some Limerick merchants to form a company and have a steamer built for the Shannon. When the construction of this boat was completed, his backers withdrew their support, leaving him responsible for the payment for it. He had already been in correspondence with the Directors General about it and in November 1824 the Directors General had asked him when his steamer would commence plying. In August 1826 Grantham told them: 'Circumstances have arisen that will prevent him carrying into Execution the Plan he had formed of working a Steam Boat between Dublin and Limerick.' The fact that this was a reference to the withdrawal of support is confirmed in the *Dublin Evening Mail* of 26 July 1826, which set out the whole story, adding: 'We cannot avoid crying shame on the Limerick merchants who would thus compromise their own characters and the public good.' However, he must have decided that his best option was to go ahead because, in the following month, he told the Grand Canal Company, which was still in control of the middle Shannon at this time, that the government had refused financial help but that he had decided to operate a steamer between Limerick and Shannon Harbour. He was looking to operate toll free on the middle Shannon for one year and he added: 'I confidently hope this proposition will be acceded to, and without it, I must give up the undertaking, as I cannot venture to fight the battle single handed without it, if it is granted, the boat shall be immediately brought over and set to work.' He was also granted permission by the Directors General to operate toll free for one year through the Limerick Navigation.

Having secured free tolls for one year, on 21 November 1826 Grantham asked the Grand Canal Company for permission to put his steamer, the *Marquis Wellesley* into the dry dock at Portobello in Dublin 'to take off some iron plates and clean her bottom from the effects of sea water. That I wish to accomplish tomorrow that she may proceed to the Lake so as to arrive there before Sunday'. In December he told the Directors General that his steamer had arrived on the Shannon and that she had travelled down Lough Derg with a slight head wind in six hours. She had been built by the Horseley Iron Works in Staffordshire under his superintendence; the design was twin iron hulls with the paddle wheel located between the hulls.[2] The *Limerick Chronicle* of 3 February 1827, announcing the arrival on the previous day of the *Marquis Wellesley* from Dublin, added that this was 'the first instance of the application of Steam to the navigation of the interior waters of this Country'.

In the meantime, on the 24 October 1826, another company, the Shannon Steam Navigation Company, had requested that its steamer the *Mountaineer* drawing 4ft 8ins (1.35m) and trade boat No. 803 could have a pass through to the Shannon. This company is referred to as a 'Joint Stock Company'. It is also not clear which boat actually became operational first. There was a memorial erected subsequently to Grantham in Killaloe Cathedral stating that he introduced steam navigation to the Shannon in 1825, which based on this evidence would appear to be a mistaken date. There was a long letter from Grantham to the canal company in March 1827:

We are here [Shannon Harbour] since Saturday with dreadful weather, and the Shannon much higher than during the winter. I am in great apprehension I cannot get under Banagher Bridge [the road bridge on the canal], indeed I am sure I cannot, we have never yet gone through it without mischief . . . We have encountered one dreadful gale of wind on the Lake with a boat in tow, we did not mind it and every day we gain confidence and skill. My competitors are at work, we are great friends. There is business for us both, and we cannot hurt each other. . . I stuck fast below Branagans [Hamilton Lock] the other night and kept three unfortunate people out all night.

Grantham was greatly annoyed when he learnt that the other company had been given the same toll remission and was operating with freight rates lower than his. He seems to have decided not to operate a service through the Limerick Navigation because of his fears about the passage through O'Brien's Bridge and the decayed state of the lock gates. However, he was then given permission to operate 'his light passage boat' on this navigation at a reduced rate, but it is not clear what boat this was.

THE CITY OF DUBLIN STEAM PACKET COMPANY

The names of the companies are confusing at this time; Grantham's original company was called the Shannon Navigation Company and the other company was referred to as the Shannon Steam Navigation Company. They were both absorbed into C.W. Williams's Irish Inland Steam Navigation Company. Williams and Francis Carleton had also set up the City of Dublin Steam Packet Company in 1829, which was based at 15 Eden Quay in Dublin, to operate between Dublin and Liverpool and eventually both Irish Sea and inland companies came together and operated under this name. The steam companies also had horse-drawn trading canal boats operating on the Grand Canal and Limerick Navigation, providing a through service between Dublin and Limerick, towing with their steamers between Shannon Harbour and Killaloe. The *Mountaineer* had a wooden hull and the last mention of her in the records of the Grand Canal Company was in March 1829, but she is still listed as part of the City of Dublin Steam Packet Company's fleet in the 1833 Act 'for regulating and enabling the City of Dublin Steam Packet Company to sue and be sued'.[3] It is a safe assumption that there must be some connection between the steamer and a rock on Lough Derg which was named the Mountaineer Rock by the R.N. surveyors, Wolfe and Beechey, in 1837-1839. Whether she hit this rock and foundered on Lough Derg or struck the rock and subsequently left the Shannon is difficult to establish.

Before long, in 1829, the company was reported to be adding two new steamers to the fleet. One of these was the *Lady Clanricarde,* a wooden paddle steamer 80ft (24.3m) long, which had to be assembled in the dry dock in Killaloe because she was too large to fit in the Grand Canal locks. The dry dock in Killaloe had been constructed by the Limerick Navigation Company, funded by a public grant, and the Shannon Commissioners assumed it had been part of the transfer of the company to them and so Williams had to get permission to use the dry dock. A dispute subsequently arose later, in 1841, with Williams about the land it had been constructed on which he said was part of the steam company's station. In the end Williams agreed to hand over £1,000, the original cost of the dock, if the commissioners gave up all claim to it. The second boat was the *Lady Dunally,* which was a smaller iron paddle steamer, built by Fawcett Preston & Co. of Liverpool, similar in design to the *Marquis Wellesley.* She is described as having 'exactly the appearance of two vessels joined together by the deck, but separated in every other respect. The paddles instead of being at the sides, are placed in the middle, between the vessels, so that in working they will not be likely to injure the banks of the canal, which has always been the principal obstacle to steam boats being employed in canal navigation'.[4]

Grantham continued to act for Williams as manager and superintendent for the Shannon business based in Killaloe. In 1830 he produced *The Traveller's Map of the River Shannon* for the company using his original 1822 charts. This advertised a service from Killaloe to Banagher for a fare of 6s 4d: 'To invalids the above route presents the most desirable conveyance, as the journey is performed without fatigue, and in the most agreeable manner. . . Carriages and horses are carefully shipped and carried at modest charges.' For the convenience of passengers the company had built the Ponsonby Arms Hotel in Killaloe. It was pointed out that travellers for Killarney or Tralee could continue on by the company's steamers to Limerick, down the estuary to Tarbert and from thence 'the drive to Killarney is over a very fine country'. In addition, linking with the Grand Canal to Dublin, goods, cattle and produce of all kinds were carried with agents at each station to receive and forward the goods 'with great expedition and at half the rate of land carriage. .

. . . To Graziers and Cattle Dealers this mode of conveyance presents great advantages. Stock of all kinds may be brought to Dublin at moderate rates, and without delay, fatigue loss of weight and condition necessarily attendant on overland driving.' It added that the services would be extended to the upper Shannon when suitable steamers were acquired.

Grantham appears to have ceased his involvement with Williams after a short period because in 1830 he approached the Royal Canal Company about establishing steamers on the north Shannon. He told that canal company in 1832 that he was no longer connected with the steam company but he died a short time later in 1833. As already mentioned, he had gained a detailed knowledge of the river in the course of the survey he had carried out in 1822. His comments about the strong link between navigation and flooding issues that called for the removal of the shoal areas in the river had proved very accurate and his charts are an important source of information today on the early navigation works.

As already indicated, by 1833 the City of Dublin Steam Packet Company was listed as having five boats on the Shannon, *Clanricarde, Dunally, Mountaineer, Wellesley* and the *Wye.* The *Wye* had recently been added to the fleet: she was also an iron steamer, built at Birkenhead Iron Works in 1826, and was small enough to fit in the Grand Canal where she was used for towing on the canal. In the same year Williams ordered what was to be the largest boat on the river from William Laird & Sons of Birkenhead, to be called the *Lady Lansdowne.* She was shipped in individual pieces to Dublin and then she and her assemblers, twenty men and six boys, were brought by Grand Canal Company canal boats to Killaloe in October 1833 for assembly in the dry dock from where she was launched on 4 March 1834. She was 133ft (40.5m) long and with her side paddle wheels was 17ft (5m) wide with a draught of 5ft 6ins (1.6m). For safety reasons she was divided into five watertight compartments. Her cost was said to have been £2,926 12s 2d for the hull and fittings and another £4,200 for her two 45hp engines.

The *Lady Lansdowne* could travel at about 13mph, making the direct journey from Killaloe to Portumna in under two hours. Her timetable was a bit more flexible; she left Killaloe at 9 am on the arrival of the flyboat from Limerick which had left there at 6 am. Arriving at Portumna at between noon-1 pm, having called at Williamstown on the way, the passengers transferred to a smaller steamer to make the journey to Shannon Harbour to join the flyboat to Dublin.[5] Having picked up the passengers from the smaller steamer, she then made the return trip arriving back in Killaloe about 4 pm to 5 pm. Making this trip up and down the lake once each day except Sundays, she required 120 tons of coal a month and later, when a switch to turf was made to save money, about 250 tons per month. She could also tow up to four laden canal boats on each trip. The company also had stations at Garrykennedy, Dromineer, Terryglass and

A drawing of the PS Avonmore with her paddle wheels in the stern by William Wakeman.

Cloondavaun, which were served by the *Avonmore*, which was a stern paddle wheeler added to the fleet in 1835. She also operated some of the time up the river as there were a number of accidents reported when she was towing boats through the horse bridge near Shannon Harbour and the new bridge at Banagher. In that year it was reported that 31,562 passengers had been carried by the City of Dublin Steam Packet Company on its Shannon routes. This company also operated a service between Shannon Harbour and Athlone and in 1840 it was reported to the Shannon Commissioners that a total of 18,544.5 passengers had been carried between Killaloe and Athlone (children being counted as a half passenger).

Earlier, in 1834, Williams had also launched a new iron ship, the *Garryowen*, built by Lairds, to operate a service on the estuary between Limerick and Kilrush. She was fitted with watertight bulkheads, later to be used in the *Great Britain*. Williams also added the *Erin-go-bragh* and the *Dover Castle* for service on the estuary. In addition to providing transport for local people, the services were also used by visiting travellers. Mary John Knott gave an account of a voyage in 1835 describing the beacon towers, erected by the Limerick Chamber of Commerce, and the many large houses including Bolton Waller's Shannon Grove, John Waller's Castletown and the Knight of Glin's Castle.[6] Other operators, including William Dargan, subsequently started services on the estuary but Williams withdrew his services in the late 1850s. *Black's Guide* in 1888 reported that there were no longer regular services but that boats could be hired for excursions and 'if desired, a night may be spent at one of the towns adjoining the river's bank'.[7]

Because of the limitations of size of the locks on the Limerick Navigation and the fact that there was less need for steamers because there were towpaths, Williams designed a horse-drawn canal boat, the *Nonsuch*. She was 80ft (24m) long but her bow and her stern were designed to hinge to enable her to fit in the smaller locks. She could carry sixty passengers at a speed of 9mph, the bow and the stern sections being held down by the weight of one man.[8] There is also a reference to Captain Tully's packet-boat steamer, the *Wellington*. William Watson, who later became managing director of the CDSPCo, also patented a canal boat 120ft (36m) long that divided into two sections to fit in the locks side by side, possibly the *Gazelle*.[9]

Limerick: the arrival of steamers led to busy scenes at the quays. (Courtesy of the National Library of Ireland)

In the meantime the Railway Commissioners had been surveying the country in the mid-1830s and they produced some useful information about the steamers.[10] They reported that C.W. Williams was operating a steamer three days a week on the estuary between Limerick and Kilrush, calling at Tarbert and returning on alternate days. Passengers were the principal source of revenue with 21,270 travelling in one year. On the Limerick Navigation in 1836, 14,600 passengers had been carried. The journey between Limerick and Killaloe took 3½ hours but only 2½ hours with the light Scotch boat; fifty minutes of this time was spent locking. In addition to the steam-company passenger boats it also had two trade boats that carried livestock for the Dublin

market and general merchandise, with British and Irish manufactured goods from Dublin. There were three other boats owned by private proprietors carrying slates, turf, and foreign and native timber, with manure carried free, and also four boats carrying turf to Limerick Distillery. The total of 28,212 tons carried in 1831 had risen to 36,018 in 1836 bringing in £1,514 in tolls in that year. On the middle Shannon, the Railway Commissioners said that the *Lady Lansdowne* and the *Clanricarde* were operating on Lough Derg with the *Avonmore* and *Dunally* running between Portumna and Shannon Harbour and the *Wellesley* between Shannon Harbour and Athlone. The steamers also towed lumber boats and the revenue from tolls had risen to £5,425 in 1833. There were no passenger boats on the upper river and boats travelled from ten to forty miles a day depending on the weather, carrying 9,770 tons in 1835.

CONTEMPORARY ACCOUNTS

There are a number of references to travelling on the steamers during their period of operation on the river. Although many of the passengers used the steamers as a convenient way to travel, some of them were visitors enjoying the trips on the river as tourists. Reference has been made to the comments of Henry Inglis about the lack

The PS Shannon *operated on the Shannon Estuary to and from Limerick. (Courtesy of the National Library of Ireland)*

of boats to be seen on Lough Ree.[11] In the course of the trip made aboard the steamer placed at his disposal by the steam company he had landed at Rindoon and enjoyed a picnic on Hare Island which he said was 'charmingly diversified with corn-fields, pasture and wood.'

Inglis's description of the lack of use of Lough Ree was also mentioned by Commander Wolfe in the sailing directions accompanying the Admiralty charts: 'The lake is but little used in a commercial way, not a trading vessel of any description crosses its surface, and even the boats for carrying turf, which are occasionally seen passing to and fro, merely supply the islands or other places where this necessary article cannot be more easily obtained.'[12] Wolfe described how a small steamer towed 'lumber boats' twice a week to Shannon Harbour but that the boats for the Royal Canal had to be poled or sailed.

In 1842 Johann George Kohl joined the steamer in Shannon Harbour and went down the river to Limerick.[13] His description of what happened when they reached Killaloe, where work was still going on to improve the Killaloe canal stretch of the navigation, is remarkable:

Beyond Killaloe we come again to rocks and whirlpools, and as the canal was not yet finished, by means of which this part of the river is to be avoided, we had the amusement of landing bag and baggage, and proceeding with jaunting cars to the spot where it was possible to embark for Limerick. The Captain of the steamer and his mates shipped themselves on the backs of some cantering nags, and, thus caparisoned, rattled away in front as commanders and escorts to the caravan. At the end of a few miles we embarked again, but this time in a long canal boat drawn by a couple of horses. All this sounds rather wild and Irish; in England such a variegated mode of transport is scarcely to be found.

He went on to describe another incident in the Limerick Navigation:

A small steamer, which came alongside our vessel, was making its first experimental trip, and had on board some members of the Shannon Steam Navigation Company. It was built on a new plan, and consisted of two round shaped boats shaped like cigars, and connected above by a common deck. The steam engine was fixed upon deck, and the paddles struck the water quickly but not deeply. The people termed it "the cigar boat".

Kohl had been describing the oddly-designed iron paddle steamer, the *Gazelle*, which was also described by another traveller, James Johnson:

One paddle, and that in the centre of her stern, propelled the boat at a very slow rate, along a dull canal, and through flat meadows; but to make up for the deficiency of paddles, she sported a couple of rudders, worked with one rope. The steamer, in fact, is composed of two boats, joined side by side, the quarterdeck being a platform in the place of a forecastle, which was hoisted up perpendicularly, in front of the best cabin, while passing through the locks.[14]

Another large steamer had been added in 1843, the *Lady Burgoyne*. She had been built in the Ringsend Iron Works in square compartments so that she could be shipped to Killaloe for assembly. The *Clare Journal* described a visit to the yard on 5 September 1842 by the Shannon Commissioners to see her being built, when it was announced that she was to be named *Lady Burgoyne* in honour of the chairman's wife. She was 130ft (39.5m) long and 36ft (11m) breadth overall, with two 40hp engines and was said to be a faster boat than the *Lady Lansdowne*, averaging 12mph. Williams was planning to use the new boat up to Athlone and the issue of the size of the lock there had not yet arisen. He now asked could he operate the new vessel up to Shannon Harbour through the new navigation at Meelick in the coming winter. He was told that he could but that the navigation might have to be closed for some weeks in the following spring to complete some works there. In the following year it was suggested that she would operate a regular service between Killaloe and Banagher, and the company sought permission for the *Gazelle* to enter the old canal at Meelick every day free of toll to operate a service up to Athlone. She was advertised in 1846 as running a service daily except Sundays at 6.30 am from Athlone to Shannon Harbour where the passengers transferred to the *Lady Burgoyne* or *Lady Lansdowne*.[15] The total fare in that year from Limerick to Athlone, changing boats three times, was 7s 10d cabin and 4s 4d deck. However, in November of that year a notice appeared in the *Westmeath Independent* indicating that the *Gazelle* would cease to ply until further notice but that the *Dunally* would continue to take passengers as usual.[16]

When the commissioners had opened up the new navigation to Athlone, they anticipated that the *Lady Lansdowne* and larger steamers would make trips up river. In addition to making the locks large enough, the depth of water off the new quay at Banagher was made to accommodate boats drawing 6ft (1.8m). The *Westmeath Independent* recorded in June 1849:

The appearance on Thursday of one of the City of Dublin Steam Company's large vessels, the Lady Lansdowne on the upper Shannon was a novelty which came unexpectedly upon the inhabitants of Athlone. As she steamed up the noble river a large number of spectators congregated on

Killaloe: a drawing by William Stokes in 1842 of a steamer with trade boats alongside at the Pierhead. It is suggested that this is the Lady Clanricarde *and not the* Lady Lansdowne *as previously thought.*

the bridge and quays and by hearty cheers welcomed this, the first attempt to open the navigation for vessels of any burden above Shannonbridge. We are happy to learn that in future the company's steamers will ply regularly between Limerick and Athlone with passengers and freight.

This report is puzzling because while she could fit easily in the new lock in Meelick, Athlone lock, which only measured 127ft (38.7m) from lower mitre to upper sill, would not have been long enough for her to lock through. There had been a degree of indecision about the size of the lock, and it is hard to understand why the commissioners made the lock just too short for her and the *Lady Burgoyne*. It is possible she just entered the lock chamber before returning downstream. In any event her visit to Athlone appears to have been a one-off event and she principally operated on Lough Derg.

Dr John Forbes described the scene as he joined the steamer in Killaloe for the journey up river to Athlone in 1852, in which he makes a very interesting reference to the steamer's freight:

We found the steamer waiting for us, and the little pier thickly crowded with people waiting to go on board or to see their friends on board. The deck was indeed so crowded that it was not an easy matter to get from one part of it to another and the crowding and confusion were still further increased by the whole fore part of the vessel

being occupied by cattle. It was soon seen that a party of emigrants had come or were coming on board, and were now taking leave of their friends with every token of the most passionate distress. With that utter unconsciousness which characterises authentic sorrow, these warm-hearted and simple-minded people demeaned themselves entirely, as if they had been shrouded in all the privacy of home, clinging to and kissing and embracing each other with the utmost ardour, calling out aloud in broken tones, the endeared names of brother, sister, mother, sobbing and crying as if the very heart would burst, while the unheeded tears ran down from the red and swollen eyes literally in streams. . . And when the final orders were given to clear the ship and withdraw the gangway, the howl of agony that rose at once from the parting deck and the abandoned pier, was perfectly over powering. . . There were about twenty of*

A Paul Gauci drawing of a steamer passing down the lower end of Lough Derg in the 1860s.

these emigrants, all destined in the first place to Liverpool by way of Dublin. The majority of them were going to the United States, but several, particularly the young women, were bound for Australia. Every one was going out on funds supplied by the friends who had preceded them to the land of their exile. [17]

Forbes recounted that it took seven hours to reach Athlone and he was surprised by the immense quantity of turf consumed on the voyage. There were also tourists on board and 'bankers, merchants, doctors, county squires, fishers with their rods, sketchers with their tablets and professors with their pupils'. There was much political talk about the state of the country and one passenger told him 'it was absurd to think of treating the Irish like a civilised people, that savages must be tamed and taught before they are made the subject of legislation; that the only law-giver suited to them was another Cromwell, that, in a word they were only fit to be treated like wild beasts or slaves'. This illustrates at first hand the state of the country at the time and the attitude of some people towards the ordinary country people. There was also a farmer on board from Scotland with a view to settling in Ireland but 'his professional eye was shocked beyond measure by the wretched state of the cultivation everywhere prevalent'. Many visitors enjoyed the boat trips; it was reported that 'the ex-President of the USA Mr Van Bruen and his son, General Cooper and Lady' took a trip from Athlone in 1853. [18]

WORKING STEAMERS

Steam dredgers had been used for some time. As early as 1816 John Hughes, a London-based engineer, had won a contract to deepen the channel in the River Suir when it was reported that he was the proprietor of a 'new machine called an Excavator' worked by steam. [19] As already indicated the Shannon Commissioners had purchased steam dredgers and hoppers at an early stage of the works. They first contacted the Corporation for the Improvement of the River Clyde for information about its river-deepening operations. They then ordered the hulls of three steam dredgers, known as A, B and C, but, as mentioned earlier, actually named *Victoria*, *Albert* and *Prince*. They were supplied by Grantham Page of Liverpool for £1,000 each and were brought in sections by canal to Shannon Harbour where they were assembled on canal-company land; the latter had asked an exorbitant price for the land and so the commissioners invoked the Act to acquire the land. A fourth dredger was added later, the *Princess Alice*. The dredgers and hoppers were leased out to the contractors at a weekly rate. A number of accidents were reported and in 1841 the commissioners obtained insurance quotations from the London Union Assurance Company for cover of £1,000 per vessel at a cost of 10s 6d

for three months or 15s 9d for six months. It has already been shown that the dredgers were able only to carry out limited removal of shoals because of the difficult nature of the material and that dams, sometimes formed by wooden planks and sometimes by earthworks, had to be erected in many cases to dry out areas to be worked on. They were, however, extensively used where possible and in particular to remove the temporary earthwork dams after the work was completed. The Shannon Commissioners also used the regular services of Williams's steamers on their inspections. The *Marquis Wellesley* was used in the river and the *Avonmore* on Lough Derg.

There was continuing dispute with the Grand Canal Company about drawbacks and tolls and in 1845 a further meeting was held: 'a very lengthened and important conversation ensued on the subject of the several matters affecting the interests of both companies'. The steam company was also looking for further reductions in tolls and drawbacks and increased bounties on passengers. In 1846 the Grand Canal Company launched its own steamer for towing on the Shannon called the *Shannon*, which made the canal company much less dependent on the steam company. She was a wooden boat, 72ft (22m) long, built for them by Wakefield Pim of Hull for £3,580, and the interesting thing about her was that she was driven by a screw propeller. It is worth noting that in 1843, when there was some discussion about the dimensions of the new locks and the width required for side paddle wheelers, Williams and William Watson, who was also involved in the company, met the commissioners and had stated that 'the screw is quite unfitted for canal and small river navigation, having adduced results of many experiments confirming this view'. The canal company established a towing service between Athlone and Killaloe with rates determined by the tonnage carried in the canal boats. After operating for a few months the *Shannon* had engine problems and the decision was made to lay her up for a while because of the lack of trade in agricultural produce 'under the present circumstances of the country, arising out of the failure of the potato crop', but she was operational again in the spring of 1847 with a smaller crew.

Relations between the City of Dublin Steam Packet Company and the Grand Canal Company deteriorated. In 1850 the steam company said it was withdrawing trade between Dublin, Limerick and Dromineer without notice and that they were going to start an establishment on the Royal Canal. All communications with the canal company were broken off in December 1850, which led to undercutting in toll charges between the two canal companies with the trade from Athlone, Ballinalsoe and Lanesborough routed through the Royal Canal. They advertised in 1850 that their steamer *Avonmore* would ply regularly to Tarmonbarry, the junction with the Royal Canal, and the *Lady Burgoyne* would continue on her present route between Athlone and Killaloe. It was claimed that the total time for trade boats to reach Dublin from Athlone had been reduced by five hours by this new route. The first screw boats had been tried out on the Grand Canal in 1850, and another steamer, the *Brian Boru*, 90ft (27.4m) long, was added on the Shannon. Three more screw steamers, 72ft (22m) long, the *Dublin, Limerick* and *Athlone*, were introduced on the Shannon in 1851 by the canal company.

These new boats carried cargo and towed canal boats, but the canal company also decided to convert the *Shannon* into a passenger-carrying boat. In 1851 that service was advertised:

Public Notice to Emigrants and all Others Travelling on the Shannon. Cheap and Comfortable Travelling Limerick to Liverpool. By steamer, passage boat and railway. Fare throughout, including all charges, 5s. The passage boat leaves Limerick from the Canal Bank every evening in winter at 3.00pm, arriving in Killaloe at 6.00pm where passengers can get comfortable lodgings on very reasonable terms and start by the company's steamer for Dublin on Mondays, Wednesdays and Fridays. Agent at Killaloe, Mr Sylvester Hurley.

The railway part of the above offer was the arrangement between the canal company and the Great Southern & Western Railway Company made in 1847 to cease operating the passage boats to and from Dublin and to transfer the passengers to the railway at Sallins. Eventually, a truce was called to the freight war from January 1852 when it was agreed that the Grand Canal Company would operate the trade between Limerick and Athlone and cease trading north of Athlone, the steam company would operate all the passenger traffic and freight rates would return to the former levels. The canal company finally gave up the unequal struggle with the railway company in 1852 and all the passage-boat services ceased on the canal but the passenger service operated by the *Shannon* continued on the river and their other steamers continued to act as towing steamers for the trade boats.

THE IMPACT OF THE RAILWAY AGE

With the completion of the Shannon navigation works it might have been expected that things would only get better. However, the writing had already been on the wall for some time. As early as 1844 it had been reported at a meeting of the Shannon Commissioners that there was information now available about a proposed railway crossing of the river at Athlone and that they would be dissenting to it. With a number of railway bills coming before parliament the commissioners were seeking the insertion of clauses for the protection of navigation works. They were fighting a losing battle and by September 1845 they were in negotiation with Sir John Macneill insisting that the railway bridge at Athlone must have an opening span and be 40ft (12m) wide with headroom when closed of 22ft (6.6m) and with a minimum of 14ft (3.1m) width on the other arches. The bridge was eventually completed in 1850, designed by George Hemans and built by Messrs Fox and Henderson using a new experimental way of sinking the columns using compressed air. In 1845 they were also already in discussion with the Great Hibernian Railway Company about a crossing near Jamestown. The commissioners turned down a request to supply information about trade on the river and Rhodes, Long and Mulvany were all told in no uncertain terms that they were not to respond to offers of work from railway companies. By the end of the year it was reported that there were nine railway companies seeking bills involving river crossings and once again the commissioners appealed for protection clauses.

It was ironic that the invention of steam, which had directly led to the decision to improve the navigation to a size that would accommodate the steamers, was now leading to the beginning in earnest of the Railway Age, which was to seriously affect trade on the river. The two canal companies became pawns in the struggle between the railway companies. With the takeover of the Royal Canal by the Midland Great Western Railway Company in 1845 and with the Grand Canal Company at first heavily engaged with it in a rates war, and then even negotiating a seven-year lease with the Great Southern & Western Railway Company in 1853, the impact on the passenger traffic on the river had been inevitable. The total number of passengers carried by the City of Dublin Steam Packet Company on the Shannon between Killaloe and Athlone, from the records supplied to the commissioners for their annual reports, averaged about 16,000 in the early 1840s. It showed an increase in the years of the famine, rising to a peak of 23,767 in 1847, then falling to 10,645 in 1848, followed by a big fall to 4,033 in 1849, when the services were cut to boats running every second day.

The Midland Great Western Railway Company had been compelled to maintain the Royal Canal as a going concern by the terms of the takeover and it now showed an interest in the steamer services on the Shannon. In 1855 it had been decided to put two steamers on the river, the *Midland* and the *Lorton*. They were cargo-carrying boats but did carry some passengers and both were removed after a few years. In the same year the City of Dublin Steam Packet Company was obviously suffering from the opposition from the railways because it was advertising its store in Athlone for sale and a reduced fare for the river trip of 12s 6d 1st class

RIVER SHANNON PASSENGER TRAFFIC.

The Duchess of Argyle and Artizan Steamers

PLY EVERY DAY, EXCEPT SUNDAY, (WEATHER PERMITTING) UNTIL FURTHER NOTICE.

Through Tickets are issued at Limerick, Nenagh, and on board the Steamer, and *from Dublin* at the Broadstone Terminus, as underneath.

THE STEAMER STARTS FROM ATHLONE EVERY MORNING, (SUNDAY EXCEPTED), ON ARRIVAL OF TRAIN LEAVING DUBLIN AT 7 O'CLOCK, A.M., AND FROM KILLALOE AT 8.20 A.M., TO MEET THE TRAIN ARRIVING IN DUBLIN AT 6 O'CLOCK, P.M.

Tourists will find this route preferable to any other to Killarney, as they will have an opportunity of seeing the splendid Scenery of Lough Derg and the River Shannon.

THROUGH FARES.							Distance from Athlone.	Week days only.
SINGLE TICKETS.			Return Tickets. Available for a Week to Limerick, and 4 days to all other stations.		FROM DUBLIN.			
3rd Class	2nd Class	1st Class	2nd Class	1st Class				
s. d.	s. d.	s. d.	s. d.	s. d.			Miles.	Departure.
					DUBLIN			7.0 A.M. from Broadstone Terminus
					ATHLONE			10.10 ,, arrival by Train.
					,,			10.15 ,, departure by Steamer
6 6	10 6	13 6	15 9	20 0	SHANNON BRIDGE		13½	11.45 ,,
6 9	10 9	13 9	16 0	20 6	BANAGHER		22	1.30 P.M.
7 6	11 6	14 6	17 6	21 6	PORTUMNA		35	2.45 ,,
7 9	12 0	15 6	18 0	23 6	WILLIAMSTOWN		47	3.45 ,,
7 9	12 0	15 6	18 0	23 6	NENAGH		—	4.45 ,, Omnibus from Drumineer
7 9	12 6	16 6	18 9	24 9	KILLALOE		62	5.0 ,, arrival by Steamer
							—	5.10 ,, Departure by Coach
8 0	13 0	17 6	19 6	26 3	LIMERICK		77	6.40 ,, arrival

THROUGH FARES						TO DUBLIN.		Distance from Limerick.	Week days only.
								Miles.	6.45 A.M. from Cruise's Hotel, by ... loe
8 0	13 0	17 6	19 6	26 3		LIMERICK		15	8.15 ,,
7 9	12 6	16 6	18 9	24 9		KILLALOE		—	8.20 ,,
						,,		—	8.15 ,, ...m
7 9	12 0	15 6	18 0	23 6		NENAGH		—	9.15 ,,
7 9	12 0	15 6	18 0	23 6		WILLIAMSTOWN		42	10.15 ,,
7 6	11 6	14 6	17 6	21 6		PORTUMNA		55	11.45 ,,
6 9	10 9	13 9	16 0	20 6		BANAGHER		63½	12.45 P.M.
6 6	10 6	13 6	15 9	20 0		SHANNON BRIDGE		77	2.30 ,, arrival by Steamer
						ATHLONE			3.0 ,, departure by train
						,,			6.0 ,, arrival
						DUBLIN			

	First Class. s. d.	Second Class. s. d.	Third Class. s. d.
LIMERICK TO GALWAY	15 0	13 6	9 0
,, TO CAVAN	17 6	15 4	10 3
,, TO LONGFORD	16 4	14 3	9 0

NOTE.—The Ticket-Office in Limerick closes 5 minutes before starting of Coach. Passengers holding Return Through Tickets should either send a notice to the Company's Office in Limerick, previously, or attend at the Office a quarter of an hour before starting of Coaches to secure seats.

Through Passengers, to or from Dublin, may break the journey at Athlone and Killaloe.

☞ **See next page.**

A Midland Great Western Railway Company timetable for its steamer service.

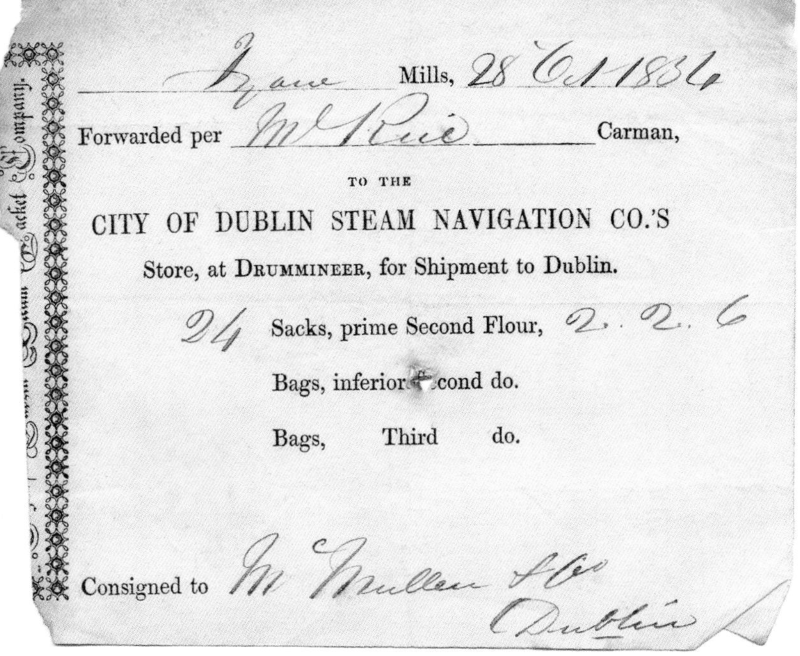

Docket 1 (top left):

Mills, 28 Oct 1854

Forwarded per _Mc Rue_ Carman,

TO THE

CITY OF DUBLIN STEAM NAVIGATION CO.'S

Store, at DRUMMINEER, for Shipment to Dublin.

24 Sacks, prime Second Flour, 2. 2. 6

Bags, inferior Second do.

Bags, Third do.

Consigned to _W. Mullen & Co_
Dublin

Docket 2 (top right):

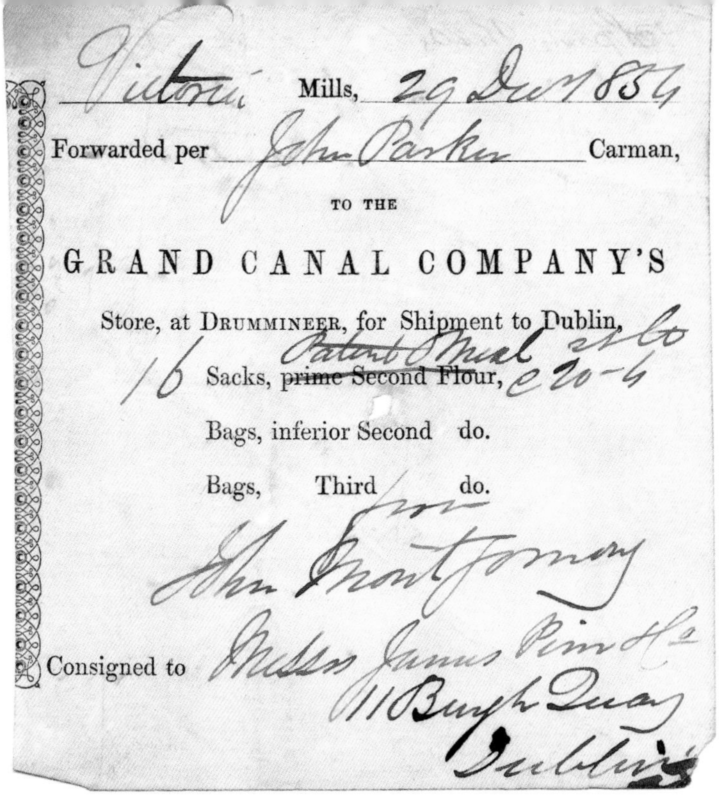

Victoria Mills, 29 Dec 1854

Forwarded per _John Parker_ Carman,

TO THE

GRAND CANAL COMPANY'S

Store, at DRUMMINEER, for Shipment to Dublin.

16 Sacks, prime Second Flour, @ 20-6

Bags, inferior Second do.

Bags, Third do.

John Montgomery

Consigned to _Messrs James Pim & Co_
11 Burgh Quay
Dublin

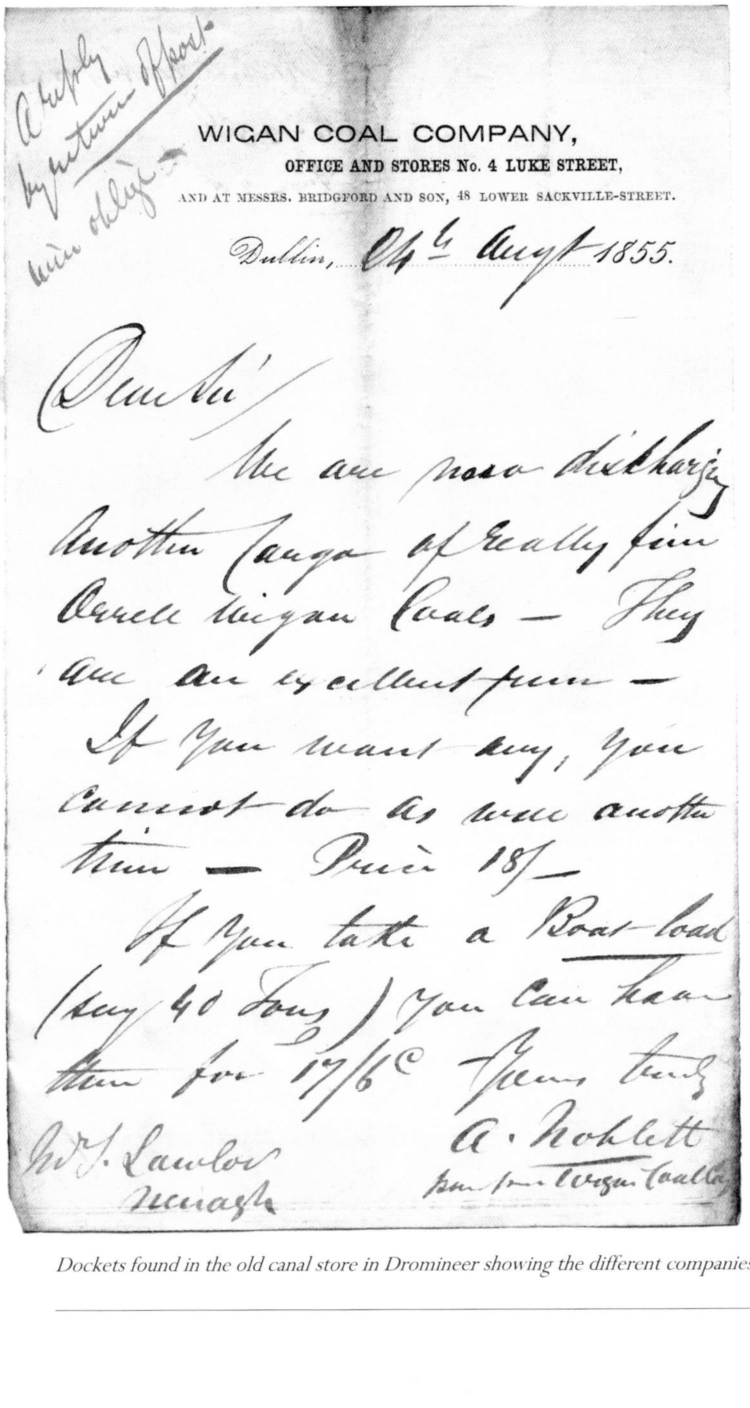

Docket 3 (bottom left):

A reply by return of post will oblige

WIGAN COAL COMPANY,

OFFICE AND STORES No. 4 LUKE STREET,

AND AT MESSRS. BRIDGFORD AND SON, 48 LOWER SACKVILLE-STREET.

Dublin, 04th Augt 1855.

Dear Sir,

We are now discharging Another Cargo of Really fine Arrell Wigan Coals — They are an excellent firm —

If you want any, you cannot do as well another time — Price 18/—

If you take a Boat load (say 40 Tons) you can have them for 17/6 Yours truly

A. Noblett
pro Wigan Coal Co.

Mr. Lawlor
Nenagh

Docket 4 (bottom right):

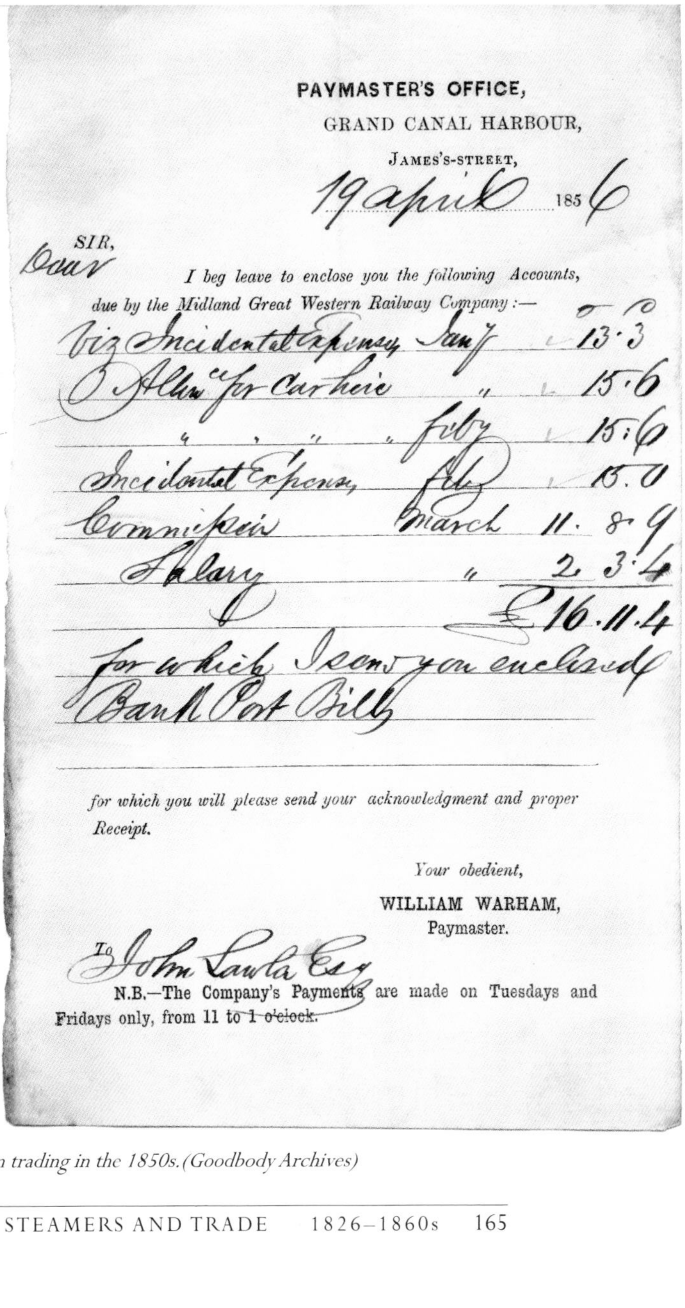

PAYMASTER'S OFFICE,

GRAND CANAL HARBOUR,

JAMES'S-STREET,

19 April 185 6

SIR,
Dear

I beg leave to enclose you the following Accounts, due by the Midland Great Western Railway Company:—

viz Incidental Expensy Jany — 13. 3
Allow. for Car hire " — 15. 6
" " " Feby — 15. 6
Incidental Expensy Feby — 15. 0
Commission March — 11. 8. 9
Salary " — 2. 3. 4
£ 16. 11. 4

for which I send you enclosed Bank Post Bill

for which you will please send your acknowledgment and proper Receipt.

Your obedient,

WILLIAM WARHAM,
Paymaster.

To John Lawlor Esqr

N.B.—The Company's Payments are made on Tuesdays and Fridays only, from 11 to 1 o'clock.

Dockets found in the old canal store in Dromineer showing the different companies engaged in trading in the 1850s. (Goodbody Archives)

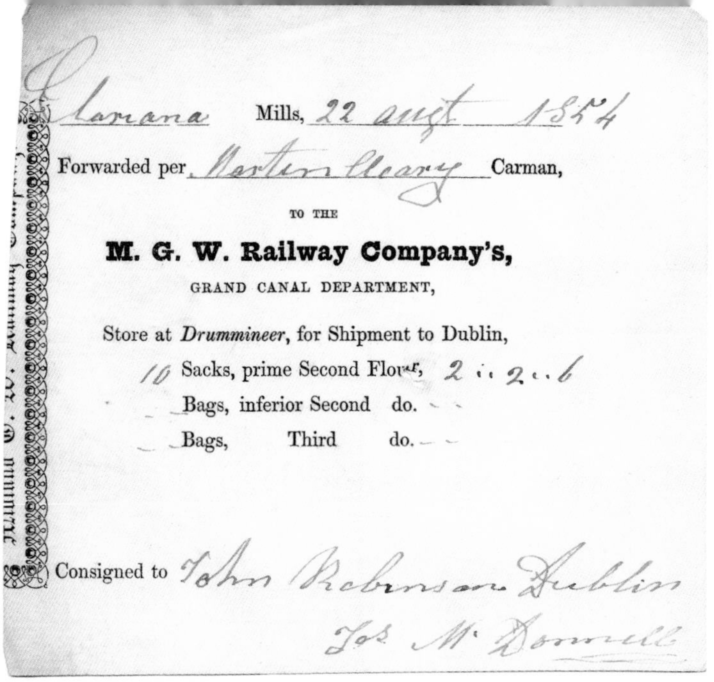
Clarana Mills, 22 aug^t 1854

Forwarded per Martin Cleary Carman,

TO THE

M. G. W. Railway Company's,

GRAND CANAL DEPARTMENT,

Store at *Drummineer*, for Shipment to Dublin,

10 Sacks, prime Second Flour, 2 .. 2 .. 6

Bags, inferior Second do.

Bags, Third do.

Consigned to John Robinson Dublin

Jos. McDonnell

Docket found in the old canal store in Dromineer. (Goodbody Archives)

and 6s 3rd class.[20]

The Midland Great Western Railway Company offered patronage to William Wakeman to publish a guide to the river in 1852.[21] He gave details of the steamer services from Killaloe to Athlone and Athlone to Carrick-on-Shannon operating every second day. The Killaloe boat was served by a coach service from Limerick: 'No mode of travelling can be more delightful than that afforded by the Dublin Steam Company's boats.' He said that the steamers travelled at about 12mph and he described how at Williamstown on Lough Derg a small tender comes out to take passengers ashore who wish to stay in the Williamstown hotel, 'a popular place for fishermen with a promise of salmon or a pike upwards of 40lbs'.

Wakeman gave a vivid description of sailing regattas on Lough Ree:

In August of each year, for a considerable time past, a regatta has been held upon Lough Ree. Hither flock the fashion and beauty of the district for miles around; and once more a fleet enlivens the aspect of the usually deserted lake. Gay vessels, decorated with many-coloured streamers, accompanied by bands of music, and laden with gentlest ladies and gallant gentlemen, glide tranquilly over the scene of many a well-contested battle.

More detail of these regattas is found in a report in the *Westmeath Independent* in August 1858. The regatta was held at Ballyglass over two days with races as well for fishing boats (with spitsail) and 'punt chases'. The report described the scene on the shore:

Tents and standings plentifully supplied with refreshments, were filled with welcome visitors. Fiddlers and pipers were in great requisition . . . The Midland Great Western Railway Company allowed their steamers to ply to and from the town and occasionally to follow yachts around the courses. The regatta concluded with a splendid ball in the Assembly Room of Rourke's Hotel.

Then in 1857 the Midland Great Western Railway Company made the decision to bring two passenger boats to the river to compete with the City of Dublin Steam Packet Company. and also in order to attract passengers from the Limerick area to travel to Dublin via the river and the train from Athlone. These boats came over from the Clyde under their own steam, they then had to be cut in sections for transport by canal and river to Athlone where they had to be reassembled. *The Duchess of Argyle* was a conventional iron paddle wheeler, which had been built originally in Scotland as a private yacht called *Jenny Lind*. She had then been lengthened to150ft 11in (48.5m) and became a passenger boat on the Clyde. When she was being reassembled in Athlone she was shortened again to fit in the lock.[22] The second boat, the *Artizan*, was also an iron paddle wheeler, 113ft (34.4m) long, which had been built as a passenger boat for the Clyde. It was reported that she was 'built for speed, with high pressure engines, and beautifully fitted up with every convenience for passengers'. They operated the service between Athlone and Killaloe, making connections with the Dublin to Athlone train and with a four-horse coach/omnibus conveying the passengers between Killaloe and Limerick. The *Argyle* covered the 58 miles from Athlone to Killaloe in 4½ hours at about 13mph and the *Artizan* in 6 hours. The steamers also called at Dromineer on request offering a service by water to Athlone and rail to Dublin leaving at 9.00am and arriving in Dublin at 5.00pm travelling deck and 3rd class for 6s and cabin and 1st class for 12s 6d with similar return journey arrangements.[23]

The City of Dublin Steam Packet Company was advertising a service in competition on the *Lady Burgoyne* between Killaloe and Athlone three days a week each way, linking with the Great Southern & Western Railway Company. The fare for the boat trip was 7s 6d cabin and 5s deck with a four-day return offer of 11s 3d cabin and 7s 6d deck.[24] Special trips were laid on for events such as the Banagher Fair with the boat leaving Athlone at 6.30 am, arriving at Banagher at 8.30 am and returning to Athlone in the afternoon.[25] The total time to make the journey between Dublin and Limerick on the Midland Great Western Railway Company and its boats was just under twelve hours, double the time taken by the direct train by the rival company but the former was able to offer fares of 12s 6d first and cabin and 6s third and deck against the latter's fare of 23s 9d first and 10s 9d third. A day trip from Athlone to Banagher and back was also on offer for 2s 6d cabin class and 1s 8d deck.

The City of Dublin Steam Packet Company appears to have decided to give up the struggle and it ceased to operate its boats in 1859; the boats were just laid up afloat in Killaloe. In 1862 the Grand Canal Company was still advertising that its screw steamer *Shannon* was making the journey from Killaloe to Athlone three days a week, calling at Williamstown, Portumna, Banagher and Shannonbridge, carrying passengers on board, 6s cabin and 4s 6d deck. It was stated that there was a stewardess on board but reports of the conditions for the passengers were not very good.[26] It was also suggested that at times she was towing one of the canal passenger boats alongside for the comfort of the passengers.[27] In 1862 the canal company complained that four of the steam company's old boats were blocking the entrance to the canal at the pierhead in Killaloe. The two railway companies had entered into an agreement in 1860 and the former agreed as part of this deal to withdraw all the passenger services with the exception of a summer service. The Great Southern & Western Railway Company operated this until 1862 with the *Duchess of Argyle*, which it had purchased from their former rivals in 1860.

Almost all the steamers ended their days laid up afloat in Killaloe. Giving evidence before a select committee of the House of Lords in 1868, Captain Winder, who had skippered one of the boats, said that he had been placed in charge of looking after some of the boats when they were laid up in Killaloe.[28] He confirmed that neither the *Lady Lansdowne* nor the *Lady Burgoyne* had been in service since 1859. He added that some of them were too large to leave the river, they could not be sold and they were not worth breaking up. Another witness remarked: 'They are a wretched exhibition of the expenditure of money thrown away; they are rotting at Killaloe.' W.R. Potts visiting Killaloe aboard his yacht *Audax* in 1874 had commented: 'Killaloe looks more dilapidated than ever, the steamers once the pride of the Shannon, were sunk and going to pieces. The piers fast hastening to decay.' A survey of the remains of a large steamer, probably the *Lady Lansdowne*, was made by Professor P.N. Davies with a team from Liverpool University. They recovered a number of items including two Cantrell & Cochrane bottles containing the names of two local men, John McEvoy and John Brosnan with the date 30 July 1867, which might indicate that she was scuttled on that date.

The *Shannon* was sold in 1869 by which time the canal company had purchased more steamers for towing on both the canal and the Shannon. It is not clear how long the company continued to operate the passenger service. The only further reference to the subject of carrying passengers was a discussion some years later, in 1889, as to whether the *Ballymurtagh*, one of the Grand Canal Company's steamers, which it had acquired from the mining company in County Wicklow, should be fitted up to carry passengers. This was not followed up; towing the canal boats would have made it difficult to maintain a regular service for which there was

The Grand Canal Company's towing steamer Ballymurtagh. *(Molloy, Portumna)*

Killaloe: an early photograph of the steamers out of commission in the mid-to late 1860s with a key to their identity deduced by Andrew Bowcock. (Courtesy of the Irish Picture Library)

probably little demand by this time because of the railways.

Thus this period of the early Shannon passenger steamers had come to an end. It was before the days of general photography but there are some artist's drawings of the steamers even if artistic licence was used in the detail. William Stokes in his *Pictorial Guide to Lough Derg* (London, 1842) shows a steamer alongside at Killaloe, which Andrew Bowcock judges in view of her size and the position of her funnel was probably the *Lady Clanricarde* and not the *Lady Lansdowne* as previously thought. Paul Gauci also shows steamers in his *Select Views of Lough Derg and the River*

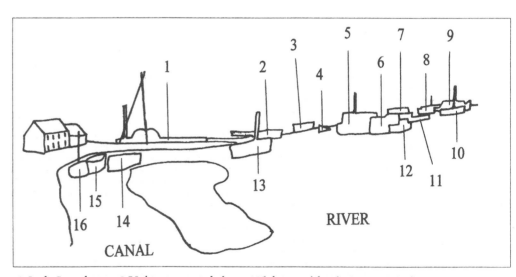

1 *Lady Lansdowne.* 2 Unknown vessel about 60ft long, with what appears to be a superstructure at the stern. 3 Barge. 4 What appears to be part of a sunken barge. 5 *Lady Burgoyne.* 6 *Avonmore.* 7 Dredger, probably one of the four *Victoria, Albert, Prince* and *Princess Alice.* 8 Unknown. 9 *Duchess of Argyle.* 10 Unknown. 11 Unknown. 12 *Lady Dunally* or *Marquess Wellesley.* 13 *Shannon* (the name is clearly visible on the stern). 14 Barge, with what appears to be part of a ship's engine on board. 15 Barge. 16 Vessel with a mast.

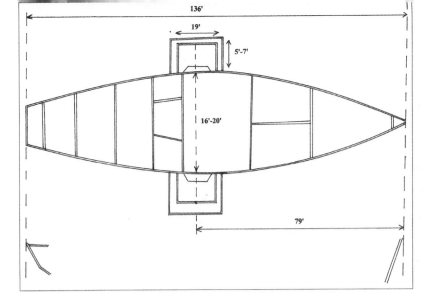

Killaloe: a drawing made by Vincent Delany following a brief survey in 1957 of a submerged steamer thought to be the Lady Lansdowne.

Shannon (Wm. Spooner, 1831) and there is a drawing of the *Avonmore* in Wakeman's guide. There is also a drawing of a steamer passing through Banagher Bridge on the day of its opening on 12 August 1843, drawn by the contractor William Mackenzie. A unique early photograph was taken at Killaloe of the steamers, already laid up there; Andrew Bowcock has drawn up a key identifying them. It was a sad fact that within a little more than ten years of the completion of the major works on the Shannon, passenger traffic had all but ceased because of the railways. However, the story with regard to trading was to be a more positive one.

TRADING ON THE RIVER UP TO THE 1860s

It is possible to trace how trade had developed on the three main divisions of the river leading up to the 1840 works. On the Limerick Navigation, which had the benefit of towpaths once it had been put into repair by the Directors General, trade had increased from the time the navigation had been handed back to the company from 28,212 tons in 1831 to 36,018 in 1836, just prior to being taken over by the Shannon Commissioners. On the middle Shannon, which had been restored by the Grand Canal Company and was being operated by it, tolls had been charged from 1810. The tonnage gradually increased to and from Shannon Harbour from 3,120 tons in 1822 to 20,534 tons in 1837, producing revenue from tolls of £5,669. Most of this trade was downstream to and from Shannon Harbour with only a small proportion operating to and from Athlone.

On the upper river trading was limited, which is not surprising because of the extremely bad state of the navigation and the fact that boats had to be sailed or poled. After the completion of the Royal Canal in 1817 and Lough Allen Canal in 1821 there was some increase in trading. Encouragement was given in that year to the coal and iron trade; boats carrying 30 tons or upwards were allowed to pass toll free on the canal and river for a period of three years. However, the income from tolls on the upper river for 1821 was under £80. By 1835 the tonnage carried on the upper river had risen to 9,770 tons, some of which would have been coal and iron from Lough Allen. The Board of Works collected the tolls on the upper Shannon, which did not even cover the lock keepers' wages and maintenance costs.

During the period of the works under the Shannon Commission, detailed statistics were included in the annual reports for the entire river. In the first year, 1840, a total of 40,882 tons was carried to places on the river, with over one third of this to Limerick, and 31,180 tons was exported, with again about one third from Limerick. Of these totals, 27,425 tons were to and from the Grand Canal and only 3,308 tons to and from the Royal Canal. There was

also a breakdown of the type of cargo carried. Turf made up a little over a quarter of the tonnage 'landed' with slates, coal, timber, grain, flour products and general merchandise being the other main items. Of the loaded tonnage, the principal cargo was grain, with slates, coal, timber, flour products and general merchandise making up the other large amounts. The coal and iron trade from Lough Allen amounted to less than a quarter of the tonnage of English coal finding its way up and down the river from the Grand Canal at Shannon Harbour.

Despite the continuing works on the river involving temporary closures the trade was improving and by 1845 the total tonnage had risen to 51,661 tons landed and 53,423 tons loaded. Athlone was now taking in nearly as much as Limerick but the latter was still sending out by far the most tonnage. The tonnage to and from the Royal Canal had actually dropped with virtually no coal going out and even some coal arriving on the river from Dublin. The total tonnage carried on the river reached a peak in 1847 of 121,702½ tons before railway competition began to take effect. A breakdown of the tonnage carried in that year shows that about three-quarters of the trade was imports and that Limerick was the destination of nearly two-thirds of this trade, most of which had come down the Grand Canal from Dublin.[29] Limerick was also the station from which more than half of the goods were exported. The emphasis was now on the heavier and bulkier goods such as building materials, agricultural produce, coal, turf and manure. In 1849, the final year in which returns were made to the Shannon Commissioners, the tonnage of landed goods was 54,627 tons and of loaded goods 34,292 tons. The completion of the works and the effect of steam towage did not lead to any sort of dramatic increase and there was still no sign of any coal or iron trade picking up from the Lough Allen district.

Over the period of the works the revenue from tolls had averaged about £1,600 after which the administration of the navigation reverted to the Board of Works. The railways prevented much increase with tolls averaging about £2,200 per year. The war of rates between railway companies and the Board of Works led to a fluctuation in toll charges. For example in 1853 tolls were reduced to try to encourage trade but this actually led to a loss in revenue and only a small increase in tonnage. In that same period salaries and the limited amount of maintenance required amounted to an average of £4,000 per year. Some documents salvaged from the canal store in Dromineer by Michel Goodbody covering the 1850s give some idea of how the trade operated from the smaller stations. In 1856 the agent, John Lawler, received a small salary of £2 3s 4d per month but earned £8 15s in commission. As part of his duties he organized deliveries of coal to customers in Nenagh and the surrounding countryside: for example in 1855 he was offered a special price by Wigan Coal Company of 17s 6d per ton if he accepted a boat load of 40 tons. The cargoes being landed at Dromineer were largely for the merchants of Nenagh and the surrounding area: general groceries, porter, wine, flour, meal etc. In 1853 the Midland Great Western Railway Company had leased the Grand Canal Company carrying trade for a seven-year period and Lawler was written to in 1856 by Samuel Healy from the railway company's Grand Canal Department in Dublin advising him of the termination of the rates agreement with the Great Southern & Western Railway Company and requesting Lawler to keep the Dublin office advised of rate changes to enable them to be matched.

A boat registration certificate, 1860.

Bellisle House

A drawing by William Stokes of yachts at Bellisle, near Portumna in 1842.

By the 1860s the total tonnage had risen to over 90,000 tons, 30,000 tons of which was landed or loaded in Limerick, and about 15,000 tons landed or loaded in Athlone, with under 25,000 tons landed or loaded upstream of Lough Ree. Receipts from tolls fell as low as £1,347 but in 1872 another new schedule of tolls was introduced, which brought about a small increase to £2,129. The high expectations for the navigation, which had motivated the government's investment in the works, had not materialized and this in turn was to lead to a renewed focus on flooding issues and calls for drainage schemes.

CHAPTER ELEVEN
THE CHANGING SCENE 1860s–1940s

1860s–1890s

The annual reports of the Board of Works give some indication of what was involved in the management of the Shannon from the 1860s to the 1890s.[1] The income from tolls, wharfage and rents in each year after they assumed control of the river just about met the expenditure and maintenance, leaving very little for any extra work. In the 1860s the only record of any work was the lengthening of Annabeg lock on the Limerick Navigation by 3ft 6in (1m) to accommodate the new Grand Canal Company steamers in 1862. These were the *Dublin, Limerick* and *Athlone*, which carried 60 tons cargo in addition to acting as towing vessels and the *Brian Boru* which carried 80 tons. The company also acquired the *Ballymurtagh* in 1868 from the Wicklow Copper Mining Company; the older *Shannon*, which could carry 100 tons was sold in 1869. Severe weather increased maintenance costs, especially damage from floods and in 1867 a particularly cold winter caused damage to markers from ice. In 1874 it was reported that the coal trade on the Lough Allen Canal was increasing rising to 2,102 tons but two years later with the level of Lough Allen at its highest for fifty years, the canal bank burst upstream of Drumleague lock and in 1878 the canal here was frozen from 9 December to 18 January. At this time it was recorded that much of the Boyle trade was being carried by rail to Sligo.

When the major flood mitigation works and installation of the new sluices were nearing completion in 1882, the Board of Works decided to raise the tolls on the Shannon. The Grand Canal Company's response was that if these increases came into force they would have to cease trading on the river.[2] The increase involved was 50 per cent and in some instances this represented a 400 per cent increase on the charges of ten years earlier. The company said that this meant that freight charges would have to be increased, which in turn would lead to a further transfer of business to the railways and, although trade was showing some signs of improving, it was still not at present 'in a prosperous state'. The deputation attending the Board of Works said that the company would be looking for compensation of £6,300 for their Shannon steamers if they could no longer trade. The controversy rumbled on with lengthy correspondence back and forth, and no tolls were paid for a period of nine months pending the outcome. The Board of Works suggested that the navigation might become a trust and it did not want to diminish the solvency of such a trust but it felt that the canal company should not abandon its Shannon trade in a hasty decision. The canal company's response was that it would continue to trade at the old rates but, when this was not accepted, a decision was made to cease trading at the end of June 1883. In any event the trade had never been very

Boats owned by the Delany family, Chang-Sha, La Vague II *and* Oudra, *wintering in Richmond Harbour. (Alf Delany archives)*

profitable. The company was then asked 'frankly to submit to them any suggestions for the establishment of such a scale of tolls and charges as shall be consistent with the solvency of the Trust'. Eventually, the Board of Works agreed to retain the tolls at the 1882 level pending any future reorganization of the navigation's administration. The canal company promised to attempt to increase trade and help to make any future trust self-supporting. The trust did not materialize and that seems to have been the end of the matter. Although the traffic was very small on the upper river, the board was maintaining the works reasonably well: for example, new tail gates were fitted to the Albert lock in 1883.

In 1875 the Midland Great Western Railway Company had also decided to purchase five steamers for towing on the canal and river: the *Rambler, Rattler, Mermaid, Conqueror* and *Pioneer.* The *Rambler* and *Rattler* were built in Scotland and appear to have started out originally as passenger steamers.[3] The railway company had entered the carrying business in 1871 using horse-drawn boats and now they used the two larger steamers, the *Rambler* and *Rattler,* to carry cargo up to 30 tons and tow on both the river and canal and the three smaller boats to tow on the canal. The experiment was not a success and the railway company ceased to act as carriers in 1886. It is possible that the *Rambler,* which was 70ft (21.4m) long, continued to be used as an inspection boat on the Royal Canal; she was too long to fit in the Grand Canal. From 1920 to 1923 she was used by the Department of Agriculture and converted into a laboratory for an extensive fishery survey of Lough Derg together with a boat called the *Chang-Sha,* which was used as extra accommodation. The *Rambler* was then sold to T.W. Delany in 1923, who converted her into a comfortable house-boat and at the same time his brother, Dr V. S. Delany, bought the *Chang-Sha*; the two boats often cruised in company. The latter was a 'personal yacht', known

as 'Sankey's Steamer', which had been built for a gentleman called Sankey in 1846 who was later chairman of the Board of Works. She was constructed with iron from the Lowmoor pits, which had a very low percentage (.016) of carbon in its composition, giving it a high resistance to rusting. She was bought by Major Lloyd of Knockvicar House around the turn of the century, who removed her steam engine and named her the *Chang-Sha,* the Chinese for 'river house'. Both these boats changed hands several times over the years.[4] One of the owners of the *Chang-Sha* from 1942 to 1957 was the well-known Syd Shine of Athlone, who restored her and lived aboard her during those years. Both boats experienced changing fortunes but are still active on the waterways today, with the Becker family owning *Chang-Sha* and John and Siobhan Connon the *Rambler.* While there is no record of what became of the *Rattler,* it is just possible that she was one of the boats that remained on the Royal Canal as a maintenance boat, Float No 1, and then fell into disuse. Gay Boylan purchased this boat in the late 1960s and cut a section out of the middle so that she would fit in the Grand Canal. She was subsequently bought by John Dolan and refurbished as a family boat for the waterways.

The Chang-Sha *today now owned by the Becker family. (Colin Becker)*

The original Fox *owned today by Syd Shine.*

Two more boats, which still survive today, were also constructed of the long-lasting Lowmoor iron. These were the *Fox* and *Bat*, two of four steam tugs built for the Grand Canal Company in 1865-1866 by Grendons foundry in Drogheda, the others being the *Bee* and *Fly*. Because of the time it took to lock through long trains of boats on the canal, the company chiefly used the small steamers to tow boats on the long levels and these boats subsequently had varied histories. The *Fox* was purchased by the Board of Works and served as a maintenance boat from 1910 until 1957. Syd Shine bought her and fitted her out as his

floating home and still lives aboard today. In 1927 the *Bat* was purchased and used in the construction of Ardnacrusha. She was subsequently abandoned, rescued, restored and converted by Mick Donaghue, the Grand Canal lock keeper at Ballycommon. Also known as *25M*, she has had a number of owners and is now owned by Kieran and Kay Walsh and is called *Shantrek*. The *Bee* had her steam engine removed in 1905 and became a horse-drawn trading boat. She was later fitted with a bolinder diesel in 1913 and became *24M* and was subsequently sold to a by-trader in 1938 and became *115B*.[5] Another boat that has survived was the *Naas*. She and her sister ship, *Athy*, were built in 1895 in Wales for Odlums, millers, to work between Waterford and St Mullins. In 1947 the *Athy* was scrapped and the *Naas* was scuttled to shore up the weir at Milford on the River Barrow. The *Naas* was subsequently raised, fitted out and renamed *Jarra* and still travels the waterways today.

In 1887 the Allport Commission on Irish Public Works, mentioned in the previous chapter in connection with drainage issues, had delivered its report.[6] It recommended the setting up of Conservancy Boards as guardians of rivers, invested with powers and duties to rate the catchments areas for maintenance and improvements. However, in relation to the Shannon it suggested that further works were needed as already indicated to control flooding and these

The Grand Canal Company's towing steamer Bee *in Athlone lock in about 1910 with the canal boat she had under tow.*
(Courtesy of the National Library of Ireland)

would have to be funded by the government and in future a general rate applied to the catchment for maintenance. Its gloomy assessment that the river should be considered as a channel for arterial drainage rather than a navigation was an indication of government thinking about the Shannon at that time.

In 1891 it was recorded that the floods were as bad as they had been in 1861 but the benefit of installing sluices in the weirs had been clearly shown and the new sluices at Lough Allen were completed by 1893. In the 1890s the total tonnage carried on the river, having fallen away sharply, had risen again to nearly 90,000 tons but, although this brought up the total revenue, the expenditure had also increased. In 1897 the Grand Canal Company directors complained that their competitors were doing better than they were in the Shannon trade.[7] They said there were five other privately operated steamers, the *Corbally* owned by the Killaloe Slate Company, the *Marina* and the *Monarch* owned by King of Portumna, the *Lady of the Lake* operated by the Waterford & Limerick Railway Company and the *Ida* owned by Hynes of Scarriff. The canal company complained that while the railway company was working with the principal trader in Scarriff, 'we have an ex-policeman who until recently was protecting an unpopular landlord within a few miles of the town'. A circular letter was sent out to their agents advising them of the increasing threat from rail competition, requesting to be advised about customers changing over to rail transport and impressing on them the need to canvas for business.[8] The canal company then bought the *Lady of the Lake* from the railway company for £395. The fleet of steamers was constantly changing at this time with boats being sold and replaced and also moved backwards and

The steamer Monarch *owned by King of Portumna.*

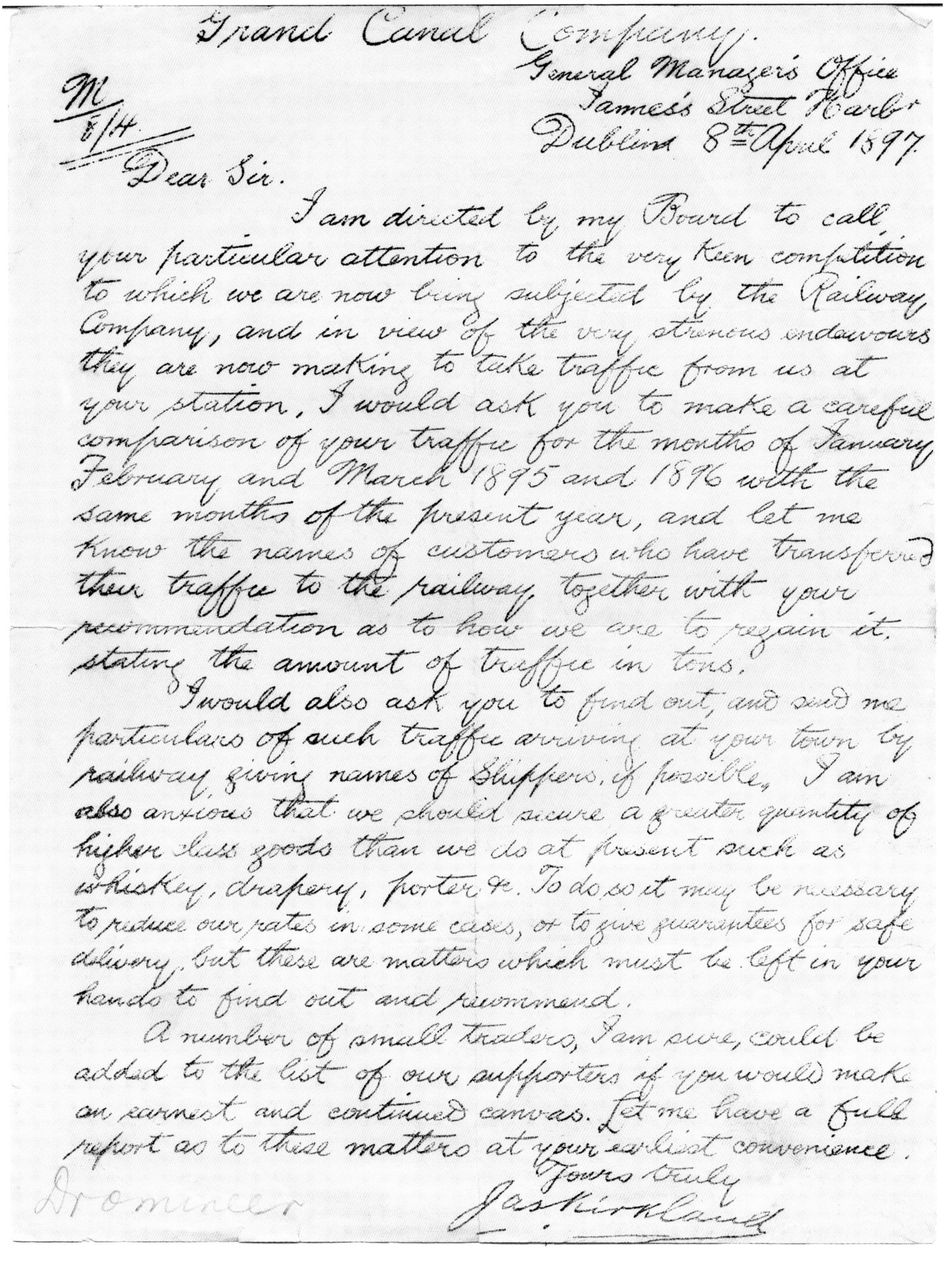

Grand Canal Company.

General Manager's Office
James's Street Harbr
Dublin 8th April 1897

M
6/4.

Dear Sir.

I am directed by my Board to call your particular attention to the very keen competition to which we are now being subjected by the Railway Company, and in view of the very strenuous endeavours they are now making to take traffic from us at your station, I would ask you to make a careful comparison of your traffic for the months of January February and March 1895 and 1896 with the same months of the present year, and let me know the names of customers who have transferred their traffic to the railway, together with your recommendation as to how we are to regain it. stating the amount of traffic in tons.

I would also ask you to find out, and send me particulars of such traffic arriving at your town by railway, giving names of Shippers, if possible, I am also anxious that we should secure a greater quantity of higher class goods than we do at present such as whiskey, drapery, porter &c. To do so it may be necessary to reduce our rates in some cases, or to give guarantees for safe delivery, but these are matters which must be left in your hands to find out and recommend.

A number of small traders, I am sure, could be added to the list of our supporters if you would make an earnest and continued canvas. Let me have a full report as to these matters at your earliest convenience.

Yours truly
Jas Kirkland

Dromineer

The increasing threat from rail competition in the 1890s is reflected in this circular letter found in the canal store in Dromineer. (Goodbody Archives)

A Shannon Navigation poster, 1894

forwards from towing duties between the Grand Canal, the Barrow Navigation and the Shannon.

THE SHANNON DEVELOPMENT COMPANY

A new company, the Shannon Development Company, had been set up in 1897 and a colourful but, sadly, a rather short period in the long history of the navigation followed.

A Railway Act in 1896 had made available loans and grants for railways and ancilliary works. The new company intended to operate a steamer service on the estuary between Tarbert and Kilrush and also that steamers would operate between Killaloe and Dromod connecting with the railways.[9] £15,000 of the capital was to be subscribed by shareholders with a subsidy of £9,500 together with a guaranteed payment of £1,700 p.a. levied on eight of the adjoining counties for a period of seven years. The company undertook to place two steamers on the river 'fully equipped for both passengers and light goods traffic and capable of steaming at least ten miles per hour'. A daily weekday service was promised during the tourist season, with a bi-weekly service the rest of the year. In 1897 the Duke of York, later to become George V, travelled with a party on the *Countess of Mayo* from Portumna to Banagher where he was received by Lord Rosse and presented with an illuminated address.[10] The event recorded in the *Illustrated London News* was accompanied by an illustration that showed the royal party on the deck sheltering under a tarpaulin, looking as if they were encountering less than kind weather. From there the royal party boarded a train on the Clara – Banagher branch of the GS&WR Co. It is recorded that he was 'graciously pleased' to accept the honour of the naming of the stretch of

From snapshot by]   [*M. J. Fitz-Patrick.*

MEELICK LOCK.

D

The Countess of Cadogan *in the lock at Meelick.*

river the 'Duke of York Route', a title which the company subsequently extended to the entire route from Killaloe to Dromod.[11]

However, the Killaloe to Dromod route did not work out very well because of the time taken to pass through the locks and bridges. Roosky was substituted for Dromod with a coach to the railway station from the lock. The daily service was found to be impractical and the service was split into a second route to and from Athlone. The number of passengers was so limited that the upper-river service was reduced to one trip per week between Athlone and Carrick but an extension of the services across the lake on Lough Derg was provided. In the following year a further modification was sought in the timetables with the abandonment of the winter service because of lack of use, although the service

The Countess of Cadogan *passing through the bridge at Banagher. (Courtesy of the National Library of Ireland)*

BOAT PIER. KILLALOE. 5589. W. L.

The Countess of Cadogan *at the Pierhead, Killaloe. (Courtesy of the National Library of Ireland)*

in the estuary was doing well in the summer. The company built a hotel in Custume Place in Athlone, which was known as 'The Shannon Pension' but it was not a success and was subsequently sold. The Board of Works had provided a site for a slip and repair yard in Athlone and also for a hotel in Killaloe for £300. The hotel, named the Lake Hotel, was opened in 1900 and the steamers operated from the end of May to the end of September running daily between Killaloe and Athlone, Athlone and Roosky, Roosky and Carrick and also on Lough Derg, with a modified winter service.

When fully expanded, the company possessed six vessels, three of them fine boats capable of carrying 200 passengers at 15mph. These were the *Countess of Mayo, Countess of Cadogan* and *Lady Betty Balfour* with two smaller boats, the *Fairy Queen* and *Shannon Queen* working upstream of Athlone while the sixth boat, the *Olga*, operated the cross-lake service on Lough Derg. In a guide book produced by the Great Southern & Western Railway Company in 1898 there is an account of a trip on the Shannon.[12] Another guide, produced by the same company, The Duke of York

The Countess of Mayo. *(Courtesy of the National Library of Ireland)*

THE ROYAL VISIT TO IRELAND.— THE TRIP ON THE RIVER SHANNON: THE DUKE AND DUCHESS OF YORK AND PARTY ON BOARD THE STEAM-SHIP "COUNTESS OF MAYO."

The Duke and Duchess of York aboard the Countess of Mayo *in 1897.*(Illustrated London News)

of Wales' Route.					30th May to 30th September.	
...VICE.			July and Aug. only.	DOWN SERVICE.		July & Aug. only.
...Y	dep.	9 0 a.m.	1 30 p.m.	BANTRY dep.	— 7 0 p.m.	—
	arr.	11 0 ,,	3 30 ,,	GLENGARRIFF arr.	8 0 ,,	
	dep.	11 15 ,,	4 0 ,,	dep. 1 45 p.m.	—	9 0 a.m.
...IFF	arr.	1 0 p.m.	5 45 ,,	KENMARE arr. 3 30 ,,	—	10 45 ,,
	dep.	5 55 p.m.		dep. 4 0 ,,	—	10 50 ,,
	arr.	6 50		KILLARNEY arr. 6 15 ,,	—	12 50 p.m.

...t Route.				1st June to 30th September.	
UP SERVICE.		July and Aug. only.	DOWN SERVICE.		
...Y	dep.	9 0 a.m.	1 30 p.m.	MACROOM dep.	10 30 a.m.
...IFF	arr.	1 0 p.m.	5 45 ,,		Via the Lakes of Inchigeela and the Pass of Keimaneigh and stopping at Gougane Barra.
	dep.		3 0 p.m.		
		Via the Pass of Keimaneigh, and stopping at Gougane Barra and at Inchigeela for Tea.	GLENGARRIFF arr.	2 15 p.m.	
					July & Aug only.
	arr.		7 15 p.m.	(next day) dep.	9 0 a.m. 6 15 ,,
				KILLARNEY arr.	12 50 p.m. 6 15 p.m.

Atlantic Coast Route.				1st June to 30th September.	
UP SERVICE.			DOWN SERVICE.		
...EEN	..	dep. 1 45 p.m.	PARKNASILLA	..	dep. 9 0 a.m.
...LLE	..	arr. 3 30 ,,	WATERVILLE	..	arr. 11 0 ,,
		dep. 4 0 ,,		..	dep. 11 15 ,,
...LLA	..	arr. 6 0 ,,	CAHIRCIVEEN	..	arr. 12 50 p.m.

...l Kenmare-Parknasilla Service.				30th May to 30th September.			
UP SERVICE.				DOWN SERVICE.			
...LLA dep.	9 15 a.m.	12 35 p.m.	3 20 p.m.	KENMARE dep.	11 45 a.m.	2 0 p.m.	4 40 p.m.
...arr.	10 30 ,,	1 50 ,,	4 35 ,,	PARKNASILLA arr.	12 25 p.m.	3 15 ,,	5 55 ,,

See also P.O.W.R. Service.

NOTICES.

...rs do not run on Sundays. ... uld be reserved the evening before, with the local ... ise they cannot be guaranteed. ... are allowed 25 lbs. of luggage only on the Motors ... ed free at owner's risk. All heavy baggage, trunks, etc., must be sent by rail, for which special arrangements have been made. The above times are subject to alteration without notice, and the Tourist Development (I.), Ltd., cannot accept any responsibility for any delays or other departure from the service shown above.

A Shannon Development Company timetable for the Duke of York Route.

The Lady Betty Balfour *with an excursion party aboard.*

Route via the Shannon Lakes, showed illustrations of the steamers and stated that circular tickets were issued from Dublin by it, which included the river trip and lunch; it also gave details of the scale of charges for the carriage of parcels and light goods.

For various reasons the undertaking did not prosper, the most profitable business was in taking excursion groups.

The Fairy Queen.

In 1902 it was stated that the receipts amounted to £1,403 but the total receipts since the opening of the services had only amounted to £9,519. After 1903 the vessels only plied in the summer. A 1904 timetable shows a daily service leaving Athlone at 9.30 am and arriving at Killaloe at 5.45 pm. It stated that the steamer also calls at stations on Lough

The Olga. *(Courtesy of the National Library of Ireland)*

THE SHANNON DEVELOPMENT COMPANY, LTD.

In Your Reply

61
99

give this reference.

In Reply to your

MEMORANDUM—From *Athlone* to *Dromineer*

6th day of *January* 1899.

Mr Burgess.

Dear Sir,
Direct steamer will call for any passenger for Killaloe. If there are none please show Red flag, and oblige

Yours truly,
J. McCormick,
Supt.

A telegram with instructions about signalling if there were passengers to be picked up. (Goodbody Archives)

Derg when landing passengers or when signalled for by a flag that there were intending passengers. The service between Athlone and Dromod took five hours with rail connections with Dublin at either end and luncheons and tea provided on the steamer. In 1906, when the seven-year period of subsidy ended, the services were further curtailed. After the end of the 1906 season the *Fairy Queen* went to the Corrib. She was replaced on that lake by the *Countess of Cadogan* in 1913, when the former steamer was sold to Fulton of Glasgow and, when the Corrib service was suspended, she went to Aberdeen. The *Countess of Mayo* was sold to Warrenpoint and subsequently ended up in Jarrow-on-Tyne. The *Olga* was lost at sea on her way to England in 1909.

The *Shannon Queen* was the last of the company's boats to operate and then she was sold to Mr Holmes of Athlunkard. From a timetable dated June 1914 it appears that the service had been reduced to one trip daily each way between Killaloe and Banagher. The timetable stated that it was possible to travel by train from Dublin to Banagher and by steamer to Killaloe where a branch line met the boat to link with the main line back to Dublin. The fare was 14s 6d first class and 11s third class, with luncheon and tea on board the steamer. The river trip lasted five hours calling at Meelick, Portumna, Rossmore, Williamstown and Dromineer. Even this service ceased after the outbreak

The Shannon Development Company's new hotel at Killaloe, later to become the Lakeside Hotel.
(Courtesy of the National Library of Ireland)

Steamers alongside at Athlone.

of the 1914-1918 war. The directors of the Grand Canal Company considered taking over the *Lady Betty Balfour* in 1915 for £400 with two-thirds of any profits paid to the Shannon Development Company but, not surprisingly, negotiations broke down largely because of the mortgage on the steamer. She subsequently went briefly to Bantry Bay and then to Warrenpoint, ending up in Aberdeen. There was no attempt to revive the service after the war although for a short period in about 1927 the Portumna Pleasure Boat Company, spearheaded by Major Bertie Waller, operated the *Jolly Roger* without any success.

Steamers alongside at Athlone.

EARLY HYDRO-ELECTIC PROPOSALS

The Board of Works continued to carry out some maintenance on the river in the 1890s, replacing the lock gates of the Clarendon lock at Knockvicar, carrying out some dredging and repairs to bridges, locks and sluices. A new pier was built at Williamstown, under an arrangement with the owner, and wooden piers were erected at Rossmore and Dromineer. The Shannon Water & Power Act in 1901 was a cause of concern because it envisaged lowering Lough Derg up to 7ft (2.1m), which the Board of Works said was totally unacceptable.[13] New plans proposed building a weir at Castleconnell, directing the water into a headrace canal to a single fall at a power station with a tailrace to lead the water back into the Shannon. In order to protect fishery interests the amount of water flowing down the river channel had to be guaranteed and this meant that at certain times of the year there would not be sufficient water to run the power station, which would need auxiliary steam power to generate. It is suggested that this difficulty effectively killed the initiative. Messrs Guinness, who relied heavily on water transport, had also petitioned against it. That the threat to the navigation was taken very seriously is reflected in some investigations conducted by the 'Intelligence Department, St James's Gate Brewery', which revealed that the rate paid per ton from Dublin to Limerick was 10s against a railway rate of 13s 6d. In 1899 16,444 tons had been sent by water at a cost of £12,396 in tolls to the canal company and if this 35 per cent increase had to be paid it would have resulted in a payment of £16,734 to the railway company. The point was also stressed that if water-transport competition was removed increases in railway rates would occur and places like Scarriff, which were some distance from railheads, would suffer and increasing costs would adversely affect exports in heavy goods such as grain and timber.

A Shannon Electric Power Syndicate Ltd. certificate, 1900.

Lengthy negotiations and investigations continued on the whole issue of a hydro-electric scheme for the river. Another scheme in 1915 also failed to materialize. In 1918, the Board of Trade was instructed to investigate the natural sources of energy in both Great Britain and Ireland arising out of the problem of shortages that had been experienced during the 1914-1918 war. In 1919 the Irish waterpower sub-committee of this Board of Trade inquiry, under the chairmanship of Sir John Purser Griffith, looked at the potential of the Shannon, Erne, Bann and Liffey and recommended that any future scheme on the Shannon should be state controlled, but questioned the output capacity of the Shannon; a report by Theodore Stevens proposed that four hydroelectric stations should be erected along the course of the river.[14] At the same time Sinn Fein established a Commission of Enquiry into the Resources and Industries of Ireland.[15] No action followed and it was to be left to the new Irish Free State government to finally take some action.

THE BINNIE AND SHUTTLEWORTH COMMISSIONS

In 1905 a Commission on Arterial Drainage, under the chairmanship of Sir Alexander Binnie, saw no reason to differ from the findings of the Allport Commission and from the earlier Monck Commission, which had taken exhaustive evidence. It recommended that drainage should remain under the control of a government department that would be in a position to consider the conflicting interests of drainage, navigation, fisheries and power.[16] In 1906 a Royal Commission on Canals and Waterways was appointed, which could be said to have been the first comprehensive survey of water transportation in the British Isles.[17] Lord Shuttleworth was appointed chairman with eighteen members, seven of them titled and three with Irish connections: J.P. Griffith, a member of the Council of the Institution of Civil Engineers who had done consultancy work for the government, Laurence Waldron, chairman of the Grand Canal Company, and M.J. Minch, a director of the Grand Canal Company. The commission had a very wide brief and, with regard to Ireland, the most important issues were the organization and development of the waterways. Eighty-two witnesses were examined about the Irish waterways between 21 March and 31 July 1906, sitting in Dublin for eight days and Belfast for three days, with further evidence called later in London. Those called to give evidence were divided into two sections: Municipal Bodies or Local Authorities and Traders or Agriculturalists, who were given specific questions to answer in advance confining them to navigational issues.

Limerick Navigation: the harbour above the 1st lock in the 1930s.

Limerick Navigation: the Limerick to Ennis train crossing the Park Canal.

The Shannon did not figure very much in the deliberations. Harry Lefroy gave evidence that he was a miller in Killaloe and operated his own boats but he said that, apart from one other private trader, the Grand Canal Company was the only operator. A good deal of attention was given to the fact that the navigation was 'throttled' by smaller locks at either end, between Limerick and Killaloe and in the Lough Allen canal. An estimate was put in for lengthening six locks (two of them double locks) on the Limerick Navigation to 82ft (25m) at a cost of £6,000 to bring them in line with the other five locks. The difficulty caused by the low bridges and strong current in the Abbey river below the last lock in Limerick was one of the issues raised so that easier access could be provided to and from the canal to the floating docks. A point frequently made was the importance of waterway competition in keeping down railway rates. E.J. Long, the owner of a tannery in Limerick, produced a table indicating that the cost per ton for transporting hides between Limerick and Dublin was cheaper by rail (17s 1d against 25s 11d) but from Limerick to Athlone the position was reversed (22s 1d against 18s 7d).

The final conclusions and recommendations of the commission stated:

The only hope for the successful treatment of the problems connected with drainage and inland navigation in Ireland depends on their being under the control of some central authority possessing technical knowledge and having full powers to deal with them. This authority should not be exclusively identified with any one of the interests above mentioned [navigation, drainage, water power and fisheries], but should act as an impartial tribunal to decide conflicting questions arising between them.

The commissioners drew attention to the small volume of traffic in general on the Irish waterways compared to the large volumes in England and was not prepared to recommend the expensive scheme that they were putting forward for English waterways but they did suggest a moderate expenditure. With regard to specifying actual work to be carried out on the Shannon, they recommended the lengthening of the locks on the Limerick Navigation and that this work should be funded by the state at the estimated cost of £6,000. Some other minor works were recommended on the Limerick Navigation amounting to £24,410 and a sum of £2,000 to be spent on essential dredging upstream on the river. With reference to the struggling Shannon Development Company it was suggested that if an efficient steamer service were to be restarted on the river at least four steamers would be required at a cost of approximately £20,000. Neither the recommendation of a Waterway Authority, nor of even the modest expenditure on works suggested, resulted in any action by the government.

TRADE IN THE EARLY 1900s

The tonnage carried on the river had been increasing but an application from the Grand Canal Company for a reduction in tolls was refused. The canal company had purchased more new steamers in the 1890s and early 1900s, the *Portumna*, the *Killaloe*, the *Tullamore* and the *Carrick*. By 1910 the tonnage on the river had almost reached 100,000 tons. From 1911 the existing horse-drawn canal boats were gradually fitted with bolinder diesel engines and, although they could now proceed under their own power, towing by steamer on the river was still much faster. Despite all these efforts of the canal company the tonnage carried on the river was to fall steeply, by nearly a half, in the war years and the older steamers gradually ceased to operate. The *Tullamore* had been sold in 1896, the *Dublin* was scrapped in 1910, the *Athlone* and *Carrick* in 1916, and subsequently the last two of the steamers, the *Portumna* and *Ballymurtagh*, in 1928. The *Killaloe* was employed doing towage on the Liffey for a while and was fitted with a bolinder diesel engine in 1925, returning to the Shannon for a few years until she was scrapped at Shannon Harbour.

Documents found in the canal store in Dromineer dating from 1897. (Goodbody Archives)

A steamer alongside at Mountshannon on Lough Derg.(Courtesy of the National Library of Ireland)

Steam Tug and Train, near Killina.

A Grand Canal Company steamer towing on the Grand Canal in the 1890s.(Shackleton Archives)

Shannon Harbour in the 1890s.(Shackleton Archives)

CONTEMPORARY ACCOUNTS

Writing in 1897, T.O. Russell described Lough Ree: 'The glories of Loch Ree, with its almost countless islands, and the glories of Loch Dearg, with its mountain-girded shores, are now nearly as unknown to tourists and to the Irish public in general as are the reaches of the Congo or the Niger.'[18] R. Harvey, who lived in Kilteelagh, in Dromineer Bay on Lough Derg, published an account of the river in 1896.[19] It is mostly descriptive and historical with very occasional glimpses of the use being made of the navigation. He referred to the Grand Canal Company steamers arriving daily at Dromineer and described steamers unloading at Scarriff Harbour. He commented on the lack of use being made of the shores of Lough Ree, with what traffic there

was passing straight up and down the lake between Athlone and Lanesborough: 'the lake is a scene of solitude, silence and melancholy'. The harbour at Lanesborough, 'built at the time when it was thought that the Shannon would be the highway of Ireland', was dry and silted up. The Lough Allen Canal he described as being 'just navigable' but in a very bad state with the locks 'in a ruinous condition'.

SHANNON NAVIGATION,

Act 2nd & 3rd Vic., cap. 61.

The Commissioners of Public Works hereby call attention to the following

EXTRACT FROM SECTION XXXVIII., 2nd & 3rd VIC., CAP. 61 :—

" And be it enacted, That it shall not be lawful for any Person whomsoever, from and after the passing of this Act, to fish upon or from any of the Weirs or any Dams or other Work or Works which shall be erected by the said Commissioners, without the Consent of the said Commissioners, which Consent shall be signified by Warrant, and shall continue in force for Three Years and not for any longer Period."

Persons offending against this are liable to a fine not exceeding **TEN POUNDS.**

BY ORDER,

H. WILLIAMS,

Office of the Board of Public Works,
Dublin, 1st July, 1907.

Secretary.

A Shannon Navigation poster, 1907.

A canal boat locking through Tarmonbarry lock with a steamer waiting to tow her above the lock.(Alf Delany Archives)

Small sailing boats were used on the lakes and G.T. Stokes described 'cotts' seen on the river between Athlone and Clonmacnois at this time:

Here the tourist can see many a specimen of the cotts used locally from pre-historic times. They are impelled by poles and remain unchanged, like the coracles of the Isles of Aran, for 2000 years. They are only used on the river, as Lough Ree is too deep for a pole. They are often mentioned in ancient documents as they were much used in warfare, being at the same time noiseless in movement, and capable of conveying a large load. [20]

This would have been similar to the fast rowing boat described in 1779 by Gabriel Beranger and Angelo Bigari for their trip from Athlone to Clonmacnois. [21]

FISHING

In the 1890s and early 1900s there were a number of families living on some of the islands of Lough Ree and Lough Derg. [22] In addition to farming, they relied on an income from fishing, netting trout and setting eel lines to supply the English market. They used an ingenious way of getting around the restrictions of the closed season by creating fish ponds and continuing to fish illegally. When the closed season ended they then had a ready supply of fish available at once for the market. A comment was made in 1895 by Sylvester Hurley of Abbey View Hotel, Killaloe, on the impact on the fishing from all the works:

Now for more than half a century those so-called "Shannon Improvements" have been going on with a cost to the country of countless hundreds of pounds, and we challenge any man to say that six pence worth of good has been effected by this outlay. The land along the course of the river been relieved from floods, the navigation has not been improved, whilst the salmon, trout and eel fisheries of our noble river have been greatly injured. [23]

There was an interesting account of fishing and shooting on Lough Derg and the Estuary published by an Englishman, John Bickerdyke, in 1897. [24] The winters appear to have been very cold and he describes encountering problems with ice in some of shallower bays of Lough Derg. He was treated to stories of the great salmon that used to be caught on the lake in addition to 'large trout and monster pike'. In the previous season it had been reported at a fishery inquiry in Limerick that only about ten salmon had been caught on Lough Derg and he posed two reasons for the falling away in numbers. Firstly the tidal waters were being over-netted and secondly the spawning grounds in the brooks and tributaries

were unprotected and heavily poached. The river stretches around Castleconnell were reckoned to be the only place where good fishing was to be had.

In that year, 1897, public meetings were held and frustrated by the lack of action on the part of the Limerick Board of Conservators, in an attempt to curb poachers on Lough Derg and its tributaries, the landowners around the lake formed a Lough Derg Preservation Society with the subscriptions used to employ bailiffs. [25] The suggestion that a licence fee of 10s should be imposed on boats 'dapping' for trout to create funding was greeted with universal indignation: 'and it is nothing short of downright impudence and tyranny to tax anglers for what has been their right and privilege from time immemorial' – sentiments that were to surface again in recent times. It had become an issue as to whether the riparian owners actually owned the fishing rights of the lake because it was a public navigation. Poachers operating in the closed season were destroying thousands of trout fry. It was also maintained that arterial drainage had deprived fish of many of their natural feeding grounds.

Another booklet from this period that dealt with fishing and shooting on the river was produced by R.D. Levinge. Referring to the three large lakes, Allen, Ree and Derg, he wrote:

Fishing on these lakes is very good, and all the way up the river duck, snipe, plover, and other kind of wild fowl are very plentiful. The people along the banks will be found most obliging and seldom object to your shooting over their lands. As regards fishing it is again quite free. Salmon to be got under the weirs or other shallow parts of the river; trout, pike and perch, large and very plentiful, on the lakes. [26]

Augustus Grimble, a well-known fisherman who wrote a series on fishing in these islands, published an account of his Irish experiences in 1903 with a revised edition in 1913. [27] He included valuable information obtained from some of the owners of fisheries in addition to his own experiences. Of the River Suck he wrote: 'Its waters hold salmon, trout and pike, but the former are so severely poached that no angler would go especially to the Suck for his sport.' He also recorded that there was much poaching of trout during the closed season in winter: 'It is to be regretted that there is no licence imposed on the trout rods, which would form the nucleus of a protection fund.' Killaloe and Castleconnell were the only places of interest to the salmon fisherman. He found that the fishing had gradually deteriorated through the 1890s. He listed eight different way in which salmon were being caught as the reason for the decline: stake nets, seine nets, drift nets in tidal waters, snap nets, rods and nets in the river and finally poachers. Poachers were operating in the tributaries: 'the destruction is wholesale from cartfuls to sackfuls'. The 1863 Act had done away with some of the problems but there had been an increase in drift netting. By 1882 there were 148 of them: 'the ravages of these new nets far exceeded those of the abolished stake-nets, and they are to blame for a great deal of the present scarcity of fish, for wherever they have appeared the fish have decreased . . . It will be a day of rejoicing for the Shannon if the drift nets can be abolished.' He criticized the 1901 report of the Inland Fishery Commission, which had said that catching salmon and trout in the open sea did not interfere with the free passage of the fish into the rivers. He also blamed the removal of the natural rapids in the river and the installing of sluices in the weir at Killaloe, which had brought about the sudden release of water instead of the natural gradual flow.

Another well-known angler and contributor to *The Field*, an Irishman, Joseph Adams, wrote a book based on his experience of fishing in Ireland over a period of forty years.[28] He subsequently brought out a revised edition after the establishment of the Irish Free State but prior to the hydro-electric scheme. He gave a number of reasons for a fall-off in the fishing on the Shannon. He blamed the exploitation of the fisheries as a commercial asset, over netting, drift netting and, above all, poaching. He gave detailed descriptions of fishing the falls at Castleconnell and at Killaloe where there was no longer the steep fall in the river. His second edition praised the fact that the new government had increased the stamping out of illegal fishing and fishing in the closed season; the civic guards were now being used to assist with this work. He pointed out that the new Minister for Fisheries had called a conference to liaise

on all the issues at which it was stressed that the proceeds from angling would be far more remunerative than netting in transforming the economic value of the river. Quoting the example of what had taken place on the River Wye, he added that it would be 'far better to buy out all the netting than allow the abuses to continue that have led to such disasters in the past or be a *laissez faire* policy to crystallise them in the future'.

A fishery survey of Lough Derg, which had been initiated by the British government in August 1920, was completed in March 1923.[29] It is suggested that it was in response to food shortages during the 1914-1918 war, when access to sea fisheries was difficult, and the idea was to investigate stocks of fish on large inland lakes. A limnological laboratory was set up in the east channel below Portumna Bridge.[30] As already mentioned, the *Rambler* and the *Chang - Sha* were moored there to provide a laboratory and accommodation for the two resident naturalists, R. Southern and A.C. Gardiner, a record keeper and a crew of five, including two fishermen, one of whom was an expert netsman. They also had two small boats for getting around the lake, *Ruby* and *Nora*, and a temporary laboratory and store on Hayes's Island. The very detailed data collected is an extremely useful source of information about the condition of Lough Derg at this time, which led to a number of scientific publications that are still quoted today. One of the most important conclusions was that two large trout hatcheries should be established, a suggestion that was to be taken up for Lough Corrib but not for Lough Derg.

The Shannon hydro-electric works in the 1920s were to have a disastrous effect on both eel and salmon fishing and nothing else much seemed to change in the new government's approach to all the other continuing issues. A Commission on Inland Fisheries was held in 1933-1935 but Peter Liddell in a report prepared for Bord Failte in 1971 suggested that there was a 'virtual interment of the Report' imposed by the government because of a minority report contained in it.[31] Liddell, who had prepared his own report before he had sight of this earlier report, noted that there were many points of agreement including the need to run down netting, create a central management body, increase protection measures, license trout fishing and protect the rivers from pollution and the impact of drainage schemes. With reference to yet another Inland Fisheries Commission that had recently been appointed he said that widespread cynicism had been voiced about its usefulness: 'It is generally

John Quigley and his father, Peter, ferrying the donkey across from Killinure Point to bring vegetables into the market in Athlone in 1910. (Peter Quigley, Quigley's Marina)

Landing-Place at Hare Island, Lough Ree.

Pleasure boating at Hare Island on Lough Ree.

William Bulfin's often quoted description of his visit to a regatta at Gailey Bay in the early 1900s demonstrated the great divide that existed at that time between what he called the 'masses' or the 'country' and the 'gentry' or 'the classes' who were organizing the event.[33] He gave a wonderful account of the occasion. There was a marquee for the committees of men who wore red badges and 'were all busy doing nothing in particular'. They held consultations in the marquee 'in which they refreshed themselves with whiskey obtained for that special purpose by public subscription'. There were several Union Jacks around and all the yachts sported them, as did 'two wheezing steam launches'. There were also about a dozen tents selling 'sugar stick, ginger bread and gooseberries' and two or three tents for the sale of drink. Five policemen were on duty and about three hundred people were present. One of the committee with a double-barrelled shotgun eventually fired a shot to start the race for two competing yachts, after which little attention was paid to their progress. He recorded a conversation between two of the 'country' who he described as well-to-do farmers: 'Isn't this regatta a mi-adh of a thing with all them English flags and curicaries . . . what the dickens is the likes of us doin' here at all?' His companion had no idea and Bulfin remarked neither had anyone else: 'What were the likes of them doing there? What indeed!' He described the ladies, some of them in panama hats and others carrying walking sticks and huge racing glasses, who shook hands with each other as if there was a five-bar gate between them. In a more serious vein he goes on to comment on the complete lack of Irishness about the 'classes' and how they looked on 'while their common country grew poorer year by year under a foreign rule that was economically calamitous to both'.

thought to be far too large, and so unlikely to hold hearings often enough in the remoter parts of the country; to have too much emphasis on commercial representation; to have too small a proportion of members with a wide knowledge of riverine problems, and so unlikely to be capable of producing a strong unanimous report leading to the vitally necessary legislation.'

RECREATIONAL BOATING

The sport of sailing goes back a long way on the River Shannon and there is evidence of regattas being held at various venues. On Lough Ree the Athlone Yacht Club had emerged from the Killinure Yacht Club in the 1830s, with Ballyglass the usual rendezvous for the regattas; the Killinure Yacht Club was said to date back to 1770.[32] Sailing on the lake at that time is remembered in the names given to shoals that the boats must have grounded on: for example the Adelaide Rock and the Louisa Shoal. The club became more formalized in 1895 with Rule 1 stating: 'This Club shall be called the Lough Ree Yacht Club and shall consist of gentlemen desirous of encouraging yachting, match sailing and boating on Lough Ree.' In 1914 a clubhouse was erected at Ballyglass, which as already indicated had already been one of the venues for regattas. Regattas were also held in Athlone over the years which were for rowing and other races. In addition there were two-day regattas held at Gailey Bay in the early 1900s preceding the Lough Ree Yacht Club regatta.

On the Shannon, Athlone

Athlone: a postcard of a town regatta.

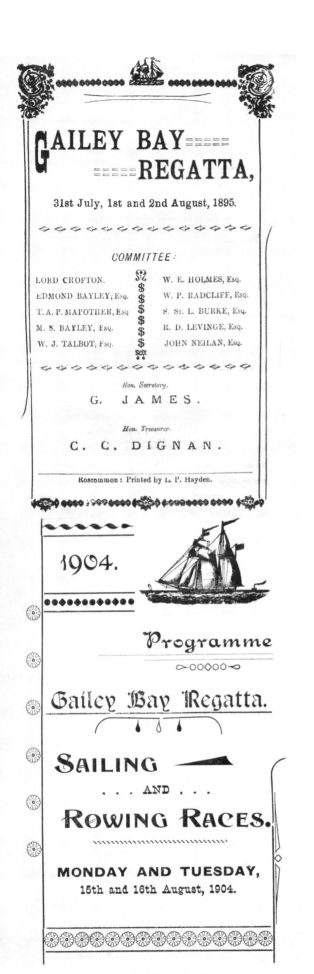

Athlone Yacht Club regatta programme, 1836.(Alf Delany Archives)

Galey Bay regatta programmes for 1895 and 1905.
(Alf Delany Archives)

There are no surviving records of the Lough Derg Yacht Club before 1883. Until then the rendezvous for sailing under the burgee of the Lough Derg Yacht Club seems to have alternated between Kilteelagh in Dromineer Bay and Portumna. The regattas were revived in the 1870s after they been abandoned for a number of years, with six to eight yachts competing and a time allowance system being used as usual for the boats of a smaller tonnage.[34] Hospitality was provided by the various gentleman with estates on the lake including a ball given by Lord and Lady Avonmore at Bellisle. In 1883 the club was reconstituted in Dromineer Bay and its affairs continued to prosper.[35] Then in 1895 a bitter dispute arose between the Commodore and Hon. Secretary on the one hand and Traherne Holmes on the other. There had been a protest between *Knockrockery*, the yacht owned by Traherne Holmes and W.R. Minchin and *Achilla* owned by Robert Harvey. The club awarded the decision to the latter but this was reversed on appeal to the Yacht Racing Association. The dispute spilled over into the local press and ultimately led to the resignation of Holmes and his supporters, who set up a rival Lough Derg Corinthian Yacht Club. This situation lasted until 1904 with neither clubs prospering. Protracted negotiations followed and eventually in 1908, by which time some of the protagonists were dead,

Dromineer: Lough Derg Boat Club premises before the amalgamation with the Lough Derg Yacht Club.(Courtesy of the National Library of Ireland)

the members of the Corinthian Club were elected en bloc to the original club. In 1922 the club amalgamated with the Lough Derg Boat Club and moved to their spacious premises where it is still based today, having recently rebuilt the premises in a similar style.

There is evidence that sailing regattas were held at various other venues on the river including on Lough Allen and on Lough Key in the early 1860s.[36] A regatta on Lough Allen in 1861 was centred on the island which was the summer residence of M. O'Conor where 'a considerable party of spectators assembled as usual'. The wind 'was exceedingly high with occasional squalls' and the racing for the four yachts was close. Luncheon was provided in a spacious marquee on the island and in the evening a ball was held at Blackrock, 'the beautiful residence of A.J.V. Birchall Esq, which was attended by the elite of the vicinity and most of the visitors to the regatta. Dancing was kept up until an early hour on Wednesday morning'.

The Hon. Robert King was the host for the Lough Key regatta in 1862 when all the gates of the demesne were thrown open from an early hour in the morning and the band of the county regiment played on the lawn in front of the Rockingham House and on Castle Island. There were five large yachts competing, with King's new boat *Meta* winning the first two races and Captain Holmes's *Corsair* from Lough Derg doing well in the subsequent races. There were also races for smaller craft. However, judging by the small number of yachts that competed at each of the regattas in

Lough Derg Yacht Club.

ANNUAL REGATTA 1894.

Second day, Thursday, September 6th.

RENDEZVOUS, DROMINEER BAY.

1st Race (B), 11 a.m.—a Challenge Cup, value £15, presented by Major General W. S. Open to all yachts belonging to any recognised Yacht Club; and to be steered by a member cognised Yacht Club. A sealed Handicap. Course No. 2,—four times round—about 20 mile prize. 2nd yacht to take entrance fees. Entrance fee—10s.

STARTERS.			HANDICAP.		
			hrs.	min.	sec.
Messrs. Holmes' & Minchin's " Knockcrockery,"	...		0	0	0
Mr. G. James's " Seadrift."	...	...	0	40	0
Mr. R. Harvey's " Achilla "	...	...	1	20	0

The "Seadrift" gave up the race at first round.

Time at first round :—

	hrs.	min.	sec.
"Achilla,"	2	45	0
" Knockcrockery,"	2	45	2

The yachts were stopped by the committee at the second round, owing to calm weather.

Time at second round—a finish of race :—

	h.	min.	sec.
" Knockcrockery,"	5	25	20
" Achilla,"	5	26	46

PROTEST BY " KNOCKCROCKERY " V. " ACHILLA."

" We, the owners of the 'Knockcrockery,' protest against the owners of the 'Achilla,' Mr. R. on the ground that he did not comply with the conditions of the 1st Race, 2nd day, September that his yacht was steered by one of his crew, who was not a member of a recognised yacht club.

"W. R. MINCHIN,

" (Owner).

" September 6th, 1894."

PROTEST BY " ACHILLA " V. " KNOCKCROCKERY "

" I, the owner of the " Achilla," protest against the owners of the Knockcrockery," Messrs. H and Minchin, in that they did not comply with rule 30 of the Y.R.A., and display an ensig spicuously in the main rigging when lodging the protest against the 'Achilla.'

"R. HARVEY,

" (Owner).

" September 6th, 1894, 6.10 p.m."

Lough Derg Yacht Club regatta programme for 1894, the year of the controversial protest that was to split the club for a number of years. (Alf Delany Archives)

The Tessa *owned by Traherne Holmes. (Alf Delany Archives)*

the early years, the annual events were actually more social occasions for the gentry and a day out for the local people. Boats could work their way down river taking in a number of events ending up on Lough Derg. The large yachts were owned by the landed gentry and, with the installation of opening bridges in the 1840s, they could move freely up and down as far upstream as Lough Bofin and Boderg.

The North Shannon Yacht Club was formed in 1896 and records of the club would suggest that its principal function

PROGRAMME
OF
North Shannon
★ Regatta ★
To be held in Lough Bofin
ON
1st, 2nd, 3rd & 4th August,
1922.

Commodore—Right Hon. the Earl of Kingston.

Vice Commodore—Dr. Kieran Delany.

COMMITTEE—Messrs E. O'Neill Clarke, T. W. Delany, Major Hunt, R. Lonsdale, J. W. Hogan, C. J. P. Farrell, J. C. Healy, Louis Fee, Major Lauder, Major Hon. W. Ormsby Gore, M.P., James P. Maguire.

Hon. Treasurer—Dr Vincent S. Delany, Longford.

Hon. Secretary—Robert Devenish, Esq., Drumsna.

Official Timekeeper—Henry Reuss Newland, Esq.

C. Dann, Printer, Longford.

North Shannon Yacht Club regatta programme, Lough Boderg, 1914. (Alf Delany Archives)

The North Shannon Regatta.

PROGRAMME

First Day—Tuesday, 1st August.

FIRST MATCH.—A Handicap for Open Boats not exceeding 18ft. O.A. and 5ft. beam, the property of Members.
First Prize—£2.   Second Prize—£1.   Third Prize—10s.
Entrance 5s.

SECOND MATCH—An Open Handicap for all Yachts which have at any time been rated.
First Prize—£3.   Second Prize—£2.   Third Prize—£1.
Entrance Fee 5s.

THIRD MATCH—For Motor Boats.   A Handicap for Perpetual Challenge Cup.   Entrance Fee for four days racing 5s.   First, Second and Third (3-2-1) to count for aggregate score for Challenge Cup and Money Prizes.

FOURTH MATCH—The Annesley Challenge Cup for Out-Board Motors. A Handicap.   This Cup to be won three times in succession or four times in all.   First, Second and Third (3 2-1) to count towards aggregate Score for Challenge Cup and Money Prizes.   Entrance Fee for four day's racing 5s.

Second Day—Wednesday, 2nd August.

FIRST MATCH—The Longford Cup.   A Handicap for Yachts and Boats the property of Longford Members.   The Cup to be won three times in succession or four times in all.   Entrance Fee 5s.

SECOND MATCH—The Visitor's Challenge Cup to be won three times in succession or four times in all.   A Handicap for all Yachts and Boats any Rig or Rating.
First Prize—Cup and £2.   Second Prize—£1.   Third Prize—10s.
Entrance Fee 5s.

THIRD MATCH—The Derrycarne Perpetual Challenge Cup.   A Handicap for open boats not exceeding 18 feet O.A. and 5 feet Beam, the property of Members.
First Prize—Cup and £2.   Second Prize—£1.   Third Prize—10s.
Entrance Fee 5s.

FOURTH MATCH—The Second Heat for Motor Boats.

FIFTH MATCH—The Second Heat for the Annesley Challenge Cup for boats with Out-Board Motors.

Third Day—Thursday, 3rd August.

FIRST MATCH—For Boats of the "Shannon One Design Class."
First Prize—Silver Cup.   Second Prize—£1.   Third Prize—10s.
Entrance Fee 5s.

SECOND MATCH—The North Shannon Challenge Cup.   An open Handicap for all Yachts and Boats any Rig or Rating.   This Cup to be won three times in succession or four times in all.
First Prize—Cup and £2.   Second Prize—£1.   Third Prize—10s.
Entrance Fee 10s.

THIRD MATCH—The Ladies' Cup.   A Handicap for all Yachts and Boats, to be steered by Ladies.
First Prize—Cup and Rope of Pearls.   Second Prize—A Rope of Pearls.
No Entrance Fee.

FOURTH MATCH—The Third Heat for Motor Boats.

FIFTH MATCH—The Third Heat for the Annesley Challenge Cup, for Out-Board Motor Boats.

Fourth Day—Friday, 4th August.

FIRST MATCH—The Bartly Walker Challenge Cup.   A Handicap for Half Decked Boats, the property of Members.   To be won three times in succession or four times in all.
First Prize—Cup and £2.   Second Prize £1.   Third Prize—10s.

SECOND MATCH—An Open Handicap for all Yachts that have at any time been Rated.
First Prize—£2.   Second Prize £1.   Third Prize—10s.
Entrance Fee 5s.

THIRD MATCH—A Handicap for Open Boats not exceeding 18 feet O.A. and 5 feet Beam.
First Prize—£2.   Second Prize—£1.   Third Prize—10s.
Entrance Fee 5s.

FOURTH MATCH—The Fourth Heat for Motor Boats.

FIFTH MATCH—The Final Heat for the Annesley Challenge Cup, for Out-Board Motor Boats.

CONDITIONS.—1.   The Regatta to be held under the Y.R.A. Rules. All Yachts and Boats to be steered by members of Recognised or Shannon Yacht Clubs.   Open Boats not to carry more than three hands, or 140 sq. feet of sail.   North Shannon Challenge Cup excepted.
2.   The decision of the Committee to be final.   They also reserve to themselves the right to refusing or accepting any entry, altering the Programme, conditions and course, in any way they consider necessary.
3.   Entries for all Matches accompanied by Entrance Fees to be made with the Hon. Sec., (R. Devenish Esq., Drumsna) on or before 1 o'clock, on Thursday, 27th July, on form of entry as prescribed by Rule 6 Y.R.A. which may be had from the Hon. Secretary.
4.   All protests to be made to the Hon. Sec. in writing within two hours after arrival of the protesting Yacht accompanied by £1, which will be forfeited to the fund if the Committee consider the protest frivolous or vexatious.
5.   The Matches for Challenge Cups, the winners are entitled to hold the cups for one year, giving them up to the Committee on the day proceeding next year's Regatta.   A sail over not counting as a win.
6.   Unless three Yachts or Boats start and go over half the course, no second prize will be given, and third prizes will not be given unless five yachts or boats start.
7.   All Yachts and Boats to start under weigh.

North Shannon Yacht Club regatta in 1922 moved to Lough Bofin when racing resumed after the Great War and the regatta was postponed in that year because of the death of Michael Collins.(Alf Delany Archives)

was the organization of an annual regatta.[37] Lough Boderg was the venue for the racing until 1914 and there were races for yachts, half-decked boats, open boats up to 18ft (5.5m), motor boats and open boats with outboard engines. Handicaps were applied in all the races, which were agreed by the committees running the regattas. During the regatta 1914 a telegram arrived for Lord Kingston advising him to rejoin his regiment immediately as war had been declared. The racing continued but some of those attending also had to head away. Hospitality was offered at various houses in the vicinity including Belmont, the home of the McKeons, which was to be burnt down in 1921. There were no regattas held during the war years and in 1919 the venue was no longer available on Lough Boderg and the club moved to Lough Bofin, where regattas were held from 1919 until 1928; in 1922 the regatta, which had been scheduled to take place on 1st to 4th August, was postponed because of the death of Michael Collins. In 1929 the North Shannon Yacht Club regatta was held on Lough Forbes with races for yachts, centreboard boats and inboard and outboard motor boats. After the 1929 regatta on Lough Forbes a lack of members caused the North Shannon Yacht Club to cease to hold sailing regattas although races for speed boats and racing for hydroplanes did continue into the 1930s under the auspices of the North Shannon Yacht Club and the Motor Yacht Club of Ireland.

North Shannon Yacht Club regatta, Lough Bofin, 1925. (Alf Delany Archives)

North Shannon Yacht Club regatta, Lough Boderg, 1903.(Alf Delany Archives)

A number of Water Wags, a one-design dinghy from Dun Laoghaire (or Kingstown as it was then called), visited the north Shannon on several occasions.[38] In 1903 nine boats came down by rail to Drumsna station and were carried by horse and cart and launched into the Jamestown canal from where they sailed down to join in the North Shannon Yacht Club regatta on Lough Boderg. They continued to join in this regatta on a number of occasions and in 1925 the Water Wags went on from Lough Bofin to join in a one-day event at Lanesborough and then on to Ballyglass for a week's racing at the Lough Ree Yacht Club. Races were also held for them at the Lough Forbes regatta in 1929. In 1931, instead of using rail transport, a number of them were towed down the Royal Canal and in 1948 some of them came in the hold of a canal boat for the Irish Dinghy Racing Association's dinghy week at the Lough Ree Yacht Club. With the advent of road trailers, the club's visits to the Shannon were revived in the 1970s and are now held on an annual basis.

Group at the Lough Boderg regatta in 1903.(Alf Delany Archives)

The Water Wags, having travelled down by rail from Dublin, are launched into the Jamestown Canal on their way to the Lough Boderg regatta in 1903. (Alf Delany Archives)

The larger yachts gradually became fewer in number and were replaced by smaller, more modern-rated boats. Keel-boat racing continued at various venues on the river until 1914, particularly on Lough Derg. In all some sixty keel boats sailed at one time or another on Lough Derg between 1850 and 1914 and some forty on Lough Ree; the fact that Athlone was a garrison town also provided a steady supply of members. Although keel-boat racing did revive in a small way after the 1914-1918 war it gradually declined and the emphasis changed to centreboard boats. In the early 1900s

Regatta at the Lough Ree Yacht Club in the mid-1920s. (Alf Delany Archives)

Yachts racing on Lough Ree in the mid-1920s : Syringa *(General Coe, LDYC) and* Foam *(Norman & Lionel Lyster, LRYC) in the foreground.*
(Alf Delany Archives)

racing for the centreboard boats was very uneven with owners attempting to design faster boats and in May 1914 it was reported that there were now twenty of these boats on the river 'and the boat builders are having an exceptionally busy season'. While there were no regattas during the war years some local racing took place and, in 1920, a decision was made to ask Morgan Giles to design a one-design dinghy to establish more evenly matched racing for the centreboard boats.[39] This class, the Shannon One Design, proved very successful and is very active today with new boats being added to the numbers each year.

The Lough Ree Yacht Club in the 1930s. (Alf Delany Archvies)

Lough Forbes
REGATTA

Under the auspices of the North Shannon Yacht Club Flag and the
Motor Yacht Club of Ireland

(Established 1896)

TO BE HELD AT LOUGH FORBES,
Newtownforbes, County Longford, Irish Free State,

On 13th, 14th, 15th & 16th Aug., '29

Commodore—Right Hon. the Earl of Granard, K.P., G.C.V.O.
Vice Commodore—T. W. Delany, Esq., S.S.
Rear Commodore—J. W. Hogan, Esq

COMMITTEE — Messrs W. Levinge, Major General Koe, Major
Kirkwood, J. J. Stafford, George Shackleton, Supt. Sean Liddy,
W. Norris, J. P. Kenny, D.J., Major E Cooney, H. G. Small,
Rev. J. Egan, M. J. Ryan, Alfred F. J. Delany, W. J. O'F. Clery,
J. P. Prior, James Fleming, J. C. Healy, J. W. Hogan, P. V. C.
Murtagh, J. J. Moran.

SAILING AND MOTOR BOAT COMMITTEE —Lord Granard, Messrs Sir
Thomas Myles, Viscount Forbes, Senator Oliver St. J. Gogarty,
Major-Gen. Koe, Major Blake, Major G. Handcock, Chas. C.
Dignan, James Fleming, T. Craig, Jocelyn Waller, F. Dudley
Fletcher, W. Newburgh Tisdall and Dairmuid Murtagh.

HANDICAPPING COMMITTEE—Lord Granard, Messrs T. W. Delany,
M. J Ryan, Jocelyn Waller, Rev. J. Egan, T. Craig, James
Fleming and Dr Stevens, M.D , T.C.D.

Official Time-keeper—Henry Reus Newland, M.A., T.C.D.

Hon. Treasurer—Dr Vincent S. Delany.

Hon. Secretary—F. J. Gearty, B.A., B.Comm. N.U.I.

The last North Shannon Yacht Club regatta (until the revival in recent years) on Lough Forbes in 1929. (Alf Delany Archives)

Speed-boat racing at the Lough Ree Yacht Club with the winning boat, Fiend *from England in 1929. (Rosaleen Miller)*

Lough Ree Yacht Club during Dinghy Week, 1948. (Alf Delany Archives)

Kiwi's best regatta

Lough Derg Yacht Club,

ESTABLISHED 1836.

ANNUAL REGATTA,

14th TO 19th AUGUST, 1939.

Excluding 15th—date of Nenagh Show.

COMMODORE :
A. E. MOERAN, Esq.

VICE-COMMODORE
W. JOCELYN WALLER, Esq.

REAR-COMMODORE :
MISS E. A. MILLS.

COMMITTEE :

MISS HOLMES,	MAJOR E. H. WALLER,
C. JACKSON, Esq.	COMMANDER G. WHITFIELD,
F. H. KORTRIGHT, Esq.	R. U. B. WHITE, Esq.
REV. F. F. S. SMITHWICK.	D. J. G. WEBB, Esq.

AND THE

HON. SECRETARY AND TREASURER :
CHAS. F. MINNITT,
ANNAGHBEG, NENAGH.

Gleeson & Son. Printers, Nenagh

Lough Derg Yacht Club regatta programme, 1939. (Alf Delany Archives)

Athlone: Steam launch returning from Lough Ree Yacht Club in the 1920s. (Tom Kelly)

3 p.m.   **First Race—For Annesley Perpetual Challenge Cup.** A Scratch Race for Engines up to 350 cc. capacity on Hydroplanes. Distance 6 miles.

Name	Engine	Owner
3ʳᵈ Ouida	327 c.c. Johnson	F. H. McCann
2ⁿᵈ Star IV.	327 c.c. Johnson	Viscount Forbes
capsized Three Points	327 c.c Johnson	Col. H. Mansfield
N.S. Lightnin'	327 c.c. Johnson	Cyril McCormack
1ˢᵗ Hold Everythin'	327 c.c. Johnson	A. F. Delany
N.S. Crafty	322 c.c Elto	Miss G. McCormack
N.S. Benibus	347 c.c Sharland	F. B. Booker
N.S. Nelt	327 c.c Marston	F. B. Booker
4ᵗʰ Scuse Me	322 c.c Evinrude	R. W. Arches
N.S. Bob-a-long	322 c.c. Johnson	J. Power

3.30 p.m.   **Second Race—For the Commodore's Perpetual Challenge Cup.** A Scratch Race for Engines up to 500 c.c. capacity on Hydroplanes. Distance 6 miles.

Name	Engine	Owner
1ˢᵗ Star V.	486 c.c. Johnson	Viscount Forbes
2ⁿᵈ Green-Fly	486 c.c. Elto	David P. C. Plunket
N.S. Baby Power	500 c.c. Dunelt	F. B. Booker
N.S. Hold Everythin' III	486 c.c. Elto	A. F. Delany
N.S. ____	485 c.c. Evinrude	John J. Flood

4 p.m.   **Third Race—For the Forbes Perpetual Challenge Cup.** A Scratch Race for Engines up to 1,000 c.c. capacity on Hydroplanes. Distance 6 miles.

Name	Engine	Owner
D.N.F. Whoopee II.	655 c.c. Johnson	J. C. Healy
N.S. Roselle VI.	655 c.c. Johnson	P. B. Webb
N.S. Lightnin'	972 c.c. Elto	C. McCormack
2ⁿᵈ 646	815 c.c. Elto	Geo. Robinson
N.S. ____	815 c.c. Elto	D. McMorrough
1ˢᵗ Star IV	486 c.c. Johnson	Viscount Forbes
2ⁿᵈ N.S. III	486 c.c. Elto	A.F.D.

INTERVAL—Surf-board Riding.

4.45 p.m.   **Fourth Race—Tarmon Cup, presented by N.S.Y.C.** A Handicap open to all Hydroplanes. Distance 6 miles.

1ˢᵗ Whoopee II
2ⁿᵈ Ouida
3ʳᵈ N.S. III

5.15 p.m.   **Fifth Race—Bolderg Perpetual Challenge Cup.** A Handicap open to all Hydroplanes. Distance 6 miles.

1ˢᵗ N.S. III
2ⁿᵈ Ouida
3ʳᵈ 646

5.45 p.m.   **Sixth Race—Bofin Perpetual Challenge Cup.** A Handicap open to all Hydroplanes. Distance 6 miles.

1ˢᵗ 646
2ⁿᵈ Star IV
3ʳᵈ Ouida
4ᵗʰ N.S. III

Distribution of Prizes at conclusion of Regatta.

Speed-boat racing at Tarmonbarry in 1932. (Alf Delany Archives)

CONTEMPORARY LOGS

A number of interesting logs exist of sailing at regattas and trips up and down the river.[40] The log of the *Audax* owned by W.R. Potts extended over three summers 1874-1876. On the first cruise they left Athlone and got a tow from the Grand Canal Company's *Ballymurtagh* intending to travel up the Grand Canal to Dublin but, finding water levels in the canal low, they decided to head downstream. The writer of the log, a member of the Potts family, was very critical about the commissioners for Public Works: 'those worthies give very little value for probably a large salary as neither buoy nor posts are properly coloured and many dangers not marked'. Having reached Killaloe they attended worship in Killaloe cathedral where the singing was 'very fair', and they opted to hire a car to visit Limerick. Cruising around Lough Derg they encountered a number of yachts before heading back upstream in a strong southerly gale, negotiating Meelick lock and arriving back safely in Athlone. They paid a second visit to Lough Derg in August to compete in sailing races. They eventually arrived at Meelick and 'having liquored up the lock man passed thro' and beat to Portumna. The racing was punctuated by parties ashore and they remarked, 'the Tipperary folk know how to take their liquor'. Proceeding back up the river they recorded passing three steamers in rapid succession, 'one of which was Mr Waller's which we had seen sunk in the river when on our passage south'. At Banagher they managed to get their mast entangled in the telegraph wires watched by 'a lot of fashionables.' Another trip to Lough Derg in 1876 was recorded in the log. This time the water was very low in the river and they were constantly going aground. Another entry gave some details about the regatta on Lough Ree in 1876: 'The Lough Ree regatta being fixed for the following Monday, September 11th, gave us little time for preparation. All the yacht owners from Lough Derg having promised to attend. On Sunday 11th, we had the satisfaction of seeing *Corsair, Countess, Haidee, Virago, Surprise, Meerschaum* arrive and of having owners and friends to rendezvous for lunch at New Court.' A description of the sailing races over subsequent days followed. It is known that the *Audax* subsequently was crushed and badly damaged by ice and sank in Portlick Bay about 1900.

The Audax, *owner William Potts. (Alf Delany Archives)*

The Audax *with her mast entangled in telegraph wires at the bridge at Banagher on her way down river to the regatta on Lough Derg. (John Lefroy)*

The log of R.J. Waller's *Surprise*, which he is said to have built in front of his house, Prior Park, by excavating a hole in the ground as a mould, recorded some details about racing at the Lough Derg regatta in 1886. He names nine yachts competing in the races and also taking part in 'naval manoeuvres'. A list of 'evolution signals' by code flags was drawn up together with signalling instructions and he recorded: '*The Battleship Surprise* will cruise today off the Port of Dromineer between the Point off the Hare and Islandmore and endeavour to capture merchantmen and other craft.'

'Midge' McGrath, B.W. Holmes's boatman on Corsair. *(Alf Delany Archives)*

A page from a letter written by 'Midge' McGrath to Posie Holmes later Posie Goodbody. (Alf Delany Archives)

The log of W.R. Minchin's *Torfreda* described a trip up the river from Lough Derg to compete in the Lough Ree Yacht Club's regatta on Lough Ree, and it is illustrated by fine drawings. It must have been quite a feat to sail these boats up the river and on this occasion they did manage to get a tow from the Grand Canal Company's *Ballymurtagh* from Shannonbridge to Athlone. There are a number of amusing comments: at Meelick the lock keeper 'Brannigan receives us kindly and also takes kindly to refreshment'. They had to lower the mainsail at Banagher 'owing to the tardiness of the natives' in opening the bridge and they had problems with the station master in Athlone in getting the railway bridge opened. When moored in Athlone they had to forego their morning swim because 'there were too many natives about'. On the return trip they once again were towed by the *Ballymurtagh* as far as Shannon Harbour and then by the *Athlone* to Meelick.

A drawing from the log of W.R. Minchin's Torfreda *illustrating an incident at the start of a race on Lough Ree. (Alf Delany Archives)*

There is an account written by J. Witham of a trip on the river in 1896 by five young men who acquired a boat in Athlone and had it sent by water to Carrick where they arrived by train to take it over. The boat was an 18-ft (5.5m) half-decked boat with sails and they camped at night in a bell tent. They travelled up river to Lough Key where they had an encounter with a man with a gun who told them they had no right to camp on an island without a permit and must remain in the navigation channel. They then headed downstream and came on the annual sailing regatta on Lough Boderg:

A race was visible at the far end about 2 miles off, while the upper and windward end of the lake was dotted over with craft of various build, house boats and open boats, sailing and steam yachts, anchored or in motion, while on the shore beyond conveniently situated on a slight elevation were visible eight or ten tents belonging to the owners of some of the smaller yachts. On the immediate shore itself was a crowd of persons mostly from the country round, and booths at which a pretty brisk trade seemed to be going on.

In the thirteen days they spent on the river they managed to get as far south as Killaloe with no mention of meeting traffic on the river. There they delivered the boat to the Grand Canal Company agent for transfer back to Athlone while they returned to Dublin by train via Birdhill and Limerick: 'Need I mention we stopped three quarters of an hour at Birdhill station. Anyone who has ever been there will understand about it. It seems to be the right thing to do.'

Another log recorded the cruise of the *Gipsy* in 1898 from Athlone to Lough Key. She was a 25-ton boat owned by Canon Gilligan, parish priest of Carrick-on-Shannon. Having picked up his visitors in Athlone, who had arrived by train from Dublin, they were taken on a tour of Lough Ree including Quaker Island. Here a notice informed them that Mr Johnson would be expecting a tribute of 3d per person to visit his island although they did not encounter anyone to enforce this. On the journey up the river the boat was anchored to allow for some duck shooting. Arriving at Roosky lock they found the *Shannon Queen* 'whistling imperiously'. At Carrick the skipper and his guests retired to the parochial house and the next day they travelled up the Boyle Water where she ran aground and had to be

days of Her Majesty Queen Elizabeth'.

In that same year, 1898, a group from the British Canoe Association visited the river.[41] They obviously enjoyed their visit and remarked on the fact that others had not visited Ireland: 'We are a little surprised to find that it has not been taken advantage of by more of those who are ever on the look out for fresh waters to explore than was, we understand, the case

hauled off by 'some stalwart members of the Royal Irish Constabulary'. On Lough Key they passed Rockingham, and the canon's political views are reflected in his comment that it was 'the residence of the invading family which took possession of MacDermot's stronghold and MacDermot's territory and have kept tenacious hold of both since the

last season. It is almost impossible to say how highly the noble river is esteemed locally.' They described witnessing well-attended regattas and 'some good little ships too on the Shannon. . . matches are keenly fought out, providing instances of plucky sailing and as smart handling as one could wish to meet with'.

Jane Shackleton visited Inisfail (also known as O'Reilly's Island) on Lough Allen and photographed Major & Mrs O'Conor's cottage and boathouse-cum-workshop. (Shackleton Archives)

The Shackleton family boat Seagull. *(Shackleton Archives)*

Yet another log written by Mrs Jane Shackleton described a trip in 1899, which she made with her three sons in an 18-ft (5.5m) Norwegian boat, sleeping each night beneath a canvas cover; during this trip she took some fascinating photographs. The boat was conveyed by rail from Leixlip to Carrick on two special trucks provided by the railway company. They travelled downstream with the current, obtaining a permit from the lock keeper at the Albert lock costing 4s to take them down the river to Killaloe. At Roosky: 'the lock keeper, an aged man, and very much the worse for drink, was very complimentary, addressing me as My Lady and the Duchess. W. and J. had to open and close the lock gates as he was quite incapable'. The only boat they passed on the journey down to Athlone was a canal boat called the *Pride of Westmeath*, propelled by sail and poles. They passed through some yachts racing on Lough Ree on the way to Athlone where there were a number of soldiers boating and fishing. Rowing down the

The Harriet *owned by Major Reeves. (Tom Kelly)*

A tea party aboard the Harriet *in 1914. (Tom Kelly)*

river they were overtaken by some of the yachts returning to Lough Derg after the regatta. While moored in Banagher a steamer arrived and discharged some cargo of porter and flour. Above Meelick, they went down the wrong channel and found their way blocked by flood gates and had to turn back. After some quite windy weather on Lough Derg, they reached Killaloe from where they arranged for the boat to be returned to Lucan by canal boat. On another occasion they travelled upstream to Lough Allen and she wrote: 'The canal is in a very bad condition, full of weeds and with overhanging trees in some places nearly meeting across.' She described visiting Innisfail, an island on Lough Allen, were Major and Mrs O'Conor had built themselves a cottage and harbour. She explained that is was also known as O'Reilly's Island; three O'Reilly brothers had started iron works in the area in 1788 using the local coal for smelting but they did not have much success and the business had been resuscitated from time to time under different companies. The coal mining she said was only 'on a limited scale'. The poor condition of the canal and her references to the iron and coal industries reflect the earlier gloomy views expressed about their potential.

The cruise of Ralph Smyth of Glasson's *Lallie* from Lough Ree to the north Shannon in 1911 again records the relief at being able to get a tow for some of the way, on this occasion from the *Portumna*, although for much of the time in the river stretches they had to tow with their own rowing boat. These visits must have been happening less often because at Roosky it is recorded that they created quite a stir: 'Quite a crowd gathered on the wharf and gazed at us and the yacht as if we had come from the lower regions.' However, the regatta was on in Lough Boderg, which was 'looking quite festive with yachts, steamers, motor boats and house boats and the hill covered with tents'. Drumsna was dismissed as 'the most God forsaken looking place I ever put foot in'. On the way back down river they visited the two churches in Roosky: 'The Protestant Church, which was the

John Johnson, manager of the Grand Canal Company office in Limerick, aboard his boat Ibis.

A boat registration certificate, 1911.(Tom Kelly)

most ill kept place I ever saw, rank weeds up to the door
. . . the R.C. Church was better kept but cattle evidently
had been around the place and there was evidence of their
being inside also.' On the tow back down river, again by the
Portumna, she had fifteen boats in tow and he remarked:
'It was very exciting getting through the locks.' They took
in the Gailey Bay regatta on the way back to Athlone and
the Lough Ree Yacht Club regatta at Ballyglass, where they
enjoyed hospitality in the 'military tent' that was there for
the week. Finally they attended the Athlone town regatta
day and were invited to tea at Abbey House by Robert Kelly,
where there was a big crowd and they stayed to watch the
fireworks. The other point of interest in this and other logs
was that although they took place mostly in July and August
there were frequent storms and heavy rain recorded.

The log of P.V.C. Murtagh's 8-metre *Truant*, kept by
his son, Diarmuid, records some racing on Lough Ree in
1923. There is a wonderful description of a race in which a
number of the yachts went aground near Yew Point:

*Mick Donlon, known as 'ould Mick', the Delany boatman, travelling
between regattas.*

Diarmuid also records the trip down river from Athlone
in 1923 to attend the Lough Derg Yacht Club regatta. The
Truant was towed by the motor yacht *La Vague II*, which Dr
V.S. Delany had purchased from Vyvyan Stewart in Dublin
the previous year. He had brought her down the Grand
Canal during the height of the Civil War and had to receive
a pass from the Free State government as far as Tullamore
and get permission to proceed down to Shannon Harbour
from the other side who were in control of that part of
Offaly. It is remarkable that the Civil War does not seem to
have concerned him sufficiently to change his plans to bring
the boat to the Shannon. The *Rambler*, which he had just
purchased for his brother had a very large tow, including
the *Chang - Sha*, which had Dr Delany's brother-in-law and
his wife on board, Major Bertie Waller's *Ark* and several
yachts and Shannon One-Designs. The spent a number of
days racing at the latter's place at Bellisle, Portumna, and
eventually set off for Dromineer. The *Rambler* and her tow
did not get away until 11.30 pm that night and had adventures
that have been remembered and recorded by a number of
people.[42] The wind freshened, the *Rambler's* engine failed,
boats went adrift and they ended up frantically trying to
anchor until daybreak when with the engine restored they
were able to gather up the boats. Miraculously, apart from
minor damage to boats, no one was injured. The incident
does reflect the risks that those who knew the river and its
lakes well were prepared to take.

The Delany family boat La Vague II.

*. . . one on top of the other and all hard aground with every
stitch drawing in a half-gale from the south. Their heads were
buried with the press of canvas and their counters stood up
in the air. We missed by inches and the whole scene was so
terrible – boats piled on top of each other – canvas tearing
– ropes and spars flying in all directions – the shouts and
curses of the crews – the seas breaking over all – the whole
effect was so terrifying that almost all our crew gave a wild
hysterical cheer as we passed and found we had missed the
shoal.*

*'Ould Mick' Donlon's son, Mick, who later became the Delany family
boatman with Vincent Delany.*

Another boat, which had received mention in one of the logs as 'a handsome little steamer belonging to Mr Spaight', was the *Phoenix*. She had been built in Waterford for General Spaight of Derry Castle, near Killaloe, in 1872. She was designed by Hearne, the champion of the Archimedes screw propellor, and was constructed with Lowmoor iron. Subsequently, in 1903, on the death of the General, she was sold to Major Harry Lefroy. Her ship's log exists from 1903 –1911, which mostly reads like a social diary, taking friends for outings and tea parties on board. 'Coaling' the steamer was a constant chore and he described a visit to Lough Allen when they walked up to the coal mines at Arigna and bought 12cwt of coal for 6s. They then went up the Boyle Water and visited a saw mill in Boyle, which was generating electric light. In 1907 the Major became a trader, purchasing the house boat *Australia*, turning her into a trading boat to carry coal and flour for Messrs Bannatyne of Limerick. Major Lefroy and his family built a number of stores along the river. In 1927 he removed the steam engine from the *Phoenix* and installed a Swedish two-stroke Ellwe diesel engine; it had a compressed-air start mechanism, which was known to be temperamental. On his death the boat had a number of owners before she passed back into the Lefroy family in 1961 and is still in active commission, owned by the Lefroy family of Killaloe who claim that Uncle Harry makes his presence felt on occasions.

In 1910 a book was published by an Englishman, R.A. Scott-James, describing a journey with a canoe across Ireland from Belfast, mostly by water but partly by road,

The Grand Canal Company's towing steamer Portumna *in Athlone lock with a canal boat she had under tow. (Alf Delany Archives)*

and eventually down the Shannon to Killaloe.[43] When he arrived at the Shannon, he launched his canoe into Lough Allen. He encountered some very windy weather but was lucky enough to get a tow for some of the journey from Harry Lefroy in the *Phoenix*. Upstream of Lough Ree he encountered no commercial traffic except the Grand Canal Company's *Portumna* towing four canal boats, which he learnt made the passage between Portumna and Carrick once a week. Rather than set out to cross the lake he decided to walk to Athlone and arrange for the steamer to pick up his canoe on its return from Carrick and meet up again with it at Athlone. He then paddled to Banagher and parting again with his canoe he took the steamer, which plied daily between Banagher and Killaloe. Again this is a picture of a river with very little traffic on it and it was the people he encountered along the way who fill the pages of his book.

The *Phoenix* owned today once again by the Lefroy family.

The Royal Yacht Squadron Grania *visiting Lough Key in 1925.*
(Athlone Branch IWAI)

These contemporary logs and accounts conjure up a very good idea of the river at this time with an interesting contrast between the comments of those of the gentry, most of whom appear to have had military titles, who refer to the people as 'countrymen', compared with the nationalist view of the parish priest. The writers of logs in those days in addition to frequently illustrating them with drawings, in one case wrote the log in verse. One of these was a trip by R. Purcell in his large yacht *Grania* in 1925.[44] He made the trip from Cowes to the Shannon Estuary and all the way up the river to Lough Key:

And we undertook the Shannon, locks and bridges
of the river Hauling, squeezing, through those spaces
Which the German scheme replaces
But in time arriving.

The opening span of the new bridge at Portumna built in 1910-1905
with the Phoenix *passing through.*

J.A. Synnott wrote extolling the Shannon in *The Motor Boat* in 1932. He described the interesting trip for a visitor from across the water down the Grand Canal and then from Shannon Harbour to Carrick, 'passing through beautiful Irish Lakeland at a cost of only 9s in lock dues, and everywhere he will find courteous officials ready to help him, whilst there are no irritating formalities'. The Synnott family, who came from Cork, kept their family boat *Inistiog* on the Shannon and cruised widely for many years.

BOARD OF WORKS ADMINISTRATION 1910–1922

Concern had been expressed for some time about the condition of the bridge at Portumna. A report in a local paper in 1907 referred to a recent accident when two men fell over the parapet and were drowned.[45] It was suggested that the pillars supporting the bridge were rotten and if the parapet was raised and sheeted 'owing to the rotten condition of the whole structure a good gale would blow the bridge over altogether'. Following a Royal Commission of inquiry a new bridge was under construction by 1910, which took five years to complete. The original estimate was put at £21,500 but the final cost was nearer £30,000. It replaced the wooden bridge built by the Shannon Commissioners in the 1840s, which in turn had replaced Lamuel Cox's wooden bridge built in 1796. Shortage of funds had prevented the commissioners putting in a more substantial bridge and the wooden structure was only intended to last about twenty-five years when, in fact, it had stood for seventy-five. The stone piers built to support Rhodes's swing bridge in the 1840s were retained to carry the new single opening span and concrete-filled cast iron cylinders carried the long steel girders supporting the roadway. John Moynan, county surveyor for Tipperary, was responsible for the construction, with N.H. Wilson the engineer in charge.[46] The bridge was designed to Moynan's specification by an English architect, C.E. Stanier of London, and constructed in Manchester. The driving force for operating the opening bridge was provided by a falling weight in a tower, one half of the fall opened it and the other half closed it. Before the next opening the weight had to be winched back up to the top of the tower. This was replaced by geared winding handles but it was hard work to open the bridge in windy conditions and eventually it was fitted with hydraulic controls. Another interesting new bridge was erected at the ford of Hartley, on the upper river a short distance upstream of the junction with the Boyle Water. The 1911-1912 report recorded that plans had been submitted for this bridge, which was to be constructed 'to a new system in ferro-concrete', said to be the first of this type in Ireland.

Severe flooding was reported in 1912 'and careful

consideration was given to the working of the sluices with the view to the early relief of the flooded lands'. Some figures produced demonstrated the good that had resulted from the measures already adopted, showing the average number of days in a year when the lands below Athlone were flooded 'to a large extent'. Between 1836 and 1844 the figure was 258, between 1849 and 1880 (after the Shannon Commission works) the figure was 78, and after additional works from 1883 to 1912 the number had dropped to 28.

The ferro-concrete bridge, Hartley Bridge, on the upper Shannon built in 1911-1912.

The former bridge keeper's control room at Portumna Bridge.

The tonnage carried on the river fell sharply during the war years and was down to 55,664 tons in 1918, making the Board of Works increasingly dependent on financial support for the administration and maintenance of the river by parliamentary vote. These were troubled times throughout the country but trade did build up again slowly, despite the fact that there were steep increases in tolls when government control on charges was removed in 1920. The Grand Canal Company was allowed to increase its tolls on the canal by 150 per cent and the Board of Works was permitted to increase by the same rate.

THE 1923 COMMISSION
The 'Democratic Programme' of the Republican Dail, issued in 1919, emphasized the necessity of developing the country's navigations. The Board of Works, from this time usually referred to as the Office of Public Works, was transferred to the Irish Free State under the terms of the Treaty on 6 December 1921 but the actual transfer of functions was made on 1 April 1922. It took some time for its duties to be clarified, particularly with regard to financing, which had been handled by the British Treasury.[47] Because of the importance of the Office of Public Works in the administration of public works and loan schemes since the mid-1800s, the Irish Free State government was taking

over a very comprehensive organization. In relation to the administration of the Shannon Navigation nothing actually changed except that the parliamentary vote, amounting to about £3,000 each year, which had been necessary to supplement the income from tolls, wharfage and rents, now had to be approved by the new Irish government. One of this government's earliest actions, in April 1922, was to set up a commission to investigate the future of the Grand Canal and, in June, this commission was reconstituted and its terms extended to cover the 'Utilisation of Inland Waterways for Purposes of Transport'.[48]

These were troubled and difficult years. One of the lock gates of Cussane lock was blown up in July 1922 and a number of bridges, including swivel bridges, were damaged 'by the Irregulars'. The timber flooring of Banagher Bridge was set alight and the gearing for operating the opening span at Shannonbridge was damaged. The SS *Shannon*, the Office of Public Works steamer, was taken over by the Free State forces to patrol the lower river. However, the tonnage carried actually rose by over 7,000 tons in 1922 and this was despite a milling strike, but the tonnage was to suffer in the following year because of the lock-out on the Grand Canal for several months from August to November due to the General Strike.

The Office of Public Works steamer Shannon *at Athlone.*

The membership of this commission was very different and a great deal smaller than the earlier Shuttleworth Commission. Robert Tweedy, a consultant engineer, was appointed as chairman with four other members: William Davin T.D., Patrick Leonard, who was a member of the Dublin Port & Docks Board, Patrick McCarthy, consultant engineer and past president of the Institution of Civil Engineers of Ireland, and John Moynan, another past president of the institution, county surveyor for County Tipperary, mentioned above in connection with the new Portumna Bridge. Thomas Flynn from the new Ministry of Industry & Commerce was appointed as secretary. The commissioners subsequently were to praise him in glowing terms referring to 'the combination in Mr Flynn of tact, urbanity, specialised knowledge and almost incredible industry'. The commission's terms of reference were to examine (1) the service rendered to the community at present; (2) conditions and rates of employment incidental to upkeep and operation; (3) measures necessary to secure maximum utility, having due regard to (a) sound national economy (b) the relation of the waterways to other means of transport and (c) their functions in respect of drainage, fisheries and power. The commission's role was clearly a direct follow-on from the Shuttleworth Commission's principal recommendation for a Waterways Authority that would embrace all these issues.

Evidence was heard from eighty witnesses, ranging from government departments and agencies to private boat owners, using a system of providing a questionnaire so that 'there was no adumbration of visionary schemes'. They made a detailed study of the history of the various navigations and the findings of the earlier commissions that had dealt with them over the years. They referred to the Shannon Navigation as having 'the advantages of an ocean highway' and stressed the importance of access to the sea at all states of the tide, adding: 'The failure to connect several of our waterways adequately with the sea has probably prejudiced our industrial development appreciably.' Expressing surprise that the Shannon Commissioners had failed to achieve good access at that time, they recommended improving access to and from the river and the port of Limerick at a cost of £99,000 and improvements to the Limerick Navigation, by lengthening the locks to the same length as the upper Shannon locks, at a cost of £146,050. With reference to the opening bridge on the Maigue, originally installed back in 1817, they heard evidence that it had been destroyed recently but that as it had not been opened for many years it was not necessary to replace it: 'the insignificant traffic that exists is obliged to avail of the fixed masonry arch, the barge used being too wide for the opening of the movable portion'.

Some excavation works in Lough Derg and in the main channel of the river they costed at a further £12,533. They saw great potential in the development of the coal and mineral deposits in the Lough Allen area, given good water transportation, and they recommended lengthening the two locks on the Lough Allen Canal to the same as the upper river locks and improving the canal at a cost of £52,280. All these works came to a total of £310,000 and they said they anticipated 'a large trade through Limerick as far north as Lough Allen' would follow if these improvements were carried out. They pointed out that greater income could be derived by charging tolls based on distance travelled, including the lakes, rather than on the weight of goods carried.

They saw the impact of the railways as 'artificial rather than natural. . . in our opinion inland navigation is not antagonistic to the railway and the road, and the object should be to secure the harmonious co-operation of all three'. In order to initiate waterway development they indicated that it would probably be necessary that the greater part of the funds should be provided by the state. They supported the Shuttleworth Commission's concept of a new Waterway Board, embracing the administration of all the inland navigations (except the regulation of navigation tolls and charges), which would co-ordinate drainage, fisheries and power issues, but existing Drainage Boards and Boards of Conservators of Fisheries should continue to discharge their functions, subject to the control of this Waterway Board.

In relation to water-power, they heard evidence from John Chaloner Smith, an assistant engineer in the Office of Public Works, who over a period of thirty years had gathered records of the flow in the river leading him to support the view that an auxiliary plant would be needed to make up deficiencies.[49] These detailed records were to become a significant element subsequently in enabling the government to reach a decision about harnessing the Shannon for water-power. In regard to fisheries they noted that it was fishery interests that had effectually obstructed earlier attempts to develop water-power. They saw no reason why drainage issues had to conflict with navigation, pointing to the small expenditure that would be involved in carrying out excavation in Lough Derg in order to preserve the required navigation depth, if the level was to be reduced by 2ft (0.6m) to facilitate drainage.

HYDRO-ELECTRIC WORKS

It is hardly surprising that the new government was not prepared to put up public funding of £472,000, as suggested by the 1923 Commission, to improve inland waterways, of which the Shannon was to absorb about three-quarters of

the total. However, the whole question of harnessing the Shannon in a hydro-electric scheme had resurfaced at this time, which not only had implications for the navigation works proposed by the commission, but offered a much more interesting investment in public funds for the government.[50]

A committee had been set up to investigate water-power resources, which reported in 1922.[51] With regard to the Shannon, the committee suggested that the main problem was how the required storage of water could be achieved, which would involve the construction of weirs to increase

The headrace for the hydro-electric works for Ardnacrusha under construction. (ESB Archives)

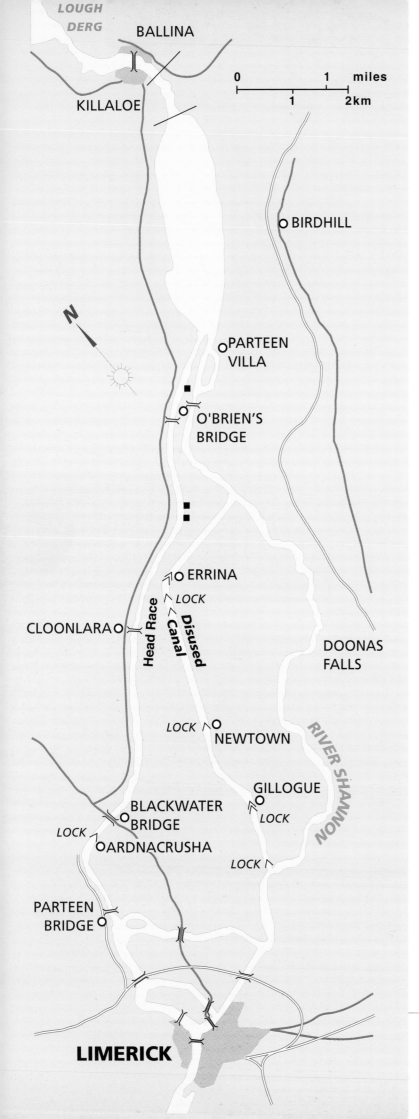

water levels in the lakes and the paying of compensation for any flooded lands. In the meantime Dr Thomas MacLoughlin, while an engineering student under Professor Rishworth at University College, Galway, had developed an interest in the idea of a Shannon scheme. In December 1922 he took up a position with Siemens-Schuckert in Berlin where he was encouraged to explore the viability of such a scheme.[52] Backed by his firm, he approached the Irish government and Siemens-Schuckert was asked to submit detailed proposals that were examined by a group of experts in 1925.[53]

The cost-effectiveness of the scheme, which was designed to develop the full fall of approximately 100ft (30.5m) in a single stage, was immediately questioned, in particular by Sir John Purser Griffith.[54] He advocated that the earlier plan put forward back in 1919 by Theodore Stevens should be adopted, which had recommended the use of the fall spread over three or four locations, but the government approved MacLoughlin's scheme and the Shannon Electricity Act was passed in June 1925 in the face of determined opposition in the Dail. Despite the high costs (£5.2 million from a total budget for the year 1925 of only £25 million), they had approved the scheme with certain modifications. It has been suggested that a fellow student of MacLoughlin's at UCG was Patrick McGilligan, who at this crucial period became Minister for Industry and Commerce, and that senior civil servants in the Department of Finance were unaware of the government's commitment and when they found out, were furious.[55]

The contract, based on MacLoughlin's plan, was signed with Siemens-Schuckert in August allowing three and a half years for completion of the works. With work on the scheme already in progress, the government decided to establish a semi-state body, Ireland's first, to carry out and manage a programme of national electrification to co-ordinate the many small local private electric supply schemes in operation by this time, and the Electricity Supply Board (ESB) was established.[56] The Shannon Scheme was an enormous and brave undertaking by the new state, in a country slowly emerging from the years of the War of Independence and the Civil War. The vision was justified and it was a proud moment, on 22 July 1929, when the official opening took place and the sluices at Parteen were opened to fill the headrace canal.[57]

Much has been written about the carrying out of the works that were achieved virtually on time and almost within budget. Much also has been written about the workers and the conditions they had to suffer.[58] Although some of the technical staff came in from Germany, MacLaughlin insisted that, where suitably qualified Irish people were available, they should get preference for employment. The vast majority of the workforce was Irish and came from all over the country to get employment. At the height of

Putting the new navigation arch into the bridge at Killaloe as part of the hydro-electric works. (ESB Archives)

the works some 5,000 men were employed, working in three shifts, some of whom were housed in three very basic camps and the rest had to find accommodation where they could. The work was hard, the hours long and there was an unacceptable number of fatalities.

The actual scheme followed in principal the original scheme put forward in the first Act back in 1901, which had come to nothing because of the apprehension that there would not be sufficient head of water all the year round. Now the scheme was based around the use of the three large

Putting the new navigation arch into the bridge at Killaloe as part of the hydro-electric works. (ESB Archives)

Professor Rishworth walking down the completed headrace. (ESB Archives)

lakes, Derg, Ree and Allen, acting as storage reservoirs. This involved carrying out works that were to bring about significant changes to the navigation. The ESB was given wide powers under the Act to control levels in Lough Allen, Ree and Derg in order to maintain sufficient water to generate power, which extended to interfering with the navigation if necessary. The sluices at Bellantra, controlling Lough Allen, the sluices at Athlone, controlling Lough Ree, and the new dam at Parteen, which controlled the Lough Derg level, were placed under the direct control of the ESB. The other sluices at Jamestown, Roosky, Tarmonbarry and Meelick continued to be operated by the navigation authority, the Office of Public Works. The latter also continued to operate the sluices at Athlone on behalf of the ESB, acting on daily instructions from Ardnacrusha.

The lower of the three storage reservoirs, Lough Derg, had to be regulated so that its fluctuation varied as little as possible. In order to increase the amount of water held on this level, the weir at Killaloe was removed, which created a new artificial lake below the bridge thus extending this to a level of 50 miles (80km) from Meelick and creating a single step down at the power station. The level of Lough Derg was to be held at between 99.9ft (32.8m) and 102.2ft (33.56m) OD. This was to be controlled by the new Parteen weir, a large dam with six large sluice gates and a stepped fish pass that enabled surplus water to be passed down the

old bed of the river. In time of drought a certain flow of water had to be guaranteed to pass down the river channel and in time of flood the sluices could allow as much water down as was able to pass through the confined channel and bridge at Killaloe. At the entrance to the new canal and headrace there was a large guillotine gate for the navigation and three sluice gates, controlling the water passing down to the power station. These works meant that the former Limerick Navigation canals could no longer be used. The new navigation would pass down through the bridge at Killaloe, through the flooded area and into the headrace, down through a double-chambered lock at the power station at Ardnacrusha (with a fall of 100ft (30.5m)), down the tailrace and via the Shannon and Abbey rivers to the port of Limerick.

The recent 1923 commission had recommended that the locks on the Limerick Navigation should be enlarged to the size of the smaller locks on the upper river to enable boats of larger dimensions to operate on the river and right through to Limerick port. Now none of these works would be necessary but, for some unexplained reason, they failed to make the new locks at the power station to match the width of even the smaller locks on the upper river. These locks were 102ft (22.8m) by 30ft (9.1m) and the Ardnacrusha locks were only 105ft (32m) by 19ft 6ins (6m). It is perhaps a measure of the lack of importance attached to the navigation at this time. The size of the locks was probably determined by the size of boats then operating, which in turn had been determined by the size of locks on the former Limerick Navigation. Another problem was that the navigation from the tailrace at Ardnacrusha to the port of Limerick was rendered rather hazardous because not only was it tidal when passing under the low bridges in the Abbey river, but it was now also subject to a heavy current when the power station was discharging. In addition to having control of the level of Lough Derg at Parteen, an embankment was raised on the west bank of the river from Meelick to Portumna to prevent waste of water spreading out in time of flood. Pumping stations were built at intervals, which were operated electrically to cut in automatically, thus relieving a large area of land that had been callows in the past from the threat of flooding. Minor changes were also made to the weir at Meelick by the removal of the fixed crest and its replacement by lifting boards and modifications to the sluices controlling the new cut there.

Lough Ree was to form the middle reservoir and the normal summer level was raised some 2ft (0.6m) to 121ft. O.D. Some dredging was subsequently carried out in the navigation channel so that both Ree and Derg could be drawn down further in dry periods when the upper storage

The power station at Ardnacrusha with the double-chambered lock on the left. (ESB Archives)

The dam at Parteen, controlling the water flowing down the river and the sluices and guillotine gate into the headace. (ESB Archives)

in Lough Allen fell too low. Some conflict was to arise when the level of the lake was dropped too low for safe navigation but equally farmers complained if it was held too high to allow for the absorbing of floodwater when that became necessary. The problem was that in time of flood little control could be exercised over the outflow from Lough Ree once the level reached the crest of the open part of the weir at Athlone and began to discharge over it.

In order to use Lough Allen as the upper storage reservoir more serious changes had to be made. There was a need to allow great fluctuations – as much as 15ft (4.5m) in the levels at which this lake would be held. A guaranteed supply during dry summer periods became a cause of concern and in 1930, when the anticipated opening up of the trade to and from Limerick with the enlarging of the locks did not materialize, there was even talk that traffic north of Athlone would have to be stopped because the ESB was short of water for Ardnacrusha.

In 1932 it was decided that it would be necessary to be able to lower Lough Allen further in dry seasons, which was in line with the recommendations made by John Bateman in the 1860s. The sluices erected at Bellantra as part of the flood-relief works in the early 1880s had been designed to keep the lake at 5ft (1.5m) above its previous normal summer level so that the release of water could be regulated to lessen flooding downstream. As it had now been found necessary in dry seasons to draw down Lough Allen even further, the old sluices were replaced by two large sluice gates at Bellantra together with some dredging and deepening of the river at the outlet from the lake. The works were completed in 1938 and enabled Lough Allen to be held between the levels of 154ft O.D. and 168ft O.D. However, in time of drought the lake would have to be let drop even further and in time of flood the water would pass over the top of the Bellantra sluices. A direct result of this was to lead to the abandonment of navigation through the Lough Allen Canal into the lake because navigation access into the shallow lower end of the lake from the canal would no longer be guaranteed if the level of the lake was dropped to these new lows and a dam was placed across the canal. Although the recent commission had pointed to the potential of encouraging the mining business by improving the canal there was little sign of this and it would have been difficult to justify that this would ever happen. The Cavan & Leitrim Railway Company had made a light railway extension into Arigna in the 1880s so there had been virtually no traffic on the canal and the last boat to pass through the canal did so in 1932. Initially three penstocks had been installed at Ardnacrusha to feed three turbines with provision for a further three to be added, but there was insufficient water supply for more than one further penstock and turbine, and this was added in 1934.

The great Falls of Doonass, an area famous for its salmon fishing, were deprived of much of the water that had made them such a spectacle. Efforts to divert the salmon-run up the old course of the river were not very successful but some of the salmon managed to work their way upstream by passing through the locks at Ardnacrusha when boats were locking through. With the number of boats using the locks decreasing it was found necessary to construct a fish pass. This was not very successful and there were so many complaints from fishery interests that the government handed over the fresh water and commercial fishing rights

The new sluice gates at Bellantra controlling Lough Allen built in the 1930s.

to the ESB.[59] The management of the fisheries was carried out in co-operation with the Inland Fisheries Trust; the latter was subsequently replaced by a central fishery and regional fishery boards, which in turn were to be restructured in recent times. The ESB took over the commercial eel fishing under licence and compensation was paid to those who had traditionally enjoyed the eel fishing on Lough Ree and Lough Derg. Compensation was also paid to the Abbey Guild of fishermen who had traditionally fished for salmon with drift nets below the Lax salmon weir and with snap nets from the weir to Doonass.[60] Their families had fished the river for many generations, and between 1915-1931 they had bought out the rights to establish their claim legally between the Lax Weir and Doonass. They fought a bitter battle with the ESB but were eventually forced to accept compensation based on the number of years they had been engaged in salmon fishing when the government handed over all the fishing rights to the ESB. The Lax (Scandinavian for salmon) weir, the site for salmon fishing since the thirteenth century, became another casualty of the hydro-electric works. In 1959 a new type of salmon lift was built at the power station and a fish hatchery established at Parteen, which was expanded in 1961-1962, to try to improve the salmon and eel fisheries of the river. The output from the hatchery was managed, working in partnership with the fishery boards, which administered the game fishing, under licence, and coarse fishing, under regulation.

THE DRAINAGE COMMISSION 1938–1940

This Commission of Inquiry into Land Drainage was set up in 1938 and delivered its Report in 1940.[61] While the Shannon was only one element covered by the inquiry, the comments made about the flooding problems associated with the river are of interest. They found that there had been an improvement on the upper river as a result of the new sluice gates at Bellantra but it was suggested that there was a problem with the weir at Tarmonbarry. The sluices here were unable to discharge water in time of flood without

Limerick: all that remains today of the Lax salmon weir, a casualty of the hydro-electric works.

DUNASS FALL. CASTLECONNELL. 3214. W.L.

The famous Falls of Doonass before they were deprived of their glory by the hydro-electric works. (Courtesy of the National Library of Ireland).

overtopping the weir, which led to a flood level rise of about 1ft (30.5cm) and so it was recommended that the navigation level on the stretch above Tarmonbarry should be reduced by 1ft (30.5cm) and additional sluices added. Other deepening and widening works would also improve the situation. Works to improve the Lough Ree level would not be justified but two options were put forward for improving the stretch between Athlone and Meelick: deepening and widening the river channel or embankment works with the provision of a pumping plant. However, they went on to virtually rule out both these options because the difficulties involved would make the cost prohibitive although there might be some limited areas where embanking might be an option. They suggested the reduction in the navigation level on this stretch of river by about 2ft (61cm) which would involve some deepening of the channel, pointing out that this had been a recommendation of the Allport Commission in 1887. The cost of all these works was estimated at £345,000 but further technical investigation would be needed. They added significantly: 'The works which we recommend are intended to reduce the incidence of floods in the summer and harvest months, when periodical flooding now occurs. In seasons of excessive rainfall flooding must be expected.' They spelt out in some detail the problems created by the conflicting interests of drainage, power, navigation and fisheries and while recognizing the wide powers given to the ESB under the 1927 Act, they recommended the establishment of a Joint Advisory Committee representing the three main interests of drainage, navigation and power to examine difficulties or problems and to advise the government on the appropriate action to be taken.[62] Needless to say no action followed.

BORD NA MÓNA

Another factor that was to affect the navigation was the establishment of Bord na Móna (the Turf Board) in 1946.[63] The prediction that one day the bogs would be used as a major fuel resource had been realized and the emphasis now moved from the concept of draining the bogs in order to create more land for agriculture to developing the bogs as a peat resource for fuel, principally to supply the ESB power stations. The technique developed, after years of

Lanesborough: the ESB turf-burning power station.

experimenting with different methods, was to scrape the surface of the bog and allow the turf dust to become air-dried. This dust was then collected in vast mounds but in the course of all this work, large quantities of turf dust found its way into the rivers of the Shannon catchment, causing silting. In addition, as part of the draining process to allow heavy machinery on to the bog, water was extracted and pumped into the rivers, which added to the silting. Over the years back channels have silted up and damage has been done to fish stocks and breeding grounds, particularly in the upper part of Lough Derg. It can also cause damage to soil conditions when flood waters are carried out over land. Bord na Móna has taken measures to minimize all these problems.

TRADE IN THE 1930s AND 1940s

J. Bannatyne, millers in Limerick, had a new motor barge delivered to the Shannon in 1924, the *Sunrise*, to carry on trade between Limerick and Carrick. They advertised for 'a good engineer who understands semi-diesel engines. Life job. No running at night. 75s per week'. They subsequently added the *Cambrais* and the *Eclipse Flower*. The Grand Canal Company had experimented in 1930 with a view to developing trade through to the port of Limerick. One of its former steamers, the *Fox*, which as has been mentioned above had been sold to the Office of Public Works in 1910 for use as a maintenance boat, was borrowed back. Great difficulty was experienced with the navigation through the Abbey river bridges and Professor Rishworth advised that navigation should only be undertaken three hours either side of high water and even then it was only 'barely possible'. The company decided instead to avoid the problem and develop its base above the old tidal lock. It had become important for the canal company to try to maintain its Shannon trade in the face of railway opposition. The amount paid by the company in tolls on the Shannon had dropped from £3,896 in 1929 to £1,959 in 1930. The railway companies had begun to use lorries to transport goods direct to their destinations and the canal company began to purchase lorries at this time.

In the years leading up to World War II the total tonnage carried on the river fell slowly from 67,848 tons in 1930 to 65,337 tons in 1940. The revenue varied with changes in toll charges and there was even a surplus of total revenue over expenditure in 1930 of £4,503 and again in 1940 of £2,631. It was principally the trade to and from

Shannonbridge: the ESB turf-burning power station now being replaced by a new building under construction on the right. (ESB Archives)

the Grand Canal that was helping to keep the revenue up. By 1940 the canal company had built up its trade again and, of the total of £5,396 collected in tolls, £4,042 was collected from the Grand Canal Company. During the war years, with the restriction on road transport because of the shortage of fuel, the tonnage carried on the river remained fairly constant. In 1938 the company had commissioned the Ringsend Dockyard Company to build a large new towing vessel for the Shannon, the *St James*, which cost £3,240; she was fitted with a bolinder diesel engine and could carry seventy tons. This was in response to complaints that the traffic was frequently held up waiting to cross Lough Derg in adverse weather conditions.

The shortage of fuel during the war years continued to severely curtail road transport and increase the amount of goods carried by water. The company purchased two more even larger boats for the Shannon trade in 1945. These were the *Avon King* and *Avon Queen*, which had been operating on the River Severn. They were renamed the *St Patrick* and the *St Brigid* and could carry 90 tons each as well as operating as towing vessels. The two last locks up to Shannon Harbour had to be enlarged so that they could move up and down to tranship in the harbour and a large new transhipping shed for goods was erected. Despite these efforts opposition from road transport built up again after the war and the canal company recorded a decrease in the tonnage carried, adding rather sadly: 'the reasons for the decrease were such that no action by the company would improve the position'. The total tonnage carried on the river had only dropped by about 1,000 tons in 1950 to 64,678 tons but for a number of reasons the 1950s were to become very critical years for the navigation.

CHAPTER TWELVE
'*RESURGAM:* I SHALL COME INTO MY OWN AGAIN'

TRADE IN THE 1950s

While the 'Emergency Years' during World War II had led to greater use of water transport because of fuel shortages, once road transport picked up again trade on the river reached its lowest ebb. During the years of fuel scarcity pleasure boating on the Shannon had virtually ceased. Scarce fuel supplies were rationed and allocated where most needed and those pleasure boats which were on the river, were confined to using sail and had to prove this by having their propellers removed.

In addition to the Grand Canal Company, a few private traders continued to operate such as the flour millers: Ranks of Limerick (formerly Bannatynes), had three fine vessels, *Cambrais, Sunrise* and *Eclipse Flower*, which ran between Limerick and Carrick. They subsequently sold the first two but the *Eclipse Flower* continued to ply through the 1950s. There was also the *102B*, F. A. Waller & Co's boat, which collected barley for their maltings in Banagher. The so-called 'turf boats', *Foam, Lady, Aran Queen* and *Sandlark*, carried turf from the midlands and also carried other goods such as slates, bricks, flour, meal and coal to and from Limerick. They operated under sail and pole and were said, with their sloop-rig, to have gone to windward quite well. They could carry about fifty tons with the turf built up into a high deck load; the angle of heel was measured by the number of sods of turf under water when the vessel was rail down. The *Sandlark*, which had been built for C. McGrath of Garrykennedy about 1925 by a local carpenter-turned-boat builder, John McLoughlin, did subsequently have an engine fitted and survived for many years until she went on fire and foundered in the inner harbour at Garrykennedy, where she and the *Aran Queen* lay for many years. However, with road transport restored, the tonnage carried on the river fell and lack of activity on the river by the end of the 1940s made its future as a navigation very vulnerable, which applied in particular to the upper river.

The purchase of the Royal Canal Company by the Midland Great Western Railway, back in the 1840s, had slowly brought about the demise of this canal, with ownership passing in 1938 to the Great Southern Railway and, in turn, to Córas Iompair Éireann (CIÉ).[1] What little traffic there had been had seldom passed west of Mullingar for some years. The last of the by-traders, Leech of Killucan, ceased to operate in 1951 and CIÉ was permitted to close the Royal Canal officially in 1961.

A sailing barge on Lough Derg. (Jonathan Wigham)

In August 1950 a reluctant Grand Canal Company had been forced by the government to amalgamate with the newly nationalized transport authority, CIE.[2] The total tonnage carried on the river had fallen by about 20,000 tons by 1955 to 46,622 tons, with the Grand Canal trade accounting for an increasing percentage of the tonnage and toll receipts. The total revenue was insufficient to meet the expenditure and the government had to meet the increasing deficit. The take over by a railway-dominated company of the Grand Canal was not going to do the middle Shannon trade any favours and, because so much of that trade had been supplied by the canal company, by 1960 the tonnage on the river had fallen to 33,279 tons, almost half the figure for 1950.[3] The continued fall in business had led the Beddy Inquiry into Internal Transport in 1957 to recommend that CIE should be allowed to end their carrying trade.[4] CIE subsequently withdrew most of its fleet on 31 December 1959 with some limited boats operating to Limerick for another six months to allow Messrs Guinness to make alternative warehousing arrangements there. Trading on the Shannon was consequently reduced to virtually nothing.

MORE FLOODING PROBLEMS

The 1950s also produced another problem for the navigation when, in the winter of 1954 and the early months of 1955, exceptional flooding took place once again along parts of the Shannon: 25,000 acres were inundated, roads were submerged and houses flooded. Just as had happened earlier, the fact that little use was being made of the navigation led to a renewed call to 'Drain the Shannon'. The local farmers, completely failing to understand the complexity of solving the problem of Shannon flooding, once again called for the removal of Meelick weir, even at one stage threatening to have it blown up. The government enlisted an American expert, Louis Rydell, of the US Corps of Engineers, who was asked to advise 'on the possibility of dealing effectively and permanently with the periodic flooding in the Shannon valley', and he reported in 1956.[5]

To begin with, Rydell determined that in assessing the viability of any scheme it was necessary to consider the whole Shannon basin because drainage schemes on the tributaries could not be undertaken until the main river could cope with the additional flows. Suggesting the possible diversion of the upper Suck into Lough Ree by way of the River Hind, he noted that in the floods of 1954-1955 the Suck

A sailing barge under tow by the Eclipse. *(Alf Delany Archives)*

was contributing to one third of the total amount of water the river had to cope with between Shannonbridge and Meelick. He also stressed that the implications for a whole range of issues in addition to drainage had to be considered such as power generation, agriculture, navigation, fisheries and recreation. In regard to the latter he reckoned that the Shannon with its navigable tributaries was one of the outstanding rivers in the world and he believed that its recreational use could be developed into a tremendous asset far beyond its present status, thus replacing the commercial traffic, which it had lost to road and rail competition. In addition to recreational developments, he pointed to the need for reforestation schemes on poorer land, relocations of houses and roads out of the flood plains, improved agricultural practice and land use, assisted by engineering solutions. What he was advocating, therefore, was a comprehensive and co-ordinated plan, and to achieve this a Shannon River Basin Interagency Committee or what might be termed a Shannon Valley Authority was needed to carry out the overall investigations and co-ordinate its effective prosecution.

He recommended that investigations should fall into two stages: a desk study in the first instance followed by more detailed fieldwork. He came up with two options: a more limited 'summer relief scheme' costing a total of an estimated £15 million, which included work on tributaries already ongoing, and secondly 'a full relief scheme', which he estimated would cost £19, 500,000. He admitted that the schemes were not economically viable, and the expenditure would not be justified by the acreage that would be improved for agriculture on the main river but, taking into account the lands that could then be drained around the tributaries, there would be considerable economic benefit.

His suggested works were based largely on increasing the holding capacity of Lough Allen and Lough Ree, raising the former, which currently fluctuated between 151 and 163 O.D. from the maximum up to 170.0'O.D. and allowing a range on Lough Ree of a low of 112.0' O.D. to a high of 128.0' O.D. However, all this depended on increasing the flow of water and he indicated that the way to achieve this was to increase the channel capacity at bottlenecks where required. He pointed out that taking figures from 1893 to 1955, the flow in the river had always exceeded the discharge capacity of the river channel. He was thus

Former sailing barges, Sandlark *and* Arran Queen *abandoned at Garrykennedy.*

drawing attention yet again to the problem, identified by the Shannon Commissioners all those years ago, something they did not have the funds to complete and which they realized would at some future time need to be done. It would also require replacing Athlone weir to permit the greater draw-down that would be needed, and removing the weir at Meelick, making it one long level from Athlone all the way to the headrace to Ardnacrusha. With regard to the use of embankments to reduce the amount of excavating required in improving the channel capacity, he drew attention to the problems that the ESB had experienced with the new embankments between Meelick and Portumna, which because of the poor foundation had settled by as much as a third of their height and subsequently required major reconstruction. It is hardly surprising that, in the absence of immediate further exceptional flooding, the government, with an eye to the high estimates involved, shelved the idea of taking any immediate action along the lines suggested by Rydell.

In 1961 a joint report was issued by the OPW and the ESB, which considered Rydell's conclusions and set out the options and costs involved.[6] Rydell's frequently quoted statement with reference to previous investigations sums up the situation very well: 'No simple or obvious solution has heretofore been found nor, said Mr Rydell, had he found one. Investigators have generally concluded that any solution physically practicable for accomplishment would involve extensive and costly engineering works with which he wholly agreed.' Once again no action was taken by the government. It was clear that temporary or piecemeal solutions were not likely to produce the relief being sought in extreme weather conditions, and the high estimates and lack of economic viability made the undertaking of any major scheme an unlikely option.

WHERE THE RIVER SHANNON FLOWS

Not much was being written about the Shannon at this time but one book, which is sometimes overlooked, was Richard Hayward's *Where the River Shannon Flows*. This described his travels along the river in 1939, giving a good indication of traffic in the year leading up to the World War II years.[7] Maybe the reason why less notice has been taken of this book is that the journey he made was by 12hp car, towing a caravan, rather than by boat, although they did manage to make some boat trips along the way. His stated aim was threefold: 'to make a travel picture of the River Shannon from its source to its mouth; to write a book of similar scope; and to enjoy ourselves'. He travelled with two companions: Germain Burger to make the film and Louis Morrison to take still pictures for the book. Both the film and photographs are a wonderful record of the river at that time and his well-researched book is full of history and legends, providing glimpses of the river but not very many references to the navigation. He did say that moored in the river above the bridge in Athlone 'you will usually find a number of cabin cruisers and house-boats available for hire at moderate prices'. During a boat trip on Lough Ree he described seeing all sorts of boats: 'great powerful motor-barges operated by the Grand Canal Company, small rowing-boats with hopeful anglers aboard, house-boats and cabin cruisers moored among the tall reeds at the water-margin, and a strange contraption from Banagher which looked like a ship's longboat converted into a floating caravan'. Some idea of the common perception of the waterways can be seen in Hayward's comments when he referred to 'that tragic craze for canal-building which took hold of the Irish people early in the nineteenth century and caused them to waste millions of pounds upon the construction of inland waterways which within a few years became utterly useless, and which are now to be seen all over the country, for the most part weed-grown and forlorn'.

GREEN & SILVER

In 1949 Tom Rolt, who had made the circular journey with his wife, Angela, along both the Grand and Royal canals and parts of the Shannon, published an account of his trip, which he called *Green & Silver*, indicating the silvery glint of the water as it passed through the green fields.[8] Just as his earlier book, *Narrow Boat*, had drawn attention to the threat to the waterways in England, his book on his Irish travels drew the public's attention to what a wonderful waterway system was out there waiting to be explored. The actual journey had taken place in 1946 and he had found it quite difficult to get information about boats for hire. Eventually it was suggested that he should contact the 'Irish Tourist Association' and it not only sent him information about the waterways but a list of names and addresses of boat owners and the craft available. Because fuel was still very scarce, all but one of those he contacted said that they did not expect to be given any fuel that year and their boats were still laid up. However, John Beahan of Athlone said he would get his boat, *Le Coq*, into commission in the hopes that his application for fuel would be approved.

The petrol allocation did eventually come through; how sad it would have been if his trip had not been able to go ahead and we would have been deprived of this classic book. The only commercial boats they encountered between Athlone and Shannon Harbour were the *Eclipse Flower* and a canal boat. Having completed the journey along the two canals, they re-entered the Shannon at Tarmonbarry and headed upstream. He described Clarendon lock at Knockvicar: 'The lock sides were overgrown. The gates on one side were chained up, being obviously rotten and unusable, while their opposite numbers looked little better.' The inactivity of the

Tom Rolt with Le Coq *in the 13th lock on the Grand Canal on his trip in 1946 which led to his book* Green & Silver. *(Athlone Branch IWAI)*

REPLACING RHODES'S SWIVEL BRIDGES

Rydell had also drawn attention to one other issue that was to have wide implications: the need for the replacement of the opening bridges. Rhodes's swivel bridges had stood the test of time but, with road transport gathering momentum after the war, their load-carrying capacity was being called into question. The local authorities, aware of the low volume of traffic on the river, were reluctant to spend the additional money needed to replace them with opening spans and were planning to put in fixed structures which would be a much cheaper option. Rydell, quite rightly, suggested that the final decision about these bridges should not be made until plans to solve the flooding problem evolved, which would have implications for the levels in the river. There is little doubt that the Shannon Navigation was under great threat. A number of waterway enthusiasts were particularly worried about this development. The war years had reduced the number of pleasure boats on the river and the era of the large yachts was over, although the recreational use of the river was slowly beginning to build up again. Road and rail transport was taking its toll on the commercial traffic and the situation was soon to worsen with the ending of the CIE carrying trade.

war years had led to neglect. Arriving at Battlebridge, at the entrance to the now-defunct Lough Allen canal, they learnt that *Le Coq* was the first boat to visit there for seven years. In Roosky lock they met the OPW maintenance boat *Fox*, which they learnt was the only such vessel on the river and was trying manfully to keep up the maintenance duties. Rolt, more used to the English canals, saw the big lakes on the Shannon as a deterrent to developing cruising facilities: 'to encourage those without previous experience to hire craft and take them out on the lakes would be folly'. In the foreword to a new edition of his book in 1968 Rolt was able to point to the fact that his book had 'become a part of history', a very true comment for much had happened over the course of the intervening twenty-one years.

Athlone: the opening span operating on the bridge. (Simmons Photography)

Roosky: the dragon yacht Firedrake *passing through the bridge in 1952.(Reggie Lee)*

The threat of the strangling of the navigation by the insertion of low fixed bridges to replace the swivel bridges was not going to be easy to counter. With the gradual disappearance of almost all of the large-masted boats there had been virtually no demand for some time to have the bridges opened, because many of them had relatively good headroom. The opening mechanism of the bridge in Athlone, for example, which was carrying much heavy traffic, no longer worked. However, farther upstream, the opening bridges at Tarmonbarry and Roosky had much less headroom when closed and they were also under threat for replacement by fixed spans because of the low volume of river traffic. Just as it seems unthinkable now that it was seriously suggested in the 1860s that the gates should be taken off the upper Shannon locks to allow the water to flow freely, it is equally hard to understand that in the 1950s local authorities were seriously thinking of closing off the upper river navigation and almost succeeded in doing so, thanks to a complete lack of interest by the people and apathy by the government.

In 1951 a letter was written to the *Irish Times* by J.J. Johnson of Limerick pointing out the tourist potential of the Shannon and calling on the Tourist Board to use some of its funding to develop this potential: 'to place within the means of those visiting our shores the way to see and admire what has been truly described as the "hidden Ireland"'. This was followed up by a leading article supporting this concept. A small group of enthusiasts had become aware that the navigation was facing threat, in particular the need to replace the swivel bridges, and they decided to mobilise support. In 1949 an Inland Waterways Association

Banagher: Rory O'Hanlon (centre) and Vincent Delany (left) have a dispute in 1952 with the bridge keeper(right) who was reluctant to open the bridge which had not been opened since 1939. (Reggie Lee)

had been formed in England to fight a similar apathy and threat to the waterways. Two people in particular, Harry Rice and Vincent Delany, both of whom knew and loved the waterways, and in particular the Shannon, carried on a correspondence with their friends in the English IWA and sought support in Ireland to set up a similar organization here. In January 1952, following up the leading article in the *Irish Times*, Vincent Delany wrote a letter suggesting that an Inland Waterways Association of Ireland should be established. He received an enthusiastic response and Harry Rice described how he, Vincent Delany and one other person met and each put £1 on the table as a subscription and declared the association founded.

That summer, Rory O'Hanlon, aided and abetted by Vincent Delany, agreed to bring his dragon yacht, *Firedrake*, to the Shannon and proceed up the river having put in a request for the bridges to be opened. Knowing that it was no longer possible to operate the bridge at Athlone, and being informed by the railway company that the railway bridge could not be opened until the following day, they carried the mast on deck from Shannon Harbour through Shannonbridge and Athlone bridges and, passing under the railway bridge in Athlone, stepped the mast from it. Lanesborough Bridge was swung for them, despite the fact that a water-main had been laid across it and had to be disconnected, then Tarmonbarry Bridge, where they had to lower their burgee to get under the telegraph wires, a portent for what was to follow. Roosky Bridge was negotiated and they approached the railway bridge at Lough Tap, which again they had arranged to have opened. This bridge had not been swung since 1904 but CIE had provided the necessary crew (twenty-three men) and it was considered that the telegraph wires would not be a problem. The mail train passed over, the bridge was opened and they began to pass through, towed by a cruiser. This time her mast struck the wires, they were forced to let go the tow and were left spinning in the bridge striking one of the piers and causing a small amount of damage. Having disentangled themselves they decided to abandon the idea of going through to Lough Key, which involved taking down the mast because none of the upstream bridges had swivel spans, even though they had been tempted by the information that there had not been a keel boat on Lough Key for many years.

They headed downstream for Lough Derg, having all the bridges opened again except Athlone and Banagher, where they had to repeat taking down and re-stepping the mast. On arrival at Banagher they had discovered that the bridge had not been opened since 1939, when great difficulty had been experienced closing it again. However, after some rather heated discussion that also involved the local Garda sergeant, the bridge keeper agreed to try to open it but all efforts to do so failed. The cruise was deemed to have been a success although an action subsequently brought against the Minister for Posts & Telegraphs for the damage caused to the boat at the Lough Tap railway bridge was lost. Vincent Delany and Sean MacBride (who had been giving the tow), both of whom were lawyers, had persuaded Rory that the Minister was infringing his statutory right to navigation. He had won in the circuit court and was awarded £42 damages but lost on appeal when the judge suggested that they had not taken reasonable precautions to ensure that the wires were high enough. Nothing daunted, Rory O'Hanlon subsequently persuaded a group of Dragon owners to bring their boats to the Shannon by rail to Banagher and down to Lough Derg for some racing there.

THANKS FOR THE MEMORY
In the same year (1952) Harry Rice published *Thanks for the Memory* – mostly an account of Lough Ree, illustrated with his own beautifully hand-drawn charts of the lake, which he had explored with his wife, Peggy. Legends are interwoven with descriptive material and history to make a memorable read. He also provided a short account of the navigation upstream to Lough Key and Battlebridge and downstream to visit Clonmacnois and Clonfert. His love and concern for the river is evident: 'This mighty river is our national heritage. There are indications that we are coming to appreciate this fact more and more. It is to be hoped that we

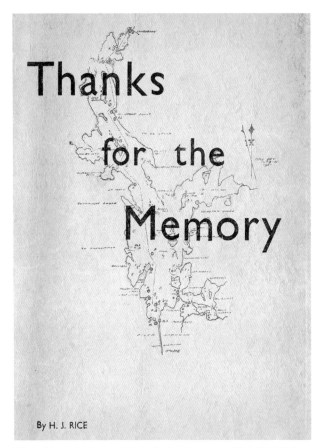

Harry Rice's classic book Thanks for the Memory *published in 1952 (Athlone Branch IWAI)*

Harry Rice's house, Dunrovin, a war-surplus Nissen hut built in the mid'-1940s, at Coosan in the Inner Lakes, where the plans to set up the Inland Waterways Association of Ireland were hatched.

have not left things too late.' He had the vision to see what could come to pass in the future: 'Those with prudence will, however, envisage the possibility of a time when tyres, petrol and coal will be in short supply. It would be then that this great trade route through Ireland might act as the nation's life-line. . . *Resurgam* – "I shall come into my own again" should be the motto of the Shannon.' In an appendix a reference was made to the fact that the Inland Waterways Association of Ireland 'is well on the way towards the active implementation of its aims and objects'.

'STRANGLING THE SHANNON'

Harry Rice's book, together with Tom Rolt's, were to become classics of the Irish waterways. In February 1952 a public inquiry was held in Athlone about replacing the bridge, which resulted in the decision being made that it should be replaced with a fixed structure. It was obvious that something had to be done quickly. The Minister for Local Government was considering bringing in a 'Bridge Order', but this was postponed when it was pointed out that the Shannon Navigation Acts would have to be repealed to replace the opening bridges with fixed structures. It was estimated that an opening bridge would cost £35,000 and a fixed structure about half this figure, the additional cost of which would have to be borne by the ratepayers. In April 1953 Vincent Delany wrote two articles for the Irish Times describing the long history of how the inland waterways had developed and the importance of maintaining this national asset. A series of letters was orchestrated in the *Irish Times* under the heading 'Strangling the Shannon',

which included support from Robert Aickman of the Inland Waterways Association in England and from Tom Rolt. Although a founder member of the IWA, he had broken off his connection with that association a few years earlier over a dispute about administrative matters.

Harry Rice wrote that if a fixed bridge was built it would:

... lie, functioning like so many planks across a bog drain, barring the passage of anything much bigger than a lifeboat. If that happens, the closing ceremony of the Shannon will be performed to the applause of its suicidal sponsors, and the great river will sneak humbly through an ungrateful town that it could have helped to make a thriving city, neglected and forlorn, leaving behind it a great future.

The suggestion that the bridge had not been opened since 1937 was denied; it was stated that it had been opened as recently as 1942 and the reason it had not subsequently been opened was not because there was no demand but because it was known that the mechanism had become defective and that it could no longer be operated. More and more letters followed to such an extent that the editor eventually stated: 'Contributors to this correspondence are asked to confine their letters to 200 words.' The matter was debated in the Dail where some support for the campaign had been enlisted and an amendment to the new Local Government Act calling for the preservation of the navigation rights on the Shannon was passed.

THE INLAND WATERWAYS ASSOCIATION OF IRELAND

In January 1954 the inaugural meeting of the Inland Waterways Association of Ireland (IWAI) was finally held, making official the formation of the association. Harry Rice was elected as President, Vincent Delany and L.M. Goodbody as joint honorary secretaries and members of a Council were also elected. The four stated aims were: to encourage water transport; to collaborate with tourism interests in encouraging pleasure boating, publishing guides etc.; to encourage cruising under sail and power; to compile historical records and data on development. The following resolution was passed at the inaugural meeting: 'That this Association is resolutely opposed to any attempt to amend the Shannon Navigation Acts so as to permit the obstruction of the Shannon Navigation and, in particular, its obstruction by the erection of a fixed bridge at Athlone.' The association followed the same type of structure as the IWA across the water by creating branches in the various areas; the Athlone branch was formed that year followed by branches along the Shannon in Killaloe and Portumna, later amalgamated as the Lough Derg Branch, and in Carrick.

Harry Rice addresses the inaugural meeting of the IWAI in Dublin in 1954.

Despite failing health Harry Rice continued to keep up the campaign. Some idea of the efforts he made becomes apparent from his correspondence with various people.[9] He described how he saw a letter in the *Irish Press* written on behalf of the South Westmeath Ratepayers Association suggesting that those seeking an opening bridge at Athlone were not the people who were going to have to pay for it. Harry, who was a member of this Ratepayers Association, turned up at the next meeting and questioned whether the letter had been written on behalf of the members and suggested it was implying that he was not paying his rates. He claimed: 'I am not a big ratepayer. Oh no. I own just less than one acre of Ireland. I saved up to buy that acre and to erect the modest house in which I live [a war surplus Nissen hut] and I pay rates for it and am entitled to speak.'

The meeting developed into an uproar and the letter was repudiated by those present. A motion was passed demanding that the county council seek a grant from central funds for an opening bridge and Harry was nominated to represent the association at a meeting of the local authority. It was suggested that the bridge was in a dangerous condition: CIE was making bus passengers walk across the bridge, the state of the bridge was caused by the heavy traffic now being carried on an arterial highway, and it was not a cost that should be borne by local ratepayers. There was, however, strong opposition from Westmeath county council, which voted that the bridge should be condemned and replaced by a fixed bridge. This was supported by Offaly county council, which was anticipating having to replace Banagher Bridge. Despite all the effort and publicity it was a clear that this was going to be an uphill battle.

The Tanaiste, William Norton, and party aboard the St Clair *in 1954.*

THE CIE PASSENGER SERVICE

In November 1954 a Local Government Act was drafted that contained a clause permitting the Minister to sanction the replacing of bridges even where rights of navigation prevailed. However, in December, due to pressure of business the Minister moved an amendment excluding the Shannon but retaining the threat to bridges over other navigable waterways. A bridge over the Munster Blackwater was also under threat and the IWAI called for the exclusion of bridges on all public navigable rivers but they did not succeed in achieving this. Harry Rice and Vincent Delany had received much encouragement and support for the IWAI from Sean McBride T.D.[10] Sean had owned a boat on the river since the 1930s, the *Lady Di*, a former steam pilot boat from Dun Laoghaire. He and his family had enjoyed the waterways over the years, even exciting the interest of the Special Branch at one time, who could not work out why a well-known Republican was spending so much time moving around in a boat and felt that he must be up to some subversive activity. He supported the campaign to preserve the waterways from 'the faceless technocrats and uninformed civil servants that wanted to destroy them in the name of progress'. He had first met Harry Rice in 1948 when he was Minister for External Affairs and Harry was building his home at Coosan. Together they now decided that it was important that the tourist potential of the river should be realized. In June 1954 Sean helped to arrange for the Tanaiste, William Norton, and the chairman of CIE, Ted Courtney, to be invited to make a trip on the river aboard the *St Clair*, an ex-air-sea-rescue launch that was owned by Harry Rice's daughter Betty and her husband, John Williams. John was later to make his boat available to carry Rydell on his flood assessment trip. For two days John brought the Tanaiste up the river from Killaloe to Athlone in ideal weather conditions and everywhere they were received enthusiastically. They had to finish the trip at Athlone but he returned a few months later to travel up from Athlone to Boyle. The result was that the Tanaiste was sufficiently impressed by what the river had to offer to encourage CIE to consider putting a passenger service into operation as a tourist attraction.

CIE acted with commendable speed and purchased two large boats in England, which were renamed the *St Brendan* and the *St Ciaran*. The former, originally the *Cardinal Wolsley*, arrived first in 1955 and operated from Athlone, and the *St Ciaran*, formerly the *Wroxham Belle*, arrived one year later and operated from Killaloe. She was built in 1936 and had had a colourful existence. She was the first motor-driven passenger boat on the Norfolk Broads, where she was commandeered for patrol work during the war, shipped out to Sierra Leone and later returned to the Thames. The service was begun in June 1955 and the significant factor was that they needed headroom under the bridges of at least 14ft (4m), which was to determine the minimum height of any new fixed bridges. This was more than any of the boats on the river at the time would need. Although the service was subsequently withdrawn in 1974 it had played an important role; the boats were sold, with both of them eventually ending up in New Ross where Dick Fletcher ran a successful floating restaurant service.

The IWAI now reluctantly withdrew its opposition to the opening bridge being replaced with a fixed structures at Athlone and at the other higher-level swivel bridges at Shannonbridge, Banagher and Lanesborough, on condition that the replacements for the lower bridges at Tarmonbarry and Roosky would have opening spans. In retrospect, with the return today of many masted boats to the river, it was a pity that this concession had to be agreed to, but it was hard to fight for opening spans at that time when there were virtually no masted boats left on the river. There had been references made at local authority meetings to 'yachts owned by the privileged few'. Public money was involved and, as the association was fighting for the very survival of the navigation, it had to agree to the compromise. In many ways the introduction of the passenger boats could be said to have been the turning point as far as the Shannon Navigation was concerned, although there were still going to be difficult times ahead for inland waterways in general.

The passenger boat St Brendan *which arrived on the river in 1955.*

Meelick lock: boats moving between regattas in the 1950s.
(Terence Cleeve)

EARLY SHANNON RALLIES

Knockvicar lock had been found to be in a dangerous condition and was closed in 1953. Temporary repairs were carried out and then, in response to pressure from the IWAI, the gates were eventually replaced. In August 1956 Harry Rice led a group of small boats with outboards from Athlone to Lough Key. This was directly in response to the local development group's call for help to oppose the Rockingham Estate Company's efforts to exercise control over the navigation of the lake. The rights to the navigation of the lake were quickly re-established by the OPW but landing rights had to be respected. Harry was to lead further expeditions and, in 1961, the first of what was to become an annual rally of cruisers and small boats, set off from Athlone for Lough Key. As a gesture of support Esso had agreed to provide free fuel for the rally, which encouraged seventy-one boats to participate, 'the greatest mustering of craft ever seen on an Irish inland waterway' according to the *Westmeath Independent*. These early rallies were very important because they demonstrated the potential of the river for development as a recreational and tourist resource. The Shannon rallies still continue on an annual basis, together with an annual Lough Derg rally, and the emphasis now is very much on encouraging competency and emphasizing the importance of safety measures. Both the Shannon and Derg rallies came together in a monster rally in Athlone in 2000 to celebrate the Millennium, and the 47th Shannon rally and the 33nd Lough Derg rally will be held in 2007.

THE TOURISM POTENTIAL

In addition to the successful encouragement of the CIE tourist/passenger boat service, some members of the IWAI had also looked into the building up of a hire-boat business.

Roosky: an early rally in 1964 with the swivel bridge which had been under threat. (L.A. Edwards)

In 1949 T.E. Hagenbach of Graham Bunn of Wroxham on the Norfolk Broads had come to Ireland by invitation to give advice about the prospects of establishing a hire-boat firm. At this time there were some 750 boats for hire on the Broads. He did a trip along the river in November 1949 and produced a memorandum.[11] In many ways it was a positive document: 'there is certainly no question but that the beauty of the countryside greatly surpasses any other known area where Motor Cruisers are operated'. He suggested that activities should be confined to the north Shannon because the large lakes, Ree and Derg, were unsuitable. He considered the infrastructure such as quays was good but additional marking of the navigation was needed and other amenities would tend to improve when the demand was made for them. He was obviously concerned about the implications of weather conditions, which, when it is considered that he made his trip in November, is not surprising. He prepared a table of data over a three-year period comparing rainfall on the Broads and on the Shannon and indicated that, while there was a twenty-week season on the former, sixteen weeks would be the maximum possible on the Shannon. However, he added: 'From the study there would appear to be no reason to believe that the weather in the Shannon area should be any worse than that in the Avon and Severn area', both being subject to prevailing westerlies. It was probably his information about the financial implications and the small returns, which he estimated could be expected, which discouraged any further action at this time.

An early rally at Hodson Bay Lough Ree in 1962. (John Breen)

Recognizing that increasing boating on the river was vital prompted the IWAI group to investigate the situation further in 1953. Contact was made both with Blakes and Graham Bunn on the Broads. Blakes showed an interest but said that they would need to take a 15 per cent commission on bookings. Mr Hagenbach was also contacted and he sent over a copy of his 1949 Memorandum. Again he was encouraging, offering them a good deal on four of his 1947-8 'Windboats' but the net revenue figures he estimated were not very good, showing a small net profit of £743 in the first year, rising to £1,038 in the fifth year. He also admitted that the weather data he had compiled was 'not encouraging'. There is no record in the correspondence of his previously quoted remark about the Shannon needing a giant umbrella to make a hire-boat business viable, but a meeting was held with him in England at which he might have said this.

Some of the rally boats locking through Knockvicar lock in 1963.

Nothing came of these negotiations but the IWAI found itself having to fight on a number of other fronts. They made a submission to the Beddy Commission on Transport in 1957, pointing out the many advantages of water transport over road and rail. However, this fell on deaf ears and CIE was allowed to give up its carrying trade in 1959, thereby depriving the Shannon of almost all of its remaining commercial traffic.

THE CAMPAIGN CONTINUES

In the meantime Bord Failte, the Irish Tourist Board, was showing more interest and this was to give a significant boost to the campaign. It gave financial assistance to the IWAI to publish a small guide to the navigation, the *Shannon Pilot*, written by Vincent Delany, with basic fold-out maps of the river, at the princely price of 2s 6d. The Admiralty charts of Lough Ree and Lough Derg had been reprinted and, although they dated back to the 1830s, they were very accurate and the fact that the levels of both Ree and Derg had since been raised meant that the clearance on the shoals was

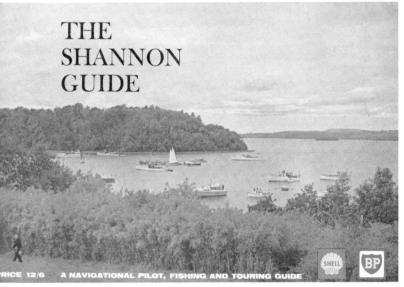

The first Shell and BP Guide to the Shannon published in 1963.

slightly better than that shown on the charts. Other apects of developing the Shannon as a tourism and recreational resource were being encouraged and Shell and BP published the *The Shannon Guide* in 1963, a full navigational pilot, based on charts prepared by John Weaving, together with a fishing and touring guide; many editions of Shell guides were to follow over the years. Geoffrey Dibb of Norfolk also brought out a guide, *The Shannon Book*, in 1967.

With the ending of its carrying trade in 1960 CIE began to dispose of most of its fleet of Shannon barges and canal boats. In 1961-1962 the Kearsleys purchased first the *St Patrick* and then the *St James* from CIE and fitted them out as 'floatels'; they operated the two boats as Irish River Floatels, travelling in company with the sleeping

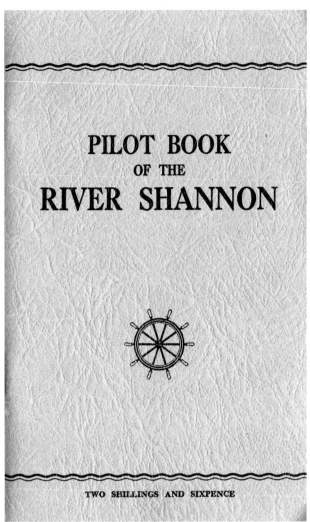

The first Shannon guide, The Shannon Pilot, edited by Vincent Delany and published with assistance from Bord Failte in 1956.

accommodation on one of the boats. They charged twenty-six guineas per week, which included some coach trips from a number of places; they added to the fleet in 1964 bringing in the *Linquenda* from Holland. CIE sold off most of the canal boats in the 1970s, which were purchased by private individuals for conversion. Donnaca Kennedy of Carrick-on-Shannon purchased five of these and converted them, selling on some of them and chartering two of them as Weaver Boats.

THE HIRE FLEET DEVELOPS

Word was spreading across the water about the Irish waterways. In 1958 Hugh Malet had travelled extensively in his little boat, *Mary Ann*, and published two books and R. Gardner wrote about his time on the river in 1977.[12] Some efforts to make boats available for hire had been made over the post-war years. J.B. and M. O'Driscoll had set up Irish Cruises Ltd on Lough Derg with a number of boats and there were still a few fairly small individual cruisers for hire of various sorts in places like Athlone. The number of private cruisers was also gradually increasing through the 1950s. Then, far away in India, George O'Brien Kennedy, a naval architect, began to think of returning to Ireland and asked his mother to see if she could find a book about the Shannon.[13] She sent him out *Green & Silver* and he records how he and his wife, Christine, read it and 'we knew what we wanted to do! Start a Hire Boat business on the Shannon!' They made a preliminary excursion to the river while on holiday and, in 1960, they returned to Ireland.

He and his wife had two small children and a few thousand pounds and they planned to design and build their own boats for the hire company. Bord Failte was not prepared to give them financial help but did agree to guarantee a loan of £10,000, which they turned down as too big a risk. They managed to secure a site at Jamestown Bridge for £250 and they rented a tiny flat and yard in Killiney, County Dublin, where they built their first boat. While this boat was under construction, as CIE had closed down their water transport operations, they purchased the CIE boat, *St Brigid*, for £320 and one canal boat, the *52M*, for £120, at the auctioning off of the carrying fleet, converting *St Brigid* first and using her as a home at Shannon Harbour. Here they took a lease of the big transhipping shed from CIE, no longer needed for their carrying trade. Thus, on a shoestring, by designing and building their own boats, they put together a fleet of two cruisers and two motor sailers. Eventually they moved their floating home to Jamestown, where they set about building a house and at the same time established K Line Cruisers in 1964. They sold the *52M* and bought one of the by-trader boats, the *Peter Farrell*, which had been in turn *1B, 30M* and then *125B*. They employed John Weaving to operate her laying markers and, subsequently, sold her to John who lived on her with his two dogs very happily for many years until his death in May 1987. As John moved up and down the river, carrying out various dredging and small harbour works, he became very much a part of the Shannon legend.

Canal boats at James's Street harbour before being auctioned in 1960. (Oliver Lovell)

Royal Canal: Richmond Harbour was re-opened to boats from the Shannon in 1968 and the canal from Dublin seen in the middle of the picture approaching the harbour is due to be reopened in 2008. The old Shannon Navigation passed up through Clondara lock on the left and up the River Camlin. (Photograph Kevin Dwyer AIPPA)

The hire fleet began to expand further. Dick McGarry of Roosky had some cruisers built for him by Hickey's of Galway. O'Brien Kennedy, in addition to his own fleet, built four boats for James O'Connor's Flag Line operating in Carrick. Most significantly O'Brien Kennedy had a visit from Derek Dann, of Messrs Guinness, which had begun to investigate the possibility of starting a fleet. Bord Failte now stepped in and offered to give grants of one third of the cost of imported boats from England and Guinness set up Emerald Star, with bases in Carrick and Portumna; by 1970 they had a fleet of twenty-three cruisers. Another English company, Carrick Craft, also benefited from the grant scheme. Marina facilities were installed at Carrick, Banagher and Portumna by the local authorities and leased to the new firms. The unfair thing was that grants were not made retrospective and so the pioneers of boat hiring got nothing. Not only that but, with numbers of new boats for hire arriving on the river, supported by well-financed companies, K Line Cruisers found they could not compete and, handicapped by debts from borrowed money, they were forced to sell off their fleet; the same fate was experienced by other small firms. However, it was all good news for the future development of the Shannon Navigation and the arrival of the large hire-boat firms firmly placed the river on the map as a perfect destination for a waterway holiday.

THE O'CLEARY REPORT

In 1963 Dermot O'Cleary, who had been President of the IWAI from 1962-1967, produced a report on the future development of the Shannon that had been commissioned by Bord Failte. He indicated that it was necessary to improve facilities to cater for the increasing recreational and tourist use of the river. Heretofore the infrastructure had been designed for commercial traffic but now different facilities were needed. The plans put forward would require funding and Bord Failte, by this time fully realizing the potential of the river, guaranteed the estimated funding of £140,000, which also included the grants to assist in building up the new hire-boat fleets. Almost all the suggested improvements in the O'Cleary report, which had been very well laid out by someone who had a good practical knowledge of the river, were carried out over the next number of years. Amongst other things the Lecarrow canal was re-opened in 1966, providing an important refuge harbour on Lough Ree; Richmond Harbour, the terminus of the Royal Canal, was opened up and considerable improvements were carried out to the markers, particularly on the larger lakes where more easily visible buoys were laid.

PROGRESS IS MAINTAINED

Several branches of the IWAI had been set up including branches at Athlone, Lough Derg and Carrick; the latter earned the name of 'the friendly branch' by making a point of visiting the quays in summer to welcome boats and offer help to visitors. Both Harry Rice and Vincent Delany died in 1964. They had the satisfaction of seeing the river come alive and they left behind them a good team of dedicated people. Year by year improvements were carried out by the OPW. The low swivel bridges at Tarmonbarry and Roosky, which had caused so much anxiety, had been replaced by lifting spans in 1968; the potential of the river had become obvious by this time and it was no longer an issue. In 1975 Terence Mallagh, an active member of the IWAI and an engineer with experience in marine works, produced a report on the commercial potential of the river, recommending using containers that would be carried by barge between Dublin and Limerick and transferred to and from sea-going ships. The report was a bit ahead of its time; but now with the issue of cutting down on greenhouse gases and achieving sustainable development on the agenda, there is a good case that the option of water transport should once again be considered.

The early hire boat companies came together to form the Penguin Group in 1967 and produced a brochure advertising boats available.

John Weaving. (National Geographic)

*Stephen McGarry, lock keeper at Meelick holds
a ladder for Vincent Delany.*

Sean Butler, bridge keeper at Portumna for many years.

Michael Bourke, son of Mattie, lock keeper at the Albert lock talking to Ted Croxon.(Jan de Fouw)

Bernard McGarry, son of Stephen, lock keeper at Meelick and his nephew, Brendan McGarry, with Alf Delany. (Jan de Fouw)

Mattie Bourke, lock keeper at the Albert lock for many years talking to Peter Denham.

Denis Madigan, skipper of the OPW maintenance boat, preparing to carry out an underwater inspection.

Tarmonbarry: the low opening span which was threatened with a fixed replacement span.

In 1975 Brady Shipman Martin carried out a study for Bord Failte on the tourist and recreational potential of the Shannon, which recognized it as 'a uniquely valuable resource'.[14] By this time there were 231 boats available for hire representing nearly 5,000 boat weeks. Less than one quarter of the hirers were from Ireland and 35 per cent were from Germany. Encouraged by the Bord Failte grants the boat-hire business had expanded rapidly: in 1970 there had been 5,590 visitors rising to 12,200 in 1975. It was estimated that there were now between 200 and 250 privately owned 'power, decked, private craft' on the river. The study identified twenty different political and administrative divisions involved in one way or another with the river but it suggested that the option of creating a Shannon Authority was neither feasible nor practical. What was needed was advance planning and they suggested the introduction of 'special planning zones' in which the extent of recommended development would be recognized. Working on the estimate of the OPW that over the years more than £7.3 million had been spent on arterial drainage schemes in the catchment area, the report recognized that it was not possible to separate the concepts of conservation and development and that the conservation/management of the whole river needed to be undertaken at a national level.

An interesting two-day conference had been held in Athlone in 1976, organized by the Institution of Civil Engineers of Ireland (Midlands Region) and the Midlands

Tarmonbarry: the new opening bridge which replaced Rhodes's swivel bridge.(Walter Borner)

Roosky: the mechanism for operating the old swivel bridge.

Region Development Organization. The theme was 'The Management of the River Shannon in the 1980s'; the papers delivered give a good idea of the positive thinking about the future of the river at that time.[15] By that time there were about 300 boats for hire and about 250 private boats on the river and the total number of lock passages recorded had risen from 16,700 in 1970 to 31,500 in 1975. Paul Byrne,

Roosky: Rhodes's swivel bridge is dismantled in 1968.

Roosky: the new bridge is installed.

county manager of County Roscommon, spoke of the role of local authorities, making this comment: 'Some form of controls or zoning on the waterways may also need to be considered at some future time so that those developments which of their nature will generate increased people activity will not destroy the sense of solitude and peace which to my mind is one of the major attractions of the river itself.' Another prophetic comment was made by John Carty, the principal OPW engineer in charge of the river: 'The

attraction of the Shannon can only be maintained for as long as its water quality is not allowed to deteriorate, its shoreline development controlled and the uncrowded nature of the waterway retained by the planned spacing of new hire-base centres.' John Carty had also shown vision in advising that the Grand Canal system and the Barrow Navigation should be transferred to the OPW, and he also saw the potential in re-opening the Ballinamore & Ballyconnell Canal to connect the Shannon and the Erne and carried out the first detailed survey of this navigation. George Bagnall, Bord Fáilte, stressed the importance of the associated land-based tourism and that improving shore facilities was 'an integral part of any waterway development'. The regional development organizations produced a submission in 1979 also calling for an overall plan for the resource.[16] Sadly, the government failed to act on the concept of the overall strategic development of the Shannon and it was left to the adjoining counties to continue to manage planning on an individual basis.

Terryglass on Lough Derg in 1972 before the new harbour was made.

The Canals Act, 1986, saw the transfer of the Grand Canal system and the Royal Canal to the OPW, thus placing almost all the waterways under a single authority, something that had frequently been suggested by earlier commissions. Although it did not alter the position of the Shannon Navigation within the OPW, the Act stressed the wider recreational role of the waterways and demonstrated an acceptance by the government that the inland waterways were part of the nation's heritage. This led to a new approach in the way in which the Shannon was being administered. Since the Board of Works had assumed responsibility for the river in 1831 it had seen its role principally as a navigation authority. Now, in the 1980s major works were undertaken: new harbours were constructed at Dromod on Lough Bofin and at Dromaan, Williamstown, on Lough Derg (which later had to have its outer protecting wall increased) and floating jetties were provided at Clonmacnois.

Portumna Castle harbour under construction in 1978.

MORE FLOODING, THE SHANNON FORUM AND WATER MANAGEMENT

As might be expected the flooding issue did not go away. Promises to 'Drain the Shannon' had formed a popular plank in the platform for political parties in successive

Canal boats assembled in the Jamestown Canal in 1972 to take part in an expedition to try to reach the 1st lock from the Shannon on the Ballinamore & Ballyconnell Canal.

John Weaving and friends clearing a passage through the bridge at Leitrim in 1972 to access the 1st lock which was to draw attention to the potential in re-opening the canal to link the Shannon and the Erne.

general elections. Following some difficult years of winter flooding between Athlone and Meelick, the government established a Shannon Forum in 1989 with the aim of bringing together the Irish Farmers Association, the various government departments and agencies and some of the non-governmental organizations to discuss the management of the river. Once again the lack of a proper understanding of the issue led to calls for the removal of Meelick weir. The forum continued to meet over a period of years but nothing emerged other than a call for a Shannon Authority. The IWAI had also called for such a Shannon Authority over the years because it found that the large number of departments and agencies involved in one way or another made it difficult to achieve overall co-ordination and planning. However, it was obvious that to create such an authority would have been extremely difficult to implement and the government opted for the easy way out and took no action.

John Weaving, aboard the Peter Farrell *passing the Shannon Rally in Cootehall in 1984.*

Hodson Bay, Lough Ree: the new harbour, one of the few places to moor on the lake. (Walter Borner)

THE SHANNON NAVIGATION ACT

The Shannon Navigation Act passed in 1990 enabled the OPW to introduce new by-laws to replace the existing ones, which had been framed back in 1911, for the commercial traffic days. Amongst other things it was intended to bring in registration of boats together with a charge. Up to then, boat owners had enjoyed free use of the river, paying only for passing through locks and opening bridges. This sparked off a major confrontation with the IWAI, which represented many of the boat owners. The government had just emerged from a difficult nationwide period of confrontation with fishermen over rod licences in which the latter had scored a victory and so showed little taste for a new struggle. It was finally agreed that registration would be introduced, so that the navigation authority would have some means of identifying boats and their owners, but there would be no charge for registration. The new by-laws, introduced in 1992, among other things brought in restrictions on the number of days boats that could avail of public moorings to overcome the practice of 'harbour hogging', which was preventing visitors in hire craft finding moorings. New harbours had been constructed at Dromineer and Mountshannon in 1991 and subsequently at Terryglass, Banagher, Hodson Bay and Lecarrow. Quays were extended at Lanesborough, Drumsna and elsewhere and the locks and bridges were gradually converted to hydraulic operation, which helped to cater for the increasing numbers of boats.

A Lough Derg rally in Dromineer in 1982 indicating the increase in the number of masted boats on the river.

The Lough Derg Yacht Club during the annual regatta.

THE WATERWAYS SERVICE AND DUCHAS WATERWAYS

In 1993 policy for the development of the Shannon Navigation, along with all the other waterways, was transferred from the OPW to the new Department of Arts, Culture & the Gaeltacht (AC&G) under Minister Michael D. Higgins. There had been some suggestion that waterways should remain with OPW, which was to continue to manage drainage when all the other heritage sections were transferred, but it was considered that waterways were an important part of the country's heritage and as such should be transferred. This decision was to prove an essential element in the way in which the river was to be managed and developed. Under the Programme for Government of the Fianna Fail and Labour parties, one of the commitments for the new minister was to formally establish the Heritage Council, with inland waterways listed as part of its brief.[17] In the meantime although policy decisions had been transferred, operational procedures for the waterways had remained for a time within the Waterways Division of the OPW until the official transfer was completed in 1996, and it then became the Waterways Service with policy and operations now within the Department of AC&G.

Shannon One Designs racing on Lough Derg.

The OPW maintenance boats Coill an Eo *and the new* Fox *at Portumna in 1970.*

Carrick-on-Shannon: the re-opening of the link with the Erne has made Carrick an important hub. The Boyle Water branches off into Lough Drumharlow on the left of the picture and the Shannon passes up towards Lough Allen on the right. (Photograph Kevin Dwyer AIPPA)

Ballyconnell: the ceremony to mark the re-opening of the Ballinamore & Ballyconnell Canal, renamed the Shannon Erne Waterway in 1994.

In 1978 the Lough Allen Canal had been re-opened to Acres Lake, just short of Lough Allen, after years of pressure by Joseph Mooney, IWAI member in Drumshanbo. In 1992 the ESB accepted that Ardnacrusha was no longer such an important part of the national grid and that it would be possible to minimize the variation in levels on Lough Allen. By constructing a two-way lock into the lake to allow for these variations in levels it would be possible to restore the navigation into the lake. The scheme was completed and opened by Minister Higgins in 1996. The re-opening of

Lough Allen Canal: the overgrown harbour at Battlebridge in 1975 before restoration to Acres Lake.

Lough Allen Canal: the restored harbour. (Walter Borner)

the Ballinamore & Ballyconnell Canal linking the Shannon and the Erne systems in 1994 (renamed the Shannon Erne Waterway) by the two governments as a cross-border flagship scheme, has also brought considerable additional activity to the north Shannon.

The River Suck had been surveyed with a view to extending the navigation to Ballinasloe back in 1988. It is interesting to recall that the Grand Canal Company had suggested this in 1802 when it was carrying out the works on the middle Shannon but when this offer was not accepted the canal company eventually decided to make the Ballinasloe

Lough Allen Canal: dredging out the canal in 1975 prior to the re-opening to Acres Lake.

Lough Allen Canal: the canal was re-opened into Lough Allen in 1996.(Ian Bath)

River Suck: the new lock near Ballinasloe under construction. (John Keane)

The decision to allow Masonite to erect a large plant on the river near Drumsna in 1995 must be questioned. The IWAI had fought an intense campaign against it. At the public inquiry the IWAI's counsel had likened the impact of the factory to 'beaching a battleship on the banks on the river'. There had been quite strong support for the new plant in the Carrick area, as it was seen to be a source of new jobs, and the threat that the firm would seek a site outside the country frightened the government. An Bord Pleanála, the final arbiter in planning appeals, approved it, ignoring its own inspectors' advice.

Lough Allen Canal: Michael D. Higgins, Minister for Arts, Culture & the Gaeltacht (centre), who showed a great interest in the waterways during his time in office, performed the re-opening ceremony in 1996. (Ian Bath)

canal instead because of the expense of constructing towpaths along the river at that time. Ironically, this canal was not opened until 1829, three years after steamers arrived on the river, making towpaths unnecessary. Now the Ballinasloe canal, which was closed in 1961, had largely disappeared in bog workings. Work began on the Suck scheme in 1994, which involved dredging obstructions in the river channel, constructing a new lock and the creation of a harbour; the work was completed and it opened to navigation in 2001.

Under the Fianna Fail and Progressive Democrat Coalition Government, the Department was restructured as the Department of Arts, Heritage, Gaeltacht & the Islands. Duchas, the Heritage Service, was established within this department and the waterways section became Duchas Waterways. With EU structural funding allocated under the Operational Programme for Tourism 1994-1999, it was possible to draw up plans for improving facilities on the Shannon.

River Suck: the navigation to Ballinasloe was opened in 2001. (John Keane)

Despite protests by the IWAI, Masonite was given planning permission to build a factory on the banks of the Shannon near Drumsna in 1995.

The pilot Rural Tax Incentive scheme for the north Shannon corridor was introduced in 1998, which while it may have brought prosperity did lead to some ill-advised development. Having achieved its aim the decision was made in 2006 to phase it out. One new type of development that has emerged as a result of this scheme is the marina surrounded by apartments or housing estates, which have sprung up in places such as Leitrim, Dromod and Tarmonbarry. The Business Enterprise Scheme (BES), which offered tax relief for the purchase of craft for hire, is also ending, but a new BES scheme has been announced by the government for tourism-related schemes in the middle Shannon region from Lough Ree to Lough Derg. This time a certification body is to be established to vet proposed developments to provide quality assurance for the scheme and it will not cover stand-alone hotel or holiday-cottage developments; this should lead to better control and integrated planning decisions by the local authorities.

WATERWAYS IRELAND

In yet another transfer, the Shannon Navigation, together with the other navigable waterways in Ireland, North and South, have now become the responsibility of Waterways Ireland, one of the North/South Implementation Bodies under the terms of the 'Good Friday Agreement' 1999; some of them were transferred in December 1991 and the final transfer of the remaining waterways was completed on 1 April 2000.[18] It was envisaged that these new implementation bodies would report to the North/South Ministerial Council. Waterways Ireland was to be administered by the Department of Culture, Arts & Leisure in the North and the Department of Arts, Heritage, Gaeltacht & the Islands in the South. Subsequently, in the course of a change in how heritage was managed in the South, responsibility for Waterways Ireland was transferred to the Department of Community, Gaeltacht & Rural Affairs. A keen interest was shown by some of the Members of the Local Assembly (MLAs) in Northern Ireland but, with the dissolution of the Assembly and the imposition of Direct Rule, responsibility for Waterways Ireland was transferred to the relevant minister appointed by Westminster pending the restoration of the Assembly. The headquarters of Waterways Ireland is located in Enniskillen with regional offices in Dublin, Carrick and Scarriff. The majority of the staff were designated and transferred to the new body and continuity was also assisted by the appointment of John Martin, the former Director of Duchas Waterways, as Chief Executive, Martin Dennany as Director of Marketing and Communications, and Ray Dunne as Regional Manager responsible for the Shannon Navigation.

Limerick: the combined drainage and navigation scheme was completed in 2001 which involved putting gates in the tidal lock at Sarsfield Bridge, the 1st lock on the old Limerick Navigation and the construction of a new weir at the entrance to the Abbey River increasing the tidal window for accessing the navigation. (Eamon Horgan, Waterways Ireland)

Limerick: the harbour area above the 1st lock before the recent scheme began. (Paul Duffy)

None of these changes in the way the Shannon Navigation was operated slowed progress in carrying out improvements on the river. In 2001 some major schemes were completed. In addition to the River Suck Navigation mentioned above, a new length of canal with a harbour was opened from Lough Key to Boyle. This replaced the former stretch of navigation up the Boyle river to Boathouse Ford, which had been cut off by a new ring road, and brought the navigation closer to Boyle. Work was completed on a major drainage and navigation scheme in Limerick. This actually was similar to the original scheme planned by Nimmo all those years ago in 1822 of making a new weir across from Sarsfield Bridge lock to the entrance to the Abbey river. The new scheme carried the weir farther across to include the entrance to the Abbey river and made this difficult stretch of the navigation non-tidal except for a short period either side of high water when the tide tops the weir. Yet another of the major difficulties with the navigation, identified many years earlier, had now been addressed, although the current when the power station is generating is still causing problems.

Limerick: the 1st lock on the old Limerick Navigation with the former Navigation Company offices on the left before the recent scheme began. (Paul Duffy)

Subsequently further harbour schemes were carried out at Scarriff Harbour, where a new building has been erected for the Waterways Ireland regional office, at Ballyleague, Lanesborough, at Portrunny on Lough Ree and at Garrykennedy on Lough Derg, all reaching completion in 2005-2006. There is continuing work to improve mooring, particularly above and below the locks, and at the towns and villages like Shannonbridge and Killaloe. Limerick City Council is carrying out a scheme in co-operation with Waterways Ireland to restore the Park Canal in Limerick, for which the local authority obtained EU funding. This is the realization of a scheme that had been spearheaded back in 1980 by Mrs Reale and a local community group. This stretch of canal is the downstream canal of the old Limerick Navigation with two locks, and it will give access once more to a stretch of the river at the University College Limerick campus. A pre-feasibility study was also carried out in 2001 by ESB International for the Plassy Campus Company into the restoration of the Plassy to Errina stretch of the old Limerick Navigation with a second phase extending up the river to Parteen and inserting a lock in the weir. It was found that no major technical barriers existed but it would be a costly scheme, estimated at some 13.5 millions euro for phase one and 4 million euro for phase two. New moorings have been made on the west shore of Lough Allen at Cleighranmore, and plans are being drawn up to open up the Shannon river towards Dowra at the north end of the lake. Passenger boats have reappeared on Lough Derg, at Banagher, on Lough Ree and at Carrick, where the *Moon River* provides popular trips.

Limerick: the lock and harbour area after restoration which is being carried out by Limerick City Council as part of the EU Interreg programme, Water in Historic City Centres. (Brian Goggin)

FURTHER FLOODING

Following some further heavy flooding both on the north and middle Shannon in December 1999 and again in the following year, the issue had been raised in the Dail and an inter-party committee was established to investigate and report back.[19] It found that there was a lack of integrated management and co-ordination by the various bodies involved and recommended that the functions of the Western Development Commission should be extended to make it the co-ordinating body. There was further flooding in the summer of 2002, particularly on the north Shannon, which also caused major problems and damage to boats trying to cope with the heavy stream. In 2003 the Minister of State with responsibility for the OPW, Tom Parlon, instigated yet

another inquiry to look into the feasibility of carrying out a more detailed examination of the problem. There were calls yet again for a Shannon Authority to co-ordinate all the various interests involved on the river. It is hard to understand why each time there are exceptional floods, all the same ground is explored over and over again when it is quite clear that the river channel is too constricted in places to let the water pass freely, causing it to back up. To excavate all these places would be extremely costly and there is now no longer any reason to free up more land for agriculture. It makes no difference what authority manages the river. There is absolutely nothing the ESB or Waterways Ireland can do to relieve the situation when there are exceptional floods and the best option is for them to continue to manage water levels through daily consultation, as has been the position down the years.

There will probably continue to be inquiries each time flooding occurs. In the meantime, Tom Parlon's promised flood-plain maps have been produced so that at least housing development should now be excluded from problem areas. This was carrying out what had been recognized in the past - that re-housing and re-routing roads out of the flood plain was one practical thing that could be done. In fact, it was too little water that was as much a concern to the ESB. It is equally impossible to manage levels in dry conditions, and the ESB has to keep the Lough Derg level up in such conditions. It is legally entitled to close the navigation if necessary to provide Ardnacrusha with sufficient water, which it did on parts of the river in the very dry summer of 1957. It is becoming increasingly difficult to close the navigation with the enormous increase in recreational boating on the river. Low water in the dry summer of 2005 and again in 2006 led to problems when levels were run down to a limited degree without closing the navigation, causing numbers of damaged propellers. It is not easy to avoid these problems in dry summers and good water management is essential by the ESB and Waterways Ireland. There has been some interest shown in developing small hydro-electric schemes on the upper river, reverting to what was one of the ideas back in the 1920s of tapping the river for power at a number of locations.

THE FUTURE

There is always a danger that the very resource that makes the Shannon special today as a recreation and tourism asset could be destroyed by the lack of integrated planning and unco-ordinated development. Equal weight must be given to the economic, social and environmental/heritage demands. The establishment of an environmental division within Waterways Ireland and heritage officers in the local authorities has helped to focus attention on sustainable development.

The Heritage Council, established in 1995 with the navigable inland waterways as one of its standing committees, initiated a series of Corridor Studies in 2002 with the final Shannon study being produced in 2007.[20] These studies complemented other earlier studies. A submission had been made by the midlands regional development organizations in 1979, which had called for an overall plan for the development of the River Shannon, listing the seven government departments, twenty agencies and ten NGOs that were involved in one way or another. In the same year Athlone Chamber of Commerce had commissioned a study on the development of the Lough Ree area, which pointed to the lack of consistency and co-ordination in

planning between the local authorities. A working group had been established in 1993-1934 of the local authorities and other agencies in the Lough Derg area with a view to developing the tourism potential, which had led in turn to the commissioning of two reports.[21] Building on all this work, the Heritage Council brought together the relevant local authorities and Waterways Ireland as a steering group and consultants were engaged to consider how the corridors should be developed in a co-ordinated and sustainable way. Wide consultation with stakeholders and local communities was carried out for each of the studies; objectives and recommended actions were identified together with a timescale and indicating who should carry them out. The Heritage Council is now embarking on carrying out an audit to monitor how many of the objectives are being followed up and will continue to work with the local authorities and other stakeholders to encourage their implementation. One of the issues that was raised in the corridor studies was the impact of boat wash on the heritage of the waterways, and the Heritage Council has carried out a Literature Review as a first step to investigate this problem.[22] Further research is now required to examine traffic data and quantifying the actual impact at various locations. It is considered that this programme will raise important issues in relation to the management of the inland waterways if usage continues to increase.

It is to be hoped that the EU Water Framework Directive 2002, which calls for the establishment of River Basin Districts to draw up management plans for each catchment area, will help in water management and pollution control on the Shannon. Some progress had already been made in this area. In the light of increasing pollution in the river, and particularly in Lough Derg which acts as a sort of sump for the river, the relevant local authorities had come together to commission a study on the management and monitoring of the Lough Ree and Lough Derg catchment in 1996, and its final report had been issued in 2001. A detailed study was carried out at this time and there was wide consultation. The main problem of eutrophication or over-enrichment was found to be largely caused by phosphates. Agricultural non-point pollution sources caused by over-use of fertilisers and poor farmyard management and municipal waste discharges were identified as among the offenders. Two of the local authorities, Cavan and North Tipperary, introduced by-laws to try to reduce agricultural sources of pollution, which was a positive step.

The non-governmental organization, Save Our Lough Derg (SOLD), is active in following up on the findings of the Final Report. More towns are installing sewage treatment plants but the gradual introduction of holding tanks in boats with the necessary infrastructure of pump-out installations is taking time to achieve. Boats currently account for only a small percentage of pollution but are responsible for a major problem in harbours and confined mooring places. The EU Water Framework Directive is looking for not just a holding operation but improvement within a given timeframe. The Directive should also help to ensure that the implementation of plans such as Dublin City Council's proposed scheme to extract drinking water for the capital from Lough Ree is fully investigated, particularly in the light of recent water shortages in the river mentioned above.

Invasive species, in particular the Zebra mussel, are also a problem and there is an active Lough Derg Science Group monitoring the mussels and the growth in both algal bloom and a recently identified new invasive weed. The long term impact of invasive species is a cause of concern. It is recognized that the zebra mussels are now controlling the planktonic and blue-green algae in the lakes, which they consume and deposit in the sediment on the bottom. This is leading to improved water transparency, which in turn will encourage greater weed growth and cause a change in the ecosystem. With regard to fisheries management the present model comprising the Central Fisheries Board and regional boards is being restructured. A new single National Inland Fisheries Authority is to be established subsuming all the former boards, with regional advisory boards to provide stakeholder input into policy formulation and sectoral development of the fisheries.

There is a great deal of activity on the river today with substantial hire fleets, some 6,500 private boats registered and more and more private marinas coming on stream. The Shannon Commissioners of the mid-nineteenth century would be most impressed with current use of their expansive engineering works. They might be surprised by the fact that, as Stephen Heery has pointed out, The callows on the middle Shannon are recognized today as one of the most natural floodplains remaining in Western Europe, 'an outdoor laboratory . . . relatively undamaged by man's activities', with intensification of grassland management and changing agricultural practices seen as the main threat to them.[23] Under the 1984 Ramsar Convention on wetlands, the callows qualified as a designated area. A voluntary system of management is operated keeping cutting of hay late to preserve nesting and controlling the use of fertilizers and herbicides, with the normal winter flooding now accepted as a part of the cycle.

The middle Shannon callows are now recognized as an important Special Area of Conservation.

Athlone: an IWAI Millennium rally brought together a large number of boats of all sizes.

Harry Rice, who had said of the great river that its motto should be '*resurgam*, I shall come into my own again', and Vincent Delany, would be well pleased with the way their vision of the river, and indeed of all the Irish inland waterways, has come to fruition. Would it be tempting providence to suggest that the metaphor of the ebbing and flowing tide, so apparent up to now in the long history of the Shannon Navigation, is no longer apt, as it would appear to be heading into a very secure future?

Jamestown: the Heritage Boat Association organised a rally in 2006 attended by fifty two canal boats and many other boats.(Heritage Boat Association)

INTRODUCTION

[1] Frank Mitchell, *Reading the Irish Landscape* (Dublin, 1986).

[2] Robert Lloyd Praeger *The Way that I Went* (London & Dublin, 1947), p.247.

[3] Tracy Collins and Frank Coyne, 'Fire and Water –Early Mesolithic Cremations at Castleconnell, Co Limerick', *Archaeology Ireland*, vol.17 No.2, 2003.

[4] *Annals of the Kingdom of Ireland by the Four Masters from the Earliest Period to the Year 1616,* edited and translated by John O'Donovan (Dublin, 1851).

[5] *The Annals of Loch Ce* , edited and translated by William M. Hennessy (London, 1871).

[6] Giraldus Cambrensis, *The Topography of Ireland*, translated by J.J.O'Meara (Dundalk, 1951).

[7] Report in the *Irish Times,* 30 June 2006.

[8] Harman Murtagh, *Athlone History & Settlement to 1800* (Athlone, 2000), pp 48-51.

[9] N.Dowdall, *A Description of the County of Longford (*1682), quoted in the *Journal of the Ardagh & Clonmanoise Antiquarian Society*, 1932.

[10] Henry Mangan, 'Sarsfield's Defence of the Shannon", *The Irish Sword*, vol.1, 1949, pp. 24-32, quotes a letter from Sarsfield to Lord Mountcashel, dated 24 February 1691, describing the winter campaign 1690-1.

[11] Aidan O'Sullivan, *Foragers, Farmers and Fishers in a Coastal Landscape – an intertidal archaeological survey of the Shannon Estuary,* Discovery Programme Monograph No.5 (Dublin, 2001).

[1] (Anon) *Exshaw's and London Magazine* (1771), p.449.

[2] Richard Lawrence, *The Interests of Ireland in its Trade and Wealth Stated* (London, 1682)

[3] Irish Commons Journal, 11 August 1697, II, p.164; 9 September 1697, II, p.190. £13 Irish currency was equal to £12 sterling.

[4] Irish Commons Journal, 29 September 1703, II, p.322; 20 May 1709, II, p.586.

[5] 2 Geo.I,c.12 (Ir), 1715

[6] 8 Geo I, c.6 (Ir), 1721.

[7] 3 Geo.II, c.3 (Ir), 1729.

[8] 25 Geo.II,c.10 (Ir), 1751.

[9] (Anon), *Great Importance of the Shannon Navigation to the Whole Kingdom of Ireland* (Dublin, 1746); Philo Senensis (Dublin, 1755).

[10] Henry Brooke, *the Interests of Ireland considered, stated and reconsidered, particularly with respect to Inland Navigation* (Dublin, 1759).

[11] The sizes of the locks were later recorded in John Brownrigg's report to the Directors General of Inland Navigation in 1802, National Archives Ireland, 1/5/7/1. The lengths are given as 'clear of the reveals' which would probably mean the same as mitre to mitre.

[12] *Reports of the Late John Smeaton F.R.S. made on various occasions in the course of his employment as a Civil Engineer* (London, 1812), vol.2.

[13] Irish Commons Journal, VIII, app.xxvii.

[14] Irish Commons Journal, VI, app.x –xiii, 13 October 1757;app. cxcix – cclxv, 24 Ocotober 1759.

[15] Quoted in Stephen Heery *The Shannon Floodlands* (Galway, 1993).

[16] The lock chamber measurements that follow, given by Brownrigg, differ from those later recorded by Rhodes (see the Summary of the System, appendix).

[17] Irish Commons Journal, 21 November 1769, VIII, app.cccxxvii.

[18] John Cowan, *A Description of the Upper Parts of the Shannon* (Dublin, 1795).

[19] Irish Commons Journal, 14th February 1785, XI, app.ccclxii

[20] Samuel Clifford *A Description of the Shannon* (Dublin, 1786).

[21] Maurice Lenihan, *Limerick: its History and Antiquities,* (Limerick, 1866, reprinted Cork, 1967), p.346.

[22] Charlotte Murphy, 'The Limerick Navigation Company, 1697 – 1836, *North Munster Archaeological Journal,* vol.XXII, 1980. This article gives a very comprehensive account of the navigation.

[23] Irish Commons Journal, 14th November 1759, VI, app. cxcix – cclxv.

[24] Irish Commons Journal, 27 October 1761, VII, app.lxvii.

[25] Irish Commons Journal, 1 November 1763, VII, p.193; 15 November1763, VII, p.219.

[26] Irish Commons Journal, 20 November 1767, VIII, app.ccii.

[27] 7 Geo.III, c.26 (Ir), 1767.

[28] Lenihan, *op.cit.* gives the full list, p.363.

[29] Irish Commons Journal, 12th December 1783, XI, p.165, app.cxxviii.

[30] Correspondence of John 4th Duke of Bedford, London, 1846

[31] 11 & 12 Geo.III, c.4 (Ir), 1771-2.

[32] 17 & 18 Geo.III, c.16 (Ir), 1777-8.

[33] Irish Parliamentary Debates, vol 2, p.57.

[34] 23 & 24 Geo.III, c.26 (Ir), 1783-4.

[35] 23 & 24 Geo.III, c.26 (Ir), 1783-4.

[36] Irish Commons Journal, 7 February 1785, XI, app.cclxxxvi.

[37] Irish Commons Journal, 4 –15 April 1785, XI, app. ccccvii.

[38] 27 Geo.III, c.30 (Ir), 1787.

[39] 29 Geo.III, c.33 (Ir), 1789.

[40] Irish Commons Journal, 31 January 1786, XII, app.cclii.

[41] Irish Commons Journal, 23 February 1787, XII, app.ccccxci.

[42] Irish Commons Journal, 29 January 1788, XII, app.dcxliv.

[43] Irish Commons Journal, 29 January 1788, XII, app. dcxl

[44] Irish Commons Journal, 5 April 1790, XIII, app.ccclvii

[45] Irish Commons Journal, 15 March 1788, XII, app.dcclxi.

[46] Irish Commons Journal, 11 March 1789, XIII, app.clxix.

[47] National Archive Ireland, Grand Canal Company minutes, vol.11, 31 January 1794 (Report dated 3 October 1791).

[48] Irish Commons Journal, 28 January 1792, XV, app.lii.

[49] Irish Commons Journal, 29 January 1793, XV, app. cclxxxvi.

[50] William Chapman, *To the Subscribers of the Limerick Navigation Company*, Dublin 26 November 1795.

[51] W.Chapman, *Report on the Navigation of the River Shannon from Lough Allen to Killaloe with an estimate of the expense of completing the whole* (Limerick, 1791).

[52] John Cowan, *Upper Parts of the Shannon* (Dublin, 1795).

[53] M.B.Mullins, 'Historical Sketch of Engineering in Ireland', *Transactions Institution of Civil Engineering in Ireland* vol.VI, (1859).

[54] Irish Commons Journal, 18 February 1794, XV, p.310; 24 February 1794, XV, p.318.

[55] Jessop's report in Irish Commons Journal, XIX, app.mviii. The missing volume of the Grand Canal Company minute books, vol.12, may have contained Killaly's report.

[56] C(J), *The Neglected Wealth of Ireland* (Dublin, 1778).

[57] Arthur Wollaston Hutton (ed.), *Arthur Young's Tour in Ireland, 1776-1779* vol. 1, pp. 432-45 (London, 1892).

[58] Journal of the Royal Society of Antiquities of Ireland, vol. 11, 1870, pp. 254-5.

[59] Reproduced in Roger Stalley, ed., *Daniel Grose, The Antiquities of Ireland, A supplement to Francis Grose* (Dublin 1991).

[60] Irish Commons Journal, 18 February 1799, XVIII, p.26.

[61] Irish Commons Journal, 23 June – 18 July, 1800, XIX, app. miv et seq.

[62] James Caldwell, *Parliamentary Register 1763*, p.142

[63] Irish Commons Journal, 23 June – 18 July, 1800, XIX, app.mviii.

[64] 40 Geo.III, c.51(Ir), 1800.

CHAPTER TWO   THE EARLY WORKS UNDER THE DIRECTORS GENERAL OF INLAND NAVIGATION 1800–1814

[1] 40 Geo.III, c.51 (Ir), 1800. The Minute and Report Books of the Directors General of Inland Navigation are in the National Archives, Dublin, in thirty volumes, 25 August 1800 – 17 July 1841, OPW 1/5/1/1 –1/5/1/30; there are three volumes of Report Books, 7 September 1800 – 28 January 1809 and also Letter Books relating to the various districts and Account books

[2] Francis Plowden, *History of Ireland 1801-10* (Dublin, 1811), vol. III.

[3] Unpublished thesis, Ruth Heard, "Public Works in Ireland 1800 –1831" (Trinity College Dublin, 1977), pp.35-72.

[4] Ruth Delany, *Ireland's Royal Canal* (Dublin, 1992), pp. 27, 34-8, 40-1.

[5] Paul Kerrigan, *Castles and Fortifications in Ireland 1485–1945* (Cork, 1995).

[6] See footnote 1 above. The information in this section is taken from the Minute Books and Report Books of the Directors General of Inland Navigation.

[7] Peter O'Keefe & Tom Simmington, *Irish Stone Bridges* (Dublin, 1991), p.240.

[8] National Archives Ireland, Minutes of Grand Canal Company , Vol. 47, December 1812, Vol. 48, March 1813, Vol. 49, October 1813, Vol. 50, September 1814.

[9] Reported in the *Limerick Chronicle* and the *Dublin Journal & Patriot*, January 1811.

[10] 53 Geo III c.144, 1813.

[11] National Archive Ireland, Minutes of the Grand Canal Company, vol.11, January 1794.

[12] National Archive Ireland, Minutes of the Directors General of Inland Navigation, vol.1, 1/5/1/1; Ruth Heard, *The Grand Canal of Ireland* (Dublin, 1995), pp.152-160; see footnote 1 & 7 above.

[13] National Archive Ireland, Grand Canal Company minutes, vol. 21, December 1801.

[14] National Archive Ireland, Grand Canal Company minutes, vol. 24, 1 February 1803.

[15] In addition to the records of the Directors General and the Grand Canal Company, an account of this controversy is given in the Journal of House of Commons, 1805 (169), IV, 331, app. B & C.

[16] National Archive Ireland, Grand Canal Company minutes, vol. 29, June 1804.

[17] National Archive Ireland, Grand Canal Company minutes, vol. 30, February 1805.

[18] National Archive Ireland, Public Works, 1/5/7/1, Directors General of Inland Navigation, Report Book, vol. 1.

[19] Edward Wakefield, *An Account of Ireland Statistical and Political* (London, 1812).

[20] Anthony Marmion, *The Ancient and Modern History of the Maritime Ports of Ireland* (London, 1855).

[21] Figures extracted from the Directors General Account books, National Archive Ireland, OPW 2/5/ 1-6; summarised in Ruth Heard, *Public Works in Ireland 1800 – 1831*, unpublished thesis, Trinity College Dublin, pp. 44 – 6.

[22] Ruth Delany, *Ireland's Royal Canal* (Dublin, 1992), ch.4.

[23] Journal of House of Commons, 1812 (366) V, 679.

[24] H.C. 1812-13 (61), VI.

CHAPTER THREE   THE DIRECTORS GENERAL 1814–1831

[1] The full details about the Directors General are in Ruth Delany, *Public Works in Ireland 1800 – 1831,* unpublished thesis, Trinity College Dublin, 1977, chapter 2 and appendix III C.

[2] 57 Geo.III, c.34, 1817.

[3] H.C. 1822 (173,174), XVIII, 372,381.

[4] Quoted in C.W.Williams, *Observations on the Inland Navigation of Ireland* (London, 1833), p.38.

[5] All references to the Directors General of Inland Navigation in this chapter are from their Minute Books, National Archive Ireland, OPW 1/5/1-30.

[6] John Cowan, *A Description of the Upper Part of the River Shannon* (Dublin, 1795).

[7] 10 Geo.IV, c.126, 1829.

[8] Ronald Cox & Michael Gould *Ireland's Bridges* (Dublin, 2003).

[9] 53 Geo.III, c.143, 1813.

[10] Quoted in Cooke, *Early History of Birr* (Dublin, 1875).

[11] Ruth Delany, *Ireland's Inland Waterways* (Dublin, 2004) , pp. 56, 93, 108.

[12] Minutes of the Royal Canal Company, Vol. 7, 27 June 1825, C.I.E., Heuston Station.

[13] Ibid Vol.8, 20 February 1826.

[14] 6 Geo.IV, c.101, 1825; 1 Will.IV, c.54, 1830.

[15] H.C. 1829 (342), IV, 127.

[16] 1 & 2 Will. IV, c.33, 1831

[17] Ruth Heard, *Public Works in Ireland 1800 – 1831,* unpublished thesis, Trinity College Dublin, chapter 2.

CHAPTER FOUR   THE WINDS OF CHANGE IN THE 1830s

[1] H.C. 1830 (589,654,655,667) VII, 173,451,649,1.

[2] H.C. 1831-2 (677) XVI, 1.

[3] H.C. 1831-2 (677) XVI, 1

[4] C.W.Williams, *Observations on the Inland Navigation of Ireland* (London, 1831); 2nd edition with additional section (London, 1833).

[5] H.C. 1834 (532) XVII, 141, p.215.

[6] J.O'Loan, 'Origin and Development of Arterial Drainage in Ireland and the Pioneers', *Department of Agriculture Journal,* vol. LIX.

[7] Thomas Rhodes (1789-1863) obituary in *Institution of Civil Engineers, Minutes of Proceedings,* vol. 28, pp.615-18, 1869; L.T.C. Rolt, *Thomas Telford* (London, 1958).

[8] Waterways Ireland Archive, Enniskillen, Letter Book of the Shannon Commission. First Report, H.C. 1831-2 (731), XLV, 333; 2nd Report, 1833 (371) XXXIV, 235.

[9] Thomas Steele *Practical Suggestions on the Navigation of the Shannon* (1828)

[10] H.C. 1859 (257 Sess.1) XVII, 245. The Admiralty charts continue to be used today and with subsequent alterations in the levels there is a little to spare on the soundings at normal summer levels.

[11] 35 Geo III c.1 (Ir), 1795.

[12] John Cowan, *A Description of the Upper Part of the River Shannon* (Dublin, 1773 & 1795).

[13] 4 & 5 Will.I, c.61, 1834.

[14] National Archive Ireland, Grand Canal minutes, vol.72, 6 July 1833.

[15] Ibid, vol.74, 30 September 1835.

[16] 1859 (257) Sess. 1, XVII 245.

[17] Peter O'Keefe & Tom Simmington, *Irish Stone Bridges* (Dublin, 1991), pp.190-6.

[18] Isaac Weld, *Statistical Survey of County Roscommon* (Dublin, 1832).

[19] Henry Inglis, *A Journey Throughout Ireland during the Spring Summer and Autumn of 1834* (London, 1835).

[20] Isaac Weld, *Statistical Survey of the County of Roscommon* (Dublin, 1832)

[21] Quoted in C.W.Williams, *Observations on the Inland Navigation of Ireland* (London, 1833), appendix.

[22] H.C. 1834 (240) XL, 233.

[23] H.C. 1834 (532) XVII, 141, evidence of C.W.Williams.

[24] H.C. !834 (532) XVII, 141, evidence of Nicholas Fanning.

[25] 5 & 6 Will. IV, c.67,1834.

CHAPTER FIVE   A NEW ERA BEGINS

[1] Gordon Herries Davies & R.Charles Mollan, *Richard Griffith 1784 – 1878* (Royal Dublin Society, 1980).

[2] H.C. 1836 (143), XLCII, 581.

[3] H.C. 1837-8 (130) XXXIV, 1.

[4] Valentine Trodd, *Banagher on the Shannon* (Banagher, 1985).

[5] H.C. 1837-8 (142), XXXIV, 203.

[6] H.C. 1839 (172) XXVII, 1; H.C 1839 (208) XXVIII, 1.

[7] 1837-8 (145)XXXV, 449.

[8] H.C. 1839 (173) XXVIII, 139, app.C.

[9] *The Nenagh Guardian,* 1 August 1838.

[10] Information supplied by Professor A.W. Skempton, London.

[11] Caesar Otway, *A Tour in Connaught* (Dublin, 1839), pp.65-6.

[12] 2 & 3 Vict.,c.61, 1839.

CHAPTER SIX   THE WORK BEGINS: ESTUARY AND LIMERICK NAVIGATION 1840–1850

[1] The information for this chapter is taken, unless otherwise indicated, from the minute books etc. of the Shannon Commissioners in the National Archive Ireland 4/7/ 1-4, from the 1st – 11th annual reports presented to Parliament, 1840 – 1850, and also from records held in the Waterways Ireland archives in Enniskillen

[2] J.O'Loan, 'Origin and Development of Arterial Drainage in Ireland and the Pioneers', *Department of Agriculture Journal,* vol.LIX

[3] John de Courcy, 'A history of Engineering in Ireland', *The Engineer's Journal,* vol. 38, nos 9 & 10, 1985.

[4] 1st Report: H.C. 1840 (64) XXVIII, 533.

[5] Shannon Commission Letter Book of Henry Renton 1 February – 16 December 1841, Waterways Ireland Archives, Enniskillen.

[6] 2nd Report: H.C. 1841 (88) XII, 315.

[7] 3rd to 11th Reports: H.C. 1842 (71) XXIV, 341; 1843 (76) XXVIII,253; 1844 (151) XXXI, 387; 1845 (178) XXVI, 367; 1846 (153) XXII, 463; 1847 (545) XVII, 607; 1847 (710 –V) LVIII, part 3 (index); 1847-8 (491) XXXVII, 633; 1849 (113) XXIII, 737; 1850 (407) XXV, 783, final report.

[8] Peter o'Keefe & Tom Simington, *Irish Stone Bridges* (Dublin, 1991), p. 240.

CHAPTER SEVEN   THE MIDDLE SHANNON: KILLALOE TO ATHLONE 1840–1850

[1] Information for this chapter continues to be taken from the minute books of the Shannon Commissioners and their parliamentary reports, as indicated in note 1 of chapter six.

[2] Grand Canal Minutes, Vol.80, January 1840, in National Archives Ireland.

[3] Shannon Commission Letter Book of Henry Renton, 1 February – 16 December 1841, Waterways Ireland archives, Enniskillen.

[4] John MacMahon, 'Construction of Centres for Bridges', *Transactions Institutions of Civil Engineers Ireland,* vol. 1, 1845.

[5] A.W. Skempton (ed.), *A Biographical Dictionary of Civil Engineers in Great Britain and Ireland,* Thomas Telford Publishing,

2001.

[6] H.C. 1867-8 (277) X, 555, app.4.

[7] Quoted in *Old Athlone Society Journal,* vol 2 (1978), p. 78.

CHAPTER EIGHT   THE UPPER SHANNON WORKS 1840–1850

[1] As in the previous chapters, 6 and 7, the information for this chapter is taken from the minute books of the Shannon Commissioners in the National Archive Ireland, 4/7/1-4, from the 1st - 11th Annual Reports presented to Parliament 1840 – 1850 and also from records held in the Waterways Ireland archives in Enniskillen.

[2] Royal Canal Company Minutes, Vol.14, October 1830, C.I.E., Heuston Station.

[3] Peter O'Keefe & Tom Simington, *Irish Stone Bridges* (Dublin, 1991), pp.107-9. John Long's description is contained in a footnote in Lenihan's *History of Limerick* p.50.

[4] H.C. 1847-8 (491) XXXVII, 633, p. 12; *Report of Shannon Commissioners to Investigate Certain Acts of Abuses,* 30 November 1847, Eamon Norton Collection, No. 611, University College Limerick

[5] 9 & 10 Vict. C.86, 1846.

[6] Ron Cox (ed.), *Engineering Ireland* (Dublin, 2006), p.24.

[7] Patrick Raftery, 'A Brief History of the Institution of Civil Engineers of Ireland' *The Engineers Journal,* vol.38 Nos 9 & 10, 1985, pp.17-19.

[8] John De Courcy 'A History of Engineering in Ireland', *The Engineers Journal,* vol.38 Nos. 9 & 10, 1985, pp.23 -35.

[9] H.C. 1847 (847) XVII, 505, 15th Report of the Office of Public Works, 1846.

[10] H.C. 1847-8 (983) XXXVII, 213, 16th Report of the Office of Public Works, 1847.

[11] Information provided by the late Billy English.

[12] H.C. 1849 (1098) XXIII, 433, 17th Report of the Office of Public Works, 1848.

[13] H.C. 1850 (1235) XXV, 509, 18th Report of the Office of Public Works, 1849.

[14] H.C. 1851 (1414) XXV, 1, 19th Report of the Office of Public Works, 1850.

CHAPTER NINE   'DRAIN THE SHANNON'

[1] Stephen Heery, *The Shannon Floodlands* (Kinvara, 1993), p.129.

[2] C.Coote, *General View of Agriculture and Manufactures of the King's County* (Dublin, 1801).

[3] H.C. 1839 (173) XXVIII, 139, app.B.

[4] H.C. 1850 (407) XXV, 783, pp. 4 & 9.

[5] J.O'Loan, 'Origin and Development of Arterial Drainage in Ireland and the Pioneers', *Department of Agriculture Journal,* vol.LIX.

[6] 5 & 6 Vict.c.89, 1842.

[7] 9 Vict.c.4, 1846

[8] H.L. 1852-3 (10) XXVI, 1.

[9] Ms letters in Larcom Papers, National Library Ireland, Ms.7746.

[10] H.C. 1854 (91) LVIII, 201.

[11] H.C. 1861 (330) LVII, 557.

[12] H.C. 1863 (292), L, 701.

[13] *Inquiry into the Extent and Causes of the Shannon Floods* held by J.F. Bateman (Dublin 1865); earlier evidence heard in Banagher, H.C. 1854 (91) LVIII, 201; evidence heard in other towns, H.C. 1861 (330) LVII, 557.

[14] H.C. 1865 (189) XLVII, 705.

[15] H.L. 1865 (130) XI..

[16] H.C. 1865 (400) XI, 1.

[17] H.C. 1866 (213) XI,617.

[18] H.C. 1867 (298) LIX, 327.

[19] H.C. 1867 (383) LIX, 309.

[20] H.C. 1867 -8 (277) X, 555.

[21] 37 & 38 Vict. C.60, 1874

[22] H.C. 1875 (206) XXI, 299.

[23] H.Tench *The Shannon Floods, Lough Derg Level,* 1879.

[24] The Monck Commission, C.3173 (1882).

[25] 51st Report of the Board of Works (1882).

[26] The Allport Commission, C.5038 (1887).

CHAPTER TEN   THE STEAMERS AND TRADE 1826–1860s

[1] Grand Canal Company Minutes, vol. 53 et seq.; Directors General of Inland Navigation, vol. 20 et seq. National Archives Ireland.

[2] Andrew Bowcock, 'Early Iron Ships on the River Shannon', *The Mariner's Mirror*, vol. 92 No.3, August 2006; John Grantham Jnr., *Iron Ship-building* (London, 1868), 5th edition, p.11. Much of the detailed information about the steamers that follows is from Andrew Bowcock's article, together with references from the records of the Grand Canal Company and the Shannon Commissioners.

[3] 3 & 4 Will.IV, c.44, 1833.

[4] Liverpool *Albion* , 14 September 1829.

[5] Sailing directions to accompany the Admiralty Chart 1838-9, H.C. 1859 (257, Sess.1) XVII, 245.

[6] Mary John Knott, *Two Months at Kilkee with an Account of a Voyage down the River* (1835).

[7] *Black's Guide to Galway, Clare and West of Ireland* (Edinburgh, 1888).

[8] *The Mechanics' Magazine*, 8 August 1840, quoted in Bowcock, see ftn 2 above.

[9] Patent 1839, No.8104, discussed in Samuel Healy, 'On the Employment of Steam Power upon the Grand Canal, Ireland' Proceedings of Civil Engineers, vol. 26, 1866-7.

[10] 1837-8 (145) XXXV, 449, app. B. See Chapter 4 pp. 61-62

[11] Henry Inglis, *A journey throughout Ireland during the Spring, Summer and Autumn of 1834* (London, 1855) See Chapter 4 p.76

[12] H.C. 1859 (257, Sess.1) XVII, 245.

[13] J.G. Kohl, *Travels in Ireland,* translated from the German (Bruce & Wyld, 1844).

[14] James Johnson, *A Tour in Ireland* (London, 1844).

[15] *Westmeath Independent,* 5 September 1846.

[16] *Westmeath Independent,* 28 November 1846.

[17] John Forbes, *Memorandums made in Ireland,* vol.1 (London, 1853).

[18] *Westmeath Independent,* 9 July 1853.

[19] National Archive Ireland, Minutes of Directors General of Inland Navigation, vol.19, July 1816.

[20] *Westmeath Independent,* 28 March 1855.

[21] William Wakeman, *Three Days on the Shannon* (Dublin 1852).

[22] *Athlone Sentinel,* 18 November 1847.

[23] Information from documents salvaged by Michael Goodbody from the canal store in Dromineer.

[24] *The Official Irish Travelling Guide: a General Conveyance Directory* (Dublin, 1858).

[25] *Westmeath Independent,* 1 September 1858.

[26] *Westmeath Independent*, 17 February 1862.

[27] H.L. 1865 (130) XI, q.132.

[28] H.L.1865 (130) XI, 57.

[29] H.C. 1847-8 (491) XXXVII, 633, pp.22-3; see appendix iv.

CHAPTER ELEVEN   THE CHANGING SCENE 1860s–1940s

[1] The references to the administration and works on the Shannon by the Board of Works are drawn from the annual reports presented to Parliament.

[2] Grand Canal Company minutes, vol.100, 1882, National Archives Ireland.

[3] Ruth Delany, *Ireland's Royal Canal* (Dublin, 1992), p.158.

[4] *Cool Metal – Clear Water*, published by the Heritage Boat Association, 2006.

[5] See note 4 above.

[6] C.5038, 1887.

[7] Grand Canal Minutes, vol. 106, et seq. National Archives Ireland. The references to the canal company throughout this chapter are drawn from the minutes.

[8] Among the documents found by Michael Goodbody in the canal store in Dromineer.

[9] H.C. 1898 (184) LXXXII.

[10] *Illustrated London News,* 11 September 1897; Valentine Trodd, *Banagher on the Shannon* (Banagher, 1985).

[11] John O'Mahony, *The Sunny Side of Ireland, How to see it by the GS&WR* (Dublin, 1898).

[12] John O'Mahony, *The Sunny Side of Ireland* (Dublin, 1898)

[13] 1 Ed.VII c.136, 1901 Shannon Water & Power Act.

[14] Canals & Inland Waterways Commission, 1923, p.18.

[15] Ron Cox (Ed), *Engineering Ireland,* (Dublin, 2006), p.258.

[16] Cd. 3374 (1907)

[17] Royal Commission on Canals & Waterways, sections dealing with Ireland, Vol. 11, part 2, Cd.3717 (1907) XXX111; Final Report vol. XI, Cd. 5626 (1911) X111; Appendices to Final Report, vol.XII, Cd. 5653 (1911) X111.

[18] T.O. Russell, *Beauties and Antquities of Ireland* (London, 1897).

[19] R. Harvey, *The Shannon and its Lakes* (Dublin, 1896).

[20] G.T. Stokes, *Athlone, the Shannon and Lough Ree* (Dublin & Athlone, 1897).

[21] *Journal of the Royal Society of Antiquities of Ireland,* vol.11, 1870, pp.254-5.

[22] Sean Cahill, Gearoid O'Brien & Jimmy Casey, *Lough Ree and its Islands,* (Athlone, 2006).

[23] Quoted in Sean Kierse, *Portraits of Killaloe,* (Killaloe, 1995), No.42.

[24] John Bickerdyke, *Wild Sports in Ireland* (London, 1897).

[25] There was a considerable spate of correspondence in the newspapers on the subject in 1897.

[26] R.D. Levinge, *Sportsman's and Tourist's Guide to the Shannon* (Athlone, n.d.), p.1.

[27] Augustus Grimble, *The Salmon Rivers of Ireland* (London, 1913), pp. 251- 279.

[28] Joseph Adams, *The Angler's Guide to the Irish Fisheries* (London, n.d.), pp. 244- 49.

[29] Frank Mackey, 'Lines on Lough Derg', *Cois Deirge,* Summer 1978, pp. 9-10.

[30] Research by Tom McDermott, Marine Institute: 'Department of Fisheries Scientific Invstigations at the Limnological Laboratory, Hayes Channel, Portumna, Co. Galway 1921-3'.

[31] *Report of the Commission on Inland Fisheries 1933-5* (Dublin, P.No.1813); Peter Liddell, *The Salmon Fisheries of Eire* (Bord Failte, 1971).

[32] N.W. English, *Lough Ree Yacht Club 1770 – 1970* (Athlone, 1970).

[33] William Bulfin, *Rambles in Eirinn* (Dublin, 1907), pp.60-1.

[34] *Hunt's Yachting Magazine,* 1873 & 1878.

[35] V.T.H. Delany, *The Lough Derg Yacht Club – a Memoir* (Athlone, 1956).

[36] These references are in *Hunt's Magazine,* 1861 & 1862.

[37] Minute books and regatta material in Alf Delany archive.

[38] A.F. Delany, *The Water Wags 1887 – 1987* (Dublin, 1987).

[39] L.M. Goodbody & Ruth Delany, *The Shannon One-Design Class* (Dublin, 2000).

[40] These logs have been made available to Waterway Archive collectors over the years by the families.

[41] The visit is recorded in *The Yachtsman,* December 1899.

[42] In addition to being recorded in the log of the *Truant,* it is recorded in L.M. Goodbody & Ruth Delany, *The Shannon One-Design Class 1922 –1999* (Dublin, 1999), pp.36-9.

[43] R.A. Scott-James, *An Englishman in Ireland, Impressions of a Journey by Canoe by River, Lough and Canal* (London, 1910).

[44] Log in the possession of Sean Fitzsimons, Athlone.

[45] *King's County Chronicle*, 2 May 1907.

[46] Inland Waterways Association of Ireland News, vol.21, No.4, 1994; vol.31, No.2, 2004.

[47] Rena Lohan, *Guide to the Archives of the Office of Public Works* (Government Publications, 1994), footnote, p.1: 'The exact original title of the Office of Public Works is obscure. It has been known as the Office of Public Works, the Board of Works and the Board of Public Works. All of these titles have appeared on letter-heads and registration stamps from 1831.

[48] Canals and Inland Waterways Commission, 1923. Minutes of evidence MS in National Library Ireland.

[49] J.C. Smith 'Notes upon the Average Volume of flow from Large Catchment Areas in Ireland: the probable duration of stated rates of flow etc., deduced from gaugings on the River Shannon at Killaloe', *Trans. Inst. Civil Engineers of Ireland,* vol.45, pp. 41-118.

[50] Paul Duffy has written widely on the Shannon Scheme: there is a good summary by him in: 'Ardnacrusha – Birthplace of the E.S.B. in *North Munster Antiquarian Journal,* vol.XXIX , 1987. There are also a number of papers on various aspects of the scheme in the *Transactions of the Institute of Civil Engineering in Ireland* vols. VL – LXXXVI.

[51] *Commission of Inquiry into the Resources and Industries of Ireland: Report on Water Power,* (Dublin, 1922).

[52] M.Manning and M. McDowell, *Electricity Supply in Ireland: the History of the E.S.B. (Dublin, 1985); The Shannon Scheme – an Inspirational Milestone,* edited by A. Bielenberg (Dublin, 2002).

[53] *The Shannon Scheme, Report of the experts appointed by the Government* (Dublin n.d.).

[54] Sir John Purser Griffith, *Notes on the Siemens-Schuckert Shannon Power Scheme* (Dublin, 1925), pp. 61 et seq.

[55] Paul Duffy, 'The Pre-history of the Shannon Scheme', *History Ireland,* vol.12 No.4, 2004.

[56] Electricity (Supply) Act, 1927.

[57] *The Shannon Hydro-Electric Scheme,* published by T.C.Carroll & Sons (Limerick, 1929).

[58] Michael McCarthy, *High Tension – Life on the Shannon Scheme* (Dublin, 2004).

[59] Shannon Fishery Acts, 1935 & 1938.

[60] William Lysaght, *The Abbey Fishermen - a Short History* (Limerick, 1964, 2nd editiom 1999).

[61] Report of the Drainage Commission 1938-40, pp 61-9 (Government Publications, 1940).

[62] The Shannon Electricity Act, 1927, section 105.

[63] Turf Development Act, 1946.

CHAPTER TWELVE   '*RESURGAM*: I SHALL COME INTO MY OWN AGAIN'

[1] Transport Act 1944; Ruth Delany, *Ireland's Royal Canal* (Dublin, 1992).

[2] Transport Act 1950.

[3] Ruth Delany, *The Grand Canal of Ireland,* (Dublin, 1995).

[4] Transport Act 1958.

[5] Louis Rydell, *River Shannon Flood Problem* (Government Publications, Dublin, 1956).

[6] *River Shannon Flood Problem – Report on the First Stage of Investigations, Prepared jointly by the Office of Public Works and Electricity Supply Board, 6th June 1961* (Government Publications, Dublin, 1961).

[7] Richard Hayward, *Where the River Shannon Flows* (Dundalgan Press, 1940).

[8] L.T.C. Rolt, *Green & Silver*, first published London, 1949, reprinted by the Athlone Branch of the IWAI (Athlone, 1993).

[9] Considerable correspondence from this period has survived in the papers of Harry Rice, Vincent Delany and others, which form an important part of the IWAI archive material now held in the Oxford Island Centre, Lough Neagh.

[10] 'Our Neglected Assets', an article by Sean MacBride in *Silver River* (IWAI, 1985).

[11] A number of copies of this Memorandum exist in IWAI archives now housed in the Oxford Island Centre on the south shore of Lough Neagh.

[12] Hugh Malet, *Voyage in a Bowler Hat* (London, 1960, reprint 1985); *In the Wake of the Gods* (London, 1970); P.J;R. Gardner *Land of Time Enough* (London, 1977).

[13] George O'Brien Kennedy, *Not All at Sea* (Morrigan, Killala, Co. Mayo, 1997).

[14] *Shannon Tourism & Recreation Study,* Brady Shipman Martin on behalf of Bord Failte, 1975.

[15] These papers were printed in a special issue of *Administration, Journal of the Institute of Public Administration of Ireland,* vol.25 No 2 1977.

[16] *Development of the Shannon,* a submission by the Midlands, North East, Mid-West, North West and Western Regional Development Organisations, 1979.

[17] The Heritage Act 1995.

[18] The British-Irish Agreement Act 1999 and the North/South Co-operation (Implementation Bodies, Northern Ireland) Order 1999.

[19] Houses of the Oireachtas Joint Committee on Public Enterprise & Transport Sub Committee on the River Shannon Authority, Interim Report on Flooding on the River Shannon, November 2000. Report on issues relating to the Management of the River Shannon, March 2002.

[20] The six corridor studies covering the River Shannon are available from the Heritage Council, Kilkenny.

[21] *The Lough Derg Study*, Shannon Development and Clare, Galway and North Tipperary County Councils, 2001; *Lough Derg International Water Park Design Guide,* as above with Ireland West Tourism, 2003.

[22] *Literature review on the impacts of boat wash on the heritage of Ireland's inland waterways,* Heritage Council, 2006.

[23] Stephen Heery, *The Shannon Floodlands, a Natural History* (Kinvara, Co. Galway, 1993), p.135, a comprehensive account of the natural history of the callows to the present day.

APPENDIX A
SUMMARY OF NAVIGATION

SUMMARY OF NAVIGATION

There were several methods of measuring the length of the locks. Sometimes they were measured from mitre to mitre, which was usually the same as the total length of the lock from one quoin where the gate hung from to the other. To establish the size of boat that could be accommodated when the lock is measured from mitre to mitre, it is necessary to deduct to allow for the upper sill depending on the size of the sill. For this reason sometimes the measurements are taken from the lower mitre to upper sill. To make an approximate conversion from mitre to mitre measurements, which was the measurement usually used by the early engineers, it is necessary to take away 8–10ft (2.5 - 3m) for the larger locks and 4–6ft (1.20 - 1.80m) for the smaller ones.

EARLY WORKS

Omer originally planned locks 112ft x 19ft (34 x 5.80m) and this was the size used for Meelick and Athlone locks. Banagher, Shannonbridge and Lanesborough just had open lock chambers with a single set of gates, Clondara, Roosky and Jamestown were not made as large. The Grand Canal Company rebuilt the middle Shannon locks in the early 1800s and the last two locks on the Grand Canal were built to conform with these Shannon locks.

SHANNON LOCKS PRE-1840 WORKS
LIMERICK NAVIGATION:

The following are measurements given by Rhodes (which appear to be mitre to mitre) for the Shannon Commission, for the 1906 Royal Commission, for the 1923 Commission and by OPW (all of which are mitre to lower sill). Some of the differences are hard to explain.

	Shannon Commission Length	1906 Commission Length	1923 Commission Length	OPW Length x Width
Limerick tidal lock	127ft 6in	125ft 6in	129ft	125ft 6in x 21ft
Park lock	72ft 3in	81ft 6in		76ft 6in x 15ft 7in
Annabeg lock	80ft	74ft	74ft 9in	74ft x 15ft 7in
Gillogue lower chamber	99ft 6in	94ft 3in	93ft 6in	94ft 3in x 15ft 11in
Gillogue upper chamber	101ft 6in	95ft	95ft 9in	95ft x 15ft 11in
Newtown lock	94ft 7in	78ft 4in	90ft	78ft x 15ft 11in
Clonlara lock	83ft	78ft 4in	78ft 3in	78ft 4in x 15ft 2in
Monaskea lock	83ft	77ft 6in	77ft 6in	77ft 6in x 15ft 7in
Errina lower chamber	88ft 4in	86ft	81ft 10in	86ft x 15ft 6in
Errina upper chamber	92ft 6in	86ft 6in	86ft 6in	86ft 6in x 15ft 7in
Cussane lower chamber	95ft 7in	77ft	76ft 6in	77ft x 16ft 7in
Cussane upper chamber	80ft 9in	75ft 4in	74ft 10in	75ft 4in x 16ft 7in
Moys lock	82ft	76ft 10in	76ft 10in	76ft 10in x 15ft 11in
Killaloe lock	81ft 6in		80ft 8in	75ft x 15ft 10in

SHANNON NAVIGATION PRE-1840-50 WORKS

Brownrigg's measurements are pre-Grand Canal Company works 'in the chamber clear of the reveals' and Rhodes's measurements, which are post-Grand Canal rebuilding are mitre to mitre which is approximately the same measurement.

	Brownrigg	Rhodes
Meelick	Omer's lock 120ft x 18ft 6ins	83ft 6in x 18ft 6in
Banagher lock	single set of gates	81ft 6in x 16ft 5in
Shannonbridge lock	single set of gates	80ft x 18ft 6in
Athlone lock	Omer's lock 120ft x 19ft	80ft x 16ft 3in
Lanesborough	single set of gates	82ft 4in x 15ft 9in
Clondara lock	85ft 8in x 18ft 4in	98ft x 18ft 1in
Roosky lock	85ft 10in x 18ft 6in	99ft x 18ft 5in
Jamestown Canal lock	66ft 6in x 14ft 3in	72ft 6in x 14ft 2in
Battlebridge lock		72ft x 14ft 5in
Drumleague lock		71ft x 14ft 4in

SHANNON NAVIGATION CURRENT LOCK SIZES

All measurements are lower mitre to upper sill and metric measurements now being used:

Sarsfield tidal lock	176ft 10in (53.9m) x 40ft (12.2m)
Ardnacrusha upper and lower chambers	105ft 9in (32.23m) x 19ft 6in (5.94m)
Victoria lock, Meelick	142ft (43.28m) x 40ft (12.19m)
Ballinasloe lock, River Suck	105ft (32m) x 27ft 10in (8.5m)
Athlone lock	127ft (38.7m) x 40ft (12.19m)
Tarmonbarry lock	102ft (31.09m) x 30ft (9.14m)
Clondara lock, River Camlin	82ft 1in (25.02m) x 18ft 6in (5.66m)
Roosky lock	102ft (31.09m) x 30ft (9.14m)
Albert lock, Jamestown Canal	102ft (31.09m) x 30ft (9.14m)
LOUGH ALLEN CANAL	4.25 miles (6.8km)
Battlebridge lock	73ft 6ins (22.4m) x 12ft (4.1m)
Drumleague lock	64ft 6ins (19.68m) x 13ft 9in (4.2m)
Drumshanbo lock (opened 1996)	68ft 9in (21m) x 14ft 8in (4.5m)
BOYLE WATER	
Clarendon lock, Knockvicar	102ft (31.09m) x 30ft (9.14m)

APPENDIX B
ACTS, PARLIAMENTARY PAPERS AND
PRIMARY SOURCES

ACTS

2 Geo.I, c.12 (Ir), 1715: Authorized the making of navigations including from Carrick-on-Shannon to Limerick.

8 Geo.I, c.6 (Ir), 1721: Appointed commissioners in the counties to carry out navigation works.

3 Geo.II, c.3 (Ir), 1729: Commissioners appointed under the 1721 Act replaced by four bodies of commissioners, one for each province, and established tillage duties to finance schemes.

25 Geo.II, c.10 (Ir), 1751: Consolidated the provincial commissioners into the Corporation for Promoting and Carrying on Inland Navigation in Ireland.

7 Geo.III, c.26 (Ir), 1767: Incorporated the Limerick Navigation Company.

11 & 12 Geo.III, c.4 (Ir), 1771-2: authorizing the transfer of canals to private companies under certain conditions.

17 & 18 Geo.III, c.16 (Ir), 1777-8: continued tillage duties but restricted expenditure.

23 & 24 Geo.III, c.26 (Ir), 1783-4: Legislation governing Navigation Board.

27 Geo.III, c.30 (Ir), 1787: Dissolved the Corporation and transferred the navigations administered by it (including the Shannon north of Killaloe) to local commissioners.

29 Geo. III, c.33 (Ir), 1789: Authorising payment of debentures with conditions.

40 Geo.III, c.51 (Ir), 1800: Established the Directors General of Inland Navigation who took over control of all the navigations administered by the State.

53 Geo.III, c.144 (Ir), 1813: Transferred the Limerick Navigation Company to the Directors General of Inland Navigation.

57 Geo.III, c.34 (Ir), 1817: Exchequer Loan Scheme.

6 Geo.IV, c.101 (Ir), 1825: Transfer of Roads and Bridges to Directors General.

10 Geo.IV, c.126 (Ir), 1829: Transferred the Limerick Navigation Company back to a re-organised Limerick Navigation Company.

1 Will. IV, c.54 (Ir), 1830: Transfer of Fisheries to Directors General.

1 & 2 Will. IV, c.33 (Ir), 1831: Directors General dissolved and powers transferred to Board of Works.

5 & 6 Will. IV, c.67 (Ir), 1834: Established a commission to survey the Shannon and prepare plans for its development.

2 & 3 Vict., c.61 (Ir), 1839: Appointed Shannon Commissioners to execute the plan.

5 & 6 Vict., c.4 (Ir), 1842: Commissioners of Public Works acting as drainage commissioners.

8 & 9 Vict., c.119 (Ir), 1845: Incorporated the MGWR and authorized it to purchase the Royal Canal.

9 Vict., c.4 (Ir), 1846: Summary Proceedings Act.

9 & 10 Vict., c.86 (Ir), 1846: Transferred the powers of the Shannon Commissioners to the Board of Public Works established in 1831 (this was a nominal transfer until the works were completed in 1850).

37 & 38 Vict., c.60 (Ir), 1874: The Shannon Navigation Act transferred all the property held by the Shannon Commissioners to the Office of Public Works.

48 & 49 Vict., c.41 (Ir), 1885: Authorized works to be carried out on the Shannon to relieve flooding.

IRISH ACTS

Shannon Electricity Act, 1925: Authorized the Shannon Hydro-Electric Scheme.

Electricity (Supply) Act, 1927: Established the Electricity Supply Board.

Shannon Fisheries Acts, 1935 & 1938.

Transport Act, 1944: Established Córas Iompair Éireann (CIE) assumed responsibility for the Royal Canal.

Turf Development Act, 1946.

Transport Act, 1950: Nationalised CIÉ and approved its merger with the Grand Canal Company.

Transport Act, 1958: Authorized CIÉ to withdraw its carrying service.

Transport Act, 1960: Authorized the closure of some waterways including the Royal Canal.

Canals Act, 1986: Authorized the transfer of the Grand Canal system, the Barrow Navigation and Royal Canal to the Office of Public Works (OPW).

Shannon Navigation Act, 1990.

Heritage Act, 1995: Placed all heritage services including inland waterways under the Department of Arts, Culture & the Gaeltacht (actual transfer of operations took place in 1996).

The British-Irish Agreement Act, 1999: International agreement to establish six North/South Implementation Bodies, including Waterways Ireland to administer inland waterways.

PARLIAMENTARY PAPERS

Irish Commons Journals

11 August & 9 Sept.1697, II, pp. 164 & 190: Petition to make the Shannon navigable. Committee appointed but no further action.

29 Sept. 1703, II, p.322: Select Committee appointed to prepare a bill but no action.

20 May 1709, II, p.586: Stephen Costello and Mortimer Heylen, who had surveyed the river, given leave to bring in heads of a bill. No further action.

13 Oct. 1757, VI, app.x – xiii; 24 Oct. app.cxcix – cclxv: Authorized payments towards the building of a bridge at Shannonbridge.

14 Nov. 1759, VI, app.cxcix – cclxv: Report on Limerick Navigation works.

14 Nov. 1759, VI, app.cxcix – cclxv: Completion of bridge at Shannonbridge reported.

27 Oct. 176I, VII, p. 21 & app.lxvii: Reports on the Limerick Navigation works.

1 & 15 Nov. 1763, VII, pp.193, 219: Reports on Limerick Navigation works.

20 Nov. 1767, VIII, app.ccii: Reports on Limerick Navigation works.

20 Nov. 1769, VIII, app.cccxxvii: Report on progress on the Shannon works.

12 Dec. 1783, XI, app.cxxviii: Report on Limerick Navigation works.

7 Feb. 1785, XI, app.cclxxxvi: Inquiry into affairs of Navigation Board.

14 Feb. 1785, XI, app.ccclxii: Report on Shannon Navigation works.

24 March 1785, XI, app.ccclxii: Report on Shannon Navigation.

4-15 April 1785, XI, app.ccccvii: Further investigation into Navigation Board affairs.

31 Jan. 1786 XII, app.cclii: Further details of affairs of Navigation Board.

23 Feb. 1787, XII, app.ccccxci: Further details of investigation into Navigation Board.

24 Jan. 1788, XII, app.dcclxi: Present state of Limerick Navigation works.

29 Jan. 1788, XII, app.dcxliv, dcxl: Further investigation of Navigation Board accounts.

15 March 1788, XII, app.dcclxi: Report on Limerick Navigation works.

11 March 1789, XIII, app.clxix: Agreement with Limerick Navigation Company.

5 April 1790, XIII, app.ccclvii: Further investigation of Navigation Board accounts.

28 Jan.1792, XV, app.lii: Certified payment to Limerick Navigation Company.

29 Jan. 1793, XV, app.cclxxxvi: Further payment to Limerick Navigation Company.

18 Feb.1794, XV, p.310; 24 Feb.1794, XV, p.318: Approach by Grand Canal Company re.middle Shannon.

18 Feb.1799, XVIII, p.26: Resolution to cease payments for further public works.

23 June 1800, XIX, app.miv et seq. 2, 3 & 6 Report on Shannon Navigation by William Jessop, proposal of Grand Canal Company re. middle Shannon and report on Limerick Navigation.

IMPERIAL PARLIAMENT

1805 (169) IV,331: Negotiations between Grand Canal Company and Directors General on middle Shannon works.

1812 (366) V, 679; 1812- 3 (61) VI, 317: References to middle Shannon and Limerick Navigation.

1818 (267) XVI, 457: John Killaly's report on a canal to Lough Allen.

1822 (173, 174) XVIII, 372, 381: Survey to be carried out on the relief of Shannon floods.

1829 (342) IV, 127: Investigation into continuation of Directors General.

1830 (589, 654, 655, 667) VII, 173, 451, 649, 1: Select Committees on State of the Poor.

1831 (175) XVII, 519: Agreement with Grand Canal Company re. middle Shannon.

1831-2 (731) XLV, 333: Shannon Commission's plans for river up to Portumna.

1831-2 (677) XVI, 1: Further inquiries into state of the poor.

1833 (75) XVII, 373: 1st Report of Commissioners of Public Works.

1833 (371) XXXIV, 235: Shannon Commission's plans for river upstream of Portumna.

1834 (532) XVII, 141: Select Committee's report on Shannon Commission's plans with minutes of evidence.

1834 (240) XL, 233: 2nd Report of Commissioners of Public Works.

1836 (143) XLCII, 581: 1st Report of Shannon Commission.

1837-8 (130) XXXIV, 1: 2nd Report with survey drawings.

1837-8 (142) XXXIV, 203: 3rd Report.

1837-8 (145) XXXV, 449: Report of Railway Commissioners.

1839 (172) XXVII, 1: 4th Report part 1 with survey drawings.

1839 (208) XXVIII, 1: 4th Report part 2 with survey drawings.

1839 (173) XXVIII, 139: 5th Report.

1840 (64) XXVIII, 533; 1841 (88) XII, 315; 1842 (71) XXIV, 341; 1843 (76) XXVIII, 253; 1844 (151) XXXI, 387; 1845 (178) XXVI, 367; 1846 (153) XXII, 463; 1847 (545) XVII, 607; 1847 (710-V) LVIII, part 3 index; 1847-8 (491) XXXVII, 633; 1849 (113) XXIII, 737; 1850 (407) XXV, 783: 1st to 11th Progress Reports of Shannon Commissioners.

1847 (847) XVII, 505: 15th Report of Board of Works.

1847-8 (983) XXXVII, 213, 16th Report of Board of Works.

1849 (1098) XXIII, 433, 17th Report of Board of Works.

1850 (1235) XXV, 509, 18th Report of Board of Works.

1851 (1414) XXV, 1, 19th Report of Board of Works.

1852-3 (10) XXVI 1: House of Lords inquiry into Shannon flooding.

1854 (91) L III, 201: Inquiry held at Banagher on Shannon flooding.

1859 (257 Sess.I) XVII, 245: Commander Wolfe's report on Shannon lakes.

1861 (330) LVII, 557: Inquiries held at other towns on Shannon flooding.

1863 (292) L, 701: Report by J.F. Bateman on Shannon flooding.

1865 (400) XI, 1: Select Committee report on Shannon flooding with minutes of evidence.

1865 (130) XI: House of Lords Select Committee on Shannon flooding with minutes of evidence.

1865 (464) XI, 57: Select Committee report on Shannon flooding.

1865 (189) XLVII, 705 : Report by J.F. Bateman on works left unfinished by Shannon Commissioners.

1866 (213) XI, 617: Select Committee report on Shannon flooding.

1867 (298) LIX, 327: James Lynam's report on Shannon flooding.

1867 (383) LIX, 309: Report by J.F. Bateman on Shannon flooding.

1867-8 (277) X, 555: Select Committee report on Shannon flooding with minutes of evidence.

1868-9 (373) L, 727: Forsyth & Brady relating to fish passes and correspondence.

1875 (206) XXI, 299: Inquiry into Shannon flooding with evidence taken at various towns.

1882, C.3173: Monck Commission to inquire into the system of navigation connecting Belfast, Coleraine and Limerick.

1887, C.5038: Allport Commission on Public Works.

1898 (184) LXXXII, 561: Details of Shannon Development Company operations.

1907, Cd.3374: Binnie Commission on Arterial Drainage.

1907, Cd. 3717: Shuttleworth Commission on Canals and Waterways with minutes of evidence.

1911, Cd.5626: Final Report of the Shuttleworth Commission.

1911, Cd.5653: Appendices to Final Report.

IRISH REPORTS

1922 Commission of Inquiry into the Resources and Industries of Ireland: Report on water power.

1923 Report of Commission on Canals and Inland Waterways (minutes of evidence in Ms. in National Library Ireland).

1933-5 Report of the Commission on Inland Fisheries (Stationary Office, Dublin, P.No.1813).

1938-40 Report of Drainage Commission.

1956 Rydell report on River Shannon Flood Problem.

1961 OPW and ESB report on first stage of flooding investigations.

1975 Brady Shipman Martin Shannon Tourism and Recreation Study.

APPENDIX C
REVENUE AND TONNAGE

THE LIMERICK NAVIGATION - KILLALOE TO LIMERICK

Year	Revenue from tolls [£]	Total Revenue [£]	Total Expenditure [£]	Tonnage [tons]	Comments
1799	102	-	-	-	Limerick Nav. Co. incorporated 1767
1807	568	-	-	-	Directors General 1803 - 1829
1810	100	-	-	-	Navigation impassable 1809 - 1814
1816	-	560	1,400	-	-
1831	1,092	-	-	28,212	Navigation handed back to Limerick Nav. Co. 1829
1836	1,514	-	-	36,018	14,600 passengers in 1836 Sh. Com. take over & company paid compensation £12,227

THE MIDDLE SHANNON

Year	Revenue from tolls [£]	Total Revenue [£]	Total Expenditure [£]	Tonnage [tons]	Comments
1806	-	-	-	-	Taken over by Grand Canal Co. Government grant £54,634. Actual cost to Co. £84,857. Tolls collected from 1810
1830	4,646	-	-	14,368	Only 1,199 of this tonnage north to Athlone
1835	5,425	-	-	19,475	Only 3,993 of this tonnage north to Athlone. Approx. 4,000 passengers p.a. Sh. Coms. take over. GCC paid compensation £5

UPPER SHANNON

Year	Revenue from tolls [£]	Total Revenue [£]	Total Expenditure [£]	Tonnage [tons]	Comments
1830	C.400	-	C.800	-	Adminstered by Dir. Gen. 1800-1831. Tolls charged from 1817
1832	121	-	831	-	Taken over by Public Works Coms. 1831
1835	100	-	445	9,770	Taken over by Sh.Coms. 1839

THE SHANNON NAVIGATION

Year	Revenue from tolls [£]	Total Revenue [£]	Total Expenditure [£]	Tonnage [tons]	Comments
1840	1,704	-	3899	72,062	To and from Grand & Royal canals 30,733 tons 18,544 passengers
1846	1,781	3,366	3,000	96,103	Tonnage reached peak of 121,702 tons in 1847 4,033 passengers in 1849
1855	1,647	2,989	3,282	-	1859 most passenger services withdrawn with summer service till 1862
1865	1,526	2,913	2,839	-	-
1875	2,020	3,675	3,141	-	-
1885	2,292	5,483	5,278	41,720	-
1895	2,446	4,985	4,794	83,688 (1898)	In 1897 Shannon Dev. Co. began passenger service
1905	2,960	5,338	5,163	88,451	Sh. Dev. Co. summer only 1904
1910	3,269	5,832	4,784	99,500	-
1915	2,703	5,182	4,492	73,092	Grand Canal Co. paid £2,171 tolls
1920	2,604	3,547	7,584	77,415	-
1930	4,360	11,707	7,204	67,848	-
1940	5,396	7,557	4,926	65,337	Grand Canal Co. paid £4,042 tolls
1950	6,997	8,393	9,964	64,678	Grand Canal Co. paid £5,728 tolls
1955	8,619	11,263	10,870	46,622	Government grant 1957-8 £4,500
1960	6,951	8,810	13,396	33,279	1961 2,152 passed through locks
1964	-	-	-	-	1964 7,576 vessels through locks

TONNAGE OF IMPORTS AND EXPORTS IN YEAR 1847 SHOWING THE TONNAGE HANDLED AT THE PRINCIPAL STATIONS

ARTICLES LANDED

	Limerick & OB'B	Killaloe & L. Derg	Portumna	Banagher	Shannon bridge	Athlone	Lanesborough & Lecarrow	N. Shannon & Carrick	Total
Slates	1,178	49	93	135	4	132	6	8	1,605
Tiles & Bricks	173	362	139	-	14	838	-	-	1,526
Coal	662	941	139	-	118	624	-	30	2,514
Iron	88	84	36	12	12	40	8	-	280
Timber	173	329	190	25	26	291	13	43	1,090
Hay & Straw	32	5	25	53	2	1	32	20	170
Ores & Minerals	-	43	-	-	-	22	-	-	65
Salt	-	56	254	22	6	93	-	-	431
Marble	12	25	-	2	-	5	-	-	44
Manure	1	774	298	-	-	9	14	1	1,097
Lime	-	716	4	-	-	-	-	-	720
Building Stone & Flags	197	90	35	-	-	3,027	220	4	3,573
Sand & Gravel	-	288	-	-	-	-	28	196	512
Turf	5,278	5,050	558	670	11	4,807	401	917	17,692
Grain	6,259	4,698	1,421	1,932	-	1,953	20	21	16,304
Flour, Meal, Malt & Starch	5,647	1,504	2,269	1,373	76	2,632	18	-	13,519
Butter	-	-	1	-	-	-	-	2	3
Black Cattle & Horses	13	1	1	-	-	-	-	-	15
Sheep	2	4	-	-	-	-	-	-	6
Pigs	-	25	4	-	-	-	-	-	29
Salted Provisions	21	24	62	22	-	77	-	-	206
Potatoes & Vegetables	5	16	11	18	-	4	-	1	55
Groceries	784	26	1	1	-	-	-	-	812
Wines & Spirits	738	4	-	-	-	-	-	-	742
Porter, Beer & Ale	1,737	31	-	5	-	-	-	-	1,773
Bale goods, Hardware General Merchandise	4,219	1,588	767	163	27	1,733	11	-	8,508
Tobacco	-	-	-	-	-	-	-	-	-
Military Baggage	42	-	-	39	-	2	-	-	83
Machinery	102	10	45	-	-	51	10	14	232
Totals	27,363	16,743	6,353	4,472	296	16,341	781	1,257	73,606

ARTICLES LOADED

	Limerick & OB'B	Killaloe & L. Derg	Portumna	Banagher	Shannon-bridge	Athlone	Lanesborough & Lecarrow	N. Shannon & Carrick	Total
Slates	-	2,468	-	-	-	2	-	-	2,470
Tiles & Bricks	229	1	1	-	-	45	-	-	276
Coal	1,135	63	7	-	1	-	27	30	1,263
Iron	63	48	1	8	-	2	-	6	128
Timber	1,132	42	9	43	7	16	20	40	1,316
Hay & Straw	4	17	15	74	-	-	2	1	113
Ores & Minerals	-	389	-	2	-	-	-	-	391
Salt	319	8	-	-	-	-	-	-	327
Marble	2	51	-	-	-	-	-	-	53
Manure	1,264	157	-	-	-	27	-	10	1,458
Lime	22	-	-	-	-	-	-	10	32
Building Stone & Flags	323	7	-	-	-	-	2,039	6	2,433
Sand & Gravel	171	124	-	-	-	-	-	292	587
Turf	-	2,264	2,751	-	-	-	-	40	5,055
Grain	17,818	296	983	54	-	619	1	120	19,891
Flour, Meal, Malt & Starch	5,849	771	112	306	7	264	4	4	7,313
Butter	71	4	1	-	-	-	-	-	75
Black Cattle & Horses	9	60	15	1	-	16	-	-	101
Sheep	1	47	20	-	-	5	-	-	73
Pigs	6	2	24	-	-	8	-	-	40
Salted Provisions	241	66	22	3	-	5	-	-	337
Potatoes & Vegetables	10	8	8	26	-	7	-	-	59
Groceries	1	-	-	-	-	-	-	-	1
Wines & Spirits	24	-	-	-	-	-	-	-	24
Porter, Beer & Ale	-	2	1	2	-	22	-	-	27
Bale goods, Hardware General Merchandise	2,378	573	190	70	6	741	6	-	3,964
Tobacco	-	-	-	-	-	-	-	-	-
Military Baggage	3	-	-	-	2	148	-	65	218
Machinery	41	2	13	-	-	5	6	-	67
Totals	31,116	7,470	4,173	589	23	1,932	2,105	68	48,096

Articles landed | 73,606

Total for 1847 | 121,702

Note that these figures produced for the 9th Report of the Shannon Commissioners (HC 1847-8 [491]),
XXXVII, 633, pp22-3) have been slightly adjusted to remove the fractions originally supplied.

APPENDIX E
BOATS ON THE SHANNON

STEAMERS

Name	Date & Place Built	Material	Dimensions (in feet)	Notes
Artizan PS	1856 Rutherglen	iron	113ft x 12ft	Out of commission C. 1862. Sunk on Shannon.
Avonmore PS	1835 Liverpool	iron		Twin stern paddle wheels. Abandoned at Killaloe.
Duchess of Argyle PS	1848 Dumbarton	iron	151ft x 15ft	Arrived on Shannon 1857 shortened to fit locks. Out of commission C. 1862. Sunk on Shannon.
Dunally PS	1829 Birkenhead			Abandoned in Killaloe.
Gazelle PS	1832 Greenock	iron		
Lady Burgoyne PS	1842 Dublin	iron	130ft x 36ft	Too large to leave the river. Abandoned in Killaloe.
Lady Clanricarde PS	1829 Liverpool	wooden	80ft long	Too large to leave the river. Abandoned in Killaloe.
Lady Lansdowne PS	1833 Birkenhead	iron	135ft x 176ft	Abandoned in Killaloe.
Lord Lorton SS	1855 Greenwich	iron	67ft x 14ft	MGWR towing vessel but carried some passengers. Remained briefly on the Shannon.
Marquis Wellesley PS	1824 Tipton	iron		Twin hulls with paddles between hulls. Abandoned in Killaloe.
Midland PS	1855			MGWR vessel but did carry some passengers. Remained briefly on the Shannon.
Mountaineer	1826	wooden		Last recorded 1833.
Nonsuch (horsedrawn)	1837	iron	80ft x 6ft 6ins	Used on Limerick Navigation.
Shannon SS	1846	wooden	72ft x 15ft	Sold by Grand Canal Company in 1869.
Wye PS	1826 Birkenhead	iron		Smaller vessel used by CDSPC for towing on Grand Canal.

LATER STEAMERS

Countess Cadogan SS	1897 Paisley	steel	70ft x 14ft	Shannon Dev. Co. Went to Corrib 1913.
Countess of Mayo SS	C 1939 Rutherglen	steel	70ft x 14ft	Shannon Dev. Co. Sold to Warrenpoint.
Fairy Queen SS	1893 Irvine	steel	63ft x 14ft	Shannon Dev.Co. Went to Corrib 1906 and subsequently Scotland.
Jolly Roger SS	C 1920	wooden		Attempt to establish passenger service failed.
Lady Betty Balfour SS	1897 Paisley	steel	70ft x 14ft	Shannon Dev. Co. Sold in 1915.
Olga SS	1894 Canning Town	steel	50ft x 12ft	Shannon Dev. Co. Lost at sea in 1913.
Shannon Queen SS	1892 Bristol	steel	54ft x 10ft	Shannon Dev. Co. Sold on Shannon in 1914.

TRADE AND TOWING STEAMERS

Aran Queen	Garrykennedy			Privately owned turf boat. Abandoned in Garrykennedy.
Athlone SS	1862 Drogheda	iron	72ft x 13ft	GCC towing steamer. Sold 1917.
Athy SS	1895 Wales	iron		Built for Odlums. Scrapped 1947.
Ballymurtagh SS		iron		Purchased in 1868 by GCC from Wicklow Copper Mining Co. Scrapped 1928.
Barrow	1902			GCC vessel sold 1917.
Bat SS	1866 Drogheda	iron		GCC vessel. Registered as motor boat In 1913. Used as a house boat on waterways today.
Bee SS	1865-6	iron		Became 18M and 110B.
Brian Boru SS	1862	iron	90ft x 14ft	GCC vessel. Sold in 1874.

Cambrais				Ranks of Limerick. Sold later.
Carrick	1901			GCC vessel. Sold in 1916.
Corbally				Killaloe Slate Co.
Dublin SS	1862 Drogheda	iron	72ft x 13ft	GCC vessel. Scrapped 1910.
Eclipse Flower				Ranks of Limerick. Operated to end of 1950s.
Fly	1876	iron		Became 24M and 115B.
Fox SS	1865	iron	61ft x 13ft	GCC vessel. Registered as motor boat in 1923.
Ida				Hynes of Scarriff.
Killaloe	1890s			GCC vessel. Registered as motor boat 1925. Scrapped Shannon Harbour.
Lady of the Lake SS	1880 Drogheda	iron	67ft x 13ft	Waterford & Limerick Railway Co. Bought by GCC.
Limerick SS	1862 Drogheda	iron	72ft x 13ft	GCC vessel.
Marina				King of Portumna.
Monarch				King of Portumna.
Naas SS	1895 Wales	iron		Built for Odlums. Registered as motor boat in 1913. Now a house boat renamed *Jarra*.
Owl	1878	iron		Became 14M and 120B.
Portumna	1890s			GCC vessel. Scrapped 1928.
Rambler SS				Brought by MGWR to Shannon in 1875. Now a house boat.

			70ft x 10ft 6ins ?	
Rattler SS			70ft x 10ft 6ins ?	Brought by MGWR to Shannon in 1875. Possibly became Float No.1 Maintenance boat on Royal Canal which was shortened 10ft to fit in Grand Canal and is now a house boat.
Sandlark				Privately owned turf boat. Abandoned in Garrykennedy.
Sunrise				Ranks of Limerick. Sold later.
Tullamore	C 1890			GCC vessel. Sold 1896.

PRIVATE 'GENTLEMAN'S STEAM YACHTS' STILL IN USE

Chang-Sha	1846 Scotland	Lowmoor iron		Built for Col Sankey. Sold to Major Lloyd who removed steam engine. Sold to Dept. Agriculture 1920 –23. Several owners. Now owned by Becker family.
Phoenix	1872 Waterford	Lowmoor iron	58ft 6ins x 10ft 6ins	Built for General Spaight. Sold to Major Lefroy 1903. Steam engine removed 1927. Several owners. Now back with Lefroy family.

LATER GCC TRADE AND TOWING BOATS

St Brigid	1931	steel	85ft 7ins x 15ft 9ins	Formerly *Avon Queen*. Purchased by GCC in 1945. Sold to O'Brien Kennedys in 1960s. Now a house boat.
St James	1938-9 Dublin	steel	73ft x 14ft 8ins	Built for GCC. Sold to Irish Floatels. Now a house boat.
St Patrick	1935	steel	84ft 4ins x 15ft 5ins	Formerly *Avon King*. Purchased by GCC in 1945. Purchased by Irish Floatels. Now a house boat.

CIE PASSENGER BOATS

St Brendan	1937			Originally *Cardinal Wolsey*. Brought by CIE to Shannon in 1955. Sold to New Ross in 1974.
St Ciaran	1936			Originally *Wroxham Belle*. Brought by CIE to Shannon 1956. Sold to New Ross in 1974.

APPENDIX E

SOME OF THE YACHTS COMPETING IN THE 1860s & 1870s

NAME	TONNAGE	OWNER
Achilla		Robert Harvey
Aphrodite	20-ton cutter	Captain Farrer
Audax		William Potts
Avenger	9 tons	Captain Sadlier/Captain Birchall
Beeswing	3 ½ tons	Morahan
Chance	5-ton yawl	J.J. O'Flanagan
Corsair	15-ton cutter	Captain Bassett Holmes
Countess	14-ton cutter	Captain Smithwick
Fairy	6-ton cutter	
Gipsy	3 tons	J. Birchall
Haidee	8-ton cutter	Henry Jackson/W.H. Sydney
Knockrockery		William Minchin/T. Holmes
Lady Louisa	10 tons	James Bond
Mary Anne	2 tons	Forde
Meta	8 tons	Hon. R.E. King
Querida	8 tons	M. O'Conor
Seadrift		H. Jackson
Surprise	9-ton cutter	W. Waller
Tallyhassie		
Torfrida	5-ton cutter	F. Minchin
Undine	12-ton cutter	Captain Esmonde
Virago	12-ton cutter	Lord Avonmore

SOURCES & BIBLIOGRAPHY

PRIMARY SOURCES

Directors General of Inland Navigation minute books, account books and reports, OPW 1/5/ 1-9, National Archive Ireland.

Grand Canal Company minute books. OPW 10/1/1 – 10/1/121, National Archive Ireland.

Royal Canal Company minute books vols. 1–26, 1810 – 1849, CIE Heuston Station.

Waterways Ireland Archive, Enniskillen: Report and Letter books, charts, plans etc

Logs of trips on the Shannon, copies of many of these in the Alf Delany archive.

Contemporary newspapers.

PUBLICATIONS AND PAMPHLETS

Bickerdyke, John, *Wild Sports in Ireland* (London, 1897).

Bielenberg, A., ed., *The Shannon Scheme – an Inspirational Milestone* (Lilliput, Dublin, 2002).

Black's Guide to Galway, Clare and West of Ireland (Edinburgh, 1888).

Brooke, Henry, *The Interests of Ireland considered, stated and reconsidered, particularly with respect to Inland Navigation* (Dublin, 1759).

Burke, Gerry, ed., *Cool Metal – Clear Water, Trading Boats of Ireland's Inland Waterways* (Heritage Boat Association, 2006).

C(J), *The Neglected Wealth of Ireland,* (Dublin, 1778).

Cahill, Sean, O'Brien, Gearoid, & Casey, Jimmy, *Lough Ree and its Islands* (Athlone, 2006).

Cambrensis, Giraldus, *The Topography of Ireland*, tanslated by J.J. O'Meara (Dundalk, 1951).

Chapman, William, *To the Subscribers of the Limerick Navigation Company* (Dublin, 1795).

Chapman, William, *Report on the Navigation of the River Shannon from Lough Allen to Killaloe* (Limerick, 1791).

Cowan, John, *A Description of the Upper Part of the River Shannon* (J.& J. Carrick, Dublin, 1795).

Cooke, *Early History of Birr* (Dublin, 1875).

Coote, C., *General View of Agriculture and Manufacture of the King's County* (Dublin, 1801).

Cox, Ron, ed., *Engineering Ireland* (Collins Press, Cork, 2006).

Cox, R.C. & Gould, M.H. *Ireland's Bridges* (Dublin, 2003).

Croker, Crofton, *Researches in the South of Ireland* (John Murray, London, 1824).

Cromwell, T., *Excursions through Ireland* (Longman, London, 1820).

D'Arcy, Gerard, *Portrait of the Grand Canal* (Transport Research Associates, 1969).

Davies, Gordon Herries and Mollan, R. Charles, *Richard Griffith 1784 – 1878* (RDS, Dublin, 1980).

Delany, A.F. *The Water Wags* 1887-1987 (Dublin, 1987).

Delany, Ruth, *Ireland's Inland Waterways* (Appletree, Belfast, 1986).

Delany, Ruth, *By Shannon Shores* (Gill & Macmillan, Dublin, 1987).

Delany, Ruth, *Ireland's Royal Canal* (Lilliput, Dublin, 1992).

Delany, Ruth, *The Grand Canal of Ireland* (Lilliput, Dublin, 1995).

Delany, V.T.H. & D.R., *The Canals of the South of Ireland* (David & Charles, Newton Abbot, 1966).

Delany, V.T.H., *The Lough Derg Yacht Club, A Memoir* (Athlone, 1956).

Dwyer, Kevin, *Ireland - the Inner Island* (Cork, 2000).

English, N.W., *The Lough Ree Yacht Club* (Athlone, 1970).

Feehan, John M., *The Magic of the Shannon* (Mercier, Cork, 1980).

Fisher, Jonathan, *Scenery of Ireland,* (1792).

Fitzpatrick, M.J., *Shannon Lake Steamers, A Guide to the Shannon Lakes, The Duke of York Route* (Crossley Publishing, Co.,Dublin, n.d.).

Forbes, John, *Memorandums Made in Ireland in the Autumn of 1852* (London, 1853).

Gardner, R., *Land of Time Enough* (Hodder & Stoughton, London, 1977).

Gauci, Paul, *Select Views of the Shannon* (William Spooner, 1831).

Goodbody L.M. & Delany, Ruth, *The Shannon One Design Class, 1922-1999* (Dublin, 2000).

Gough, John, *A Tour in Ireland in 1813 & 1814 by an Englishman* (Dublin, 1817).

Grantham, John Junior, *Iron Shipbuilding* (London, 1868).

Griffith, Sir John Purser, *Notes on the Siemens-Schuckert Shannon Power Scheme* (Dublin, 1925).

Grose, Daniel, ed. Roger Stalley, *The Antiquities of Ireland* (Dublin, 1991).

Grose, Francis, *Antiquities of Ireland* (Hooper, London, 1791).

Hadfield, Charles & Skempton, A.W., *William Jessop, Engineer* (David & Charles, Newton Abbot 1979).

Hall, Mr & Mrs, *Ireland its Scenery, Characters etc.* (How & Parsons, London, n.d.).

Harvey, R., *The Shannon and its Lakes* (Hodges Figgis, Dublin, 1896).

Hayward, R. *Where the River Shannon Flows* (Dundalgan Press, Dundalk, 1940).

Heery, Stephen, *The Shannon Floodlands* (Kinvara, 1993).

Hennesy, William ed., *The Annals of Loch Ce* (London, 1871).

Hutton, Arthur Wollaston ed., *Arthur Young's Tour in Ireland, 1771-1779* (London, 1892).

Inglis, Henry, *A Journey throughout Ireland during the Spring, Summer and Autumn of 1834* (Whittaker & Sons, London, 1835).

Johnson, James, *A Tour in Ireland,* (London, 1844).

Kerrigan, Paul, *Castles and Fortifications in Ireland 1485 – 1945* (Cork, 1995).

Kierse, Sean, *Portraits of Killaloe* (Killaloe, 1995).

Kierse, Sean, *The Killaloe Anthology* (Killaloe, 2001).

Knott, Mary John, *Two Months at Kilkee with an Account of a Voyage down the River* (1835).

Kohl, J.G., *Travels in Ireland in Autumn 1842, translated from German* (Bruce & Wyld, London, 1844).

Lawrence, Richard, *The Interests of Ireland in its Trade and Wealth Stated* (London, 1682).

Lenihan, Maurice, *Limerick: its History and Antiquities* (Limerick, 1866; reprinted Cork, 1967).

Levinge, R.A., *A Sportsman's Guide to the Shannon* (Athlone Printing Works, Athlone, n.d.).

Lewis, S., *Topographical Dictionary of Ireland* (S.Lewis & Co., London, 1837).

Lohan, Rena, *Guide to the Archives of the Office of Public Works* (Dublin, 1994).

Lysaght, William, *The Abbey Fishermen – a Short History* (Limerick, 1964, 2nd edition 1999).

McCarthy, Michael, *High Tension – Life on the Shannon Scheme* (Lilliput, Dublin, 2004).

MacLaughlin, Thomas, *The Shannon Scheme Considered in its National Economic Aspect* (Sackville Press, Dublin, n.d.).

MacMahon, John, *'Construction for Centres for Bridges', Transactions Institutions of Civil Engineers Ireland, vol. 1, 1845.*

McNeill, D.B., *Irish Passenger Steamship Services, South of Ireland* (David & Charles, Newton Abbot, 1971).

Malet, H., *Voyage in a Bowler Hat,* (Hutchinson, London, 1960) reprinted M. & M. Baldwin, 1985).

Manning, M. & McDowell, M., *Electricity Supply in Ireland: the History of the ESB* (Dublin, 1985).

Marmion, Anthony, *The Ancient & Modern History of the Maritime Ports of Ireland* (London, 1855).

Martin, Michael ed., *IWAI Silver Jubilee 1954 –79* (IWAI, Athlone, 1970).

Mitchell, Frank, *Reading the Irish Landscape* (Michael Joseph, Country House, Dublin, 1986).

Murtagh, Harman, ed., *Irish Midland Studies, Essays in Commemoration of N.W. English* (Old Athlone Society, Athlone, 1980).

Murtagh, Harman, *Athlone, History and Settlement to 1800* (Old Athlone Society, Athlone, 2000).

Nash, W.J., *Lough Ree and Around it* (Athlone Printing Works, Athlone, 1949).

Nowlan, David, ed., *Silver River, A Celebration of 25 years of the Shannon Boat Rally* (IWAI, Dublin, 1985).

O'Brien Kennedy, George, *Not all at Sea* (Killala, 1997).

O'Donovan, John, *The Annals of the Four Masters* (Hodges & Smith, Dublin, 1851).

O'Farrell, Padraic, *Shannon Through her Literature* (Mercier, Dublin & Cork, 1983).

Official Irish Travelling Guide: a General Conveyance Directory (Dublin, 1858).

O'Keefe, Peter & Simmington, Tom, *Irish Stone Bridges* (Dublin, 1991).

O'Mahony, John, *The Sunny Side of Ireland, How to see it by the GS& WR* (Dublin, 1898).

O'Sullivan, Aidan, *Foragers, Farmers and Fishers in a Coastal Landscape – an intertidal archaeological survey of the Shannon Estuary* (Dublin, 2001).

Otway, Caesar, *A Tour in Connaught* (Wm Curry, Dublin, 1839).

Plowden, Francis, *History of Ireland 1801-10* (Dublin, 1811) vol.3.

Praeger, R.L., *The Way that I Went* (Dublin, 1947 & 1969).

Raven-Hart, R. *Canoeing in Ireland* (London, 1938).

Rice, H.J. *Thanks for the Memory* (Athlone Printing Works, Athlone, 1952). Reprinted IWAI Athlone Branch (Athlone, 1974 & 1975).

Ritchie, Leith, *Ireland Picturesque and Romantic* (Longmans, London, 1838).

Rolt, L.T.C., *Green & Silver* (Allen & Unwin, London, 1949; reprinted 1968; reprinted IWAI, Athlone Branch, 1993).

Rolt, L.T.C., *Thomas Telford,* (London, 1958).

Russell, T.O. *Beauties and Antiquities of Ireland* (London, 1897).

Scott-James, R.A., *An Englishman in Ireland* (Dent, London, 1910).

Skempton, A.W. (Ed.), *A Biographical Dictionary of Civil Engineers in Great Britain and Ireland* (Thomas Telford Publishing, 2001).

Smyth, Alfred P., *Scandinavian York and Dublin* (Dublin, 1975).

Steele, Thomas, *Practical Suggestions on the Improvement of the Navigation of the Shannon between Limerick and the Atlantic* (Sherwood Gilbert, London, 1828).

Stokes, G.T. *Athlone, the Shannon and Lough Ree* (Hodges, Dublin, 1897).

Stokes, William, *A Pictorial Survey and Tourist Guide to Lough Derg* (Schulze & Co., London, 1842).

Trodd, Valentine, *Banagher on the Shannon* (Banagher, 1985).

Wakefield, Edward, *An Account of Ireland Statistical and Political* (London, 1812).

Wakeman, W.F., *Three Days on the Shannon* (Hodges & Smith, Dublin, 1852).

Walsh, Kieran, ed., *25th Shannon Boat Rally* (Shannon Harbour Canal Boat Rally Committee, 1996).

Weld, Isaac, *Statistical Survey of Co. Roscommon* (RDS, Dublin, 1832).

Williams, C.W., *Observations on the Inland Navigation of Ireland* (Vacher & Fenn, London, 1831) new edition with additional section 1833.

PERIODICALS

Bowcock, Andrew, *'Early Iron Ships on the River Shannon'*, *The Mariner's Mirror*, vol.92, no.3, 2006.

Carroll, T.C. & Sons, *The Shannon Hydro-Electric Scheme* (Limerick, 1929).

Collins, Tracy and Coyne, Frank, *'Fire and Water – Early Mesolithic Cremations at Castleconnell, Co Limerick'*, *Archaeology Ireland*, vol.17 No.2, 2003.

de Courcy, John, *'A History of Engineering in Ireland'*, *The Engineers Journal* vol.38, nos 9 & 10, 1985.

Dowdall, N., *'A Description of the County of Longford'*, reproduced from a private Manuscript in Ardagh & Clonmacnoise Antiquarian Society Journal, vol.1 No. 3, 1932.

Duffy, Paul, *'Ardnacrusha –Birthplace of the ESB'*, *North Munster Antiquarian Journal*, vol. 29, 1987.

Duffy, Paul, *'The Pre-history of the Shannon Scheme'*, *History Ireland*, vol.12 no.4, 2004.

Exshaw's *London Magazine*, 1771.

Foster Petree, J. *'Charles Wye Williams, a Pioneer of Steam Navigation' Transactions of the Liverpool Nautical Research Society*, vol.10, 1961-71.

Healy, Samuel, *'On the Employment of Steam Power upon the Grand Canal, Ireland' Proceedings of Civil Engineers*, vol.26, 1866-7.

Mackey, Frank, *'Lines on Lough Derg' Cois Deirge*, Summer 1978.

'Management of the River Shannon in the 1980s, Proceedings of a Conference held in Athlone on 16-17 September 1976', *Journal of the Institute of Public Administration*, vol.25, no.2, 1977.

Mangan, Henry, *'Sarsfield's Defence of the Shannon 1691-1'*, *Irish Sword*, vol.1, 1949.

Mullins, M.B., *'Historical Sketch of Engineering of Ireland'*, *Transactions Institution of Civil Engineers in Ireland*, vol.6, 1859.

Murphy, Charlotte, *'The Limerick Navigation Company 1697–1836'*, North Munster Archaeological Society Journal , vol.22, 1980.

O'Loan, J., *'Origin and Development of Arterial Drainage in Ireland and the Pioneers'*, Department of Agriculture Journal, vol. 59.

Old Athlone Society *Journals*.

Raftery, Patrick, *'A Brief History of the Institution of Civil Engineers in Ireland'*, The Engineers Journal, vol.38, nos. 9 & 10, 1985.

Rhodes, Thomas, *obituary in Proceedings of the Institution of Civil Engineers, Minutes of Proceedings*, vol.28, pp.616-18, 1869.

Smith, J.C., *'Notes upon the Average Volume of Flow from Large Catchment Areas In Ireland'*, Transactions Institution of Civil Engineers of Ireland, vol.45.

REPORTS

Development of the Shannon Submission by the Midlands, North East, Mid-West, North West and Western Regional Devlopment Organisations, 1979.

Lough Derg International Water Park Design Guide, Shannon Development and Clare, Galway and North Tipperary County Councils and Ireland West Tourism.

Lough Derg Study, Shannon Development and Clare, Galway and North Tipperary County Councils, 2001.

River Shannon Flood Problems, report by Louis Rydell, 1956.

River Shannon Flood Problems – Report on First Stage of Investigations, 1961.

Salmon Rivers of Eire, report prepared by Peter Liddell for Bord Failte, 1971.

Shannon Tourism & Recreation Study Brady Shipman Martin for Bord Failte.

INDEX